The Ownership Solution

Advance Praise for
The Ownership Solution

"Jeff Gates is that most unusual of individuals—the practical visionary."
—*Edward W. Kelley, Jr., Governor, U.S. Federal Reserve*

"*The Ownership Solution* succeeds brilliantly in showing how broad-based personal ownership can strengthen communities and make global sustainable development possible."
—*Dick Gephardt, Democratic Leader of the U.S. House of Representatives*

"How do we close a growing gap between successful owners and investors and an increasingly anxious underclass? One way that would help—more participants in ownership! No one knows more about how that should be done than Jeff Gates, and he offers his spectacular insight in this cornucopia of philosophical and practical ideas."
—*Mario M. Cuomo, Governor of New York (1983–1995)*

"An important proposal from which all those concerned with helping the poor will want to learn."
—*Michael J. Novak, American Enterprise Institute*

"Why does capitalism create so few capitalists? Jeff Gates asks and answers the central economic question, the source of our deepest social and political conflicts. He provides a humane and convincing blueprint for reforming capitalism, bringing clarity and humanity to the taboo subject of concentrated wealth. But the only radical element in this book is Jeff Gates's open-hearted conviction that the future will be different—and better—for all."
—*William Greider, author, One World, Ready or Not; Who Will Tell the People; Secrets of the Temple. National Editor, Rolling Stone.*

"With this book, a long-time explorer and discoverer, Jeff Gates, hands over his carefully constructed maps to direct policymakers, business and workers to a *common* destination of greater economic vitality and power. Onward!"
—*U.S. Senator John D. Rockefeller IV*

"Elegantly researched. A masterful statement by a creative author—a remarkable book."
—*David McLaughlin, President-Emeritus, The Aspen Institute*

"A brilliant and innovative exploration of new ways to spread wealth ownership and foster wealth creation. *The Ownership Solution* is a blueprint for the new age of capitalism."
—*Dr. Madsen Pirie, President, The Adam Smith Institute (U.K.)*

"An unparalleled effort by a unique individual with the mind of a chief financial officer and the heart and soul of a prophet."
> —*John Feldmann, Director, Center for Ethics, Capital Markets, and Political Economy*

"One of the most important books of this decade. *The Ownership Solution* is *really* a solution—one of the most significant contributions to restoring a civil society. . . . A monumental book that should be read by everyone concerned about human betterment."
> —*Warren Bennis, University Professor and Distinguished Professor of Business Administration, University of Southern California; author,* On Becoming a Leader *and* Organizing Genius

"A book full of original and stimulating ideas to which those who want to keep up with the times should expose themselves."
> —*Franco Modigliani, Institute Professor Emeritus, Massachusetts Institute of Technology, 1985 Recipient of Nobel Memorial Prize in Economic Science*

"The twenty-first will be the 'Century of the Corporations.' Jeff Gates gives an exciting and well-written preview of this New World and the 'owners' whose informed involvement will be essential for the continued welfare of the planet."
> —*Robert A.G. Monks, author,* Power and Accountability, Corporate Governance, *and* The Emperor's Nightingale

"In *The Ownership Solution*, Jeff Gates does more than point the way to broadening the base of ownership in society. He may have put his finger on the possibility of a historical convergence. If capitalism can be prevented from concentrating ownership and wealth, social democrats will avoid the danger which they are pledged to fight as they pursue the imperative of social equity. Equally, if social equity can be achieved without frustrating entrepreneurship and undermining market forces, the conservatives will be assured of the preservation of those sources of economic energy which they are pledged to guard. Let's both get on with it!"
> —*Michael Manley, Prime Minister of Jamaica (1972–1980; 1988–1992)*

"The world has turned its back on state ownership of the means of production, [and] the free enterprise system is the best we have for generating wealth. But there is some risk that if economic disparities widen—and there is some evidence of this happening—it may also give rise to discontent. Jeff Gates has given much thought to how this could be avoided and capitalism given a broader base of stakeholders and beneficiaries. He sets out his ideas in this stimulating and timely book."

> —*Sir Shridath Ramphal, Secretary-General of the British Commonwealth (1975–1990)*

"Development will be truly sustainable only when Jeff Gates's ideas are put into practice."

> —*Dr. Norman A. Bailey, Senior Director of National Security Planning, National Security Council (Reagan Administration)*

"In countries like my own, Nicaragua, the rich and political elites should read Jeff Gates's *The Ownership Solution* for inspiration on how to stop the impending social conflagration which we have been stirring for generations."

> —*Arturo J. Cruz, Senior, former Nicaraguan Ambassador to the U.S.*

"A very inovative, progressive idea. Sure to stimulate much good dialogue."

> —*Amitai Etzioni. Professor, George Washington University, and author,* The Spirt of Community

"Jeff Gates has provided a sweeping review of capitalism at its best and at its worst, and has skillfully shown us how a fundamentally different and better future could be shaped by weaving the thread of widespread individual responsibility through ownership into the fabric of society. How might the future be fundamentally different from the one likely to result from an extrapolation of the present? It could be what so much of mankind yearns for but finds unattainable today—a sustainable society for us and our descendants, built on the legs of social equity, environmental restoration, and progress for all. With three billion of our fellow human beings hanging on by their fingernails and billions more on the way, this is a timely and insightful work."

> —*Ray C. Anderson, Chairman and Chief Executive Officer, Interface, Inc., Co-Chair, President's Council on Sustainable Development*

"A compelling account of how widespread capital ownership is the 'missing piece' needed to strengthen both democracies and private property economies worldwide."

> —*Senator Russell B. Long (U.S. Senator, 1949–1987)*

"Jeff Gates has produced a view of sustainable growth that at last puts more faith in humans than in governments. Splendid!"

> —*Malcolm Wallop (U.S. Senator, 1977–1995); Chairman, Frontiers of Freedom Institute*

"Ownership is a *sine qua non* of sustainable development. An interesting intellectual contribution to the evolving debate."

> —*James D. Wolfensohn, President, The World Bank*

"In the dynamic age of globalization, Mr. Gates stretches the envelope of conventional thinking on the critical issues of ownership and equity. The evolving concepts of ownership in the developed world are yielding important lessons which should be helpful to developing countries as they integrate more and more into the global economic system.
—*James Gustave Speth, Administrator, United Nations Development Program*

"Jeff Gates has devoted years to discussing new patterns of distributed ownership. In this thoughtful and well researched book, he argues the increasing disparity of wealth within and among nations, the difficulties of abetting development, and the recent success of micro-financing all suggest a major role for new ownership patterns to drive local and global economic growth and stabilization of democracy. Gates may not have the whole solution. It is enough that he may well have an essential piece of it.
—*Stuart A. Kauffman, founding general partner, Bios Group, LP; Professor, Santa Fe Institute; author,* The Origins of Order *and* At Home in the Universe

"The world is increasingly being divided into those who own capital and technology and those who don't. The former group's wealth is growing; the latter's stagnates and diminishes. Instead of taking this as an inevitable trade-off capitalism imposes, Jeff Gates has made a compelling argument for an approach that can share ownership with all those who create it. Indeed, it is an approach Newt Gingrich can adopt as readily as Ted Kennedy."
—*Corey Rosen, Executive Director, National Center for Employee Ownership*

"The great value of Jeff Gates's book is that it offers proven and practical ways to restore a sense of pride and ownership to industry, and how to marry capitalism to ethical values. It couldn't be more timely."
—*Geoff Mulgan, Director, DEMOS (U.K.)*

"A thoughtful and creative approach to the problem of how to involve people most personally, productively, and with a minimum of loss to their individuality, in the rapidly forming world economy. Gates envisions an expansive and dynamic capitalism that is both market-oriented and people-oriented. [*The Ownership Solution*] can open horizons for both policymakers and entrepreneurs."
—*Jim Wright, Speaker of the U.S. House of Representatives (1987–1989)*

"An important subject, excellent thinker, good writer, thoughtfully done. Read it!"
—*Dee Hock, Founder, President and CEO Emeritus, Visa International*

"Jeff Gates's affirmation of employee ownership as a means of achieving a significant measure of human empowerment, social justice and economic success in the midst of social and technological upheaval demands our attention."

—Lynn R. Williams, President, United Steelworkers of America (retired)

"This is a unique, unusual and untried proposal to solve a vexing problem in national and international economic development. It is worth some serious consideration."

—Rev. Theodore M. Hesburgh, President Emeritus, University of Notre Dame

"Jeff Gates is one of America's most insightful analysts of worker ownership and participation; his book, The Ownership Solution, is a brilliant contribution to a broader understanding of the enormous potential of employee ownership."

—Stan Lundine, President, Worker Ownership Institute; former Congressman and Lieutenant Governor of New York

"In this important book, Jeff Gates expands and empowers the growing crusade for widening and democratizing capital ownership begun by Louis and Patricia Kelso."

—Hazel Henderson, futurist and author, Building a Win-Win World and Paradigms in Progress

"The community we all long for can't be realized with only 6 percent of the population having any share in ownership. We have a long way to go to change this, and Jeff Gates is leading the way."

—Bob Swann, President, E.F. Schumacher Society

"The Ownership Solution offers a persuasive argument for why broadened capital ownership should be a top economic priority."

—J. R. Beyster, Chairman and CEO, Science Applications International Corporation

"A timely and provocative stimulus which should be required reading for policymakers."

—Ian Taylor, MP and Parliamentary Under-Secretary for Trade and Technology (U.K.)

"A delightfully refreshing strategic overview for utilizing the vehicle of capitalism to bring us, as a people, back into compassionate community."

—Ram Dass, author and lecturer

"An erudite yet good-natured analysis of the power and possibilities of broad capital ownership."

—Joseph V. Vittoria, former Chairman and CEO, Avis, Inc.

The Ownership Solution

Toward a Shared Capitalism for the Twenty-First Century

Jeff Gates

With a foreword by
Stephan Schmidheiny,
Founder of the World Business Council
for Sustainable Development

Addison-Wesley
Reading, Massachusetts

Many of the designations used by manufacturers and sellers to distinguish their products are claimed as trademarks. Where those designations appear in this book and Addison-Wesley was aware of a trademark claim, the designations have been printed in initial capital letters.

Library of Congress Cataloging-in-Publication Data
Gates, Jeffrey R.
    The ownership solution : toward a shared capitalism for the twenty-first century / Jeffrey R. Gates : foreword by Stephan Schmidheiny.
        p.   cm.
    Includes bibliographical references and index.
    ISBN 0-201-32808-9
    1. Property.   2. Capitalism.   3. Property—United States.
4. Capitalism—United States.   5. Comparative economics.   6. Twenty-first century.   I. Title.
HB701.G38   1998
    333.3—dc21   97-43298
                                                              CIP

Addison-Wesley is an imprint of Addison Wesley Longman, Inc.

Jacket design by Suzanne Heiser
Text design by Jean Hammond
Set in 10-point Sabon by CIP

1 2 3 4 5 6 7 8 9—MA—0201009998
First printing, April 1998

Addison-Wesley books are available at special discounts for bulk purchases in the United States by corporations, institutions, and other organizations. For more information, please contact the Corporate, Government, and Special Sales Department at Addison Wesley Longman, Inc., One Jacob Way, Reading MA 01867, or call 1-800-238-9682.

Find us on the World Wide Web at
http://www.aw.com/gb/

 This book is printed on recycled paper.

For the children

Contents

Foreword

This book may save capitalism.

Let me put that in a slightly less dramatic way: this book may help us save the best of capitalism and turn the whole into a system that can actually sustain a global population expected to double next century.

Western economic society has been so busy in the twentieth century defending capitalism against other systems that it has not had time to keep improving the model, or even to criticize it creatively. Now that capitalism seems to have won globally, its very momentum as it reaches into the formerly centralized economies makes running repairs and upgrades difficult.

But repairs and improvements are needed, both at the systemic and at what might be called the personal or individual levels.

Look first at the big system. As capitalism spreads, so does democracy. This is good. But the capitalism spreading into Asia, Latin America, and Eastern Europe seems to be making the rich richer. If it is not exactly making the poor poorer, then it gives the impression of doing this, because it is not pulling many people out of poverty, while sheer population growth means that more and more people are yearly born into poverty.

But why look only at less developed countries? The United States and Western Europe also appear on the verge of becoming "winner take all" economies, in which capitalism squeezes out rather than welcomes in the majority of people who are not capitalists in the sense of being successful entrepreneurs. And the system feels remote, guided by intricate, convoluted and detached financial signals rather than by humans.

The connection between this syndrome and democracy is obvious. Unless capitalism is made to reward the majority, then the majority will turn against it—at the ballot box and perhaps by other means. The rebound will take different forms in different places. Some societies will revert to various types of central planning, in the forms of socialism, populism, monetarism or combinations of all three. Others will revert to chaos.

Looking at the same problem from the individual level, we find that the majority are not connected with capitalism, except—at best—through a job. However, even those who have jobs in wealthy nations have felt ever more strongly of late that this is a very tenuous and unsatisfactory connection indeed. Jobs might end suddenly, for reasons no one seems to understand. To advise people in general to counter this risk by being successful entrepreneurs is a little like advising people in general to be chess prodigies. We do not understand what makes an entrepreneur, but experience teaches us that such people are relatively rare in society.

So what does Jeff Gates have to say to all this? First, it is worth looking at Mr. Gates's unique background. He spent almost a decade working with the U.S. Senate Finance Committee helping to draft laws, many of these encouraging employee stock ownership plans (ESOPs). He has advised companies. He has advised governments of twenty-five countries. He is practical; he knows what works, and thus he knows what can work. It was this insider view which led him to the conclusion that present forms of capitalism are unsustainable; and it was this insider view which guided him toward suggestions for workable improvements.

Mr. Gates's basic view is that capitalism is good at creating capital but poor at creating capitalists. So he has used his background in drafting laws to devise a number of strategies for changing the present dehumanized capitalism into what he calls a more personalized, human-sized, "up-close" capitalism. He argues that widespread personal ownership of capital assets provides a way to connect people to their economy, to their community, to their workplace and to each other. He then offers a series of ways in which this ownership can be achieved—ways entirely in keeping with the best aspects of present capitalism.

For me, one of the best things about Mr. Gates and his ideas is that they are ideologically inscrutable; he will drive crazy anyone viewing the world through the old dogmas. Is he a liberal, in the present United States, rather pejorative sense a of do-gooding humanist, because he is trying to humanize capitalism? Is he a liberal, in the older, European sense, because he is trying to increase human freedom and responsibility? Is he a conservative, because he is trying to make capitalism more secure? Or is he even a socialist, in that he is trying to spread the ownership of capital assets? I like this undogmatic aspect of Mr. Gates's work because it reveals the feebleness of any *single* ideology in meeting society's current challenges, and it shows we must borrow from all points of view.

I hope we can find the maturity to do this. Our ability to survive as a civilization while preserving our environmental resource base depends upon our using the best of capitalism—its opportunities and its encouragement of innovation and efficiency—while avoiding the worst—the rich-get-richer phenomenon.

Mr. Gates has some wonderful ideas on how to go about this.

Stephan Schmidheiny
Founder, World Business
Council for Sustainable
Development

Preface

Property is merely the art of democracy. It means that every man should have something that he can shape to his own image, as he is shaped in the image of heaven.

—G. K. Chesterton

Often I feel like the botanist who excitedly invites people into his garden knowing he can see relationships that are invisible to others. The thrill for that botanist, and now for me, lies in making those relationships visible. My goal in writing *The Ownership Solution* is to offer a new framework for the way people think, by making visible a part of their world of which they are seldom aware: the world of finance and the primary fruit of its operations—capital ownership.

Throughout history, nations have been known by their patterns of ownership, whether concentrated in a monarch, in the hands of a privileged few or controlled by a bureaucratic elite. In the United States, the 1980s and 1990s saw a return to the rich-get-richer legacy of turn-of-the-century primitive capitalism. I will describe how it happened, identify those policymakers who facilitated it, and show why this trend—now the worldwide norm—is unsustainable. I will also explain how modern-day capitalism could be designed to deliver broad-based prosperity, real security and abundant leisure.

For me, this book represents what British economist John Maynard Keynes characterized as "a struggle of escape from habitual modes of thought and expression." Ownership is not an issue often discussed in polite company. And certainly not in the company of conventional economists. As we shall see, this determined, even devout avoidance plagues policymaking worldwide, though perhaps nowhere more so than in my home country, the United States. As counsel to the U.S. Senate Committee on Finance (1980–1987) and adviser to Senator Russell Long, I crafted much of the federal legislation encouraging employee stock ownership plans (ESOPs), an early and still quite popular ownership solution. For the past decade, on assignment to foreign governments whose politics span the spectrum, I have advised on a range of politically sensitive "ownership engineering" projects in more than twenty countries, typically in those "in-transition" economies shifting from state to private ownership.

The ESOP originated with a little-known book, *The Capitalist Manifesto,* published in 1958 by San Francisco lawyer Louis O. Kelso and philosopher Mortimer J. Adler, who proposed broad-based ownership as a tool for addressing an array of economic and social challenges. *The Ownership Solution* is intended as an overview rather than a detailed and exhaustive study of this remarkably broad and complex subject. My objective is to educate, to persuade readers of the necessity for change and to suggest a range of policy initiatives.

This book is written for the nonprofessional. I avoid the use of financial, legal and economic jargon. Though intended for an international readership, I draw heavily from my experience in the United States. To the extent that the United States is viewed as a "mentor" economy, I trust that my observations will help others learn both from America's abundant strengths and her many shortcomings. *The Ownership Solution* is a "work in progress." Although I have learned from many collaborators worldwide, all of us are building this road as we travel. Also, I realize that only rarely is there a genuinely new idea; more often, we uncover new ways of looking at old ideas. With this book, I offer what I hope will be a fresh viewpoint. Footnotes expand on the text while endnotes are provided for those who prefer a more in-depth analysis. It is ideas, not their faintly discernible origins, that matter most herein.

Acknowledgments

The Zurich-based AVINA Foundation provided crucial support that made this effort possible. I gratefully acknowledge my indebtedness to Stephan Schmidheiny, AVINA's founder and founder of the Business Council for Sustainable Development (now the World Business Council for Sustainable Development). His interest, encouragement and patience were critical ingredients in this effort. I also thank AVINA's Lloyd Timberlake for sharing his wealth of experience and for his helpful guidance, advice, counsel and friendship. The Scotland-based Russell Trust also provided timely supplemental support, as did Philip Baxendale, the driving force behind Baxi Partnership Ltd. (U.K.). The U.S.-based Foundation for Enterprise Development was also supportive of this work. A particular thanks is due the Aspen Institute, which has long served as a fertile training ground for thinkers, doers and leaders. The institute's "Tomorrow's Corporation" seminar provided a forum in which these ideas surfaced and were discussed. Likewise, the State of the World Forum offered a welcome environment for intellectual stimulation and fruitful inquiry.

I owe a particular thanks to Senator Russell Long of Louisiana for his many years of support, encouragement and genuine friendship. Stuart Speiser also showed an uncommon faith in me at an early age, hiring me as a freshly minted attorney to work with him on what became *A Piece of the Action* (Von Nostrand Reinhold, 1976), the first historical account of the ESOP movement in the United States. Louis O. Kelso, Mortimer J. Adler and Patricia Hetter Kelso remain an inspiration as pioneers in this area.

Helpful comments were provided by friends, acquaintances and colleagues too numerous to mention in their entirety, including Delal Baer, Bob Beyster, David Binns, Beth Bogart, Ward Bond, Harry Broadman, Mary Bush, Gordon Cain, Michael Chriszt, Harlan Cleveland, Ben Cohen, Arturo Cruz Sr., Max De Pree, David Ellerman, David Fenton, John Feldmann, Rich Ferulato, Fred Freundlich, Jeff Furman, Jim Guirard, Jim Green, Jerry Greenfield, William Greider, Peter Hannaford, Michael Keeling, Norman Kurland, Bernard Lietaer, Lance Lindblom, Russell Long, Ron Ludwig, Chris Mackin, Michael Manley, Avon Mattison, Aziz Ali Mohammed, Akihiro Monden, Tom Mullins, Paul Murray, Robert Oakeshott, Madsen Pirie, George Pillsbury, Williams Roberts, Loren Rodgers, Scott Rodrick, Corey Rosen, Allison Sander, Jim Smith, Crocker Snow, Bob Swann, John Templeton, Wayne Thevenot, Shann Turnbull, Francis Vitagliano, Mourad Wahba, Ron Walker, Susan Witt, Lynn Williams,

Jim Wright, and a stalwart group who traveled to Sintra, Portugal, in April of 1995 to critique an early draft, including David Erdal, Michael Higgins, Dee Hock, David McLaughlin, Geoff Mulgan, Robert Taylor and Steve Quick.

My agent, Joe Spieler, of the Spieler Agency, was helpful in every way, including editing several early chapters. Jon Beckmann provided invaluable advice and insight as a seasoned and accomplished editor, helping condense my lengthy tome to a more digestible size. Nick Philipson at Addison Wesley Longman ably shepherded this work to completion with the invaluable production assistance of Lynne Reed, excellent editing input from Melissa Dobson and a striking jacket design by Suzanne Heiser.

The standard disclaimer applies: any mistakes or omissions are my own. I am responsible both for what this book says and how it's said.

Introduction and Overview

A problem adequately stated is a problem well on its way to being solved.

—*Buckminster Fuller*

While the thin veneer comprising the owners of capital continues to exist above a slightly thicker layer of so-called "knowledge workers," most Americans sense they are sliding down a steepening economic slope. With the highest concentration of both wealth and income in the industrial world,[1] the United States is now the developed world's most economically stratified society, edging out even such traditional class-conscious societies as Britain, which acquired its disparities from a feudal past. Americans lack that handy excuse; we didn't inherit inequity, we chose it.

Globally, we are witnessing the most dramatic shift of ownership patterns in history. As communism wanes, those newly emerging patterns offer both promise and peril. On the one hand, they offer escape from unworkable forms of socialism. On the other hand, we see the emergence of oligarchies rivaling those of czarist Russia and reminiscent of America's early "robber baron" capitalism. It is this tension that defines our times: the clear ascendancy of private enterprise alongside a tendency for its ownership benefits to flow into the hands of a few.

Today's capitalism embodies a curious and dangerous inconsistency. It extols the necessity of private ownership. Yet while the capital is there and so is the capitalism, what's missing are people who can rightly be called capitalists. The reason for this is poorly understood: *contemporary capitalism is not designed to create capitalists, but to finance capital.* Absent political will, those dramatically different goals will never be combined. *The Ownership Solution* shows both why a new ownership alternative is needed and how to go about developing it.

Ownership: The Underutilized Feedback Loop

Financial capital in the United States today resides largely in two camps. While much of it is concentrated in the hands of an ownership aristocracy, the balance has no true owner because over the past two decades approximately $12 trillion in assets has come to be held by institutional investors: pension plans, mutual funds, insurance companies, banks, foundations and endowments of various sorts. Today's detached and disconnected capitalism is now largely "on automatic," with investment decisions based on a "by-the-numbers" process that is incapable of taking into account many longer-term concerns, including the impact those investments have on the social fabric, on the fiscal condition of the nation, and on the environment.

Adam Smith, the father of free enterprise, understood that markets make great servants but lousy masters. Thomas Jefferson, the father of democracy, understood that a disengaged citizenry could be democracy's undoing. If free-enterprise democracy is not generating the results (other than financial returns) that its citizens intend—socially, economically, environmentally—then we need to reengineer it for broader and deeper personal involvement.

If Smith were alive today, I wager he would abandon his eighteenth-century image of "the invisible hand" to explain how the pursuit of private gain becomes a public virtue. Instead, he would favor an information age metaphor—"feedback loop"—to describe that complex chain of cause and effect that results in individual self-interest advancing the greatest good for the greatest number. Smith was first and foremost a moral philosopher. Both markets and democracies trace their moral roots to individual choice. That's why both are *obliged* to respond to the preferences of the consumers and constituents who participate in them. He envisioned that the "self-design" of free enterprise would be wrought by a being (a self) with a soul embodying the complexity of purpose that makes humans uniquely human.[2] Financial calculation is part of who we are, but *only* a part. Moral man, not Dow-Jones or Moody's, was envisioned as the animating force in the marketplace. At its core, this book is about using ownership as a means for reconnecting personal conscience to market capitalism.

There was a time when economic decisions were informed by conscience and made with sensitivity to the community. That was most obviously the case when village elders held sway or when close-knit communities were the rule rather than the rarity. That richly textured, multilayered, multiple-agenda decision-making has gradually been replaced by a cool financial efficiency engineered with but one goal in mind: money-denominated returns. On that score, global capitalism displays an undeniable genius for detached reckoning in its capacity to ferret out financial returns worldwide. But that process also fosters grotesque inequities and environmental travesties. By my calculation, it is demonstrably unsustainable—socially, politically, fiscally, culturally and environmentally.

The human element that Adam Smith saw at the heart of self-design has been allowed to atrophy as return-seeking capital has been granted deference, even dominance. We are all now buffeted by a global economy in which key actors are encouraged, even mandated, to maximize financial returns in a worldwide auction of sorts in which financial values have become a substitute for the values of ethics, religion and community. At any given hour of the day, somewhere a capital market is operating. The securities traded often belong to huge, virtually stateless multinational corporations that, in turn, take their cues from the detached concerns of investment managers intent on reaping short-term financial returns. Money, not man, is fast becoming the measure of the public good.

Graffiti spotted on a wall in Warsaw captures this very modern dilemma: "We wanted democracy, but we ended up with the bond market." As we'll see, the real enemy here is our own bad habits, epitomized by our now institutionalized indifference to the common good. The new field of struggle will be in the domain of finance because it is there that mankind has lost his place as the measure of things. Instead, both man and his environment are being made to measure for this impersonal and all-pervasive force of his own creation.

The Ownership Solution shows how people and communities worldwide can regain some control over their fate. My hypothesis is simply this: people are likely to become better stewards of all those systems of which they are a part—social, political, fiscal, cultural and natural—as they gain a personal stake in the economic system, with all the rights and responsibilities that implies. It is unproductive to complain about overly large or remote economic forces—multinational corporations, global trade, cross-border capital flows and such—absent efforts to implement ownership patterns that support strong local communities. Current ownership patterns not only offend our collective conscience; they also endanger our capacities by reducing decision-making to the lowest common denominator.

Serendipitously, this ownership reengineering resonates particularly well with Americans because decentralized systems play directly to our historic strengths. Democracies and markets are self-organizing systems; the challenge lies in how to engage more "selves" in that self-design. At present, many Americans' concerns are not addressed by our dynamic social fabric. People feel alienated, left out and cut off, and with good cause—they've been separated from responsibility for the actions of a system they were told was designed to respond to them.

A Brief History of Ownership—The Core of the Social Contract

American democracy was founded by property owners who limited the vote to property owners. Given that history, it's remarkable that property patterns have not received more attention as a way to strengthen the nation. Rousseau, the eighteenth-century political theorist, characterized property as the "foundation of the social contract." That remains the case. Modern property traces its origins to the seventeenth-century writings of the English philosopher John Locke. Writing at a time when divine right was embodied in the king, he proposed the radical notion that rights to personal property arose whenever man "mixed his labor" with whatever he removed from nature, because " 'tis labor indeed that puts the difference of value on everything." As we shall see, that simple observation served as the foundation on which political philosophers built a variety of ownership solutions worldwide over the ensuing centuries.

Locke saw property as encompassing not only rights to material things fashioned by man's effort but also personal rights embodied in "lives, liberties and estates." Those rights, he argued, were so much a part of the human personality that they could not be "alienated," because they belonged to mankind in posterity. That notion, now commonly known as "human rights," so impressed America's founders that Jefferson included an adaptation of Locke's trilogy in the "natural law" preamble to the Declaration of Independence, proclaiming that "all Men are created equal, that they are endowed by their Creator with certain unalienable Rights, that among these are Life, Liberty and the Pursuit of Happiness."[3]

Seven decades later, German philosophers Karl Marx and Friedrich Engels also adapted Locke's analysis, in publishing *The Communist Manifesto* in 1848. Only they argued that property's origins in labor required the *abolition* of personal ("bourgeois") property in the means of production, because the owners of industrial property "appropriated" the workers' efforts that lay "congealed" in that machinery. Their "labor theory of value" became the moral catalyst for the worker-led Russian Revolution of 1917, which relieved Russia's nobility of their property, transferring it not to the workers individually but to the Communist Party collectively, as a representative of the workers.

In 1862, fourteen years after publication of *The Communist Manifesto*, Abraham Lincoln proposed another revolutionary ownership solution with his Emancipation Proclamation declaring freedom for slaves as of New Year's Day 1863—in the hope that this would strip the American South of a primary means of production during the Civil War. He proposed a second ownership solution that same year when he signed the Homestead Act enticing settlers (including potential Confederate enlistees) to migrate westward, where they would be granted a 160-acre parcel that would become their "freehold" once they homesteaded the land (mixed their labor with it) for five years.[4] The first homestead title was granted to Kansas farmer Daniel Freeman. An avid reader, Lincoln was familiar with the advice offered by Alexis de Tocqueville following de Tocqueville's study of the United States of the 1830s, in which he observed:

"Nations are less disposed to make revolutions in proportion as personal property is augmented and distributed among them, and as the number of those possessing it is increased."[5]

The industrial revolution of the eighteenth century was itself fueled by an ownership solution. Professor Douglass North, economic historian and 1993 Nobel laureate in economic science, chronicles the correlation between the "social invention" of patent rights (included in the U.S. Constitution) and the beginning of a wave of agricultural and industrial inventions.[6] For instance, Eli Whitney applied for the first patent for a cotton gin in 1793.[7] With the protection of intellectual property rights, North documents, people became more willing to invest in research and development, secure in the knowledge that their costs could be recouped.[8]

Innovation and investment were also encouraged by Locke's proposal to divorce property from politics. Imagine the disincentive for a farmer to improve or even maintain his acreage if he could be evicted at the whim of the landlord (or the lord himself, in feudal times). History confirms that a freehold farmer is more willing than a sharecropper to invest, and is a far better steward. Despite the importance of technical innovations in production, North documents why they are much less important than those innovations embedded in legal and social institutions. Fully functioning property rights, he argues, are particularly crucial to support a market economy.

Property rights held in common also played a role, even though this was the key philosophical conundrum Locke had to solve to justify the transformation of the goods of nature (common to all men) into personal property that could be "beneficial to any particular man." The enclosure movement of nineteenth-century Europe marked a watershed in the evolution of property, when common fields and pastures (the "commons") were transformed into hedged fields and consolidated farms owned by the well-to-do. That drove property-deprived peasants into the mills and slums of the city, providing pools of cheap labor to fuel the industrial revolution.[9]

From Security to Securities

The common and the personal inevitably worked hand in hand. As social institutions (a type of commons) evolved to support personal contracts with the force of law, contracts themselves became an ownable and exchangeable form of property. At first the law recognized letters of credit, promissory notes and such. Initially these contracts were personal—"pay to the order of John Smith." Gradually they were made out to whoever held them ("the bearer"). This innovation enhanced efficiency by enabling a creditor to sell to a third party an enforceable obligation even though the parties were unknown to each other.

In today's sophisticated capital markets (another commons), this "securitization" process now includes bearer securities backed by home mortgages, credit card receipts, car loans,* student loans and other contractual claims.[10] This property-ization process is spreading rapidly. In 1985, just fifty-six nations had significant securities markets with total capitalization of $6.5 trillion. Ten years later, eighty-five nations had stock markets valued at nearly $18 trillion while global bond markets topped $18.5 trillion.

Over time, the nature of the "person" entering into these contracts also changed, becoming more "institutional" as the corporation (a legal "person") emerged as the most prevalent of these new entities. This transformation parallels mankind's steady evolution away from descriptions denoting social status (monarch, lord, serf, slave) and toward a terminology where relationships are based more on contract. Over time, "worker" (with its sociopolitical implications) became "employee," suggesting employment contracts, pension agreements and such. However, it is the contractual notion of "owner"— a concept based solely on contract—that remains the key legacy of this steady evolution from the days of John Locke. While property retains its status as the foundation of the social contract, the corporation has emerged as its primary expression; it has become the social person (the "corpus") through which a majority of the world's productive assets are now held.[11] Thus, it is with the corporate form of property that an ownership solution must be most concerned.

The corporation is itself best understood as a social contract, its most significant element dependent on the perspective of the viewer. Pointing to its origins in the granting of royal charters to English trading companies, such as the Hudson Bay Company that helped settle North America, an economic historian would see the corporation as a contract for the receipt of royal favors, the pooling of commercial risks and the limiting of personal liabilities. A finance-oriented historian, on the other hand, would note that it was in the United States, not Europe, that the corporate form first flourished, reflecting America's lack of large family fortunes and the need to raise funds from investors. A lawyer-economist, such as 1991 Nobel laureate Ronald Coase, would see the corporation as a way to reduce "transaction costs" by coordinating contracts for such commercial activities as employment, production, distribution and so on.†

---

* The Ford Motor Company earned more as a banker than as a car builder from 1991 to 1996; its banking profits in 1995 were higher than all but two of the nation's commercial banks. In the third quarter of 1996, Ford Credit earned $299 million while the company's worldwide automotive operations earned profits of only $15 million.

† As we will see in a later chapter, information technologies have greatly reduced these costs, with an accompanying increase in outsourcing and other noncorporate, nonemployment work arrangements. Similarly, the cost of maintaining liaison with others in order to coordinate work (the origins of corporate middle management) is falling rapidly with the spread of information and networked communication technologies capable of facilitating many of those tasks.

History's Two Fateful Near-Misses

We've come a long way since Locke proposed personal property as a social innovation meant to help mankind evolve out of a state of nature.* The labor-based notion on which Locke based his rationale for personal property (" 'tis labor indeed that puts the difference of value on everything") continues its steady decline in real-world relevance. A seventeenth-century farmer can be visualized "mixing" his labor with whatever man "removes out of the State that Nature hath provided." But for those of us living in a post-agrarian, postindustrial information age, both Locke's imagery of labor-based property and Marx's metaphysical notion of "congealed labor" are badly outdated. A visit to any capital-intensive, robotized and reengineered manufacturing facility quickly dispels any notion of just who is being "mixed" with what. For example, in a Japanese factory outside Toyota City, 66 humans and 310 robots assemble 300 Lexus sedans each day.

In order to effect the ownership solution, we have to acknowledge the modern reality that property is now more often accessed through corporate finance than through personal toil. Oddly enough, though Marx is rightly viewed as the world's greatest destroyer of property rights (and the greatest critic of "finance capitalism"), few historians realize just how close he may have come to advocating not communism but a radically decentralized form of capitalism.

A close reading of Marx reveals three equally plausible remedies to the two key concerns he identified: the concentration of wealth and the exploitation of working people by the forces of finance capital. His first solution, abolishing private property, is the best known. His second remedy is less well known but more widely applied: the steady erosion of property rights by what is today known as "creeping socialism." The ten "erosive" measures he recommended are now commonly accepted features of even the most avowedly capitalist countries; they include the abolition of child factory labor, free primary school education and progressive income taxes.

Philosopher Mortimer Adler points to "a third and quite distinct remedy, not recognized by Marx, but equally appropriate to his purpose—that is, neither the erosion of private property rights, nor the abolition of private property itself, but the extension of the ownership of capital from the few to the many."[12] In support of this premise, Adler points to *The Communist Manifesto*, where Marx implies that broad-based personal ownership would have provided an equally satisfactory solution:

---

* In *The Social Contract,* Rousseau argued that man's bargain with himself (i.e., his agreement to subject himself to civil order) required that he forfeit his *natural liberty,* where the enjoyment of property was based on his strength, in order to gain *civil liberty.* This social contract transformed his enjoyment into genuine "proprietorship" where his possession was made secure by the rule of law rather than through brute force and usurpation.

You are horrified at our intending to do away with private property. But in your existing society private property is already done away with for nine-tenths of the population; its existence for the few is solely due to its nonexistence in the hands of those nine-tenths. You reproach us, therefore, with intending to do away with a form of property, the necessary condition for whose existence is the nonexistence of any property for the immense majority of society.

Whether Marx and Engels missed the point or simply chose to ignore it is an issue best left to the late-night ruminations of scholars. One fact is clear: Marx was not only a critic of capitalism, he was also a begrudging admirer, conceding that it "has created more massive and more colossal productive forces than have all preceding generations together. . . . It has accomplished wonders far surpassing Egyptian pyramids, Roman aqueducts, and Gothic cathedrals; it has conducted expeditions that put in the shade all former Exoduses of nations and crusades."

From an ownership perspective, the second fateful near miss was authored by the hugely influential John Maynard Keynes and his publication of *The General Theory of Employment, Interest and Money* (1935). Though Keynes acknowledged that patterns of ownership could affect his economic theory, he chose to place this thorny issue beyond the scope of his analysis, conceding:

In so far as the distribution of wealth is determined by the more or less permanent social structure of the community, this also can be reckoned a factor, subject only to slow change and over a long period, which we can take as given in our present context.[13]

Reconnecting Capitalism—A Review of What Follows

Though concentrated ownership has long been capitalism's least savory feature, decision-makers—in both the private and the public sectors—are cautioned to proceed with care in nudging the system to become more inclusive. That's because property's value derives largely from the confidence people place in its security. It seems to me implausible to build a widely participatory private property economy for tomorrow by first undermining confidence in the private property system we enjoy today. With that as a first step, neither the old nor the new owners could have confidence in capitalism. Policy initiatives are likely to be more fruitful, and their results more robust, if efforts are focused on a steady broadening of ownership, in the knowledge that a vigorous effort in that direction will, in time, correct the current concentration.

Through policy initiatives that are adaptable throughout the world, I show how a more participatory capitalism could gradually displace today's exclusive, detached and socially erosive ownership patterns. Drawing on imagery common to systems analysts, I demonstrate why broad-based personal ownership is capitalism's missing "feedback system," and why a component of "up-close ownership" is required to link a nation's people to their workplace, their community, their economy, their environment—and to each other. Lacking a reliable *human-based* signaling system for identifying investments that have damaging, even transgenerational effects, today's capitalism—indifferent, remote and numbers-driven—continues to direct resources into projects that endanger our planetary resources. In a worldwide review, I describe hopeful ownership solutions afoot in such hot spots as Russia, China, Cuba, South Africa and the Middle East.

An ownership strategy could fill the current policy void in either the Republican or Democratic Parties. The same holds true for Britain's Tories and Labor. Free enterprise policymakers can no longer afford to be agnostic about ownership patterns; leaving most citizens assetless is certain to result in ever greater fiscal strains. Before my seven-year-old son graduates from college, he will feel the full fiscal impact of a demographic tidal wave as the first baby boomers go on the receiving end of entitlement programs that are already unaffordable. The only way out, I submit, is a sensible ownership policy.

Ownership breeds a certain conservatism. Yet few politicians have made the leap from concept to policy, even though ownership advocates hail from across the American political spectrum, including Ronald Reagan, Jim Wright, Jack Kemp, Mario Cuomo, Dick Gephardt, Newt Gingrich and Ted Kennedy. An ownership solution offers a unique political platform. The policies lend themselves to progressive, even populist rhetoric while the prescriptions are typically rock-ribbed conservative. I offer the reader a seasoned in-the-trenches political realism born of legislative battles that both span the ideological spectrum and circle the globe. In contrast to the handwringers who fuss without offering feasible solutions, I show how a pragmatic ownership strategy could weave a broader web of personal, economic and civic participation. My hope is to inspire bold, forceful leaders in both the private and the public realm who are willing to act with a sense of purpose equal to the scope of the historic forces at work.

Why Capitalism Creates
So Few Capitalists

CHAPTER 1

Disconnected Capitalism

> If we do not change our direction, we are likely to end up
> where we are going.
>
> —*Chinese proverb*

For the first time in human history, a single economic system encircles the globe. This global capitalism is both good news and bad. The good news is that more so than ever before, capitalism has proven its capacity to produce untold riches. The bad news is that many people are now victimized by forces seemingly beyond their control, including an ongoing globalization of finance that benefits the few while marginalizing the many. Those same forces could be harnessed to the advantage of everyone, but this will come about only if, as and when more of us become connected to capitalism—*as capitalists.*

As the world's largest market economy, the United States provides a dramatic example of how modern capitalism is rapidly becoming "disconnected" from those who live in its midst. America's institutional investors—pension funds, mutual funds, insurance companies, banks, foundations and university endowments—held $11,100,000,000,000 ($11.1 *trillion*) in assets as of 1 July 1996.[1] Due to the booming stock market, those holdings doubtless crossed the $12 trillion threshold by early 1998.

Fidelity Management and Research Company oversees more than $600 billion in assets; Boston's State Street Bank manages $300 billion.[2] The December 1997 announcement of a merger between Union Bank of Switzerland and the Swiss Bank Corporation was the first sign of what is likely to be a series of megamergers that reflect the structural changes sweeping global capital markets. It not only created the world's second largest bank with $595 billion in assets; it also created a money management behemoth with $920 billion in assets. Worldwide, the top half-dozen investment managers now direct $3.5 trillion in combined assets.[3] These are the equivalent J. P. Morgans, Pilkingtons and Krupps of today, but with a key difference: where those legendary "silk hat" capitalists were hands-on managers both of companies and the financial capital those companies represented, today's megacapitalists manage only one thing—money. Money management focused on maximizing financial returns is not new. What *is* new is the vast scale and the skyrocketing growth of contemporary "disconnected" capital. Institutional assets totaled just $673 billion in 1970 and still only $1.9 trillion by 1980. For the next ten years, an American will turn age fifty every seven seconds. Aging baby boomers (born between 1946 and 1964) ensure a continued growth in retirement savings, along with a steady flow of funds into institutional hands.

What is also new is the enormous deference granted the information reflected in financial returns, especially when one considers how dramatically people's lives are affected by the decisions based on those numbers. To an alarming extent, short-term share prices are the compass by which the course is set. The result is a sort of secular sanctification of market forces, with the result that these vast sums are invested to reflect only those values contained within a very narrow band of very specialized feedback. This preference for financial indicators, in turn, neglects the impact this capital has on many other key indicators of economic and social health.

Those include the nation's social structure, including the steadily widening gap between rich and poor; the environment (financial data inadequately signals ecological costs that are distant in time and place); and the steadily growing number of households left out of this wealth accumulation process altogether who, in turn, become dependent on government support. This escalating dependency, in turn, imperils the nation's fiscal health as claims for support (income, services, public-sector jobs, etc.) "crowd out" budget resources essential to the general welfare, including funds needed for education, health, infrastructure and the cleanup and restoration of the environment.

This trend toward institutionalized, disconnected capital is gaining momentum worldwide as governments privatize state-run pension plans and enhance incentives for retirement savings. One school of experts sees this trend contributing both to development and political stability as growing pools of capital support dynamic "emerging markets" worldwide. These analysts foresee a steady lessening in the vulnerability of developing countries to the whims of foreign investors and the volatility of quick-trigger capital flows. Others worry that the dictates of financial capital will diminish both the will and the means for societies to pursue fundamental notions of equity, dignity and individual self-realization. While experts disagree on the impact of this trend, there is little disagreement on one key feature of the trend itself: the ongoing concentration of wealth in the hands of either the already-rich or institutions.

The Widening Gap Between the Haves and the Have-Nots

Between 1980 and 1992, total assets in the United States increased nearly threefold while institutional assets grew 4.5 times. By mid-1997, American mutual funds held $4.0 trillion, almost six times the total of just a decade earlier.[4] While it's true that more American adults own stocks and stock mutual funds than at any time in history (51.3 million in 1995), 71 percent of households own no shares at all or hold less than $2,000 in any form, including mutual funds, popular 401(k) plans and traditional pensions, according to a 1995 study by M.I.T. economist James M. Poterba and Dartmouth economist Andrew A. Samwick.[5]

Though stories of "401(k) millionaires" abound, such individuals are a rarity. For instance, a mid-1997 survey of the records at one fund group, T. Rowe Price Associates Inc. in Baltimore, found just 308 millionaires among their seven hundred thousand company-sponsored retirement accounts (i.e., four-hundredths of 1 percent). Even though the United States now has 2.7 millionaires in a 1996 population of 265 million (1 percent), it would be a mistake to conclude that wealth ownership is broadening in any appreciable way. Indeed, surveys suggest quite the opposite. For example,

- Research by Harvard University economic historians found that the share of the nation's overall net worth held by the wealthiest 1 percent of American households jumped from below 20 percent in 1979 to more than 36 percent in 1989.[6]

- Although the national net worth expanded $5 trillion from 1983 to 1989, New York University professor Ed Wolff found that 54 percent of that was claimed by the half million families who make up the top one-half of 1 percent of the U.S. population. That works out to an average $5.4 million *gain* per already-wealthy household. That's three-quarters of a million dollars each year, $65,000 per month, or $90 per hour, twenty-four hours a day. And that's when the Dow-Jones industrial average was a fraction of what it is today.

- Research by scholars at the Federal Reserve and the Internal Revenue Service found that the net worth of that top 1 percent is now greater than that of the bottom 90 percent.

- Professor Wolff characterizes the current era as the most extreme level of wealth concentration since the late 1920s. Census Bureau data (1996) confirm that impression, documenting that the gap between America's haves and have-nots is the widest since the end of World War II.

Those who own financial capital also benefited disproportionately from a record-breaking inflow of funds into the stock market, due in substantial part to more funds (dominantly baby-boomer retirement savings) chasing a relatively limited number of securities. That fueled a steady increase in share values far higher than what could be justified by underlying economic activity. For instance, following the stock market "correction" of October 1987 (when the Dow-Jones industrial average fell from 2,700 to 1,700), the Dow index climbed to 5,000 by November 1995 and soared beyond 8,000 by mid-1997. In other words, according to financial market reckoning, the value of these companies more than quadrupled in less than a decade.

Accompanying this steady increase in wealth concentration was a steady increase in income disparities:

- According to the Congressional Budget Office, the top 1 percent of U.S. households claimed 70 percent of the total $250 billion net increase in household income during the 1977–1989 period.

- The Census Bureau reported in 1996 record levels of inequality, with the top fifth of American households now claiming 48.2 percent of the nation's income while the bottom fifth gets by on just 3.6 percent.

- Though average household income climbed 10 percent between 1979 and 1994, 97 percent of that gain was claimed by the most well-to-do 20 percent. In 1973, the income of the top 20 percent of American families was 7.5 times that of the bottom 20 percent.[7] By 1996, it was more than 13 times.

- Between 1989 and 1993, median household income in the United States fell more than 7 percent after correcting for family size and inflation. Recent data suggest that this erosion is accelerating. After adjusting for inflation, the annual income of households in the lowest quintile rose only $87 from 1975 to 1994, while the median wage is nearly 3 percent below what it was in 1979.[8] For those in the bottom tenth percentile—someone earning just above the minimum wage—their inflation-adjusted wages fell by an astounding 16 percent between 1979 and 1989.[9] Three-quarters of Americans have weathered two decades of stagnant living standards.

- Meanwhile, income tax returns for 1995 show that 87,000 Americans reported adjusted gross income of $1 million or more. This upper-upper income group's income soared 25 percent from 1994 to $227.6 billion, outpacing the overall 7 percent increase in income reported for the nation's 118.2 million individual returns.[10]

These trends led William McDonough, chairman of the Federal Reserve Bank of New York, to issue a strongly worded caution: "Issues of equity and social cohesion [are] issues that affect the very temperament of the country. We are forced to face the question of whether we will be able to go forward together as a unified society with a confident outlook or as a society of diverse economic groups suspicious of both the future and each other."[11] M.I.T. economist Lester Thurow shares that concern, cautioning that we have entered a realm where "[T]he system that has held democracy and capitalism together for the last century has started to unravel."[12]

Two-Tier Markets for a Two-Tier Society

The marketplace is fundamentally indifferent to this record-breaking inequality in wealth and income. Retailers have adjusted to this social polarization by turning to a "Tiffany/Kmart" marketing strategy that tailors their products and pitches to two very different Americas. Saatchi & Saatchi Advertising Worldwide warns its clients of "a continuing erosion of our traditional mass market—the middle class," while Paine Webber Inc. cautions investors to "avoid companies that cater to the 'middle' of the consumer market." In 1997, both Kmart and Tiffany reported earning surges while the midscale chains such as J. C. Penney suffered.

This dual society means that separate and decidedly unequal markets are becoming the norm, such as private banking for the well-to-do alongside record levels of check-cashing outlets (the number of Americans without checking accounts has surged from 9 percent to 13 percent since 1977). The United States now has fifty-five hundred check-cashing outlets, versus less than half that in 1988. The Gap recently remodeled and expanded its upscale Banana Republic clothing stores, adding sixty-eight new outlets since 1992. Meanwhile, it created a lower-end chain called Old Navy, opening two hundred outlets since 1993 (compared with just twenty-one new middle-income Gap outlets).

This phenomenon cuts across industries. The top-earning 20 percent of Americans now account for 54 percent of new-car sales, up from 40 percent in 1980. Meanwhile, since 1994 growth in the "secondhand" industry has tripled the pace of more traditional retail sales. Used-car sales are at record levels. Pawnshop activity is booming. Prepaid phone cards have become a must for those who cannot afford their own telephone. This trend is poised to accelerate. The Atlanta-based Affluent Market Institute predicts that by 2005 America's millionaires will control 60 percent of the nation's purchasing dollars. Sales of high-end luxury yachts are already at record levels.[13]

The Index of Social Well-Being is at a twenty-five-year low. Working with research dating back to 1970, Fordham University's Institute for Social Policy annually compares government statistics on sixteen troublesome topics such as teen suicide, children in poverty and the gap between rich and poor. The nation's best year was 1973 when (on a scale of 100) the index stood at 77.5. In the Nixon-Ford era, the index averaged 73. Under President Carter, it fell to 60. Under President Reagan it plummeted to 43, and to 40 under George Bush, where it has since stabilized. Noting that the index has dropped steadily since its inception, Institute Director Marc L. Miringoff concludes: "Despite a range of stated differences in philosophy and policy, neither political party has been able to achieve significant progress in social health over 25 years."[14]

UN Assessment: "World Heads for Grotesque Inequalities"

A worldwide widening of disparities in wealth and income led the United Nations Development Program to conclude in 1996 that the world is heading for "grotesque inequalities," noting that "100 countries are worse off today than 15 years ago." According to UN figures, the poorest 20 percent of the world's people saw their share of global income decline from 2.3 percent to 1.4 percent over the past thirty years. Meanwhile, among the world's 5.7 billion people, the top 20 percent hold 83 percent of worldwide wealth. While global GNP grew 40 percent between 1970 and 1985 (suggesting widening prosperity), the number of poor grew by 17 percent. Although 200 million people saw their incomes fall between 1965 and 1980, more than 1 billion people experienced a drop from 1980 to 1993. In sub-Saharan Africa, twenty countries remain below their per capita incomes of two decades ago. Among Latin American and Caribbean countries, eighteen are below their per capita incomes of ten years ago.[15] Even within the developed countries, more than 100 million people live below national poverty standards and more than 5 million are homeless.[16]

Meanwhile, the UN reported in 1996 that the assets held by the world's 358 billionaires now exceed the combined incomes of countries with 45 percent of the world's people.[17] These findings led UN development experts to conclude "Development that perpetuates today's inequalities is neither sustainable *nor worth sustaining*" (emphasis added). This pattern—pockets of prosperity alongside widespread deprivation—has become the worldwide trend both within and among nations. Over the past thirty years, those countries that are home to the richest 20 percent of the world's people increased their share of gross world product from 70 percent to 85 percent. Three decades ago, the people in these well-to-do countries were thirty times better off than those in countries where the poorest 20 percent of the world's people live. This gap has since more than doubled (to sixty-one times) and is certain to widen further. The UN offers the most dramatic assessment, concluding that, if this rich-poor divide continues, it will produce a world "gargantuan in its excesses and grotesque in its human and economic inequalities."[18]

Chronicling the Cost of Economic Disparity

This global growth in economic disparity and "disconnectedness" creates an array of challenges to the health of entire nations and, indeed, to global capitalism. Mexico evidenced an early symptom in the armed uprising of the "Zapatistas" on New Year's Day 1994 in impoverished Chiapas state, home to one-third of Mexico's population though host to 70 percent of its extreme poor, its highest illiteracy rate (60 percent) and childhood mortality rate (46 percent) and its lowest life expectancy (35 years for women, 45 for men).[19] Similarly, in the Islamic world, the shift to fundamentalism and occasional extremism is fueled, in part, by those concerned about steadily worsening poverty and fast-accelerating economic disparities. Yet the Islam-phobic West points to fundamentalist fervor as the cause rather than a symptom of discontent.

Frances Moore Lappe, author of *Diet for a Small Planet*, documents the correlation between concentrated ownership in agrarian economies and the high incidence of hunger, malnutrition and infant mortality. In Latin America, for instance, large landowners are notorious for allowing vast stretches of arable acreage to lie fallow while landless peasants eke out a hardscrabble existence. She cites a Central American study where only 14 percent of the land held by the largest landowners was under cultivation.[20] A UN study of eighty-three nations found that 5 percent of rural landholders controlled three-quarters of the land. Reflecting a common pattern, a mid-1980s study disclosed that six families in El Salvador controlled as much land as three hundred thousand peasants.

In the United States, the most obvious challenge is the ongoing deterioration in social cohesiveness and the erosion in civil society, made worse by the fast-growing economic separation between the haves and have-nots. Fully one-third of American men between the ages of twenty-five and thirty-four do not earn enough to keep a family of four out of poverty, with all that implies for the strains on marriage and the prospects for young families. This growing rift is also racial. The Census Bureau found in 1991 that the meager median wealth of white households is eight times that of Hispanic households and ten times that of African-American households.[21]

Based on a 1995 survey, the Federal Reserve found that the typical American family had a net worth of $56,400, including home equity, down from $56,500 six years earlier. This ever widening gap has well-known social and political implications. Two-tier societies and two-tier marketplaces are not the fertile ground in which robust democracies take root. Historians have long documented the threat posed to open political systems by extreme disparities in wealth, as the possession of great wealth by a few confers on their holders inordinate power, which they may be tempted to use in ways that run counter to the general welfare.[22]

The Trend Accelerates

There remains yet much fuel for a continued widening of this two-class system. For instance, in order to boost short-term earnings, corporations can unleash what the *Wall Street Journal* characterizes as the "four horsemen of the workplace": (1) downsizing, (2) moving operations to low-wage countries, (3) increased automation and (4) the use of temporary workers. Other factors are also at work, including the growth in demand for high-skilled labor,[23] the spread of networked computers, immigration, the shift from a manufacturing to a service economy, flatter tax rates, cutbacks in assistance to the poor, an increase in single-parent families, a decline in unionization, an erosion in the value of the minimum wage and the steady rise in the stock and bond markets (and speculation) in which the wealthy are disproportionately represented.

Widespread assetlessness and eroding incomes also imply large and growing fiscal strains. That's because, absent broad-based economic self-reliance, a nation's citizens tend to look to their government not only for services they cannot afford but also for income they cannot generate. For example, absent a major shift in policy, a 1994 Bipartisan Commission on Entitlements and Tax Reform concluded that outlays for entitlements (Social Security, Medicare and Medicaid) plus interest on the national debt will by the year 2012 consume 100 percent of federal tax receipts. Social Security and Medicare alone cost Americans $591.4 billion in 1996[24] while other outlays to boost household incomes (such as military and federal employee pensions) cost an additional $247.5 billion.

That's a single year total of $838.9 billion in income redistribution. And that's before the retirement needs of the baby boomers begin to kick in. Also, in January 1998, President Clinton proposed an expansion of Medicare to those aged 55 to 65. This trend is not limited to the United States. As wealth disparities have widened within developed economies, the ratio of public to private spending has grown, on average, from 30 percent of gross domestic product in 1960 to 46 percent in 1997,[25] belying the notion that the worldwide expansion of free enterprise will necessarily reduce the size of government. Other countries are also struggling under the fiscal strains associated with this widespread assetlessness.

America's hugely regressive Social Security tax (levied on a flat percentage of payroll) is now the largest single tax paid by most U.S. taxpayers. For a majority of American workers in private industry, Social Security entitlements are their *only* old-age pension. Most revealing of all, those anticipated payments now represent the most significant "wealth" for a majority of U.S. households. Thus, in the world's avowedly most "capitalist" economy, the most important asset for a majority of its citizens is an assurance that someone else will be taxed on their behalf. Adding insult to injury, that tax is levied on jobs, the sole link that most Americans have to their economy. Perhaps most ominous of all: U.S.-trained economists now advise in-transition socialist countries worldwide, spreading this suspect ownership formula abroad.

Cracks in the Facade

As I suggest in the introduction, the main "systemic" deficiency in today's capitalism lies in its faulty "feedback" system. The system is not engineered—wired, if you will—to anticipate and respond to the needs of those who populate it.

Rather (as we shall see), it is steadily being rewired to reflect the peculiar dictates of financial capital. It is useful to recall that the very concept of free enterprise is itself a feedback notion, a term unknown two centuries ago when Adam Smith opened *The Wealth of Nations* with his parable of how the market's "invisible hand" of voluntary exchange and freely determined prices would assure the optimum results for its participants.

> *It is not from the benevolence of the butcher, the brewer, or the baker that we expect our dinner, but from their regard to their own interest. We address ourselves, not to their humanity but to their self-love, and never talk to them of our own necessities but of their advantages.*[26]

History has proven Smith largely correct. The dismal results achieved in "command economies" (such as the Soviet Union) offer eloquent testimony to the need for markets. However, two major cracks are beginning to show in the free-enterprise facade. They share a common trait: faulty feedback. The first: the bulk of people participating in free enterprise today are not connected to the system in a fully appropriate manner. Jobs alone are proving inadequate. For instance, Jacques Delors, president of the European Commission, advised that Europe's disadvantaged would have to learn to cope with "a whole new relationship with leisure time" (i.e., unemployment). In the United States, more flexible wages assure more jobs, but at the cost of soaring inequality and growing poverty. Both Americans and Europeans suffer from a Faustian bargain: Americans with their high rate of job creation alongside their "working poor"; Europeans with their government-protected jobs alongside a growing "leisure class." Despite capitalism's roots in private property, little thought has yet been given to reengineering free enterprise to make it possible for more people to participate as capitalists.

The second crack: environmental hazards continue to mount. For example, the market-driven search for "cheap" energy has left radioactive waste worldwide, creating health and genetic dangers that will last for millennia. The cost of hydrocarbon-fueled development has resulted in 1.3 billion people breathing air below the minimum standard considered acceptable by the World Health Organization. None of the largest twenty cities in the world meet international clean-air standards. The environment will come under even greater assault as industrialization continues in the Asian Tigers and as China's development hastens resource consumption among its 1.2 billion people. Similar costs accompany the spread of industrial-scale farming and modern production techniques that contaminate aquifers, degrade watersheds, waste precious topsoil and imperil rivers and oceans with the runoff of agricultural chemicals.

These two cracks are destined to widen if ownership continues to become ever more institutionalized, concentrated and disconnected—and if financial capital continues to become ever more directed solely "by the numbers" (i.e., to the lowest-cost, highest-return production). Because the broader impact of investment decisions typically lie in a faraway part of some larger system, today's finance-dominated capitalism is limited in its ability to learn from those consequences. The impact often is too distant in both place and time. Precisely because the economy lacks a way to incorporate more personalized, localized, genuinely humanized feedback, Adam Smith's vision of a seamless, *self*-designed system has begun to fray. As yet, there is no countervailing signaling system capable of ensuring that capitalism is sufficiently well informed except in a limited, financially myopic manner.

Policymakers are searching for a comprehensive "design science" capable of organizing economic activity in a way that both promotes human well-being and reflects sound ecological, ethical and fiscal principles. Today's finance-dominated free enterprise is simply incapable of detecting, much less responding to, those self-correcting signals for which Adam Smith envisioned the market so well suited. Smith could not have foreseen how financial capital, the lifeblood of capitalism, would become both (*a*) concentrated in so few hands and (*b*) disconnected from the concerns of those whose lives it affects.

Happily, private ownership is uniquely well suited to provide today's missing "connectivity." Why? Because at their core, property rights operate as a signaling system, connecting people to their economy in a way that enables them to register their personal concerns so that free enterprise performs in a genuinely people-responsive fashion. That, in a nutshell, is the premise behind *The Ownership Solution*.

A Sustainable Capitalism Requires a People-ized Signaling System

At present, free enterprise responds to three types of feedback:

- *Product pricing.* Consumers "vote" for the best quality at the best price.

- *Share pricing.* Capital markets "vote" by directing investment capital to those firms with the best financial returns.

- *Corporate governance.* This feedback is provided both by hands-on managers and by the monitoring of those managers by boards of directors who, in turn, are voted in or out of office by shareholders.

As we shall see, each of these signals has significant limitations. Yet each could be improved if the underlying ownership pattern were more participatory. As Smith envisioned, pricing serves as free enterprise's dominant "feedback loop"—both product pricing and the prices at which a company's shares trade hands in the marketplace. Consumers have long assumed that the price of a product includes the full cost of its production plus a profit. Similarly, shareholders assume that share prices reflect the company's success in selling products on a profitable basis. Yet neither assumption may be true where, for example, a company treats the environment as a cost-free subsidy.

Environmental costs are often imposed neither on the customer (through higher product prices) nor on shareholders (through lower share values) but on the public in the form of reduced air quality, increased needs for health care, depleted stocks of natural resources (clean water, fishes, forests, etc.) and a poisonous and depleted legacy for future generations. Even the notion of "profit" may be illusory where private gain is generated by shifting such costs to the public. When free enterprise signals us that the invaluable (breathable air, drinkable water) lacks value, then our feedback system is flawed. Further, when product costs show up not as a business expense but as a social cost (pollution, illness and such), this flaw undermines free enterprise by ensuring higher taxes (for environmental cleanup, health care, etc.), more intrusive government regulation and, eventually, less consumer purchasing power.

Further, it is impossible to "cost" certain types of environmental damage. How does one set a price on lumber when its harvesting destroys a centuries-old stand of virgin forest? Or cost the use of industrial chemicals when their disposal damages an aquifer? Or do a cost-benefit analysis on the use of chemicals that disrupt the endocrine system?[27] Or put a price tag on the enhanced likelihood of childhood cancer? Such questions raise both commercial and ethical concerns.

Microbiologist Theo Colborn documents five hundred measurable chemicals in our bodies that were never in anyone's body before the 1920s, including a range of endocrine-disrupting chemicals (EDCs) associated with a litany of adverse health effects, including weakened immune systems, reproductive problems, metabolic maladies and functional deficits in intelligence, sexual function and behavior. As explained by Michael Lerner, president of Commonweal, a health and environmental research institute: "Before EDCs, we used to worry most about toxic chemicals' increased cancer risk. The higher the dosage/exposure, the greater the cancer risk. The new research shows that EDCs have a wide range of serious effects beyond cancer; that they cause these effects at infinitely lower levels than are necessary to cause cancer; that these effects are fundamentally intergenerational (the health effects are in our children and grandchildren)."[28]

Lastly, experience suggests that the current feedback between directors and managers often fails to provide the oversight needed to protect either the financial interests of shareholders or the personal interests of "stakeholders"— those who are put at risk by the company's activities but have no voice. Although stockholders, at least, have ownership rights (ineffective though they may be), stakeholders typically lack any property right through which they can either communicate their concerns or pursue corrective action.

What free enterprise requires is another signaling mechanism. The feedback conveyed by prices is essential, but it's insufficient to meet even the most rudimentary standards of sustainability. Further, as a creature of law, the corporate entity's "license to operate" is put at risk when decisions affecting a broad base of stakeholders are reserved solely for shareholders—who may not even reside in the community where the effects are felt.[29] In the constant balancing of the interests of stockholders and stakeholders, the solution is often regulation or litigation. I suggest that the solution may lie in a more inclusive style of feedback-intensive decision-making, one that takes into account the concerns of *both* shareholders and stakeholders.

Capitalism Needs More "Up-Close" Capitalists

While that may sound reasonable in the abstract, what does it mean in operation? Consider, for instance, the case of a power-generating facility organized as an investor-owned utility with rates set by a public utility commission. Because investors are assured a minimum return, these companies are seen as prudent blue-chip investments favored by institutional investors. Consequently, a power utility's shareholders commonly reside far from the community where the physical impact of its operations are felt. Thus, if the company becomes an environmental scoundrel, the most a local consumer can do is complain—to the company, to the public utility commission, to a local politician—an indirect, after-the-fact and, at best, tenuous form of feedback.

However, that company *could* be financially reengineered so that a portion of its shares are owned by its consumers and its employees. Converting those stakeholders into shareholders could change things. For instance, where dissatisfied local residents now depend on a circuitous feedback system to register their concerns, an ownership stake would transform them from concerned (but disconnected) stakeholders into property-empowered owners. Even if local consumers and employees owned only a small quantity of the utility's total shares, this *qualitative* change in the composition of that ownership could transform the company's capacity to anticipate and respond to legitimate local concerns.

As an example of the benefits of such "up-close capitalism," Nobel laureate economist Myron Scholes touts the positive effect that employee stock ownership can have on corporate decision-making. In his view, such "inside" ownership improves performance both directly (by encouraging insider challenges to poorly conceived management decisions) and indirectly—by influencing managers who know that the firm's owners are now working among them.[30] Similarly, by including a component of *consumer* ownership, the utility's managers (and their families) would live among shareholders who are also neighbors, schoolmates and teammates. Such a community-focused ownership stake could change the quality of business relationships across a broad spectrum because local, up-close capitalists have more at stake than do remote investors. They are also more likely to raise a hue and cry when the company makes an environmental misstep (or is about to make one). Dumping solvents into the local watershed, for instance, looks very different from up close—when it's your family, not just your financial return, that's at risk.

If a Little Capitalism Is So Good, Why Not a Lot?

What contemporary capitalism needs most is to be consistent with itself. If the private ownership of capital is a "public good" worthy of promotion and protection, then surely the nation will be much improved as more people gain an opportunity to directly experience just how good ownership can be. That will happen only when the culture underlying capitalism includes as a goal the creation of a free enterprise broadly populated with capitalists.

The intentional engineering of up-close ownership patterns is something new for modern-day capitalism. However, the deliberate creation of feedback systems is nothing new. Democracies enjoy popular support for the very reason that they *are* engineered feedback systems. Voting provides a way for the populace to "talk back" to the system, though opinions vary regarding how well the system listens. Both pricing and voting reflect a preference for "self-designed" systems based on personal preference. "The true case for the market mechanism," *Financial Times* columnist Sam Brittan argues, "is that it is a decentralized and non-dictatorial method of conveying information, reacting to change and fostering innovation."[31]

Both Adam Smith and Thomas Jefferson proposed radically decentralized systems, along with a centralized government strong enough to ensure that decentralization. That paradox continues to this day. Winston Churchill aptly cautioned that democracy is "the worst form of government, except for all those other forms that have been tried from time to time." The same could be said of free enterprise. For relieving poverty and protecting personal freedoms, market-based democracies are a major improvement on state-controlled systems. In large part, that's because command economies fail to tap that very personal feedback that fuels the dynamism, responsiveness, robustness and, yes, the messiness of markets.

In the United States, the political foundation of free enterprise is based on what Alexander Hamilton described in *The Federalist Papers* as a "commercial republic." The goal was to encourage an environment of free economic activity as a way to counteract the erosive influences of envy, class division and the tyranny of the majority.[32] In a similar vein, Adam Smith saw commercial activity as the engine fueling the ever-widening prosperity that democracies require for their popular support. Worldwide, the resulting "capitalism" now takes many different forms, reflecting the many cultures in which it arose.[33] Individualistic, American-style capitalism is very different from that of communitarian Japan, which differs from that of corporatized Germany, egalitarian Sweden or doctrinaire Singapore. Yet each, to varying degrees, creates wealth—capitalism's primary practical goal. Each of these capitalisms also shares a common challenge: how to institutionalize a system that generates reliable, people-responsive feedback on a sustained day-to-day basis.

That, in turn, requires some attention to social engineering. I propose that societal feedback grounded in broad-based, up-close ownership is not only desirable but also feasible, affordable and perhaps even essential. However, without a sustained initiative by leaders in both the private and the public sector, the bulk of capitalism's financing will continue to flow through a highly exclusionary, ownership-concentrating "closed system of finance," which I will describe in Chapter 3.

Modern-day free enterprise has about it an internally corrosive element because it lacks a sufficiently engaged constituency with a personal ownership stake. Again, the capital is there and so is the capitalism; what is clearly missing are the capitalists. The reason for this low level of ownership participation is, I submit, a design flaw because it fails to tap the wisdom of the community. That flaw is traceable to the fact that capitalism is not yet designed to *create capitalists*. Instead it remains frozen in time, reliant on antique financing techniques that retain their very limited turn-of-the-century purpose: to finance capital. Those dramatically different goals (i.e., creating capitalists versus simply financing capital) require a conscious choice if they are to be combined. And combined they must be. A genuinely sustainable capitalism must be engineered so that, by its very operations, it steadily expands the ranks of those who can rightly be called capitalists.

CHAPTER **2**

Reconstructing Capitalism

As we shall see, apparent differences between people arise almost entirely from the action of the system they work in, not from the people themselves.

—*W. Edwards Deming*

The Ownership Solution is not intended as a critique of capitalism. Quite the contrary. I long ago tired of woe-filled leftist litanies of capitalism's alleged shortcomings, including concerns about its concentrated ownership—invariably accompanied by untried and infeasible prescriptions. Throughout this book, you'll find numerous ownership prescriptions built on a proven base of American experience. Of course I fully expect libertarian readers to find it preposterous that anyone would propose changes to an economic system in need of less rather than more intervention. Yet the right sort of intervention is required if ever we hope to reduce the size and intrusiveness of government. Absent that, capitalism's propensity to concentrate ownership will damage its dynamism, sap its vitality and eventually erode essential popular support.[1]

As Czech president Vaclav Havel warns: "People today know that they can only be saved by a new type of global responsibility. Only one small detail is missing: that responsibility must genuinely be assumed." Yet that notion risks becoming only an appealing abstraction in the absence of concrete means through which people can exercise that responsibility. In the world of commerce, responsibilities are paired with rights. In an environment where property rights reign supreme, no one can assume responsibility for the actions of a commercial enterprise without the standing that enables them to do so.

In particular, the bulk of people cannot remain outside the corporate entity, connected only as consumers and jobholders, and expect to assume responsibility for its actions. That requires that the architects of free enterprise (business leaders and policymakers alike) assume responsibility for ensuring that personalized, localized, "up-close" ownership becomes an everyday fact of life. The rights that accompany ownership are the essential "entry fee" required before people can properly assume their responsibility.

16

Havel's appeal for a new type of *global* responsibility can only emerge from the collective force of many individuals who are empowered to be *locally* responsible. That notion is reflected in the principle of "subsidiarity" which simply states that problems should be solved at the most local level possible. To contain the size, cost and intrusiveness of government requires that responsibility for problems begin with the individual, the family, civic organizations and the like, and *then* the larger community, reserving for the state the role of problem solver of last resort. Implicit in that principle is a paradox: the state must evoke an environment in which that personal responsibility can rightly be assumed.

In Search of Balance

The end of the Cold War has succeeded in making the world safe from communism, at least temporarily. Now the world must both be made safe *from capitalism*, with all its many problems, and made safe *for capitalism*, with all its promise. After all, it is market-based, capitalist economies that provide the highest standard of living worldwide. It is to market countries that refugees and emigrants flee in search of a better life. Free enterprise also provides a welcome ground for robust democracies. Economic freedom often propels a country toward more open political practices. It's difficult to imagine an open society absent an open economy.

The 1980s were an upbeat, even triumphant period for those touting the benefits of free enterprise. The decade was characterized by deregulated markets, financial liberalism and free trade. In the United States, a free enterprise–touting former California governor was twice elected president, followed by four more years under his handpicked successor. Keynesian "demand side" remedies were cast aside in favor of new "supply-side" prescriptions, while the collapse of the Soviet Union boosted the bravado of those touting market forces as a cure-all for the world's many ailments.

However, as we shall see in the next chapter, absent an accompanying ownership-participation element, unbridled free enterprise is destined to throw both the social and the economic system badly out of balance. The previous chapter chronicled the most obvious imbalances: that era's rich-get-richer legacy. While the top was flourishing, the bottom was left floundering.[2] Nor did the middle class fare well. Despite the longest, strongest economic expansion in the postwar period, Americans' wages remained stagnant for two full decades.

Laura Tyson, former chairman of President Clinton's Council of Economic Advisers, contends that, from 1978 through 1991, the inflation-adjusted median family income showed no change, despite an increase in hours worked.[3] The lower the level of skills, the worse the impact. The average inflation-adjusted earnings for nonsupervisory American workers was the same in 1993 as in 1959, when Eisenhower was president. For those with only a high school education, entry-level wages fell 39 percent from 1973 to 1993. Despite the long-heralded promise of labor-saving advances, the average American's paid work year increased by 163 hours between 1970 and 1990, equivalent to adding an extra month of toil for no additional income.[4] This is the first recorded economic boom in which the real wages of the median worker fell.[5]

The impact of this dramatic shift continues to ripple through American society. For the first time in its history, the United States has a generation destined to experience a standard of living lower than that of their parents. As two-income families become the norm, a nationwide "parenting deficit" undermines the family and tears at the core of the social fabric. An entire generation is growing up in conditions where family instability and failure are now commonplace. Crime continues to skyrocket while armed security guards emerged as the fastest growing segment of America's highly touted "service sector."

It should come as no surprise that political disenchantment is now the norm. Frustration and alienation run deeper than at any time in American political history. According to a 1995 *New York Times*/CBS poll, 79 percent of Americans believe the government is run by a few big interests looking out for themselves while 59 percent report there is not a single elected official they admire. When asked what a third political party should stand for, the most frequent answer is that it should "represent the people."

The Rising Costs of Disconnectedness

Left without the economic self-sufficiency that comes only with capital ownership, Americans turn to their political system for support. Despite the huge and growing fiscal strain of entitlement programs, policymakers have learned that even modest cutbacks could be political suicide. Bob Dole, then Senate majority leader, attributes the Republican Party's loss of the Senate in 1986 to their attempt to enact a modest two-year freeze in Social Security's cost-of-living adjustment. The "discontent of the disconnected" also shows up in other ways, including an easily tapped undercurrent of support for tariffs and trade restrictions to keep out products manufactured abroad with lower-cost labor—and to ban the entry of foreigners altogether. This can turn ugly. In 1996, it showed up as a virulent combination of xenophobia and jingoism in Pat Buchanan's failed bid for the Republican presidential nomination.[6] It's also reflected in the agonizingly slow cutback in post–Cold War defense spending with its accompanying job losses.

Over time, a remarkable array of income-support policies—many begun as social safety nets—has gradually become a fiscal noose. That spending, in turn, crowds out other competing claims on the public's purse, a key reason for the steady decline in the Index of Social Well-Being. For example, public spending on infrastructure as a percentage of GDP has been cut by half since 1975. In November 1995, the U.S. General Accounting Office cited $112 billion in pressing construction requirements in the nation's public schools but found that the states spent only $3.5 billion addressing those needs.[7]

Social Software

Ownership patterns play a supporting role in this drama. Property rights connect people to those income-producing means of production that Karl Marx rightly viewed as key components in any market economy. Marx warned that where only a few are connected and where those means become a key factor of production, private property rights will quite naturally direct the lion's share of national income to those few. What he wrongly predicted was that concentrated ownership would cause the "collapse" of capitalism, largely for lack of widespread consumer demand. Cambridge economist John Maynard Keynes nipped this dilemma in the bud, albeit not with an ownership solution but instead with an income solution. His "demand-side" bromides first surfaced during the New Deal era when President Franklin D. Roosevelt turned to public works spending as a job- and income-creating stimulus.[8] Four decades later, even Republican Richard Nixon would declare, "Now I am a Keynesian."

Nobel laureate economist Milton Friedman argues that the two authors who are read the least but influenced mankind the most are Karl Marx and John Maynard Keynes. Yet even Marx, the archenemy of capitalism, could not foresee how crucial ownership patterns would become, particularly as production was steadily shifted off man and onto his own-able inventions: his machinery, equipment, chemical processes, communication systems, computers, and so on. Marx chose for his social software not a highly *connected* ownership system but instead a system that left people even more radically *disconnected.*[9] Meanwhile, in the non-Marxist economies, economic disconnectedness steadily advanced as policymakers pretended that jobs were the only way for people to earn an income. In the Keynes-influenced view of the world, government-stimulated full employment emerged as the prevalent policy prescription. Oddly enough, this continues today, even as the unrelenting progress of labor-saving technology (including information technology) continues to squeeze human input from production at every turn.

Agriculture now employs less than 3 percent of the U.S. workforce, down from more than 20 percent in 1940. In 1988, the same output of manufactured goods could be produced as in 1973 with only 40 percent as many blue-collar man-hours. By 2010, industrial workers in developed countries will account for less than one-eighth of the workforce. Other sectors also feel the pinch. Nathan Myhrvold, head of Microsoft research, predicts the emergence of "friction-less capitalism" where the middleman (merchant, salesperson) becomes redundant as companies and customers learn to communicate directly through Internet-facilitated sales.

Early Components of a Reconstructed Capitalism

Beginning in the mid-1970s, legislators at both the federal and state level began to address this challenge, enacting an array of incentives meant to encourage more broadly based ownership, initially by employees through employee stock ownership plans (ESOPs). That kicked off a trend whereby nine million Americans in some ten thousand companies now participate as shareholders of the companies where they work. The congressional ESOP champion was Senator Russell Long, son of Louisiana's populist governor and senator Huey Long. As a member of the powerful Senate Finance Committee for twenty-six of his thirty-eight years in the Senate (he retired in 1987), Long was well positioned to act on his belief that American capitalism should become more widely populated by capitalists.

During the 1930s, Huey Long reacted to the concentrated ownership of his day by proposing to redistribute the wealth. In his son's more conservative view, the United States could not build a strong foundation for private ownership by undermining anyone's private property. Louis Kelso, a San Francisco lawyer and self-taught economist, had introduced Long to ESOPs in November 1973, casting them as a nonredistributive, ownership-broadening technique of corporate finance. Long particularly liked the idea of focusing ownership on those most closely connected to the work of capitalism—the workers, sensing that would motivate people to work harder and smarter and to stay longer with the company to reap the benefits.[10]

Despite that initial interest at the federal level, national politics alone will never be sufficient to advance a genuinely people-ized capitalism. That's because capitalism is now global. Approximately thirty-seven thousand transnational corporations control one-third of the world's private-sector capital. The largest one hundred firms account for more than $4 trillion in assets, with $2 trillion of that located outside the borders of the country where the firms are headquartered. Subject to a bewildering array of local laws yet answerable to no one internationally, these economic giants pose their own peculiar challenges to initiatives meant to reconfigure capitalism for broad-based inclusion.

New Owners, Old Patterns

Opportunities for inclusion abound. For instance, member states of the European Union proposed in 1996 to sell off $150 billion in state-owned enterprises by the year 2000. The OECD cautions that the sheer volume of planned privatization share issues may exceed the absorptive capacity of international capital markets. This suggests that these transactions, if they proceed, will go forward at bargain-basement prices, further exacerbating Western Europe's legendary concentrated ownership patterns. Similar privatization efforts are sweeping Central and South America as well as much of Asia and Africa, environments where available financial resources are likewise swamped by the magnitude of public properties for sale.

Because of the global reach of financial markets, we are in the midst of a huge fire sale of state-owned assets. That bodes ill for those who believe that capitalism desperately needs to become more broadly populated with capitalists. That's because in market economies wealth leads to more wealth, since investments depend on money, which, by definition, is most lacking in those without capital. The phrase "survival of the fittest," long attributed to Darwin to explain evolution, was borrowed by Darwin from nineteenth-century economist Herbert Spencer. Yet, as this book aims to prove, the fitness of modern-day capitalism is dramatically weakened by continuing our embrace of an economic system that limits capital ownership to the already-capitalists.

It will be an irony of historic and, I submit, tragic proportions if, in the rush to unwind state capitalism, these countries embrace turn-of-the-century plutocratic ownership patterns. Yet that is precisely what is happening. That shortsightedness could fuel the very forces that rekindle nationalization and, in the process, stall the spread of democracy. The path to durable and robust forms of free-enterprise democracy lies in the design of an array of highly participative ownership strategies that are capable of adaptation across a broad range of economic and political environments.

Vaclav Havel captured well the unique times in which we live: "Today, more than ever before in the history of mankind, everything is interrelated. Therefore the values and the prospects of contemporary civilization are everywhere subjected to great tests." One of today's most profound tests—morally, economically and socially—is whether global capitalism can be coaxed to create more haves and fewer have-nots. That, in turn, may well determine the fate of democracy—which will never realize its full potential until based on an economically just foundation in which its constituents are full participants, not simply wage earners and occasional voters.

CHAPTER 3

Why Does Capitalism Create So Few Capitalists?

Ye shall know the truth, and the truth shall make you mad.

—*Aldous Huxley*

Capitalism has long been a notoriously poor creator of capitalists. Whether we look at well-established capitalist nations or those struggling to escape a socialist past, the unsettling truth remains the same: *capitalism is not designed to create more capitalists; it is designed to finance more capital for existing capitalists.* This is because financing is accomplished within a "closed system." Stripped to its bare essentials, corporate finance can be illustrated as follows:

Sources of Funds	
Internal	{ Undistributed Earnings & Profits—Reinvested for current owners { Depreciation reserves—Reinvested for current owners
External	{ Debt—Repaid on behalf of current owners { Equity—Most affordable by current owners

To understand how tomorrow's capitalism can be encouraged to create more capitalists, it is essential first to understand why today's capitalism creates so few.[1] As an ownership-engineering rule of thumb, just remember: "where the cash flows, ownership grows."

Why Is Capitalism a "Closed System"?

A corporation has only two sources of funds: those it generates internally and those it raises externally. Internally generated funds consist of two components. The first is reinvested earnings and profits—the funds a company retains for growing the business. The second is depreciation reserves—the funds it sets aside to replace physical assets as they wear out or become obsolete. Depreciation traces its roots to private property. Income taxes cannot be levied on a firm until its owners recover the cost of replacing the property used to generate that income. Otherwise, the tax would be not on income but on the property itself. Depreciation accounts for 90 percent of internally generated funds. In combination, earnings and profits plus depreciation typically account for three-quarters of *all* funds. Thus, it's important to understand that it is the *private-property system itself* (embodied in depreciation) that is the source of two-thirds of those funds used to finance capitalism (90 percent of 75 percent = 67.5 percent).

The third and fourth sources of funds are monies raised *outside* the company. Those include both lenders (banks, bond holders) and investors (shareholders). No bank will lend without collateral. Because that collateral belongs to current owners and because it is *their* company's revenue that pays off the loan, today's owners own whatever is financed with that debt. Debt typically accounts for 20 to 25 percent of total funds.

Let's recap three of the four reasons why capital ownership is largely closed to outsiders. First, earnings and profits generated by a company belong to those who presently own the company. Second, assets qualify for depreciation only after those owners put the assets to use, because only then do they become subject to wear, tear and obsolescence. Third, debt is most accessible to those who are already "inside" this closed system, because only they have access to the collateral and the cash flow required to secure and service that debt.

The fourth and final source of funds is the sale of newly issued shares. *New* equity has long been a relatively insignificant source of funds. Not since the turn of the century has the sale of new equities accounted for more than 3 to 5 percent of overall funds raised in any year. Initial public offerings of shares (IPOs) for 1996 totaled only $46 billion (692 offerings), surpassing the record $34 billion in 1993. Those new equities are purchased largely by the well-to-do or by institutional investors. Policymakers routinely claim that capitalism is an "open" system because anyone can purchase shares. It's a free market—anyone (i.e., anyone with money) can buy those new equities.

Expecting a broad base of wage earners to *buy* their way into significant ownership (i.e., from their already stretched paychecks) is what I call "Marie Antoinette Capitalism"—only instead of urging "Let them eat cake," the modern refrain is "Let them buy shares."[2] Today's closed system of finance has much the same economic effect as the enclosure movement of the eighteenth century—creating pools of people who, deprived of any realistic chance to own, find themselves competing against each other for an ever dwindling number of well-paid jobs.

Corporate versus Personal Savings

Economists assure us that the "missing piece" is a nationwide shortage of household saving, making their case by contrasting the high personal saving in Japan (15 percent) with the low rates here (4 to 6 percent). While the political Right urges employees to save more, the political Left urges employers to *pay* more so that employees can *afford* to save more. In truth, neither strategy much advances an ownership solution. The American worker's share of national income continues its steady decline from 80 percent in the 1950s to barely 64 percent by the 1990s.[3] Employers are likewise constrained to pay more as they face pressure from low-wage foreign competition. In addition, Nobel laureate economist Paul Samuelson warns about the "paradox of thrift"—private prudence can become public folly if that saving deprives retailers of too many consumers.

Even more fundamentally, Alfred D. Chandler Jr., formerly Harvard Business School's business historian, documents that the component of savings that really counts for economic growth is not personal saving so much as *business* saving—those funds that companies generate internally. This is a critical distinction because business saving "shows up" in the economy belonging to current owners, fueling the ownership-concentrating closed system of finance. As earnings are reinvested and depreciation funds are applied to buy new and replacement assets, those assets generate *more* earnings and *more* depreciation that create *more* business saving—and on and on in a process that further enriches those fortunate enough to be cut in on this phenomenon. In this little-understood manner, today's *gross saving* (i.e., both personal and business saving) determines tomorrow's ownership pattern.

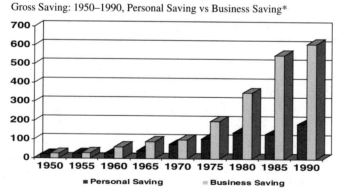

Gross Saving: 1950–1990, Personal Saving vs Business Saving*

Source: Adapted from U.S. Department of Commerce, Bureau of Economic Analysis (billions)

---

* Business saving = retained earnings and profits plus depreciation reserves

Note that as the economy became steadily more capital intensive over the four decades from 1950 to 1990, business saving became steadily more important relative to personal saving. Although early industrial capitalism was held captive by the "finance capitalists" loathed by Marx (J. P. Morgan, etc.), by the first decade of this century, 70 percent of corporate funds were being generated internally.[4] As these funds continued to finance labor-saving technologies, the substitution of capital for labor steadily widened the gap between business saving and personal saving, fueling the next round of labor-saving investment. The least understood dimension of this closed system concerns the role played by depreciation, the heart of finance in a private enterprise economy. Year after year, it accounts for nine of every ten dollars of business saving. Yet the terms for claiming depreciation are set by public policy. Recent history offers a dramatic example of how legislative changes in this arcane area can affect not only the pace and type of investment but also the pattern of ownership.

The Supply-Side Bromide

In the early 1980s, a radically new economic policy swept the country when a half century of economic theory was cast aside with the election of President Ronald Reagan, who promised to reinvigorate the economy with "supply-side" investment incentives. Since the 1930s, policymakers had relied on Keynesian "demand-side" policies to boost consumer spending, thereby indirectly expanding investment. Often this was done through deficit spending, the bane of conservatives. In a dramatic break from the past, conservative Reagan proposed tax policies aimed instead at *directly* stimulating investment spending.[5]

The key component of his proposal was dubbed "10-5-3," signifying a shortening of the time period over which business owners could write off the cost of their investments. Plus those write-offs could be "accelerated"—the bulk could be claimed in the first few years, enabling owners to recover most of their investment expense well before the asset actually wore out. Under Bob Dole's leadership as chair of the Senate Finance Committee, Congress approved this stimulus at a projected cost of $188 billion over the 1981–1986 period. The generous write-offs allowed commercial real estate kicked off an office-building boom that altered the skyline of major American cities during the 1980s. Supply-siders also campaigned successfully for a reduction in corporate tax rates, boosting corporate retained earnings. To pay for this, Washington sold bonds, many of them abroad, particularly to Japanese investors.[6]

The domestic market for these bonds was boosted by a cut in personal tax rates, initially from 70 to 50 percent.* This tax relief was targeted to high-income

---

* In 1986, the top personal income tax rate was again cut—to 28 percent.

households who supply-siders described as "effective savers"—because for them a tax cut would result in more *discretionary* income, effectively increasing the nation's supply of personal saving, thereby stimulating investment. Those tax cuts were projected to cost another $631 billion in otherwise collectible tax revenue over the 1981–1986 period.

Trickle-Up Economics

For the well-to-do, supply-side tax cuts supplied both the funds to buy those bonds and a supply of bonds to buy—quite a deal for those who were let in on it, particularly because those bonds paid relatively high interest—and tax-free too. Distressed by the clear rich-get-richer implications, columnist George Will, a staunch Reagan loyalist, balked at what he called this "regressive transfer of wealth to buyers of government bonds." Meanwhile, Washington's spending on social policy was taken hostage by record-breaking deficits due to the borrowing required to fund a combination of supply-side tax cuts and a trillion-dollar defense buildup.[7]

As documented by Reagan biographer and *Washington Post* reporter Lou Cannon, it is unfair for Reagan's detractors to claim that he balanced the budget on the backs of the poor, since "he never seriously attempted to balance the budget at all." Confirming Cannon's analysis, George Will notes that the six budgets Reagan had most control over "produced deficits totaling $1.1 trillion. The budgets Reagan sent to Congress *proposed* thirteen-fourteenths of that total. Congress added a piddling $90 billion a year."

Though Reagan's supply-side prescription was given a clean fiscal bill of health by then Budget Director David Stockman, he later admitted that his "rosy scenario" economic projections relied on figures that were "absolutely doctored," confiding to journalist William Greider that supply-side economics was really a new form of "trickle-down." That is untrue. Subsequent wealth studies confirm, as George Will conceded, that the effect was clearly "trickle-up," as the wealth of the already well-to-do expanded at a breakneck pace while most everyone else began a long period of economic backsliding.

What's since become clear is that Reagan's good intentions went badly awry with his ownership pattern–insensitive embrace of supply-side nostrums. As counsel to the Finance Committee throughout that period (1980–1987), I knew the supply-siders. Many impressed me as advocates who could be relied on to provide the same answer to practically every economic question. That served Reagan poorly. He ran for office as a fiscal conservative, yet the national debt tripled during his two terms. Interest payments on the debt more than doubled and savings declined while budget cutbacks ensured a steady deterioration in the national infrastructure that continues to this day.

Rather than "tax and spend" Democrats, American taxpayers endured a round of "borrow and spend" Republicans. The key difference: supply-side spending was done not through direct expenditures with highly transparent appropriated funds, a long-time favorite of Democrats, but through virtually invisible "tax expenditures"—targeted tax cuts and arcane investment incentives. The national debt (more than $5.5 trillion in 1997) now exceeds 70 percent of GDP, compared to 33 percent in 1980.[8]

This nation's deficit-financing capacity is a major national asset. The fiscally conservative Lincoln reluctantly turned to deficit-financing only because of its "high moral purpose" in financing the Civil War. The question now as then is to what national purpose this asset is put. World War II also saw the nation incur enormous amounts of debt, tapping this capacity to finance another high moral purpose. The question here is whether supply-side economics met that standard. Certainly the attendant shift in ownership patterns should give supporters cause for concern.

Nevertheless, the 1996 presidential race saw Republican candidates Bob Dole and Steve Forbes again touting supply-side potions as the way to cure what ails America. The economic impact of Reagan-era supply-side tax-cutting has yet to be fully resolved. And, indeed, some of its more generous investment subsidies were scaled back in subsequent years. No one, however, has yet chronicled the *ownership* impact—until now.

So, Just Who Got "Supplied" with Supply-Side Economics?

The closed system of finance provides a reliable roadmap to show who was destined to claim the ownership benefits of supply-side economics. Simply put, when public policy boosts business saving, those already inside that closed system are *certain* to be its primary beneficiaries. It's really as simple as that. The rich did get richer under supply-side economics (as, of course, did some others). However, with or without supply-side subsidies, this wealth-concentrating closed system of finance has long been "on automatic." New York University professor Edward Wolff found that 71 percent of the growth in personal wealth from 1962 to 1989 was attributable to existing holdings that simply grew.[9] That's closed-system financing.

One financial oddity must be noted. Contrary to conventional wisdom, Washington's need to borrow money to pay for supply-side deficits did not crowd out private investment. At the time, economists claimed this was largely because the Japanese bought our bonds to invest the dollars Americans were spending for Japanese cars, electronics and such. While that's true, it's only part of the story. Another factor was also at work. Testifying before the Senate Finance Committee in 1984 while the economy was booming amid record-level deficits, then Treasury Secretary Don Regan (former chief executive of Merrill Lynch) was asked, Why the lack of "crowding out" in such a deficit-burdened financial environment? The answer, he replied, lay in corporations' "capacity for self-financing." In other words, instead of government borrowing crowding out private borrowing—the usual case—the government was borrowing *to provide investment funds to private companies.**

From 1982 to 1987 (the first six years of Reaganomics), corporate tax deductions for depreciation totaled $1,653,000,000,000 ($1.65 trillion).[10] If we assume that 62 percent of all business assets (a measurement of wealth broader than corporate shares) are owned by 1 percent of the population,[11] then $1,025 billion of those tax deductions were used to finance additional (or replacement) assets for the *already-wealthiest* 1 percent of households. Assuming that 50 percent of this wealth is inherited (the low range of estimates),[12] then $513 billion of these tax deductions ($85 billion each year) were used to enhance the wealth of those *born* into this closed system. In 1982, the average wealth of those included in the *Forbes 400* list of wealthiest Americans was $200 million. By 1986, average wealth had soared to $550 million. By 1997, $475 million was required just to be included on the list.

This analysis is not meant to be unduly critical either of Ronald Reagan or of the Republican Party. Without an ownership pattern–sensitive economic policy, America's rich-get-richer trend is certain to continue regardless of whether Democrats or Republicans are in the White House. As Bruce Bartlett, senior fellow with the National Center for Policy Analysis, confirmed in 1996: "Something is going on here that's beyond politics. A lot of people have tended to draw the conclusion that we cut taxes in the 1980s, and the rich got richer. Here we've increased taxes in the 1990s, and they still got richer."[13] As the closed-system analysis confirms, this feature of free enterprise is embedded in the system itself.

That 1990s tax increase haunted New Democrat Bill Clinton during the 1996 presidential elections. Consequently, once he won the presidential race (against supply-sider Bob Dole), he readily acceded to a 1997 supply-side inspired tax cut (with a projected ten-year price tag of $270 billion) in which the share of benefits flowing to the top 5 percent tops that flowing to the bottom 60 percent. Insanity, I'm told, is doing the same thing over and over again and expecting a different result. From the perspective of someone who thinks that America's gap between the haves and the have-nots is already quite wide enough, I see both Republicans and Democrats in need of some serious therapy.

Self-Financing—The Most Feasible Road to Riches

Another curious effect also accompanied supply-side legislation.[14] This stimulus to corporate finance helped create a financial environment in which, for

---

* The "10-5-3" component of depreciation is equivalent to an interest-free loan from taxpayers to corporate shareholders because the government, in effect, advances these funds (interest-free) by allowing tax deductions sooner. Any gain on the later sale of those assets is taxed to the extent that deductions attributable to "accelerated cost recovery" exceed those available through more traditional "useful life" depreciation.

the balance of the decade, the leveraged buyout (LBO) became the nation's most notable financial phenomenon. LBOs rest on a fundamental financial principle: incoming-producing assets can repay debt used to purchase those assets. Between 1976 and 1990, the U.S. economy was host to more than thirty-five thousand ownership-transfer (merger and acquisition) transactions with a total value of $2.6 trillion. The annual value of these transactions peaked in 1988 at $340 billion, including $80 billion in LBOs.[15] It was not unusual for an LBO company to have $100 of debt for every $10 of equity, with that debt repaid (echoing Regan's comment) on a "self-financed" basis.[16]

The sometimes perverse impact of LBOs is epitomized by the 1986 buyout of California-based Pacific Lumber Company by Charles Hurwitz, a Texas savings-and-loan operative. Pacific Lumber owns 205,000 acres, including 5,600 acres of virgin redwoods in the Headwaters Forest of Northern California's scenic Humboldt County. To pay down his LBO debt, Hurwitz ordered faster cutting of that virgin acreage, a "rape-and-run" strategy that ran counter to a widely supported struggle to save part of what is left of California's ancient redwood groves.[17]

Untapped Ownership Opportunities

LBOs are feasible only because of the self-financing logic of the closed system of finance ("productive assets can pay for themselves"). Any policy tinkering that enhances the funds flowing through this closed system (such as supply-side subsidies) enhances their feasibility and finance-ability.[18] The number of LBOs completed since 1980 confirms not only the workings of the closed system but also (we may hope) just how this system could be opened to the not-yet-rich. This is the silver lining in what has to date been a wealth-concentrating financial phenomenon that continues today. In 1988, we saw 3,637 merger and acquisition ("M&A") transactions, including LBOs. Although ownership-broadening ESOP incentives were available, employees were included in less than 1 percent of the total dollar volume of transactions.[19] If employees were left out during one of the most extraordinary periods of financial engineering since publication of *The Wealth of Nations*, it is clear that opening this closed system will require a more powerful combination of political will, financial savvy and corporate leadership.

To date, most Americans have been left with access to the wrong sort of credit—that is to say, consumer credit. Whereas "investment credit"—of the LBO sort—can make you self-sufficient, even rich, consumer credit erodes your income to the extent of future interest charges.[20] Though practically anyone can qualify for consumer credit, investment credit is possible only for those who have access both to collateral and to the cash flow to service debt. In the mid-1990s, the M&A craze returned, with a similar impact on ownership patterns. The dollar volume of transactions during 1994 and 1995 exceeded the last three years of transactions during the record-breaking 1980s. Worldwide, M&A transactions totaled almost $800 billion in 1995 ($465 billion in the United States alone), for a two-year total of $1.3 trillion.[21] That torrid pace continues with a global one-year total of $1.14 trillion in 1996 ($659 billion in the United States) and a whopping $1 trillion for 1997 in the United States alone.[22]

However, regardless whether financing is structured to bring new assets on line, to transfer ownership of existing assets or to merge those assets with those of another firm, the ownership point remains the same: the purpose of finance is to enable people to acquire assets *before* they have the funds set aside to pay for them. Widely prevalent self-financing techniques can benefit either a broad or a narrow base of a nation's citizens. Recent history confirms that, without a combination of policy input and corporate leadership, this phenomenon will continue to create ownership primarily for a few.[23]

A Rising Tide Lifts All Yachts

The use of financial "leverage" can take many forms, though the LBO is its most visible use. Supply-side economics was itself a form of financial leverage, albeit on a vast scale and nationwide in scope. In effect, policymakers borrowed money to pay for tax subsidies to be paid for out of the future earnings of American taxpayers. That's a type of self-financing. In retrospect, it's clear that those subsidies were used largely to finance wealth accumulation either for those already within the closed system or for those financially sophisticated enough to gain entry.

Trickle-down theorists insist that others also did well, pointing to strong job growth and citing President Kennedy's famous quip, "A rising tide lifts all boats." In truth, supply-siders chose to ignore a key issue: who would be supplied. Though the yachts surely rose (as did yacht sales), most everyone else was left to cope with the flotsam and jetsam of this rising tide, including cutbacks in public services, an eroding infrastructure and a steadily widening gap between rich and poor. Meanwhile, the sharp increase in national debt also shifted more of the budget burden onto states and cities, putting pressure on local services—schools, public transport, libraries, playgrounds. This fiscal phenomenon also brought a transfer of obligations to state and local governments—often without any funds to pay for them (known as "unfunded mandates").*

Even hard-won civil rights victories were put at risk by this shift in fiscal priorities. In Montgomery, Alabama, for instance, Rosa Parks made history on 1 December 1965 by refusing to give up her bus seat to a white passenger.

---

* With the signing into law of a welfare reform bill in August 1996, the federal government left the states free to decide what to do about poverty, homelessness and hunger, though with less money to address them ($55 billion less over six years). The key difference: that response is not federally *mandated*; the states don't *have to* address these problems.

Her arrest and the resulting bus boycott (led by a little-known local preacher, Dr. Martin Luther King Jr.) began one of the first successful desegregation movements in the South. Three decades later, today's patrons of Montgomery's bus service are victims of a different sort as public bus service has been cut more than half due to local fiscal woes.

This ownership challenge is not insurmountable. However, for capitalism to create more capitalists, it needs a financially knowledgeable and politically engaged citizenry, as well as financially savvy political leaders and concerned leadership in the corporate sector. At present, we have none of those. A 1994 survey revealed that "most Americans simply don't possess an understanding of even the most basic financial and economic concepts."[24] Yet they intuitively know that their policy and corporate environment supports the rich getting ever richer while their own financial situation grows ever more precarious. Part of the challenge stems from the fact that the ailment's diverse symptoms are not yet setting off alarms that corporate executives and policymakers associate with something as obscure as today's highly exclusionary techniques of corporate finance. Added to that is the fact that many Americans haven't a clue how either their financial *or* their political system works. "Whether uninterested, uninformed or simply ignorant," a 1996 Harvard University study found, "millions of Americans cannot answer even basic questions about American politics."[25] This makes change a challenge.

Second-Class Capitalism

Americans instinctively know that today's ownership patterns are out of synch with the most fundamental principle on which their nation was founded: the democratic ideal of a classless society populated by politically equal citizens. Yet with expansion of America's highly touted service sector, we see the steady emergence of a modern equivalent to the era of the doffed cap and the bent knee, albeit in a different form, as growing legions of people are relegated to low-paid service jobs (no one dares call them "servants") with "Joe" or "Doris" emblazoned on their distinctly class-identifying uniforms. Servants haven't disappeared; they've just been "outsourced." The family cook has been replaced by employees at McDonald's or Pizza Hut, while the maid now works for a janitorial service cleaning office buildings at night.

The standard of living of this service class has declined since the turn of the century. In 1910 a live-in cook in major East Coast cities was paid $10 a week. After adjusting for inflation, that comes to $145 today. To net that amount after taxes, today's fast-food worker would need to make $170 per week, precisely the paycheck flowing from a forty-hour week at 1996's $4.25-an-hour minimum wage. However, today's servers must now pay for transportation, food and housing—the primary "free" benefits that accompanied the servant-sector job of nine decades ago.

Meanwhile, a small, well-propertied ownership elite (along with an inner circle of advisers) sequester themselves in havens of affluence that are geographically, socially, educationally and even culturally removed. Those who can afford to are retreating into private housing associations, private clubs and private schools. Even exposure to the arts is being "privatized" as funding is cut in a shift to "user fees" limiting access to culture to those who can afford it. The invisible bonds that bind a nation are put at risk when its financial technology is allowed to divide its people in such class-conscious ways.

The attempt to create one people out of many (*e pluribus unum*) is at a genuine crossroads. Federal legislation has gone far in securing basic political rights, protecting civil liberties and safeguarding individuals from government interference. The advancement of economic rights is more complex, requiring an activism that ensures private enterprise is opened to broader-based participation. While policymakers can help, the real responsibility lies in the private sector. Perhaps it's more accurate to say that leaders in both the private and the public sector must collaborate to create an environment where business can logically behave responsibly. At present, the two greatest enemies undermining efforts at change are (*a*) a crisis of comprehensibility (a driving force behind this book) and (*b*) the deafening silence surrounding this ongoing societal deterioration.

Much as democracy is invisible and intangible, yet palpably real (and perhaps best known by its absence), ownership, too, could become a national bonding agent. The financial technologies are at hand to create networks of ownership that could restore community and mutual commitment while helping rebuild civil society. Further delay in doing so has grave implications for the health of society, democracy and individuals. For example, recent research confirms the fact that a range of both social and physical afflictions accompany inequality, including not only a dramatic weakening in the strength of communities and civil society[26] but also an increase in the prevalence of disease and even causes of death that become more common lower down the social scale, such as infections, cancers, cardiovascular, nutritional and metabolic diseases, respiratory diseases, accidents, and nervous and mental illnesses.[27] America's widening rich/poor gap is accompanied by a widening "health gap."[28]

Renewed Capitalism Requires New Capitalists

Renewal and regeneration lie at the heart of finance, particularly through depreciation as the means by which a nation's next generation of technology is brought online. Modern productive technologies (mechanical, chemical, informational, organizational) have been hugely successful at squeezing manhours out of production—simultaneously disempowering those who work while empowering those who own. The marketplace, meanwhile, remains absolutely indifferent. It simply values productive capacity, directing income to whoever provides it, regardless of whether embodied in skilled labor or embedded in labor-saving assets.

Unsustainable symptoms of this phenomenon include stagnant incomes, weak purchasing power and precarious economic security. To date, the response from the public sector has been a mind-numbing array of "downstream" income-redistribution proposals, ignoring the need for "upstream" policies that could connect their constituents to those income-producing assets that are steadily displacing them. Those hindsight remedies include progressive income tax rates, public-sector jobs (defense remains the favorite), entitlement programs and other income-focused measures designed to blunt the impact of market-driven income patterns. While upstream ownership patterns are left largely intact, those who grow dependent on this downstream tinkering foster a fiscal inflexibility known as "demosclerosis."

This "symptomatic economics" (the tendency to address symptoms instead of causes) arises from the same school of thought that sees money as a cure for poverty or food as the solution to hunger. A lack of money is a *symptom*, not a cause, of poverty. Poverty is cured not with money but by gaining access to the productiveness—the skills and the tools—required to earn money.[29] Between 1967 and 1992 the United States spent more than $3.2 trillion on such downstream, hindsight-focused, symptom-relieving solutions. As Professor Walter Williams, an economist at George Mason University, points out: "The money spent on poverty programs since the 1960s could have bought the entire assets of the Fortune 500 companies and virtually all U.S. farmlands, and what did it do? The problems still remain and they are even worse." Yet present-day corporate finance remains designed not for inclusion but for renewal and expansion. At least we've got the prescription half right.

CHAPTER 4

Putting the "Own" Back in Ownership

The most reliable way to anticipate the future is by understanding the present.

—John Naisbitt

Over the past two decades, capitalism's historically concentrated personal ownership has been joined by a new and as yet little-understood form of concentrated wealth: concentration in the hands of institutional investors. Almost half (47.4 percent) of all outstanding shares of U.S. corporations are now held by institutions. Mutual funds alone held $4.0 trillion in mid-1997. Should this trend continue, one analyst projects that the United States will see its last individual shareholder by the year 2003. Though that overstates the phenomenon, it does raise a provocative question: at what point does this system cease to be capitalism? The *Oxford English Dictionary* defines capitalism as "a system which favors the existence of capitalists." Just what does capitalism become when it loses its capitalists—"institutionalism"?

Similar institutionalization is under way in other countries as three key factors converge. First, the World War II baby boom population is now entering its prime earning years, approaching the period when "life cycle savings" reach their peak, as Nobel laureate economist Franco Modigliani predicted. Second, policymakers worldwide are busily enacting policies to favor retirement savings—both as a means for amassing needed investment funds and as a way to promote self-reliance as an alternative to government entitlements. A third factor is also at work. A combination of closed-system financing techniques, leveraged buyouts and the globalization of finance has resulted in the amassing of immense personal fortunes over the past two decades. Investor Warren Buffett of Berkshire Hathaway has a personal portfolio that exceeded $23 billion in early 1997. The net worth of Microsoft founder Bill Gates doubled during the stock market boom of the mid-1990s, giving him more than $40 billion. Numerous LBO artisans have personal net worths exceeding $1 billion.

Inheritance laws encourage the wealthy to leave substantial sums to non-profit institutions, principally foundations. According to the Council on Foundations, in 1996 each of the twenty wealthiest foundations had assets of more than $1 billion, led by the Packard, Ford and Kellogg Foundations with more than $7 billion each. At least twenty-five others had assets of more than $500 million. That trend is certain to grow as those who did well during the go-go 1980s and 1990s begin to sense their mortality. The run-up in the stock market adds considerable fuel to this trend. When oil tycoon J. Paul Getty died in 1976, he left $661 million in Getty Oil shares to the trustees of the J. Paul Getty Museum. By mid-1997, the trust's holdings totaled $4.3 billion and that's after spending more than $2.5 billion, including more than $1 billion for the construction of a palatial museum and campus.

Bill Gates has announced his intention to transfer the bulk of his fortune to a foundation, as has Warren Buffett. That's another sizeable chunk of soon-to-be institutionalized assets with a mandatory social agenda (by law, at least 5 percent of a foundation's capital must be spent each year in the pursuit of nonprofit goals). Peter Drucker believes that this "third sector" is destined to become the economy's most dynamic sector and its largest job-creator.[1] Given the rich-get-richer legacy of the past two decades, he may well be correct as the well-to-do discover that foundation giving is both smart tax planning and a handy way to leave a personal legacy.[2] Other forces also fuel this trend. For example, when a for-profit business acquires a nonprofit organization (such as a hospital), the sale proceeds must be used for charitable purposes. Thus, when California Blue Cross converted to for-profit status, more than $3 billion was transferred to foundations.

This rapidly growing, all-pervasive institutionalization comes as a surprise to those who created the policy environment that induced this change. When the United States enacted sweeping pension reform legislation in 1974, few legislators understood that pension funds would become America's largest capitalists. Senator Russell Long, chairman of the Senate Finance Committee at the time, assured me that these huge accumulations of capital were neither foreseen nor intended.[3] Nevertheless, this institutionalization is steadily accelerating. Institutional assets grew 75 percent from 1990 to mid-1996,[4] with total assets now hovering around $12 trillion. This trend has enormous implications not only for developed countries but also for in-transition and developing countries that are busily reengineering their economic systems to mimic the more developed "mentor" economies.

For instance, many of the economies of Eastern and Central Europe are embracing mutual funds as a key component of their privatization strategy, racing from precapitalist, socialist-era "collectivization" directly into post-capitalist "institutionalization." The Czech Republic's privatization program was modeled on American mutual funds, with each Czech citizen allowed to purchase a "voucher" that could be traded for units in a mutual fund invested in privatized companies. The potential scope of institutionalization is staggering as investors worldwide move toward global diversification, creating a world characterized by increasingly global capital markets. At the end of 1995, American pension funds, endowments and mutual funds held a combined $331.2 billion in international equities, up substantially from $97.5 billion at the end of 1990.[5] One institution alone (State Street Bank) held more than $26 billion in indexed international equity.[6]

Rethinking Ownership

Historically, capitalism was based on highly concentrated, highly personalized, hands-on ownership, whether in the hands of the royal families of Europe (the Hapsburgs, etc.), the industrial empires of Western Europe and America (the Krupps, Pilkingtons, Carnegies, Mellons) or the resource extraction and financial fortunes of early America such as John D. Rockefeller (oil) and J. P. Morgan (banking). It was the exclusive nature of this ownership that socialists found so disturbing. It is difficult to imagine that Karl Marx would have insisted on the abolition of private ownership if a substantial portion of the capital of his day had been owned by workers' pension plans.

Even the word *ownership* may be an outdated word to describe these immense holdings. The simple certainties of turn-of-the-century proprietor capitalism are rapidly fading into irrelevance as ownership has evolved into something dramatically different. Though today's institutional investors try to mimic real owners, they are a long way from succeeding. They should more accurately be called fiduciaries or trustees.[7] Much as a board of directors is charged with the fiduciary duty of overseeing a company's managers on behalf of its shareholders, institutional investors are charged with the duty of overseeing investment funds set aside for pensioners, mutual fund participants and such.

In an oft-cited "Survey of Capitalism," the editor of *The Economist* characterized the difference between this new versus old-style ownership as "Punters or Proprietors?" Because institutional shareholders are not "locked-in" to their ownership (they can trade one investment for another), he likened them to those holding betting slips at a racetrack ("punters"). They place their bets on a company only so long as that company appears to be pulling ahead of the pack. Other commentators are even less charitable, comparing money managers to horse traders whose concern is not for the health of the horse but only for maximizing their proceeds when the horse is sold. This ongoing sea change in the nature of ownership has set off a search for what *The Economist*'s editor calls the corporation's "natural owners." This book is meant to aid that search.

Responsible Owners

One of the key issues facing modern capitalism is a determination of just what it means to "own" when ownership is institutionalized. Dodging rather than facing the implications, many of the large public-sector pension funds (such as those sponsored by New York and California) rely on an "index" strategy to invest. They've largely given up operating as stock pickers hoping to "beat the street" (Wall Street). Instead they maintain broadly diversified portfolios selected to match an index of companies (such as the Standard & Poor's 500 index) whose performance broadly mirrors the market as a whole. Thus, these institutions buy and sell only because a company is part of an index being tracked, not because of any knowledge about the company, its products, its markets, its employees or anything else. From 1986 to 1996, the amount of mutual-fund money invested in the most widely held stock index funds increased a hundredfold, to $65 billion, a growth rate of eighteen times that of the fund industry over all. Much of that money found its way there during the 1995–1996 period.[8]

Commenting on what economists call this "agency cost" dilemma, Professor Lester Thurow at M.I.T.'s Sloan School of Management suggests: "The only way for capitalism to work is for owners to take responsibility." As a first step, institutional investors urged companies to create an ownership stake for senior managers and directors. The hope was that these *surrogate* hands-on owners would compensate for the hands-off nature of their index investment strategy. That decade-long movement is now largely complete. The total value of shares set aside for stock options grew from some $60 billion in 1985 to $600 billion in July 1997, according to Sanford C. Bernstein & Company.

A 1996 survey of 608 firms by William M. Mercer, Inc. found that the typical large firm (with annual revenues greater than $100 million) has 5 percent of its shares set aside for top executives.[9] Consulting firms report a sharp increase in "megagrants" for top managers. In 1996, Disney Chief Executive Michael Eisner was granted eight million options (on top of his $8.7 million in salary and bonus) that were valued in 1997 at $181 million, with a future projected value (in 2007) of $583.7 million.[10] That's on top of the $127 million in reported profit from his exercise of options in 1992 and the $374 million profit realized on his sale of optioned shares in December 1997.[11] The value of Coca-Cola chief executive Roberto Goizueta's compensation— salary, bonuses and grants of stock—totaled more than $1 billion. That's without counting stock options, his interest in a 401(k) profit-sharing plan, two other deferral accounts, his $3 million a year pension and his life insurance (Goizueta died in October 1997).[12] The income ratio of chief executives to the rank-and-file in major corporations has risen steadily from an average 35:1 in the 1970s to 120:1 in 1995.[13]

Typically the justification for executive pay packages is some variant on the "great man theory," which says that a well-regarded corporate chief is required to lure capital from one investment to another—raising share value. A recent example: commentators scoffed when Alex J. Mandl received a $20 million signing bonus for quitting AT&T to run an obscure wireless telephone company. However, the owners of the new company, Associated Communications, planned to take the company public and wanted someone at the helm in whom the market had confidence. The gambit paid off. Within forty-eight hours of his appointment, the shares of Associated Group, which owns 55 percent of the wireless venture, rose almost $7 per share, making their shareholders $120 million richer and paying for the bonus.[14] It became clear some years ago that this surrogate ownership strategy was escalating wildly out of control. Thus, institutional investors began to look elsewhere in their search for a solution to their disconnected ownership.

The Search for an Ownership Voice

In determining how best to invest and manage this $12 trillion, institutional investors realized in the mid-1980s that they would be required to exercise their ownership "voice" rather than take the "Wall Street walk." Due to the sheer size of their shareholdings, money managers found they often had no feasible way to jettison their holdings in a poor-performing company. Often the very magnitude of their stake meant they could not unload without incurring a loss, because their decision to sell would cause share prices to tumble. Fund managers also became more sensitive to charges of "churning"—the constant selling and buying that incurs transaction costs without any measurable improvement in portfolio performance, another reason they turned to indexing. Also, the fact that their pension obligations often lie decades in the future persuaded them that a "buy and hold" strategy made sense, particularly if they could find ways to improve firm performance during the holding period.

Faced with that dilemma, a search began for new ways to improve corporate performance and accountability, including a search for "nonfinancial indicators" of performance. What that search discovered is that firms perform better when they have "systems for employee feedback" that grant employees "greater voice in the enterprise."[15] This, in turn, suggested a preference for firms with high-involvement workplace practices, because "companies with substandard reputations on workplace issues have lower valuations." And, indeed, "a large proportion of companies with the worst reputations on workplace issues are either taken over or experience bankruptcy."[16]

In short, an institutional investor can best exercise *its* ownership voice by encouraging companies to grant employees an opportunity to exercise *their* voice. That active, inside perspective helps compensate for the fiduciary's passive, outside role. This also suggests that insider ownership should be widespread rather than concentrated and rarefied. Retired New York State comptroller Edward V. Regan, long-time sole trustee of the state's pension fund, argues the same point:

> The widest distribution of active ownership results from ESOPs (employee stock ownership plans). The idea is very appealing, for employee ownership both closely aligns workers' self-interest with that of the corporation and provides the company with probably the ultimate source of patient capital. When managers and workers are owners, accountability pervades the company with beneficial results.[17]

Of course, employee ownership is not the same as employee voice. Many companies have one without the other. Research confirms the commonsense conclusion that where the two are combined the impact on corporate performance is stronger and longer lasting.[18] The National Center for Employee Ownership found that where employees participate in ownership alone, disillusionment eventually sets in unless managers solicit employees' views on issues important to them. Likewise, where managers involve employees in decision-making alone without also making them owners, employees gradually lose faith in these programs too, eventually wondering "What's in it for me?". This suggests that portfolio managers should look not only for workplace participation (voice) but also for employee financial participation.[19] This dual-track investment strategy could do much to put some ownership back into today's disconnected capitalism.

Nontraditional Indicators

Indirect investor activism (such as encouraging surrogate/insider ownership) is a useful adjunct to direct activism, such as pressuring companies to include more independent directors and opposing measures that insulate managers from outside accountability.[20] In a telltale sign, Ernst & Young's Center for Business Innovation found in a 1996 study of 275 portfolio managers that a surprising 35 percent of investor decisions are now driven by *nonfinancial* factors. The research identified thirty-nine people- and customer-sensitive concerns, including not only management ability and the presence of "engaged employees" but also such difficult-to-measure criteria as customer satisfaction and organizational agility. Financial measures (originally developed to meet regulatory and reporting requirements) are now widely viewed as inadequate as a benchmarking system for high-performance companies. Not only are the measures hindsight-oriented; they also lack predictive power and often reward short-termism. In addition, they fail to identify crucial business changes until it is too late, and give short shrift to hard-to-quantify key resources such as intellectual capital and research and development.

A far less traditional business organization, the Social Venture Network (SVN), recently compiled a list of corporate "standards" recommended by its members, mostly founders of high-performance companies who pride them-selves on being socially responsible. Their eight hundred U.S. members see business not only as a means to financial success but also as a potentially powerful force for creating a more just, humane and sustainable society. Thus, SVN standards include such intangible indicators as ethics, values, customer commitment and employee empowerment. Typical is SVN member Anita Roddick, founder of The Body Shop Ltd., who advocates that business should be an "incubator of the human spirit"—not your typical bottom-line concern. "Business, like it or not, is entering center stage," Roddick notes. "It is faster, it is more creative, it operates more efficiently in response to change than any other social institution, and it is capable of almost anything."

The standard critique of such business-sponsored social responsibility is voiced by Sam Brittan, award-winning *Financial Times* columnist and author: "the corporate responsibility movement lacks the legitimacy of either the market or the political process. It is up to the individual citizen to decide how much to devote to such causes, whether individually or collectively via elected representatives. It is not for managers to set themselves up as taxing authori-ties over funds which belong to shareholders—who may be their own employ-ees or other workers investing through their pension funds."[21]

On the other hand, companies are now finding that social responsibility is also prudent business practice, particularly as the labor, human rights and environmental practices of their suppliers become more closely scrutinized by consumers, shareholders and the media. One embarrassing exposé on network television and millions of dollars of goodwill and market share can be lost in the space of half an hour. Pakistani development economist Mahbub ul Haq reports that 134 million children in South Asia alone work sixteen hours, six days per week for wages of only eight cents a day.[22] Imagine the damage that could be visited on a company once the word leaks out to American parents that their child's toy, soccer ball or sports shoe is made by shockingly young indentured servants who may never have a chance to play sports or even own a toy.[23]

The New York–based Council on Economic Priorities Accreditation Agency established in 1997 a universal standard for consumers, with certified "social accountability auditors" issuing Social Accountability Standard ("SA8000") certificates in much the same way that companies now have their financial state-ments certified by public accountants. Business sector advisors to this fledgling movement include Avon, Reebok, Toys "R" Us and KPMG Peat Marwick, the international firm of accountants and auditors. SA8000 certificates are likely to take their place alongside audits for quality (ISO 9000) and environmental management (ISO 14000). Simply put, in an information age, people want to know. In the case of institutional investors, they can't afford *not* to know.

To date, the greatest growth in standards-setting has been in the environmental area. Numerous standards-certifying and auditing firms have emerged in just the past few years. For example, New York–based green activist Rena Shulsky founded both Green Audit, which provides companies with an independent assessment of their environmental performance, and Green Seal, a national environmental labeling program that recognizes environmentally superior products. Green certification is also available for environmentally conscious forestry practices from the Oaxaca, Mexico-based Forest Stewardship Council which qualifies recipients to feature an "eco-friendly" label on their products.[24] With this steady increase in consumer-driven production and product standards, institutional investors may well find that "standards barriers" begin to displace trade barriers as the focus of trade negotiations.

Institutional Capitalism Meets Social Capitalism

In *Power and Accountability,* Robert Monks, former assistant secretary of labor in the Reagan administration, chronicles a key feature accompanying these institutionalized ownership patterns. Because pension obligations are not payable for decades, pension trustees must plan their investment strategies for decades. "Unintentionally," Monks notes, "the growth of institutional investors may have reintroduced elements of stability in stock ownership."[25] Both akin to yet remarkably different from the proprietor capitalism of a century ago, this stability brings with it a new set of challenges.

For instance, as the magnitude of this trusteed capital continues to grow, advocates of "multiple bottom line" investing are destined to gain increased influence, both in the monitoring and the investment of those funds. Some of these pension trustees, such as New York's comptroller, must stand for election. That provides a tempting opportunity both for office seekers to offer voter-pleasing investment policies, and for voters to press for their preferred investment strategies. A sign of things to come: during her 1992 campaign for election to the U.S. Senate, New York City comptroller Elizabeth Holtzman touted her activist style during her term as a trustee of the city's massive retirement funds. Decisions made by the managers of such funds even have the ability to affect U.S. foreign policy. For example, in October 1997 New York City comptroller Alan Hevesi barred the Union Bank of Switzerland from participating in a billion-dollar bond offering, a move meant to signal disapproval of how the bank has been slow to respond to investigations into its dealings with "dormant" accounts opened by Jews during the Holocaust period of World War II.

Other influences are also at play. Labor strategists, have become much more financially savvy. In October 1995, the 13 million members of the AFL-CIO elected as president John Sweeney, who pledged to "put movement back in the labor movement," announcing his intention to ensure that union pension funds support union issues, a development with stunning potential to broaden the criteria portfolio managers use in selecting investments.[26] In September 1997, the AFL-CIO announced the creation of a Department of Corporate Affairs to help unions leverage their clout by developing shareholder and pension-fund initiatives. Reflecting their new Wall Street savvy, a task force called "Street Heat" will enlist volunteers to help unions during contract, organizing and legislative struggles. A new Center for Working Capital will advise on uses of worker's funds so that their capital works for them and not against them.

In a similar vein, the California Public Employees Retirement System (Calpers) is beefing up its effort to persuade portfolio companies that job security and employee loyalty are aids to productivity. Why this sudden investor concern? A 1996 survey of 3,300 employees by management consultants Towers Perrin found a dramatic rise in workforce disenchantment nationwide, particularly a feeling that managers ignore employees' interests when making decisions that affect them. The linkage between financial returns and people-responsive policies has simply become too obvious to ignore. In a similar vein, accountants Ernst & Young confirm that the more nonfinancial information investors rely on, the more accurate their forecasts.

The very immensity of these funds is destined to attract the attention of policymakers at all levels of government. Both public and private sector pension plans are equally as likely to come under scrutiny. The tax preferences provided for retirement plans are now the single largest tax expenditure, totaling $453.4 billion over the 1997–2001 period.[27] It is naive to expect that the impact of these funds will continue to be ignored. Like the quip attributed to Depression-era bank robber Willie Sutton when asked why he robbed banks ("Because that's where they keep the money"), the public is awakening to what is possible through these funds. Demands for a more socially attuned capitalism are certain to grow.[28]

A new activism is also found in funds accumulated by religious organizations, university endowments, foundations and teacher retirement funds. That first became apparent with the antiapartheid "screening" of investments in South Africa during the years preceding the election of Nelson Mandela. We now see the emergence of "multiple bottom line" banks, credit unions, insurance companies and the like. Several credit card companies pay over to social causes a portion of the interest they collect. Numerous mutual funds now offer both financial and social returns. This fledgling trend is certain to grow as people become more aware of the multidimensional impact that can accompany their savings and investments.

Multiple-Purpose Investing

Those who venture into this financial thicket are advised to proceed with caution, as few subjects better lend themselves to political mischief. Institutional investors remain leery of "social" and "economically targeted" investments because, to date, this has often meant investments yielding less than market rates of return. A job creation or job preservation agenda typically lurks in the background. Often a politically powerful union leads the charge.[29]

Multiple-purpose investing has a mixed record. A 1983 study by Alicia Munnell (then head of research at the Boston Federal Reserve) found that pension plans with social investment goals were riskier, less liquid and earned inferior returns. A 1993 study by Professor Roberta Romano of Yale Law School found a correlation between social investing and lower returns.[30] However, a more recent federal study of economically targeted investment programs (ETIs) sponsored by public pension plans found that returns were similar to other investments.[31] Opponents of such investing object that lower investment returns shift retirement costs to others: either more must be paid into the plans (through higher taxes in the case of public sector pension plans) or retirees must settle for reduced pensions or later retirement. Proponents argue that such investments can be managed to create both long-term financial value and current economic value, by supporting what the AFL-CIO's Center for Working Capital calls "high-road corporate strategies that provide good jobs at good wages."

These huge funds are already attractive targets for political tinkering. In the 1980s, New York governor Mario Cuomo massaged the actuarial assumptions underlying the state's pension plan to generate funds he needed to balance the budget.[32] In neighboring New Jersey, Republican governor Christine Todd Whitman received media accolades for the "Whitman miracle" when in 1994 she cut income taxes 30 percent while simultaneously closing the budget hole left by Jim Florio, her Democratic predecessor. Her secret ingredient: adjusting funding requirements for the state's $45 billion pension fund, "saving" $3.1 billion over the subsequent three years.

In 1997, Whitman proposed to commit the state to its largest-ever borrowing ($2.9 billion), leading opponents to charge that the bill is now coming due for her earlier tax cuts. The political attraction of these huge funds is unlikely to wane. As these strategies gain for their proponents political success, even nationwide acclaim, the word is spreading. No policymaker could miss the fact that Whitman's "miracle" propelled her into the spotlight as a potential vice-presidential candidate during the 1996 Republican Convention. Republican presidential nominee Bob Dole even promised "to do for America what Christie Whitman has done for New Jersey."

Ownerizing Capitalism

No one knows for sure what might flow from investment policies that promote widespread rather than concentrated capital ownership. For instance, pension plans were major providers of financial capital to Wal-Mart, the hugely successful chain of department stores. By traditional financial criteria, Wal-Mart was a great investment. The unasked question is this: should such pension investments be made without regard to the ownership pattern they facilitate? This is not to suggest the merits of "social investing." Social investment is often an attempt to direct funds into investments that are nonmarket worthy or that subsidize nonpension goals. This suggests something quite different. Rather than favor particular *investments* (tile versus tires, union over nonunion, Sears instead of Wal-Mart), should pension plans favor a particular type of *ownership structure*, regardless of the investment? In particular, should they favor investments structured to advance capital accumulation by a broad rather than a narrow group of shareholders?

For instance, when investing in Wal-Mart, should pension trustees have withheld their funds until persuaded that pensioners' money would build equity ownership not only for founder Sam Walton but also for a significant number of others employed by Wal-Mart? Or those supplying Wal-Mart? To oversimplify, would the economy be better off (socially, fiscally, etc.) with one Wal-Mart employee-owner accumulating $23 billion (as in the case of employee-owner Sam Walton) or with, say, ten thousand employees accumulating $2.3 million each?[33] Wal-Mart remains a favorite of portfolio investors, and rightfully so according to the usual investment standards. Unwittingly, however, those investors are fueling today's closed system of finance which, in turn, is destined to undermine the value of retirees' pensions. Why? Because they will retire into a population (like the current one, only much larger) where huge numbers of households lack economic autonomy.

Today's "agnosticism" about ownership patterns highlights a key dilemma facing money managers of every sort. Because the impact of their investment lies in a distant part of the larger economic system, they have no way to learn from their shortcomings. The corrective feedback is beyond both their investment horizon and their learning horizon. However, where these funds ignore accompanying ownership patterns, they unwittingly add to the political pressure for government spending. That's destined to show up as either higher taxes or inflationary government spending. Both are anathema to pensioners.

Much as a pension plan is a cross-generational promise, so too are the investments (and the ownership patterns) that underlie that promise. Pension trustees cannot afford the luxury of either a short-term or a narrow perspective. To put ownership-concentrating investments on a par with those that expand ownership reflects a lack of prudent fiscal foresight that can only harm retirees. To utilize an ownership pattern–sensitive investment screen is not "social" investing; it's fiscal-commonsense investing.

It's also remarkably shortsighted for institutional investors to limit their "surrogate" ownership strategies solely to those upon whom the economic system already lavishes its most handsome rewards (i.e., senior managers and directors). Far better that investment strategists ensure that their portfolio companies are permeated from top to bottom with a steadily broadening base of active, informed, inside, at-risk owners—along with management systems designed to evoke top-quality performance. More generally, unless tax-favored pension funds are invested in a way that creates a broader constituency for capitalism, it is difficult to imagine how the temptation of "social investment" can be held back. The challenge lies in how best to coordinate the long-term financial goals of institutional investors with the larger public interest in evoking long-term economic growth for a broad base of citizens.

Other, more traditional rationales also support adoption of such an investment strategy. Today's economy is increasingly global, highly competitive and high-tech. Firms must adapt quickly, innovate constantly and learn continuously, while also providing customized, consumer-sensitive services. This implies the need both for a new way of organizing work and a new attitude toward work. Experience suggests that this is far more likely to emerge where employee feedback is sought and utilized, and where a workforce is confident that it will share in the rewards that flow from this pressure-cooker environment.

In much the same way that pensions are funded over years, so too are companies built over time. Where investment managers focus solely on short-term financial results, they fail in their broader obligation to ensure that companies embrace what's required for today's marketplace: high-performance, highly adaptable, motivated workplaces. Due to the sheer magnitude of the sums involved, the future of the U.S. economy is largely in the hands of these institutional investors. Where their capital goes, so goes capitalism, including its underlying ownership pattern and its capacity to compete effectively in a global economy. One of the best ways for these investors to advance managerial accountability and environmental sustainability is to invest so that insiders have both a financial stake and legal standing to have their views heard.

Total Wealth Creation—Rethinking Ownership

In an attempt to determine why the current system so often produces less than terrific results, research by Brookings Institute economist Margaret Blair challenges the conventional wisdom that ownership should be limited to those who invest financial capital.[34] Blair notes that the dramatic changes under way—downsizing, rightsizing, outsourcing, reengineering, total quality management, learning organizations—tend "to push authority, responsibility, risk, and reward—that is, all the attributes we associate with 'ownership'—outward and downward to employees, subcontractors, and, in some cases, former employees who are now subcontractors."

Because this constituency bears many of the *risks* of ownership, Blair argues that work should be restructured to provide a greater sense of "proprietorship," pointing to employee ownership as one way this goal can be encouraged. She proposes that the search for corporate flexibility, resilience and responsiveness be combined with a movement to allocate ownership rights and responsibilities to those who control critical assets (such as suppliers, distributors) and to those who have made "firm-specific investments"—particularly employees who have invested in education and training useful to their employer. Her expansive view of ownership concludes that today's core of conventional shareholders (whether institutional or individual) should be expanded to include elements of ownership for *all* those who have put capital at risk, not just for those who risk their *financial* capital. This risk-assessment approach to ownership, Blair insists, would do a far better job of enhancing the nation's capacity for wealth creation.

Commentators in Britain offer an even more radical analysis. In a 1993 survey of the various cultures of capitalism, Cambridge University's Charles Hampden-Turner wryly notes that workers are asked to agree that the company belongs to the shareholders and that the workers' function is to earn a profit for those shareholders. Not surprisingly, this is not a wildly popular idea among those who contribute their lives while shareholders contribute their money.[35] Charles Handy, Britain's best-known business futurist, takes that yet another step: "When the assets of an enterprise are primarily its people, it is time to rethink what it means to say that those who finance the enterprise can in any sensible way 'own' those assets."[36]

Needed: Broader, Deeper Systems Feedback

In the search for a common thread that links these various themes, a careful reading brings us back to the need for a reconfiguring of the signals—the feedback—to which the corporate entity is obliged to respond. In each case, a constituency can be identified (whether inside or outside the corporation) that seeks its unique version of improved corporate performance, including a quite spirited debate concerning what the relevant measures of that performance should be. At its core, this is fundamentally a reappraisal of ownership—what it is, how it works, even *whose* it is. It's difficult as yet to discern what will emerge from this debate. It's instructive to note, however, that the $200-plus billion teacher's retirement plan (TIAA-CREF) now employs a full-time professional to call on companies in its portfolio, quietly urging managers and boards to adopt high-performance management practices.[37]

One hopeful trend lies in the use of various components of ownership to institutionalize channels of communication. High-performance firms are learning that their success depends on reliable, motivated feedback from a broad spectrum of stakeholders, including employees, suppliers, distributors, customers and even the local population. Firms that seek that feedback tend to thrive compared with those that don't. Customer satisfaction programs are becoming commonplace, as are supplier education programs, many of them organized and staffed by employees. Foresighted companies are formalizing feedback systems not only with their employees (recognizing the importance of "employee voice") but also with a wide range of others with whom the company has ongoing relationships. The boundary between firm and market grows ever fuzzier.

Required: An Inclusive Corporate Architecture

The research suggests that, by using their financial clout to "put the 'own' back in ownership," institutional investors could ensure the embrace of performance-enhancing *systems* that advance the multiple (and multigenerational) agendas to which they must begin to respond. Alan Webber, founder and editor of *Fast Company*, puts the point succinctly: "Companies don't compete on the basis of just products anymore, but on the basis of entire business models." The same is true for national economies. At a minimum, that model must include investment practices that ensure the United States does not continue its slide into fiscally unsustainable ownership patterns.

Economist David Birch suggests that the winners will be those companies that are faster, better, cheaper—what he calls the corporate "gazelles." In this ceaseless search for advantage, London Business School professor John Kay, head of the Business Strategy Center, concludes that the most important component in this complex mix is a company's "architecture." The links between a company and its employees, customers and suppliers, he insists, are the "fountainhead of institutional knowledge and adaptability."[38] At the heart of any successful architecture, Kay argues, is a network of long-term "understandings" that influence participants' behavior toward each, uniting a range of interests behind a common purpose. When successful, this network can enable quite ordinary people to perform in extraordinary ways. Why? Because the knowledge that participants in this network must go on dealing with each other constrains their short-term self-interest in favor of a mutually beneficial long-term outcome.[39] That transformed relationship results in an organizational "turbo-charging" that makes the difference between mediocrity and excellence.[40]

In a similar vein, Harvard Business School professor Michael Porter found that, in order to compete, companies must be capable of focusing on the long term.[41] This focus requires that stakeholders be transformed into shareholders by making owners not only of a company's "insiders" (managers, directors and employees) but also of others within its network of long-term relationships, including traditional "outsiders" such as customers and suppliers. Kevin Kelly, editor of *Wired*, offers a computer-age image. In his systems way of thinking, it is the coordination of information that is crucial: "The challenge is simply stated: extend the company's internal network outward to include all those with whom the company interacts in the marketplace. Spin a grand

web to include employees, suppliers, regulators, and customers; they all become part of your company's collective being: they *are* the company."[42]

Another clue is found in Peter Senge's 1990 best-seller, *The Fifth Discipline*,
which analyzes how companies transform themselves into highly adaptable
"learning organizations." Senge documents that the solution to poor corporate
performance lies in identifying core causes rather than symptoms, confirming the systems theory view that improved performance flows from addressing fundamental structural problems that often lie hidden from view. Senge
found that institutionalized, lifelong learning is an essential ingredient in the
recipe for long-term organizational resilience and performance. Professor
Peter Drucker likewise puts the performance challenge in a systems design,
feedback-oriented, learning-based context, suggesting simply that "The essence of management is to make knowledge productive." People are a
company's strongest asset, because only they have access to the information—
the front line, real-time feedback required so that the company can adapt,
learn and evolve. Drawing on an organic systems metaphor, Michael
Rothschild suggests in *Bionomics—Economy as Ecosystem*:

> In the biologic environment, genetic information, recorded in the DNA mol-
> ecule, is the basis of all life. In the economic environment, technological in-
> formation, captured in . . . the know-how of millions of individuals, is the ul-
> timate source of economic life.[43]

Self-Design or Hands-Off Design

In combination, these insights point to the necessity that institutional investors
focus on the "invisible structure" of firms, including those attitude-determining
and information-gathering relationships that companies neglect at their peril.
In *Liberation Management*, management adviser Tom Peters concludes: "Relationships really are all there is." This suggests that corporate capital structures need to be reengineered to include as owners not only traditional insiders
(managers and directors) and traditional outsiders (absentee investors) but
also others (both insiders and outsiders) with a stake in the long-term success
of the firm.

The evidence indicates that this broader, inward- *and* outward-looking
concept of the corporation is gaining ground. One indication emerges from
Britain based on a three-year "inquiry" undertaken by the Royal Society for
the Arts and sponsored by twenty blue-chip businesses (British Gas, Cable &
Wireless, Cadbury Schweppes, etc.). The inquiry dealt with how British businesses could attain "sustainable business success in the face of continuing and
substantial changes in the nature and the intensity of global competition." The
report makes the case for "the inclusive approach," arguing that companies must
be guided by "multiple bottom lines" that take into account the interests of

stakeholders, including customers, suppliers, employees, investors and the communities in which companies operate. "An exclusive concentration on any one stakeholder will not lead to sustainable competitive performance," the report concludes. Rather, sustainable success requires that managers develop a "range of nonfinancial measures of success *in all of a company's relationships*."[44]

For those who equate ownership with control, it's clear that control in this money-managed world has been divorced from the simple self-design model envisioned by Adam Smith. In part, this is natural; after all, free enterprise has long been directed by that disembodied entity Smith described as the "invisible hand." However, today's dominant manifestation of the invisible hand is not personal preference (*self*-design) but capital market preference—the market's preference for short-term financial returns. *The Ownership Solution* suggests that sustainability, by whatever measure, requires that institutional investors insist that the "own" be put back in ownership. That can best be done, I submit, by reconnecting people to this feedback-based system we call capitalism.

CHAPTER **5**

Up-Close Capitalism—The Employee Ownership Solution

> An economy which makes it easier for John Paul Getty to get a third billion dollars than it does for two-thirds of the families in the country to get $500 ahead of their debts is buying a lot of hogwash about the value of John Paul Getty. The aggregate motivation in the millions of individuals that is destroyed and frustrated by such an insane arrangement is infinitely more productive than anything that one individual could contribute, irrespective of what that may be.
>
> *—Louis O. Kelso*

ESOPs are the most visible of the newly emerging ownership solutions. For instance, it was a $5 billion ESOP that turned United Airlines into a 55 percent employee-owned company. United has since experienced both the pleasures and the perils of a company whose employees are motivated by concerns more complicated than the size of their paycheck. Following its embrace of the ESOP buyout, United became the most profitable American airline—gaining market share, tripling its share price, posting record per-employee operating revenues and confounding an initially skeptical financial community as it outperformed its competitors while also creating seven thousand new jobs during a nationwide bout of corporate downsizing. It also became the worldwide benchmark for aviation innovation, including Internet bookings, ticketless flying, redesigned meals and more comfortable seats. In addition, it established an airline-within-an-airline (Shuttle by United) to rival Southwest Airlines, a no-frills West Coast competitor.

Innovations soon emerged from a newly collaborative workforce. A task force of ramp workers, pilots and managers devised a way to use electricity instead of jet fuel while planes sit at the gate, saving $20 million a year. The only capital investment: longer ladders so that ramp workers could plug in the electrical cables. Another task force urged more flexibility for in-flight personnel to swap assignments, resulting in another $20 million saved. On the other hand, buyout-related pay concessions made employees testy. That worsened when the flight attendants declined to participate in the ESOP while benefiting from job-protecting concessions made by their coworkers.

Complex, paradoxical crosscurrents are a hallmark of employee ownership. For instance, United's exploration of a potentially profitable merger with US Air was squelched by agreement of the pilots and senior management, not only because of pilot skepticism about excessive expansion but also because they objected to the potential dilution of their hard-won ownership stake and the merging of seniority lists. United's pilots, who conceived and led the buyout, initially got what they wanted: a big ownership stake, a seat on the board and the right to handpick top managers. However, they soon chafed at management's reluctance to share United's record profits, threatening to cease their efforts to foster a new spirit of cooperation. It remains to be seen whether this is a "new paradigm for postindustrial America" (as one union official claims) or a new can of worms for modern labor relations. Jerry Greenwald, United's chairman and chief executive, concedes he underestimated the time it takes to overcome past suspicions and mistrust.

The real test for United is yet to come. Regardless of its ownership structure, the company benefited from a passenger market that was growing faster than airline capacity. Only when those elements are reversed will we know whether United's version of workplace capitalism provides a genuinely new way to operate in this intensely competitive industry. Conservative columnist George Will is optimistic, sensing that employee ownership may yet "blur the lines between, and merge the interests of, capital and labor, writing a promising new chapter in the history of capitalism." Liberal Robert Reich, Bill Clinton's first-term labor secretary, is likewise upbeat. "From here on in," he observed "it will be impossible for a board of directors not to consider employee ownership as one potential business strategy."

This U.S.-bred version of up-close capitalism has become the yardstick against which other employee ownership programs are measured worldwide where the phenomenon is more commonly found in the privatization of state-owned enterprises.[1] ESOPs occupy a peculiar niche in the unfolding of a more workable ownership system for the United States. Although Louis Kelso had much to do with their development, they may have remained only an interesting idea except for an odd synchronicity of events that unfolded nearly a half century before Kelso met ESOP-champion Senator Russell Long. This period merits a brief exposition so that what follows can be understood in the context of a rich, colorful and little-known era of American history.

The Origins of ESOPs

Despite the appeal of socialism in other countries, only during one brief period in U.S. history has its ownership patterns come under direct attack. That peaked during the Great Depression of the 1930s when huge accumulations of wealth existed alongside widespread unemployment, poverty and human misery. That environment bred a populist state governor, Huey P. Long, in the dirt-poor state of Louisiana.[2] During the late 1920s, Long anticipated the New Deal era by enacting job-stimulating programs—constructing roads, bridges, hospitals—and paying for them with increased taxes on oil and gas. In effect, this was a levy on John D. Rockefeller, the legendary monopolist and principal owner of Standard Oil. Though Louisiana's propertied elite came to fear and then loathe Long, he rode his statewide popularity to the U.S. Senate in 1931 where he quickly gained a reputation as an outspoken opponent of wealth and privilege.

In February 1934, Long made a half-hour national radio address offering his version of an ownership solution to the still-lingering Depression ("Every Man a King But No Man Wears a Crown"). In addition to a wealth tax that would prevent any family from owning a fortune of more than $5 million (equivalent to approximately $40 million in 1998 dollars), he proposed a "millionaire's tax" to limit anyone from earning more than $1 million per year. His proposals were meant to limit personal wealth to no more than three hundred times that of the average American family, and to limit personal incomes to no more than three hundred times the average family income.*

By early 1935, Long's office was receiving 60,000 letters a week, rising to 140,000 after his occasional radio speeches. In a pointed jibe at Roosevelt, a patrician yachtsman, he proposed that FDR would make an excellent secretary of the Navy in a Long administration.[3] Worried at Long's potential impact on the 1936 elections, Roosevelt's advisers commissioned the nation's first-ever political poll to gauge his populist appeal.[4] To their dismay, they found that Long would be in the position of a spoiler who might deliver the White House to the Republicans.

Long delighted in mocking Roosevelt's New Deal as the "Same Old Deal" destined to leave most Americans poor while the Rockefellers, Mellons and Roosevelts would continue to own most everything. He also began to lay plans for a vigorous presidential campaign for which he was well positioned to raise money from banks and corporations who hoped he would dislodge Roosevelt and put a Republican back in the White House. On the political defensive and stunned by the poll results, Roosevelt's "brain trust" began in

---

* To put Long's proposal in historical context, it is helpful to recall that Aristotle argued that no one should have more than five times the wealth of the poorest person. According to Plato: "The form of law which I propose would be as follows: In a state which is desirous of being saved from the greatest of all plagues—not faction, but rather distraction—there should exist among the citizens neither extreme poverty nor, again, excessive wealth, for both are productive of great evils. . . . Now the legislator should determine what is to be the limit of poverty or of wealth."

SECRET BALLOT
No Obligation
No Signature
No Stamp Required

If an election were held today, who would be your choice
FOR PRESIDENT OF THE UNITED STATES
Mark a Cross **X** in Square Opposite Name of Candidate You Would Prefer

Franklin D. Roosevelt .... ☐
A Republican Candidate .... ☐
Huey P. Long .... ☐
--- ☐
If any other candidate, write here

For Whom Did You Vote As President in 1932?

Hoover ☐   **Roosevelt** ☐   .... ☐ . **Did Not Vote** ☐
Any One Else

To assist in tabulation by states, please write the name of your state here: _____

the summer of 1935 to retool his New Deal agenda, adding a "soak the rich" tax, a hike in inheritance taxes and a graduated corporate income tax. These proposals, according to one of Roosevelt's advisors, were specifically designed to "steal Long's thunder."[5] The most radical, even "socialist" proposal in FDR's "Second New Deal" was the Social Security Act.

Populism Without Robin Hood—A Fledgling Ownership Solution

Only sixteen when his famous father was assassinated in 1935, Russell Long was elected to the U.S. Senate at age twenty-nine and quickly became known for his keen intellect, his good humor and his hilarious tales about his zany "Uncle Earl" (Huey's brother)[6] for whom Russell had served as counsel when Earl was governor. Well liked and politically astute, Russell Long rose steadily in Senate seniority, becoming chairman of the Committee on Finance in 1964. Rightly regarded as the Senate's most powerful legislative body, the Finance Committee raises 98 percent of the government's revenue and decides how more than half those funds are disbursed as it deals with all issues affecting taxation, welfare, tariffs, trade, Social Security, Medicare and Medicaid.

In November 1973, Long held an animated four-hour discussion about ESOPs with Louis Kelso and Kelso's Washington representative, Norman Kurland. The next morning, Long proposed his first ESOP idea as an amendment to Conrail legislation pending before the Senate Commerce Committee. As chairman of the Finance Committee for sixteen years and its senior Democrat for another six, Long's support of Kelso's ESOP concept resulted in enactment of twenty-five pieces of favorable legislation, including an initiative cosponsored by a bipartisan group of fifty-six of the Senate's one hundred members. Based on the incentives championed by Long, ESOPs quickly became a fixture on the American corporate scene.

In 1975, philanthropist John D. Rockefeller III published *The Second American Revolution,* advocating broad-based ownership and ESOPs and arguing that "many of the deficiencies of our economic system could be alleviated if ways were found to broaden the ownership of the means of production." Seven years later, his son, John D. ("Jay") Rockefeller IV, while governor of West Virginia, provided financial support for the use of an ESOP to rescue the state's largest private employer, the six-thousand-employee Weirton division of National Steel. Appearing together at a memorial dinner in Weirton's community center, the great-grandson of the nation's most famous capitalist and the son of his populist nemesis joined hands, jointly declaring employee ownership a "new direction for America."

Personal Wealth versus Political Entitlements

One revealing anecdote from that populist-influenced era is worth recalling to set the stage for our later crafting of an ownership solution. During his tenure in the Senate, Russell Long met Arthur Altmeyer, who had served as a principal draftsman of the Social Security Act.[7] According to Altmeyer's account of his meeting with Roosevelt, he departed uncertain whether he had been summoned to discuss Huey Long or Social Security, because each time FDR mentioned Social Security he would also say: "that damn Huey Long."

I include this anecdote to convey three primary points about legislative strategy. First, conservatives (such as Russell Long) are not likely to become advocates of redistribute-the-wealth solutions, even if their fathers were. However, Long was easily persuaded when Louis Kelso came calling, because he saw in his ideas a way to broaden wealth without jeopardizing already owned wealth.[8] Second, both the ends and the means are important. As Huey's son explained to me, Louisiana had a long history of strong and colorful politicians, but his father was the first to put the governor's office to work for the common people. However, whereas his father saw the distribution of wealth as largely a zero-sum game requiring redistribution from one group to another, Russell saw the challenge as designing policies that *evoked* rather than mandated improved ownership patterns. Lastly, Social Security is with us still, as much a legacy of Huey Long's Share Our Wealth movement as Roosevelt's New Deal initiatives. However, a government levy on the labor of its citizens is hardly an empowering notion. While a redistributive job tax may serve well as an essential safety net, it's far from the most desirable way to link people to a system founded on notions of private property.

As a matter of systems design, the key distinction lies in whether policymakers rely on foresight or hindsight. Each year the U.S. economy finances hundreds of billions of dollars in new structures and equipment (more than $800 billion in 1996), while hundreds of billions more change hands in mergers and acquisitions of successful companies ($1 trillion in 1997). All of those assets are owned by someone.[9] Without policy input and corporate leadership, today's closed system of finance is certain to continue to concentrate much of that ownership into very few hands, leaving the bulk of American adults (voters all) economically disconnected and ever more reliant on Social Security.[10] Paradoxically, the best way to reduce governmental intervention (and redistribution) is for government to intervene with a foresighted policy environment that induces capitalism to create a broader base of capitalists.

The First ESOP

With that as background, we turn to the legislative origins of employee ownership in the United States. Employee profit-sharing plans have been around since at least 1795, when Albert Gallatin, who later served as treasury secretary to both Jefferson and Madison, established a plan at his Pennsylvania Glass Works. Even railroad magnate and turn-of-the-century multimillionaire Leland Stanford took a liking to employee ownership, proclaiming worker cooperatives the "highest manifestation of self government."[11] One of the builders of the first transcontinental railroad and president of the Central Pacific from 1861 to 1883, Stanford never embraced the notion in his railroad. However, he ensured that the philosophy would be taught at the university that bears his name, inserting into Stanford University's 1885 grant of endowment a trustee duty to teach "the advantages of association and cooperation."

Around the turn of the century, American labor agreed to a social compact granting to corporations the role of initiating and controlling investment, production, employment and services. Within that compact, labor unions negotiated for their members terms and conditions of employment. That job-focused relationship continues today. During the 1920s, "welfare capitalism" enjoyed a certain cachet with profit sharing and employee ownership embraced as a way to dissuade workers of anticapitalist sentiments (Marxist-inspired revolutionaries had just ousted Russia's economic elite). In 1921, profit-sharing and stock bonus plans gained congressional encouragement as a way to help employers "attract and retain qualified employees," including servicemen returning from World War I. At the peak of welfare capitalism, more than 6 million employees owned stock in their companies.

When Louis Kelso's employee ownership publications first surfaced in the 1950s and 1960s, his analysis was based on the writings of French economist Jean-Baptiste Say (1767–1862), best known for "Say's law" of market balance, which states simply that supply creates its own demand, a central tenet of economics until the Depression, only to return to fashion in the late 1970s with the popularity of supply-side economics.[12] "Say's law is the foundation of supply-side theory," George Gilder proclaimed in *Wealth and Poverty*, the supply-sider's bible.

The power to consume, according to Say, is a by-product of the costs of production, because wages, salaries, rents, interest and dividends—all the normal expenses of production—in turn become income for someone else. Kelso injected a crucial variation on that theme. While conceding that investment can stimulate demand, he argued that this demand would broadly irrigate the economy with purchasing power only if financing techniques are used that steadily *expand* ownership because, in a private property economy, that's the only way to ensure that dividends, rents, profits and interest—the "wages of capital"—are diffused throughout the economy.* Ronald Reagan, an early Kelso fan, offered the following story in 1975 to illustrate the point:

> *Some years ago, an executive of the Ford Motor Company was showing the late Walter Reuther (head of the autoworkers union) through the Ford assembly plant in Cleveland, Ohio. Pointing to the latest in automated machinery he said, "Walter, you'll have a hard time collecting dues from those machines." Walter said, "You'll have a harder time selling them automobiles." The obvious answer neither of them thought of was that owners of machines can buy automobiles.[13]*

The first-ever ESOP demonstrates why Kelso insisted that new financing techniques are required to create new owners. In 1956, he persuaded the three principal owners of Peninsula Newspapers in Palo Alto, California, to transform the firm's profit-sharing plans into a financing vehicle to purchase 72 percent of the company's stock for its employees. The selling shareholders agreed to accept installment payments for their shares along with an IOU guaranteed by the company. Each year, the company used its profit sharing to pay off the IOU, claiming a tax deduction for funding an employee benefit plan that doubled as a shareholder buyout plan. Why is this the "first ESOP"? Because it relied on future company earnings ("self-financing") to repay company-guaranteed debt to acquire company shares. This use of financial leverage is not new. What *is* new is using a self-financing technique to empower employees.

"Open System" Finance

ESOPs often buy stock owned by the founders of a company or the heirs. At Cargill, America's largest family-owned company with more than $50 billion in annual sales, an ESOP was used in 1992 to acquire 17 percent of its shares. That satisfied cash-hungry heirs while keeping intact Cargill's close-knit ownership. Business continuity is another common use. Nolan Bushnell, founder of Atari, the first successful computer game company, turned to an ESOP to

---

* A missing ingredient in this computation is the role played by capital gains, an increasingly important source of income and economic security for those owning productive assets. This aspect of ownership is particularly important in an economy where the Dow-Jones industrial average has risen from less than 1,000 in 1982 to more than 8,000 by mid-1997.

sell some of his shares, using his proceeds to start Chucky Cheese, a chain of pizza parlors, from which he could then exit by selling to yet another ESOP. He could also raise new capital by selling to the ESOP newly issued Chucky Cheese shares, a financing technique found in one of six ESOPs.

ESOP-style "open system" financing can also be used to sell off a subsidiary or a division, much as National Steel in 1982 sold its Weirton, West Virginia operations. Academics have identified sixty American companies where employee ownership was used during the 1980s to spin off operations. Another twenty-three public companies used employee ownership to "go private."[14] ESOPs can also facilitate acquisitions. Houston investment banker Gordon Cain included an ESOP as part of a 1977 leveraged buyout of several companies in the distressed petrochemical industry. A year later he sold out to Occidental Petroleum for $2.2 billion, realizing a 4,500 percent increase in value in only one year. When the ESOP was terminated, each of Cain's thirteen hundred employees received a check for roughly four times his or her annual salary, an average $125,000 for a machine-operator or craftsman. At the Lowe's Companies, a southeastern chain of home-improvement stores, sales managers routinely retire with $1 million and truck drivers with $500,000.

Of course, employee stock can also go sour, as can other plans designed to tie employees to business results. In 1990, DuPont pulled the plug on an incentive pay program in which the company's 20,000 fibers-division employees received larger pay increases if DuPont's profit goals were exceeded, but smaller payouts or none if goals weren't met. The plan was canceled amid plummeting employee morale when the 1990 recession made it clear that for the first time, the company wouldn't meet its goals.

In the deregulated transportation environment of the early 1980s, unionized truckers agreed to substantial wage-for-stock swaps only to discover even that was not enough to stay afloat in their newly competitive industry.[15] With airline deregulation, numerous low-fare air carriers entered the market, including People's Express, where new hires were urged to "buy their jobs," typically investing funds accumulated with their previous employer. When the airline went bust, those employees lost their nest eggs.

Horror stories are rare but instructive. For instance, the same provisions that enabled employees to acquire an 82 percent stake in Charter Medical also allowed the family who ran the business to regain all but 30 percent of the shares for a nominal amount after a few years. When the company fared poorly, new investors further diluted the employees' stake to 3 percent. At textile giant Burlington Industries, investment bankers at Morgan Stanley (charging what the *Wall Street Journal* claims were twice their normal fees) set up an ESOP that borrowed funds to pay a special dividend to Morgan and the managers who hired them (and bought stock in the company). By the time the company went public three years later, its stock value had dropped by two-thirds and the ESOP's ownership had declined from 36 percent to 3 percent. In both cases, employees brought suit and won settlements.

Savings-and-loan swindler Charles Keating of Lincoln Savings and Loan fame also abused an ESOP. Lincoln's parent company funded its ESOP by transferring money from the employees' profit-sharing accounts into Lincoln shares when it was already clear that the company was shaky. The same scam emerged at several other S&Ls. In another case, evidencing the brazen ingenuity for which Americans are famed, the founder of a company with only one employee set up an ESOP that paid out all the company's earnings to himself as a dividend, thereby exempting the company from paying payroll taxes. The IRS objected and won in court. The company's name: Steel Balls.[16]

The ESOP at Corrections Corporation of America shows how even employee ownership can't redeem the perverse incentives that arise where the line is crossed between society and the market. As the nation's largest chain of privately run prisons, C.C.A.'s stock has soared from $50 million in 1986 to $3.5 billion at its peak in October 1997, leading Paine Webber to crow in its stock analysis: "Crime pays." How do the company and its employee-owners outperform its public-sector competitors: fewer inmate activities, lower-quality food, lower labor costs (accompanied by a 50 percent higher rate of violent incidents) and an early release rate for good behavior only one-eighth that of its public counterparts (every day of extra time is extra profits for the company and an extra taxpayer expense).[17] Despite these obvious perils and the always-present potential for abuse, the need remains for financing techniques that will open today's closed system of finance. ESOP financing marks a modest beginning.

Incentivized Ownership

In a "leveraged" ESOP (where shares are bought using borrowed funds), four parties are typically involved: the employees, a sponsor company, a seller and a lender. Incentives are available for each. For employees, shares accumulate untaxed until received. For companies, a tax deduction is allowed not only for its interest expense on borrowed money used to fund an ESOP but also for the expense of repaying loan principal. Plus an employer tax deduction is allowed for dividends paid on ESOP-held shares as a way to generate an ownership-based "second income"—a key Kelso-conceived rationale for ESOPs.

For sellers to an ESOP, proceeds received on the sale to an ESOP of unlisted shares may be reinvested ("rolled over") without tax. That's a key reason Avis became an ESOP company in the mid-1980s when former Treasury Secretary William Simon and his partners at Wesray Capital turned to an ESOP to sell their stake in Avis. Since 1984, "ESOP rollovers" have encouraged thousands of business owners to sell their companies to their employees. To qualify, shareholders initially need sell only 30 percent of the company's shares to the

ESOP. That allows founders (like Atari founder Nolan Bushnell) to adopt an ESOP on a step-by-step basis, generating cash for some shares while maintaining control of the company. British ESOP law has a similar tax-free reinvestment provision, though with only a 10 percent minimum-sale requirement. These ESOP rollover provisions are destined to see substantial use over the next decade. Not only will baby-boomer entrepreneurs be looking for tax-effective investment exits, but dozens of once-public American and British corporations converted to private ownership in the LBO boom of the 1980s are eligible. The financial fraternity is itching to do these deals, with the likes of Goldman Sachs, Morgan Stanley and Paine Webber staffed up with specialists offering not only advice but specialized "ESOP reinvestment securities."

In addition to employees, employers and sellers, lenders are (or were) encouraged to participate in ESOP financing. For twelve years (1984–1996), banks could exclude from their taxable income half the interest earned on ESOP loans. At one point, it was not clear that Russell Long would be able to enact this incentive. As we were walking into the Finance Committee in 1984, he was pulled aside by a Republican senator who apologized that he couldn't support Long's ESOP-lender incentive because it sounded to him like "credit allocation," an idea he opposed. Knowing the tightly closed nature of conventional finance, Long offered the ideal rejoinder: "Credit is already allocated," he countered. "It's allocated to those who have collateral." That senator later voted in support of the provision, helping Long enact it into law.[18]

Principled Capitalism

United States' ESOPs have clear advantages. That became clear to me while working in Jamaica, where a firm was touted to me as an "ESOP company." Closer inspection revealed that this fifty-employee company was founded by a husband-and-wife team, both of whom worked in the company. In combination, those two employees owned 100 percent of the shares. Although that is certainly one type of "ESOP," policymakers are increasingly reluctant to incentivize employee ownership unless participation is broad-based and the benefits broadly shared among those participating.

Those key principles were lacking at United Parcel Service (UPS) in the summer of 1997 when a fifteen-day strike hobbled shippers nationwide. Although UPS employees own one-third of the world's largest package carrier, 27,000 of UPS's supervisors and managers own a combined 29 percent of the firm's shares while some 60,000 drivers, clerks and sorters own less than 3 percent (in a total workforce exceeding 315,000). Each year the manager-owners divvy up 15 percent of pretax profits in company shares. Those shares can then be sold back to the company (during 1996, UPS purchased 22.2 million shares for $615 million). Share values have been rising more than 20 percent each year since the late 1980s. Since 1992, UPS profits have doubled to $1.15 billion on 1996 sales of $22.4 billion. In other words, it's easy to figure who was on which side of the picket line.

In addition to two core ESOP principles (widespread participation along with a widespread distribution of shares among participants), ESOPs also reflect what Kelso called a "private property principle" based on his novel "two-factor" view of economics. Kelso insists that, much as a workman is paid wages for the toil he contributes, an owner should likewise be compensated fairly for what he contributes.[19] That's why ESOP law encourages (through a tax deduction allowed for dividends) the payout to employees of a portion of the company's earnings. The goal of this "supply-side demand stimulation" (à la Say's law) is to boost broad-based purchasing power in a noninflationary way.

Stock ownership plans for those employed as managers and directors remain far more common than those provided for the rank and file. In more than half of all listed U.S. companies, management stock ownership exceeds 4 percent, while in 40 percent of such companies management ownership exceeds 10 percent. Three-quarters of the firms with 10 percent or more management ownership are listed on NASDAQ, where smaller firms tend to cluster.[20] *The Ownership Solution* suggests that the transformation of economic prosperity into social equity requires more broadly participatory patterns of ownership. Though hardly a panacea, principled employee ownership offers a promising starting point. One hopeful trend: employee benefit plans and stock brokers are of equal importance in spreading capitalism among the general population. Thirty-four percent of adults responding to a 1990 New York Stock Exchange survey report that they first acquired shares through an employee benefit plan, the same percentage who said they first bought shares through a broker.

The Reach of Employee Ownership

The National Center for Employee Ownership reports that in 1996 more than ten thousand American corporations had ESOPs and similar broad-based ownership plans covering almost 9 million employees. Ninety percent of ESOPs are in unlisted companies. Approximately 9 percent of the $8-plus trillion in corporate equity in the United States is now owned by employees, with a market value exceeding $750 billion.[21] The Center found that employee ownership has recently been growing at roughly three hundred to six hundred new plans per year (three hundred thousand to six hundred thousand new participants).[22] In unlisted companies, some two-thirds of ESOPs are used to buy shares of departing owners. The balance are an add-on benefit or a way to borrow funds. Among traded companies, three main uses dominate: to provide an employee benefit, to provide stock in lieu of fixed labor costs (20 percent of the companies),[23] and to provide employees with a voice in the event of a takeover attempt (10 percent).[24]

About a dozen publicly traded companies are majority employee-owned while 125 listed companies have at least 20 percent employee ownership. A majority of listed ESOP firms (62 percent) have less than 10 percent employee ownership. Majority employee-owned companies include United Airlines (85,000 employees), Science Applications International Corp. (30,000), The Parsons Corporation (5,900), and Amsted Industries (4,500). Brand-name companies where employees own at least 30 percent include Northwest Airlines (45,000 employees), Tandy Corp. (41,000) and Hallmark Cards (22,000). According to a 1990 study, an employee making $20,000 a year will accumulate $31,000 in stock over ten years.[25]

Stock options represent one of the fastest-growing components in employee equity participation. A 1997 study by William M. Mercer consultants found that 30 percent of the largest U.S. companies now have broad-based stock option programs covering more than half their employees, up from 17 percent five years ago.[26] Borders Group, owner of a chain of book and music stores, launched a program in 1995 while taking the company public. That plan now covers about 90 percent of its employees. According to Santa Clara, California–based ShareData, Inc., 53 percent of those companies with stock option plans offer them to rank-and-file employees.

At Wendy's International, the fast-food chain, stock options have long been offered to executives. In 1990, the firm broadened the plan to include Wendy's managers and assistant managers as well as full-time administrative personnel. As of mid-1997, 10 percent of the 50,000 employees at Wendy's-owned restaurants had participated in the stock's rise from $6 a share when the plan began to $21 in late 1997. One clear benefit for Wendy's: turnover among managers dropped from 45 percent a year in the late 1980s to 20 percent in 1997. One key reason for the growing popularity of employee stock options is a 1995 ruling by the Financial Accounting Standards Board indicating that, rather than taking a charge against earnings, sponsors could continue to disclose the cost of these plans in a footnote in their annual report. Since then, these schemes have become steadily more popular, except among other shareholders who raise concerns about dilution.

The roads to employee ownership—or a sense of ownership—are rich in variety. After dissolving its ESOP as part of a leveraged buyout, San Francisco–based Levi Struass & Co., the $7.1 billion (in sales) worldwide jeansmaker, replaced it with a novel Global Success Sharing Plan under which the company will match all 37,000 employees' 1997 pay if the company meets a $7.6 billion cash flow target by 2001. At Aramark, one of the nation's largest food service building and maintenance companies with more than $6 billion in annual sales, CEO Joseph Neubauer has seen to it that he and some 14,500 employees own 80 percent of the company (he owns 13 percent). As this book was being completed, he was completing plans to pick up the remaining 20 percent for employees while simultaneously restructuring the company to issue three new classes of stock, one for each division. Those who choose to buy stock will have to buy half in the division that employs them.[27]

Spencer Hays runs a series of companies ranging from publishing to financial planning, life insurance, real estate and the selling of suits to men in their offices or homes. Believing simply that "people have to be rewarded," he developed in the publishing firm a share incentive plan linked to each individual's contribution to annual profits. Employees can purchase the shares with an interest-free loan from the company over ten years, with the company retaining a right of first refusal to repurchase the shares from any employee-owner wishing to sell.[28]

ESOPs: The Two-Sided Coin

Employee ownership is not without its risks. While detractors worry that employees will "put all their eggs in one basket," supporters worry that employees frequently have neither eggs nor a basket.[29] There is little that employee ownership alone can do to insulate companies from competition, technological change or shifting markets. Nor is there anything "magical" about employees owning shares if the company is in the wrong business. On the other hand, some companies embrace employee ownership as a component of their competitiveness strategy, figuring that at-risk employee-owners are more likely to exhibit the entrepreneurial drive and the flexibility required to identify and make the changes required as technology changes and markets shift.

At San Diego–headquartered Science Applications International Corporation (SAIC), founder and chief executive Bob Beyster sees employee ownership as a key to their success in identifying new opportunities (health care, the environment) as they began to lose their largest customer, the Department of Defense. With its eclectic mix of a dozen different employee stock plans, including stock grants for employees who bring in new business and for those identified as future leaders, SAIC has almost tripled its workforce since the early 1990s while cutbacks have been the hallmark of most defense firms. Success, they found, was not just about market share; it was also about creating new markets—markets that at-risk, motivated employees proved adept at creating. *Inc.* magazine, in whose pages employee ownership is often extrolled, reports "there's considerable evidence that eliminating the employee mentality and creating companies of businesspeople, of owners, has become a kind of Hidden Secret of Success in the American marketplace."[30] That's certainly the case at SAIC where, as *Forbes* reports, CEO Beyster, with his spread-the-wealth management, "doesn't have to worry about what Wall Street analysts think of his company. His bosses work for him."[31]

Others worry that employee ownership may entrench poor managers by weakening the influence of other shareholders or, conversely, by not giving employee-shareholders enough clout to influence or remove poor management. CEO Jerry Gorde has been trying for twenty years to share both wealth and power at Vatex, Inc., first by sharing profits, later by creating an ESOP and most recently by converting to a worker-owned cooperative. Established in the heart of Richmond, Virginia's distressed urban center, Vatex has long focused its hiring on the economically disadvantaged. His original ESOP structure included a perverse incentive for employees to leave because only then could they cash in their shares. After living with an ESOP for a decade, he abandoned it, concluding, "If you can't read an income statement and balance sheet, you'll be a lousy capitalist." When the ESOP was terminated, fifty-four employees were paid a total of $750,000 (in a company where the starting wage is $6.50 an hour). While a few rolled over the funds into an individual retirement account (IRA), most spent it. Only one thanked Gorde.

Converting to a co-op in 1995 gave Gorde a chance to try sharing not only wealth but also power, a notion that appealed to his left-of-center sensibilities. Thus, he crafted the bylaws to mandate that 30 percent of the profits pass through to the workers. Workers elect the board and the board selects the president and the CEO. Committees set wage scales, employment policy and the appeals process. The governance is unusually democratic, while management is not. "That doesn't change," Gorde observes. "You still need day-to-day lines of authority. That's management." The problem is, most employees still think they're somehow being manipulated by someone somewhere. Notes Gorde: "We have what I call 'Rebels Without a Clue'—constantly rebelling against authority. They don't understand they *are* the authority."

The dynamics of employee ownership occasionally defy logic. In October 1981, a group of Clark, New Jersey, autoworkers (represented by the United Autoworkers) succeeded in using an ESOP to acquire a General Motors roller bearing plant. As part of the $53 million buyout, employees agreed to wage concessions along with work rule changes and job reductions, hoping to recover those concessions through profit sharing and stock accumulation. A few years later, the company was back in trouble when a dispute raged over whether the board should approve a profit-sharing payment at a time when the company required funds to modernize its plant and upgrade its product line. Rather than strike, local union leaders led a slowdown, ensuring that the profits were unavailable either for investment or for profit-sharing. The company subsequently failed.

Dueling Paranoia

Achieving the right level of employee participation remains a hit-and-miss proposition, more art than science. Chris Mackin, one of the few experts in the field, advises that a shift in company culture often requires dealing with the runaway images that managers have of labor (and vice versa), as well as the "dueling paranoia" of both that usually accompanies a failure to identify clear boundaries. Based on two decades of listening to workers and managers talk about the meaning of ownership, he found that while everyone has a theory about it, not everyone has the same theory. In order to reach workplace consensus, he developed an ownership vocabulary that posits two separate domains of "organizational" and "economic" life. Organizational life involves membership or "people" issues, while economic life involves business and "money" issues. Business exists simultaneously in both. Employees and managers have certain rights and responsibilities in each domain. For example, if employees are interested in having a voice, there is an accompanying responsibility to recognize when that voice must be accompanied by expertise.

Mackin has found that managers and workers often occupy different, unbalanced ends of the rights/responsibilities spectrum. Management is typically positive about the responsibilities and the risks of employee ownership but negative about the rights and the rewards. Their confusing message to workers: "Act like an owner, sit down and be quiet." Workers, on the other hand, are often positive about the rewards and the rights but negative about the risks and the responsibilities. Their confusing message to management: "Reward me like an owner but treat me like an employee." Mackin concludes that the remedy is to push this ownership conversation along so that both camps can begin to see and resolve the inconsistencies. And then to periodically survey the company to pinpoint imbalances as the workplace culture steadily shifts to become an ownership culture.

In order to determine the right participation "fit" for a company, he advises a two-part process. First comes the crafting of a common vision about what participation is—and is not. That's where his matrix of rights and responsibilities comes in handy. Second is the teaching of skills and an allocation of decision-making authority. Traditionally, the broadest decisions are made by managers while more local ones are reserved for workers and, where a union is involved, compensation and working conditions are left to collective bargaining. As workplaces become more participatory, decisions involving policy, planning and coordination often begin to involve more employee input, usually while still maintaining boundaries. If managers know they have the final call, Mackin notes, they are likely to be more open to input.[32] It's also important to occasionally redraw those boundaries—not only to make those disgruntled happier but also to recognize that, as company cultures evolve, so too should the lines of decision-making authority.

The Up-Close Ownership Debate Continues

Employee ownership has long been the focus of heated debate among economists and policymakers. Nobel laureate economist James Meade concedes that employee ownership companies provide more stable employment in the face of economic fluctuations. He questions, however, whether such firms may fail to respond to economic *expansion* by creating more jobs because employee-owners may choose instead to maximize *their* pay and *their* ownership rather than dilute their interest by bringing in newcomers. The data suggests otherwise. Research by the National Center for Employee Ownership found that America's ESOP firms create more jobs than non-ESOP firms.[33]

Others worry that employee ownership may be temporary, even ephemeral. Cain Chemical's ESOP lasted only a year before Gordon Cain sold out and terminated it. Yet those former employee-owners praise Cain, who could have left them out of that deal. Certainly that's the accepted practice in conventional investment banking circles. Other concerns arose at Avis. Although employee ownership at Avis began in 1987 as a 100 percent ESOP, the employees' stake dropped to 75 percent in the early 1990s when General Motors swapped its Avis debt for a quarter of Avis's shares. Then the company was sold in 1997, the ESOP terminated and employees paid out. The typical payout was $35,000, though long-term employees got considerably more while senior managers, with their separate stock option plans, benefited more than the rank and file.

It's important to understand that ESOPs were written into law for use as a highly pragmatic technique of corporate finance. That financing is designed to operate through an employee benefit plan because ESOP-like principles (and legal precedents) were already well settled in the employee benefit area (requiring broad-based participation, etc.). Simple in concept yet often complex and controversial in operation, ESOPs are meant to add a new player to the corporate financial scene so that those typically left out (a corporation's employees) are instead included. Very little about ESOPs is new except for the idea that self-financing (an old idea) can be used to create more up-close capitalists. The larger issue is who benefits from all that buying and selling in capital markets? Or, as Wall Street mavens say, "Who pays and who plays?" Employees have often paid; ESOPs now provide a way for them to play.

The Elusive Search for the Perfect ESOP

Employee ownership schemes share a common dilemma spawned by their success. Where the ownership stake in an unlisted company increases in value, employees may find it difficult to sell their shares back to the company without imposing on the company a financial strain. That, in turn, may persuade the company to list its shares, allowing the stock market to provide this liquidity. Yet this approach (or the outright sale of the company, as with Avis and Cain Chemical) may either dilute or terminate the employee ownership. In time, United Airlines will face this same dilemma. Sensitive to this quandary, David Erdal, chairman of Scottish paper-maker Tullis Russell and Company,

Ltd., searched for an ownership solution that could endure for the ages. After a decade-long search (the company has been in business since Napoleon's time), he settled in 1994 on a unique hybrid whereby 70 percent of Tullis Russell's shares will reside in trust.

His compromise illustrates the two-sided nature of the employee-ownership phenomenon. Locking in this perpetual ownership structure for the company's twelve hundred employees means that the company will only need to generate enough cash to buy back, at most, 30 percent of its shares as employees leave or retire. While that makes the firm financially stronger, it also means that 70 percent of the financial value of the company remains inaccessible to its employee-owners. Erdal concludes that this ownership solution offers a happy compromise as one of his goals is to minimize the effects that capital markets and external owners can work on a company and its employees, including their demands for dividends and a steady growth in earnings.[34]

In the heartland of America, McKay Nursery in Waterloo, Iowa, turned to employee ownership in 1984 not only as a tax-friendly way to pay off its investors but as a way to attract, retain and pay its migrant workers. This century-old firm decided on a 100 percent ESOP-owned arrangement that includes as participants sixty of its migrants who work at least the eight months required each year to receive yearly stock allotments along with sixty year-round staff, ten of whom are former migrants. Wages for America's migrant workers have long been shameful. And even those low wages have been declining for twenty years. Yet it's difficult to remain competitive by paying more in cash in this labor-intensive industry where the investment in labor (fifty cents for every dollar in revenue) creates a strong incentive to reduce turnover and training costs. The ESOP was McKay's answer. Each year employees receive bonuses equal to 20 to 25 percent of pay in either cash or in stock in their ESOP accounts. The company estimates that even the lowest-paid long-term employee should accumulate a nest egg of more than $100,000. Because the aim is to keep the company employee-owned, employees are required to sell their shares back to the company when they leave, a restriction allowed under U.S. law to encourage the goal that Erdal sought in Scotland.

Long-term Strategies in a Short-term World

This ongoing experimentation with up-close ownership also helps shine some light on the role that loyalty plays in corporate performance. In *The Loyalty Effect*, Frederick F. Reichheld finds a link between employee loyalty and customer loyalty, arguing that both are essential to long-term growth and profits.[35] However, he notes that, on average, American companies lose half their customers in five years, half their employees in four and half their investors in less than one. Loyalty, he insists, is "one of the great engines of business success, and it is still alive and thriving at the heart of every company with an enduring record of productivity and growth."[36]

Therein lies one of the key challenges facing capitalism. Various forms of up-close capitalism may well represent the best hope capitalism has for tapping the loyalty, motivation, dedication and sacrifice that free enterprise requires for long-term success. Yet the challenges are immense. For example, the workforce must be educated to think of significant ownership as a realistic and useful option. Oddly enough, in the world's largest capitalist economy, American education does not routinely teach ownership skills. In addition, managers must be reeducated to share authority. Much of today's downsizing and outsourcing, with its disproportionate impact on managers, traces its roots to their inability or unwillingness to make that change.

Organized labor must also play a role in facilitating that transition. For example, managers at nonunion Polaroid, where an ESOP holds 17 percent of the shares, called for volunteers to participate in an Employee Owners Influence Council to evaluate proposals for change within the company. When that 1995 initiative caught the attention of the National Labor Relations Board, established in 1935, officials complained that the process used to solicit volunteers was improper and that the council would be an illegal company-dominated "labor organization" (i.e., a company union) because it involved the discussion of terms and conditions of work.[37]

Another of the challenges: while mid-level managers must be relied on to make changes in this area, they may own little stock themselves. That saps their incentive to undertake what may be a wrenching transformation, including changes that may reduce management ranks and reshuffle managers' authority. Despite these challenges, the fact remains that broad-based ownership is preferable to its alternative. And employee ownership, the evidence confirms, is a cost-effective priority for targeting limited policy resources. The challenge lies in finding ways to advance what remains a very new idea in a policy environment constructed well before up-close capitalism was considered a desirable and feasible goal.

CHAPTER 6

New Property Paradigms

It may well be that the structure or architecture of a system determines its behavior and its fate.

—John Todd

This chapter reviews an array of promising new property paradigms that have appeared on the world scene over the past few years. *Paradigm* (from the Latin for *pattern*) was used by Plato at the end of *The Republic* to describe a basic form or image encompassing one's fate and fortune and determining one's destiny. Much as socialism put its fate in the hands of the Communist Party as an idealized representative of the will of the workers, capitalism trusts its fate to the market's "invisible hand" as an idealized representative of the will of the customer. Neither model is based on science but on faith, reflecting a form of prophecy that the paradigm chosen is a vehicle capable of transporting a people closer to their destiny. Yet neither model has proven fully satisfactory. The reason, I submit, is due to (*a*) our incomplete understanding of the role played by ownership patterns and (*b*) our reluctance to learn from the short-comings of those paradigms we've chosen to date.

At the same time, however, any ownership engineer faces what complexity theorist John Holland describes as a tradeoff between exploitation and exploration.[1] A business can thrive as it exploits an established business line; however, it may falter if it fails to innovate or to explore new technologies. If, on the other hand, a business directs all its resources to R&D, it may never build a successful production line, in which case it also may fail. Likewise for property paradigms. Our current system of ownership, warts and all, keeps us from failing—unlike those who embraced radically centralized Marxist-inspired paradigms. Yet it's also essential that we innovate, exploring new patterns, forms and models. Serendipitously, the magnitude and relative stability of institutional ownership affords us a certain freedom to experiment, to innovate and to work toward more sustainable ownership paradigms, including variations on the ESOP theme.

In the case of the Green Bay Packers, a quite old ownership paradigm has kept that hugely popular football team tied to a small Wisconsin town for almost seven decades by linking it to its natural owners—local residents and fans. Contrary to other pro football franchises, which are collected like so many expensive doodads by the well-to-do, the Packer's ownership resides in a not-for-profit corporation (first established in 1919) whose 4,634 shares are valued today at the same $25 as when issued. Shares can be left to relatives but cannot be sold to outsiders without first offering them to the team. No one can own more than 200 shares. If the team were sold (major league franchises routinely fetch upwards of $150 million), the proceeds must be used to construct a war memorial at the local post of the American Legion.

To maintain the long-term financial viability of the sport, the National Football League mandates the sharing of media and licensing receipts, acknowledging a sort of "cultural commons" based on pro football's nationwide popularity among key audiences. Evidence of that popularity gained a new price tag on 13 January 1998 when three television networks concluded a deal that will pay the NFL $17.6 billion for broadcasting rights of NFL games through the 2005 season. As three-time Super Bowl champs (and the runner-up in 1998), the Packers continue to thrive while Green Bay (a northeastern Wisconsin town of only 100,000) continues to attract tourist dollars. In an era when the "hometown team" routinely relocates based on the profit-maximizing whims of wealthy owners, several major cities—particularly those with substantial public investments in sports arenas—now wish they had embraced Green Bay's foresighted ownership solution as a way to anchor these quasi-community assets.[2]

Multinational Up-Close Capitalists

More than one hundred countries have an active interest in adapting ESOPs. Many are well advanced. However, it is the growing use of ESOPs in multinational corporations that offers potentially the most powerful short-term tool for spreading up-close ownership worldwide. According to a 1994 World Investment Report issued by the UN Conference on Trade and Development, multinational corporations now employ 12 million in developing countries, while in developed countries they employ about five times as many (61 million). Since 1985, however, two-thirds of their job growth has been in developing countries. This trend is certain to accelerate as both capital and trade flow ever more freely. An obvious ownership challenge accompanies this trend: how best to encourage these cross-border firms to include indigenous employees as partial owners of parent-company shares.

This will grow steadily more important as the multinational corporation emerges as a dominant player on the global stage. The number of such firms in the world's fourteen richest countries has more than tripled since 1969, from seven thousand to twenty-four thousand. The UN found that some thirty-seven thousand transnational corporations now operate worldwide.

They control about a third of all private-sector capital and have worldwide sales of $5.5 trillion (the 1996 GDP of the United States was $7.6 trillion). The largest three hundred firms account for 25 percent of the world's productive assets; the top one hundred hold $3.1 trillion in assets and account for about half of all foreign direct investment. Because American multinational corporations are the most thoroughly globalized, producing twice as much outside their borders as European and Japanese multinationals combined, it makes sense that U.S. firms should lead the way.

One of the first places this "internationalizing" challenge surfaced was at Kelso & Company, a New York–based investment banking firm where I served two years as special counsel. In 1988, Black & Decker, a U.S. tool manufacturer, mounted an unsolicited bid for American Standard, the world's largest producer of vitreous china (sinks, tubs, toilets). Kelso & Company's niche in the takeover arena is that of a "white knight," operating by management invitation only to fend off uninvited takeover bids. As part of our successful defense, a $3.0 billion "white knight LBO" was completed in which an ESOP enabled the domestic employees to acquire 19 percent of the equity. Another 14 percent was bought by more than four hundred managers worldwide, for a total 33 percent employee/manager ownership, an unusually inclusive ownership structure for the much-heralded "Decade of Greed." Under U.S. law, however, the ESOP could cover only U.S. employees—about 20 percent of a total workforce of thirty-five thousand in some thirty-five countries. Though we considered expanding the ESOP worldwide, a genuinely multinational ESOP was then simply too costly and too complex. Since that time, H. B. Fuller, a specialty chemicals company with fifty-nine hundred employees worldwide, implemented one of the first GESOPs (global ESOPs) in 1992. By 1997, the plan covered nineteen hundred employees in nineteen countries, plus another twenty-two hundred in the United States.

The challenge lies in making this "owner-ization" strategy attractive and feasible in a broad range of countries. Facing weak or nonexistent in-country legal and regulatory support, GESOP-minded companies are forced to cobble together a patchwork of offbeat ESOP-like structures.[3] For instance, H. B. Fuller established an ESOP in Jersey, one of the English Channel tax havens. Fuller's foreign subsidiaries are required to make an ESOP contribution once company-wide profits exceed 2.7 percent of sales, with those contributions used to buy parent-company shares. Although the legal creativity is admirable, as is their obvious determination, more multinational companies would embrace the notion if local institutional environments were more user-friendly. Thus far, what we see instead is the spread of "near-ownership" plans, typically broad-based stock options in which employees' sole ownership stake is the right to pocket any appreciated value in the parent company's shares. An early example is PepsiCo's offering of stock options to its worldwide workforce. Since 1989, 130,000 of its 480,000 employees have become participants in the company's "share power" plan.

The growing interest in GESOPs is driven by three key concerns. First is the interest in finding a way to harmonize corporate cultures across national cultures. Ownership translates. Second is the attraction of noncash compensation, particularly in today's globally competitive, cost-sensitive labor markets. Third is the emergence of genuinely global capital markets, accompanied by the threat of genuinely global hostile takeovers. This attracts corporate strategists to the notion of creating a block of "inside" friendly shareholders. Although the GESOP movement is still in its infancy, every indication suggests it will grow at a rapid pace. Major multinationals that count themselves GESOP pioneers include consumer product giants Proctor & Gamble, Colgate Palmolive and Gillette along with National Semiconductor Corporation.

This attempt to become less ethnocentric, more motivated and better coordinated is an organizational challenge faced by all multinationals. Although none of these challenges can be solved overnight, each can be addressed, at least in part, with a well-structured ownership strategy. For instance, by hitching its ESOP funding to group-wide profits, H. B. Fuller rewards employees not only for their local performance but also for coordinating operations with sister companies.[4] Where a full-blown ownership strategy proves impossible, a sense of ownership can be promoted by introducing limited components of ownership such as group-wide profit sharing or bonuses linked to share appreciation.

Next we turn to several other emerging ownership paradigms, including five hybrids of the ESOP concept: the RESOP, the CSOP, the VSOP, the GSOC and the DSOP. Because of the unusual environments from which these hybrids arose, each will be described in the setting from which it first emerged.

RESOPs (Related Enterprise Share Ownership Plans)

RESOPs provide an opportunity for employees of smaller companies to gain an ownership stake in larger, more established companies. Legislation I helped craft for Jamaica (enacted February 1994) encourages companies to include as participants in their ESOP not only their direct employees but also those employed by companies with which the ESOP sponsor has an ongoing economic relationship, such as suppliers or distributors.

The objective is fourfold. First, for a share-ownership strategy to work, there must be a corporation with shares to be shared. Oftentimes, smaller firms (such as microenterprises) are the most dynamic sector in developing countries. But they are typically unincorporated sole proprietorships with very modest assets. Second, an ownership strategy should put priority on stable companies. Smaller firms and microenterprises are legendary for their entrepreneurial energy; they are also notoriously unstable. Third, because the goal is to accumulate valuable assets, it makes sense to focus on more capital-intensive firms because such companies often perform much of the value-added production, particularly in developing countries. Perhaps most importantly, this ownership solution helps companies build a relationship-based corporate architecture.[5] Thus, for instance, where a supplier's employees own shares in a customer, their motivation is to maximize long-term wealth creation rather than maximize the profit on each transaction.

Jamaica's RESOP legislation was loosely based on the experience of Jamaica Broilers, the country's primary chicken-processer. As devout Christians, Jamaica Broilers' owners first embraced employee ownership as a way to practice their belief in prosperity sharing. Though that sentiment fostered a welcoming environment, the event that moved the company to implement that philosophy was the 1972 election of then socialist Michael Manley to his first term as prime minister. Unnerved by Manley's nationalization rhetoric, an American investor asked that the company buy out his 25 percent stake, which the company agreed to do. The company borrowed enough funds not only to buy his shares but also a little extra to create what became the first ESOP/RESOP. Let me explain in a very oversimplified way.

Jamaica Broilers has several hundred contract growers who raise chickens for processing, typically small family farmers who raise several dozen to a few hundred chickens. The company also has a dozen or so contract trucking companies (with only a few trucks each) that deliver the processed chickens to local grocers. The extra money that the company borrowed was used, in part, to help upgrade the operations of both the contract growers and the contract truckers. In the case of the growers, the aim was to help them improve their chicken-raising operation, creating uniform feeding and sanitation to provide a uniform chicken for processing. In the case of the truckers, the aim was to help upgrade the trucks to ensure uniform refrigeration and sanitation. The loan was repaid largely from future company earnings.

As the loan was repaid, the shares became owned both by the company's direct employees and by its "related" employees—its expanded network of contract growers and truckers. To assist with loan repayment, employees participated in a payroll-deduction scheme while the truckers had a small amount deducted from each invoice they presented for payment. For the growers, the company instituted a "chicken deduction" system whereby, for example, for every hundred chickens delivered, farmers were paid for ninety-eight in cash and two in Jamaica Broilers shares.

Though relatively simple and unsophisticated, this rudimentary combination of both financial and ownership engineering provides a way to emulate the Japanese *keiretsu* style of ownership in a developing-country context, drawing not on Japanese-style *corporate* cross-ownership but instead encouraging *personal* cross-ownership.* In modern corporate-speak, the strategy focuses on upgrading the firm's "organizational capital" by "reengineering" the "corporate architecture" to concentrate on "long-term relationship building" through a "vertically integrated cross-ownership structure" as a way to generate "long-term value-added development" in a company "built to last." Happily, this was all done well before that rhetoric was common corporate parlance, based on common sense exercised by values-led decision-makers.

From an ownership perspective, this ESOP/RESOP solution enabled a broad base of Jamaican workers to accumulate capital in a well-established Jamaican company.[6] Indeed, many of the microenterprise employees would not be employed but for their economic relationship with the larger firm. The RESOP also represents a natural extension of the ESOP idea, expanding not only the definition of "employee" but also utilizing the ESOP notion of "self-financing" to benefit a broader network of those who add value to the firms' operations.[7]

CSOP (Customer Stock Ownership Plan)

Certain customer groups offer another potential "natural owner." As investment bankers know so well, practically any revenue stream can be used to "owner-ize" income-producing assets over time. From a financial perspective, the value of a company is a function of the revenues it generates over time, unless the company is to be liquidated and its assets sold. Much as water moves through a whirlpool and creates it at the same time, the cash flowing through an enterprise both creates and sustains its financial value. In the case, say, of a power company or a water company, the company's value is based on its customers paying their bills for their access to energy or water. Without their patronage (which is nonoptional in the case of a natural monopoly), the company's financial value as a going concern would quickly disappear. The goal of the CSOP is to craft a capital structure that will capture some portion of that value for those whose patronage maintains that value.

For example, doubtless you pay at least two utility bills each month; power and water are the most common. Unless you are the rare exception, you probably do not own shares in those companies. Nevertheless, each bill you pay has built into it a financial return for someone who does. You can live in that utility district for one hundred years and still pay each month a return to someone who may live across the country, or even in another country. Why

---

* It is hoped that this more *personal* approach might evoke the motivational and risk/reward-sharing aspects of cross-shareholding while minimizing or avoiding relationships whereby cross-corporate ownership (particularly where a lender is involved) may result in cozy arrangements that lack sufficient market discipline, a shortcoming of both the Japanese *keiretsu* and the *chaebol* corporate groups in South Korea.

not gradually transform that capital structure so that you pay some portion of that return to yourself? That's a CSOP.

The developing world offers rich opportunities for ESOP/CSOP combinations, particularly with the worldwide boom in infrastructure development, such as power generation. For example, though China doubled its power-generating capacity over the past decade, it still plans to build thirty major power plants each year for the foreseeable future, a building program equivalent to half of today's global energy capacity. Including an ESOP/CSOP combination as part of each plant's capital structure could be helpful both in ensuring broad-based indigenous ownership (a political and fiscal plus) and in providing a much-needed environmental monitoring source comprised of nearby employee-owners and up-close consumer-owners.

In modern economies, people must have access to such fundamental services as water, energy and communication if they hope to have a chance of full participation in economic life. With electric utility companies now expanding nationwide and even worldwide, it makes even more sense for customers to be included as part owners. For example, 1996 saw Southern Company, an Atlanta-based utility, acquire Hong Kong–based Consolidated Electric Power Asia (CEPA) for $2.7 billion, one of the largest utilities in the Far East. Similarly, Duke Power Company acquired Houston-based natural gas distributor PanEnergy Corporation in a $7.7 billion deal, forming a $23 billion integrated energy company that is part of a growing trend toward convergence of the electricity and gas industries. With their heavily regulated rate structures, utilities provide a ready environment for an up-close owner-ization strategy.

Viewer-ization of the BBC

A variation of the CSOP is under consideration in conjunction with the politically sensitive privatization of the British Broadcasting Corporation. In conjunction with the former head of news and current affairs at the BBC, we proposed the "stakeowner-ization" of the BBC, using an ESOP and a "VSOP" (viewer share ownership plan) plus an equity stake for the BBC's independent producers. It comes as a shock to Americans to know that the BBC is financed with a mandatory "license fee" levied each year for the privilege of owning a television (the "telly tax"), regardless of whether the owner watches the BBC. Applying my owner-ization credo ("where the cash flows, ownership grows"), I proposed an obvious ownership strategy: gradually convert that revenue stream into BBC shares for BBC viewers. Of course, that would require that the BBC be at least partially weaned off its telly tax revenue stream, perhaps by including a component of commercial advertising, a challenging task in a country where the BBC is second only to the royal family as an object of fascination, pride and consternation.[8]

The proposal, written with then *Financial Times* deputy editor Ian Hargreaves included Australian Shann Turnbull's notion of "dynamic" property rights (what I called "boomerang equity"). If the "VSOP-ed" BBC needed to raise equity capital, it would first be required to turn to the viewers, employees and producers (the stake-owners) who would have preemptive rights on any new share offering. If that proved insufficient, only then could the company raise funds outside this preferred constituency. The ESOP/VSOP would then retain a call option allowing these insiders the right to force the sale to them of any "outsider" shares after a prescribed period. This boomerang feature was intended to ensure that any outside equity would eventually return to the BBC's "natural owners."

Also included was a "golden share" ceding limited power to the government to fend off any takeover attempt by the likes of media moguls such as Rupert Murdoch. In addition, a multivoice governance structure included a two-tiered board: a conventional managerial board overseen by a supervisory board with broad stakeholder representation. Due to the strong emotions associated with the BBC, the proposal (published in 1993) generated substantial interest, though Prime Minister Major was by then politically too weak to pursue it and Labor was still too timid to propose it. As we anticipated, everyone with a vested stake publicly opposed any change to the status quo. To our surprise, strong confidential support emerged from this same group, delighted a proposal had surfaced that was sufficiently "radical" that it actually might work. Labor prime minister Tony Blair reportedly remains intrigued by the notion. At this writing, the BBC's Royal Charter has been extended for another ten years (through 2004). As they say in the broadcasting trade, stay tuned.

GSOC (General Stock Ownership Corporation)

ESOP-like self-financing techniques can also be used to expand ownership beyond economic relationships based either on employment or consumption. One such mechanism is the GSOC (general stock ownership corporation), in which ownership is based on geography or citizenship. In the only version of the GSOC thus far enacted into federal law (in 1978), a for-profit corporation chartered by a state prior to 1984 could operate tax-free provided it complied with the ESOP's three operational principles; namely, a GSOC must

1. Include as a shareholder each citizen of the chartering state, reflecting the ESOP concept's "democratic" principle of widespread participation.

2. Limit individual ownership to ten shares, reflecting the ESOP "antimonopoly" principle ensuring that limits are imposed on relative shareholdings.

3. Pay out 90 percent of the company's earnings to shareholders on a current basis, reflecting the ESOP's "private property" principle encouraging a current distribution of income to the company's owners.

The GSOC legislation (a Kelso idea) was championed by Senator Mike Gravel of Alaska for the specific purpose of enabling Alaskan citizens to acquire British Petroleum's stake in the TransAlaska Pipeline Service Corporation, with a self-financing element designed to ensure that the acquisition costs would be paid from future dividends. Gravel's GSOC was never implemented for local political reasons, not for lack of financial or commercial feasibility. Two years prior to federal authorization of the GSOC, Alaskan voters agreed to establish the Alaska Permanent Fund Corporation to enable all Alaskans to share in the state's oil bonanza. Maintained by the state and funded with lease payments and royalty income from Prudhoe Bay and North Slope oil fields, the fund invests broadly. Since 1977, it has paid out over $5.8 billion to five hundred thousand Alaskan residents from a principal now exceeding $20 billion. The fund projects it will have paid out more than $16 billion in dividends by the year 2010. Although the fund is very different from a GSOC, with its personal (versus state) ownership, it offers another potential ownership solution (with reinvested dividends, a family of five would have 1997 savings of $94,066.71).[9]

A GSOC could readily be adapted to "owner-ize" government-owned natural resources such as mining deposits or drilling rights located on public lands. History is replete with stories of countries that experience a bust following on the heels of a natural resource-fed boom such as the discovery of oil (Venezuela, Nigeria). Time and again, the boom fuels a sudden unsustainable spurt in public sector growth, much of which is drained off by corrupt officials through contract fraud and outright theft. By one estimate, 75 percent of the oil-derived funds invested in Nigerian public-sector projects between 1970 and 1985 were diverted.[10] Corruption in the natural resource area often spreads throughout the public sector, contributing to political instability.[11]

A GSOC could, for instance, retain a royalty interest in an oil field or a mine, while a more traditional company is awarded extraction rights conditioned on sponsoring both an ESOP and a RESOP. The scope of participation in a GSOC need not be national or even statewide; it could be regional or even community-based. For instance, a GSOC could be used to create community-wide individual ownership of a local industrial or business park.[12] Some GSOC shares could be allocated to fund education or infrastructure.[13] Practically any revenue-generating activity could be "GSOC'ed," especially where the stakeholder status is reasonably clear.

For example, in 1984 the city of Santa Clara, California, acquired two hundred acres of land for $88.5 million from the Marriott Corporation. Formerly the site of a "Great America" theme park, the park was sold and the land leased to King's Entertainment for fifty years at $5.3 million per year, sufficient to recoup the cost of the land in less than twenty years. Similarly, the Washington, D.C., Metropolitan Area Transit Authority has long leased commercial space associated with its rail stations. Such efforts could be re-structured as GSOCs with broad-based personal ownership by community residents.

A GSOC might prove an ideal mechanism to reflect the tribal ethic embraced by Native Americans. Over the past two decades, as long-pending land and resource disputes have been settled, Native Americans have gained ownership of what are often vast and valuable lands rich in natural resources, including minerals, petrochemicals, timber and water. In Montana, for instance, the Crow reservation has coal reserves valued at $26 billion ($3.3 million per person).[14] One of the key challenges facing Native Americans lies in designing a commercial structure that fairly benefits all those in whose tribal name these settlements were reached. For example, the immensely successful casinos now operating tax-free on Indian reservations could be structured as GSOCs in which tribal members own shares.[15] The GSOC's unusual blend of individual ownership and community-wide participation makes it easily adaptable to situations in which people wish to have a shared stake in the development of common resources.

DSOP (Depositor Share Ownership Plan)

The DSOP idea first emerged in conjunction with a privatization project in Islamabad when John Speakman, an international banking consultant from New Zealand, was retained by the World Bank to advise on privatization strategy for Pakistan's state-owned banking sector. Speakman, who was familiar with ESOPs, knew of two partially state-owned banks in New Zealand and another in Australia that were privatized by targeting a sale of shares to the bank's customers. Thus was born an ownership solution we quickly labeled the depositor share ownership plan (DSOP).

It seems that depositors are often receptive to the notion of owning shares where they bank. That makes sense. If someone has sufficient confidence to trust a bank with his or her savings, the bank may be able to draw on that goodwill to persuade those customers to buy its shares. Initially, New Zealander policymakers were concerned that depositors would draw down their savings to make the investment. While that would help the bank's capital structure, it might come at the expense of the deposit base on which the bank earns its profits. However, New Zealanders somehow found additional savings to invest, leaving their deposits intact.

In Speakman's view, a bank privatization that includes an ESOP/DSOP component could create a positive outcome for everyone involved. The government would be seen as supporting a privatization technique that advances broad-based ownership; banks would gain an opportunity to strengthen both employee and customer loyalty; and the customers would become more knowledgeable up-close capitalists—both as savers and as potential borrowers, secure in the knowledge that their borrowing enhances the earnings of a bank in which they own a stake.

Each of these new property paradigms (ESOPs, GESOPs, RESOPs, CSOPs, VSOPs, GSOCs, DSOPs, etc.) share a common goal: the transformation of economic relationships in a way that enhances performance and sustainability across a wide range of measures. This transformation requires a combination of financial creativity, committed corporate leadership and sustained political will, along with a populace prepared to embrace change, complexity and risk. It also faces one other key challenge. It's a well-known fact that scientists (including economists) don't readily embrace new paradigms until the old ones have been thoroughly discredited ("If it ain't broke, don't fix it").[16] Physicist Max Planck, an originator of quantum mechanics, advised that "science makes progress funeral by funeral: the old are never converted by the new, they simply are replaced by a new generation." Only time will tell whether that's also the case for property paradigms.

CHAPTER 7

Toward a Workable Work Ethic

O let us love our occupations,
Bless the Squire and his relations,
Live upon our daily rations,
And always know our proper stations.

—Charles Dickens

Everyone knows someone who owns rather than works for a living. Many aspire to that condition. A few are born to it. A handful actually work themselves into that condition—our modern-day Horatio Algers being the superstar athlete (Michael Jordan, Tiger Woods), the world-class musician, the software genius, the farsighted entrepreneur or the dealmaker who happens to be in the right place at the right time. However, unless free enterprise is recast to include broad-based capital ownership as a goal, most of us will go through life not as capitalists but as workers, relying solely on our labor as our "stock in trade" to generate income. This chapter examines how the work ethic might be updated to become more relevant to an era when ownable assets now perform much of the work.

The word *work* stems from the Greek for "sacrifice," implying that a job is a "necessary evil" or what an economist would label a "disutility." A worker sacrifices his leisure and, in return, is compensated in wages. From that perspective, the ideal of the employer is to have output without employees, while the ideal of the employee is to have income without work. Yet psychologists have long known that work infuses life with meaning—providing structure, identity and a sense of place.[1] "One does not work to live," philosopher Max Weber insisted, "one lives to work."

Even the surnames in Anglo-Saxon cultures have distinctly vocational connotations—Baker, Butcher, Carpenter, Tanner, Smith. Prior to the time of William the Conqueror, names were typically more descriptive of place than occupation ("James of York"). Even the etymology of work suggests a high level of personal commitment, even devotion: *vocation* literally means a "calling," whereas *occupation* means "to be taken and seized." As Studs Terkel, the working man's philosopher, observed: "Work is about daily meaning as well as daily bread. For recognition as well as cash; for astonishment rather than torpor; in short, for a sort of life rather than a Monday through Friday sort of dying. . . . We have a right to ask of work that it include meaning, recognition, astonishment, and life."

A Question of Balance

Reflecting a combination of both morality and the market, the work ethic is captured in the Greek word *compensation*, meaning "a balancing of accounts," suggesting that a person is entitled to *take out* of the economy according to what he or she *puts in*. Usually that input is labor. This notion is reflected in the origins of property—as John Locke proposed: a man could extract personal property out of mankind's common heritage (the state of nature) only when he mixed his labor with it. This notion of balance is ancient. In indigenous cultures, it's reflected in what anthropologists call "reciprocity." When those in traditional cultures take, they also give.[2] They also believe that to take more than needed is not only selfish but dangerous; potentially impairing your ability to harvest. Life itself might thereby be jeopardized.

The ethics of balance embodied in the work ethic undergird economic policymaking worldwide, where "full employment" remains a key goal, regardless of whether the economy is socialist, capitalist, developed, underdeveloped or somewhere in between. Yet manufacturing jobs presently account for only 16 percent of U.S. employment, and British economists DeAnne Julius and Richard Brown predict this will drop to less than 10 percent in developed countries within three decades. That trend may be accelerating, judging by the combined impact of free trade, layoffs accompanying corporate reengineering and dramatic advances in information technologies and machine-based knowledge. From 1979 to 1992, American manufacturing productivity increased by 35 percent, while the manufacturing workforce shrank by 15 percent. In 1995, Chrysler manufactured 1.7 million cars in the United States, the same as in 1988, but with nine thousand fewer autoworkers.

On the other hand, certain types of human capital are becoming more valuable, particularly those associated with the development of information technology (IT). Microsoft's market capitalization in mid-1997 topped $150 billion while General Motors was valued at less than $40 billion, even though GM had far more physical capital (automaking machinery, equipment and such). In tracing the historical displacement of human muscle by a combination of mind and machine, French economist Alain Cotta found that "more than half the people are now employed in sectors where they create, release, transfer, receive and utilize information." As a result, IT poses a particularly challenging development to jobs-based economic policies.

In the early nineteenth century, the spread of labor-saving looms caused displaced workers to respond by attempting to destroy that era's technological advances. Secretive rebels who followed Ned Ludd, the Luddites were made up largely of craftsmen displaced by mechanization in the textile industry. Their smashing of machinery made them a symbol of resistance to progress. Their uprising was quickly crushed, its leaders jailed or executed. It was not that they were against progress so much as they were opposed to being excluded from it. One can only speculate at their reaction had they been made part owners of those companies employing the technology that displaced them.

Today's Luddites point out that information technology (computer software, networked computers, advanced telecom equipment) is different in at least three significant ways. First, the impact of IT is not limited to one segment of the economy, such as the Luddite weavers. Information technology can displace not only the office worker and his more highly trained boss, but also the merchant who provides them with goods and the salesman who persuades them to order. For instance, the numbers-crunching and judgment skills previously performed by bank officers who review home-mortgage applications are fast being displaced by computer-evaluated checklists.

Second, IT is being phased in much faster than were mechanical looms, particularly as measured by the plummeting price of computer power and its pervasive reach into the service sector. During the 1980s, six key services (air transport, banking, health care, insurance, retailing and telecommunications) invested an amount equal to 5.6 percent of their revenues in information technology, while manufacturers invested only 2.6 percent. Lastly, IT makes work far more portable, often negating the need for personal contact with customers or even with employers. Swissair contracts out the bulk of its paperwork to workers located in Bombay at wage rates only 4 percent those of Switzerland.[3] Atlanta-based Southern Company, one of the world's largest utilities, outsourced a major computer project to programmers in India who telecommute, transmitting their finished work to Atlanta via the Internet. This both reduces the demand for labor and increases its supply.

The impact is further amplified by the spread of new organizational systems. Middle managers, whose skills were previously needed to control, coordinate and manage information and people, are rapidly being replaced either with nothing or with networked computers and new ways of organizing work (project teams, quality circles, continuous-improvement programs, etc.). A 1994 survey by the American Management Association found that middle managers, who comprise 8 percent of the U.S. workforce, accounted for 19 percent of the layoffs due to downsizing. Eastman Kodak pared its management ranks from thirteen layers to just four. This trend will continue as companies realize better results by abandoning hierarchical, top-down management models based on command-and-control, substituting flatter, people-empowered systems based on commitment, coaching, coaxing and camaraderie.

The Input Ethic

The continuing embrace of the work ethic confirms the notion that participants in a market economy should make a productive input in order to share in the economy's output. Otherwise, economics is based not on market exchange but on charity, friendship, kinship or theft. The production of things for value requires human action. To take something of value without contributing something in return is equivalent to forcing some to work for others. The work ethic's quid pro quo reckoning reflects the sensible notion of voluntary exchange. The problem arises when this otherwise valid *exchange ethic* is interpreted as a *work ethic*, implying that the input component of this balancing act must take the form of human toil.

As a moral imperative, the work ethic is not a job ethic; it's an "input ethic" intended to scold those who would partake of the fruits of production without contributing to their production. Unfortunately, this useful notion remains frozen in time, its imagery of sweat and toil indelibly seared into the modern psyche of policymakers and business leaders. The implication is that the work ethic is a *labor* ethic when, in truth, it's an *exchange* ethic, mandating market balance and requiring not human input but *productive* input.

This is not meant to suggest that there is a shortage of human work to be done. Quite the contrary. What this does suggest, however, is that income-earning can take a form other than just employment, as owners of income-earning capital have known throughout the ages, whether that capital takes the form of fertile land, livestock, slaves, industrial machinery, chemical processes or computer software. To repeat: the work ethic is not a perspiration ethic; it's a participation ethic, mandating a balancing of the taking out with the putting in. A problem arises when, in the process of crafting economic policy, an outmoded metaphor is used that acts like a net, snaring all manner of mental associations that may not be fully appropriate to the situation at hand. Language is not only the way we think; it also shapes our possibilities and determines the pathways we choose. As semanticist Gregory Bateson cautioned: "Clarity is the correct use of metaphor." A shift in economic policy will accompany a shift in how we view economic participation.

Enshrining the Work Ethic

In the United States, this job-biased interpretation of the work ethic was first enshrined into law a half century ago. In 1945, as America was winding down from World War II, policymakers were worried about how the economy would create enough jobs for 4 million returning servicemen. Looking back, they knew it was not the New Deal but the war that pulled the economy out of the Depression with its horrendous unemployment. With the concentration required by the war effort, little thought had been given to how best to put people back to work in a civilian economy.

As the Congress began debate on its post-war economic policy, legislators initially focused on whether the government should again act as the employer of last resort. If a workman could not find a job, the Full Employment Act of 1945 proposed to pay him a salary in much the same way that New Deal public works programs provided jobs for the unemployed of the 1930s. However, the Congress decided not to make a full-employment commitment, enacting instead the Employment Act of 1946. Rather than pledging the government to create jobs, policymakers promised to promote "conditions" conducive to full employment. To that end, the legislation established a President's Council of Economic Advisers, created a Congressional Joint Economic Committee and set the stage for periodic congressional questioning of the chairman of the Federal Reserve Board, a tradition that continues to this day.

The 1946 act also committed Washington to coordinate its policies to foster "useful employment" and "to promote maximum employment, production and purchasing power."[4] More than a half century later, the only legislation altering this work ethic–enshrined legislation is civil rights legislation from the 1960s ensuring that, whenever jobs are available, they will be available without discrimination on the basis of race, sex, color, religion or national origin.[5]

Jobs at Any Cost

This full-employment policy also permeates state-level policymaking. For instance, each of the states sponsors programs meant to attract investors. In 1980, Tennessee successfully courted Nissan for an assembly plant, followed in 1985 by a General Motors Saturn plant. Kentucky won a Toyota plant in 1985, while in 1992 BMW chose South Carolina over other job-hungry suitors. In the fall of 1993, this courtship reached a fevered pitch when Mercedes Benz AG announced its intention to open a plant in the United States. Alabama entered the bidding with an incentive package that eventually topped $300 million ($200,000 per job) for the construction of a $300 million facility near Tuscaloosa, home of the University of Alabama. Among other concessions, the state will allow Mercedes to pay off its construction costs with funds the state would have collected in income taxes. The state also offered $92.2 million to buy the site and develop it, $77.5 million in sewer, water and other improvements and $5 million per year for employee training.[6] The state also agreed to pay eighteen months' wages for the plant's fifteen hundred workers ($45 million) and $5 million for a welcome center. The power company committed to buy twenty-five hundred Mercedes utility vehicles. When South

Carolina offered $80 million in tax credits over a twenty-year period, Alabama sweetened its bid, offering a tax credit available *in advance* in the form of an interest-free loan.[7]

New jobs are not the only impetus; retention of existing jobs can also set off a bidding war. In 1995, New York City awarded more than $30 million each to Morgan Stanley and Kidder, Peabody & Company, in response to their threats to move elsewhere. In 1996, after Fidelity Investments threatened to move thousands of jobs from Boston to Rhode Island, Massachusetts tempted the company to stay with $40 million. Hoping to anchor Disneyland, the state of California and the City of Anaheim (home of Disneyland) reportedly spent $800 million on roads and other improvements. Connecticut enticed the 1,300 employees of Swiss Bank from Manhattan to Stamford in 1994 with a $120 million incentive package ($92,000 per job), while Zurich Centre Group plans to move its insurance and financial services operations to Stamford in return for $190 million in tax credits ($475,000 per job).[8] In August 1995, New York City reached its second deal in six years with Bear, Stearns, granting a $75 million tax package in return for its promise to remain in Manhattan and build a new headquarters.

In August 1997, Chrysler won concessions totaling $232 million ($47,000 per job for each job retained) for building a Jeep assembly plant in Toledo, Ohio. That's on top of the $250 million Chrysler received in 1992 when it replaced a $1 billion Jeep factory in Detroit. The corporate strategy with perhaps the most chutzpah was launched in Cashmere, Washington, in 1997 when Liberty Orchards, manufacturers of Aplets and Cotlets (fruit and nut concoctions), asked the town to convert itself into a marketing arm of the company, including changing the city's road signs and its official stationery to read, "Cashmere, Home of Aplets and Cotlets." In addition, they asked that the two main streets be renamed Cotlets Avenue and Aplets Avenue. The company also proposed that the city sell to them city hall and float a municipal bond to fund a tourism campaign featuring the company.[9]

On a national basis, former Labor Secretary Robert Reich argues this is "nothing but a zero-sum game. Resources are moved around; Peter is robbed to pay Paul."[10] Though Alabama was already last in the nation in spending for elementary and secondary school education, the state turned to its education fund to pay for many of its promises to Mercedes.[11] Reich has teamed up with members of Congress to propose that these subsidies be treated as corporate taxable income, thereby gutting much of their appeal.

The Emerging Global Job Market

Worldwide, jobs have long been the currency of politics. In March 1994, the G-7 convened its first "Jobs Summit" in Detroit to address the main quandary world leaders saw facing the industrialized world: unemployment. The event was repeated in April 1996 in Lille, France. According to a November 1996 report by the Geneva-based International Labor Organization, the number of adults worldwide who were either unemployed or underemployed rose to 1 billion in 1995, an increase of 180 million people over 1993 and 1994 when the UN warned that the estimated 820 million underemployed or unemployed represented a crisis not seen since the Depression.[12]

In Europe, part of that job scarcity is due to higher and more uniform wages. A European in the lowest 10 percent of wage-earners has an income 68 percent of median European pay while his American counterpart earns just 38 percent of median U.S. pay. Lower incomes for Americans are also accompanied by a much higher likelihood of job loss. In the late 1980s, only 0.4 percent of Europeans lost their jobs each month, while five times that many Americans became unemployed. On the other hand, roughly 50 percent of America's unemployed find jobs within a month, whereas only 5 percent of Europe's unemployed do so. This gives rise to a common American refrain: "You can always find a job, but you can't always earn a living." Europe's widespread practice of mandated job benefits, job protection and costly company training are partly the culprits, along with generous and lengthy unemployment benefits. The Bank of Spain estimates that dismissal of an employee requires two years and costs an average $32,000.

Labor cost differentials can be dramatic. With benefits, American factory workers in 1996 earned $16 an hour, while just over the border Mexicans were paid that much *a day*, while Chinese workers were paid only a little more than that *each week*. Whereas it costs $25 per hour to hire a laborer in Germany, nearby Polish workers are paid $1.68, while Hungarian workers cost only 25 percent as much as comparably skilled French workers.

The Many Perils of Full Employment Policies

With job creation a top-priority policy goal worldwide, it's essential to have a clear idea of just why it is that jobs became scarce—and why they may well remain so. Economists propose a variety of reasons. In theory, if companies are unwilling to hire because wages are too high, workers will respond by lowering their wages, thereby "clearing the market" of the unemployed and achieving market "equilibrium." That's a terrific theory, but wages have never been that flexible. In addition, not only does the market never fully "clear," a certain level of "frictional" unemployment is widely seen as a desirable lubricant in the system as people change jobs, relocate, retrain and so on, a key rationale for government-sponsored unemployment compensation.[13]

In the 1930s, Lord Keynes suggested that firms would be willing to hire more workers at prevailing wages provided consumer demand was available to buy their products. That notion marked the genesis of "demand side" economics, particularly government-financed "public works" in all their many guises.[14]

Despite the protests of conservatives, both Republicans and Democrats have long supported New Deal–style, demand-stimulative spending.[15] Republican president Dwight D. Eisenhower promoted the expansion of Social Security and unemployment compensation and commenced the boldest ever public works program in American history: the interstate highway system.

In any case, high unemployment reflects an inflexibility or a "stickiness" in prices, wages or both.[16] More recently, research from the employer's perspective found that, with the exception of firms that readily accept high turnover (such as temporary employment agencies), companies are reluctant to hire well-qualified job applicants for lower wages, not only because to do so would upset the firm's current pay structure but because such people are likely to quit for a better-paying job once conditions improve.[17]

Built-in Slumps

A relatively new theory (called "structural slumps") suggests that unemployment represents an unfortunate "equilibrium" based on the underlying structure of the economy.[18] A broad range of modern workplace changes also contribute to this job-scarce phenomenon. For instance, just-in-time inventory techniques plus so-called "cycle timing" assure spurts of activity as companies mobilize to quickly fill orders, followed by slower periods when a smaller full-time workforce is sufficient. Gillette is spending $100 million during the 1995–1998 period to adjust output on an hourly basis at its sixty factories worldwide.[19] Computers now track data about the workloads companies face, enabling firms to schedule work more precisely, hiring only as needed for specific tasks. Just-in-time inventory is being wedded to just-in-time workforces. According to the Bureau of Labor Statistics, the number of Americans employed in "personnel supply services" grew 400 percent from 1983 to 1995, from 619,000 to 2,459,000. By 2005, the bureau projects, more than 3.5 million Americans will, like inventory, fall into this "supply" category.[20]

With overtime at its highest level since World War II, policymakers are even urging legislative changes meant to share the available work. Because the amount of overtime is unlimited under U.S. law, proposed amendments to the Fair Labor Standards Act would require double-time pay after only thirty or thirty-five hours a week (instead of time-and-a-half after forty hours). Other structural phenomena are more deep-seated, as a changeover to new labor-saving technology may leave people without relevant skills: witness the recent fate of long-distance telephone operators. From 1983 to 1993, automated teller machines (ATMs) enabled banks to eliminate 179,000 human tellers, 37 percent of their total workforce. This "de-jobbing" is real and far from over. *Inc.* magazine's 1996 listing of the one hundred fastest-growing firms revealed that, although their sales increased eighteenfold from 1988 to 1993, employment increased only sixfold. Owens-Corning hired eighty people when it reopened a plant in 1993 that had been closed six years earlier, when it employed five hundred.[21]

Productivity, efficiency and profitability have risen steadily as capitalism's "creative destruction" continues its steady advance, leaving in its wake personal distress as a seemingly inescapable cost of progress.* From an ownership perspective, it is clear that the financial benefit of these efficiencies is captured largely by those who are either the architects of change (managers, engineers, lawyers, accountants, consultants) or those best able to acquire a stake in this change (senior managers, investors, investment bankers).

A Question Both of Value and Values

History provides a helpful clue in resolving the quandary of steadily rising prosperity alongside steadily rising inequality—and the role played in this drama by the work ethic. I find it useful to focus on what economists call "value" because that issue lies at the very heart of market versus command economies. The difference turns on what forces are allowed to determine how someone's input is valued and how much they "should" be paid. In the classically capitalist, Adam Smith view of the world, that value is determined by free exchange in the marketplace: the price an employer is willing to pay and an employee is willing to accept. Even the word *price* comes from the Latin for "exchange." In the classically socialist, Karl Marx view of the world, that value would instead be determined by "the unit of socially useful labor," a less precise standard of pricing that assumes some market intervention by the government. The reality is oftentimes somewhere in between.

For instance, the hiring of underage children is commonly prohibited, because society has imposed its value judgment that child labor is socially nonuseful at any price. National minimum-wage laws prohibit an employer from paying less than $5.15 an hour even if a job seeker would work for less. Again, policymakers reckon it is not socially useful for people to be paid less.† Social Security taxes are also a "structural impediment" based on the rationale that it is not socially useful to allow people to work without earning an old-age

---

* The phrase "creative destruction" was first made famous by Joseph Schumpeter (1883–1950), an economist and sociologist whose *The Theory of Economic Development* (1934) has become a classic in economic science. In *Capitalism, Socialism and Democracy*, Schumpeter predicted that capitalism would eventually perish of its own success, giving rise to some type of system with more control by the public.

† If the minimum wage had kept pace with inflation since 1968, it would be 53 percent higher than the 1996 minimum of $4.25 per hour (i.e., $6.50 per hour). A nationwide movement of city councils has enacted "living wage" legislation requiring that private contractors doing business with the city pay an hourly rate that yields an annual income at least equal to the federal poverty line for a family of four. In mid-1997, that would require a minimum wage of $7.49 an hour. Variations on this theme are on the books in Boston, Los Angeles, New York, Baltimore, St. Paul, Milwaukee and Minneapolis.

pension. While it's true that the value of labor is set by free exchange, the scope of that freedom is limited.

Lifelong Disconnectedness

The conventional wisdom, as reflected in the G-7's two Job Summits, suggests that government policy should focus on employment alone as the relevant form of economic participation. Touting its own job-creation record, the United States urged the major industrial countries to embrace a variety of traditional employment-focused policies, including improved job-training programs and lifelong learning. However, despite the level of education and training that people receive, certain fundamentals in the way people participate in the economy with their labor are unlikely to change.

To provide a glimpse into this future, *Financial Times* columnist Samuel Brittan proposes a scenario comprised of a "single economy world" with freely mobile physical and financial capital. In that world, pay differentials among workers of comparable skill will tend to narrow as the owners of capital (seeking their highest return) will gravitate toward those locales with the most favorable wage rates. In this scenario, Brittan asks: "If the liberalization of the world economy is going to make northern countries richer, but make many industrial or clerical workers within them worse off, then who will gain the difference?" He concludes the obvious: those who own the capital.[22]

Robert Reich, now a professor at Brandeis University, documents that, as knowledge, problem solving and creativity have grown more valuable, we've seen the emergence of "symbolic analysts" at the pinnacle of the jobs pyramid, those who deal with numbers, ideas, problems and words—investment bankers, lawyers, doctors, journalists, architects, consultants, managers and the like. It is these "knowledge workers"[23] who reap the bulk of the job-related benefits from the emerging information age. Reich estimates that this top 20 percent of income-earners now have incomes higher than the other 80 percent of Americans combined. The other two levels in Reich's job pyramid are made up of "routine operators"—those who staff the checkout counters, drive the trucks and enter the data onto diskettes, accounting for about one-quarter of the workforce. In the middle are the "personal service providers" working in restaurants, hotels, hospitals, beauty shops, security firms and so on.

Among those who own only their labor, the symbolic analysts possess the most secure economic "connectivity" in the information age. The liberalization of trade poses a particularly vexing future for those who labor for a living. The desire and ability to work hard, albeit admirable, can be found practically anywhere on the planet. More is now required. Free trade has the potential to raise the standard of living in both developed and developing countries, at least in the limited sense of providing access to lower-cost goods made with cheaper labor. However, that is accompanied by a further widening of income differentials, as globalization advances and jobs shift to lower-cost locales. That scenario repeats itself as multinational corporations steadily integrate their production worldwide, resulting in a gradual "hollowing out" of manufacturing employment as those jobs gradually move abroad.[24] "All these forms of integration," according to the World Bank, "are creating a global labor market where wages and employment decisions in one country are increasingly influenced by conditions and decisions in others."[25]

Education and Training in the Information Age

In this context, it is helpful to recall the rationale for government-subsidized education, a policy companion to our embrace of the work ethic. As the argument goes, it is difficult for the private sector to invest adequately in education and training because a company cannot be assured of recovering its investment—for the simple reason that it cannot *own* the people (i.e., the "human capital") in whom that investment resides. If the public sector subsidizes education (as a "social good"), the resulting wealth will trickle down, as more sophisticated tools require more sophisticated operators. The emergence of intelligence *as property* reverses that causal chain. With intelligence now embedded in productive property (robotics, computer software, etc.), the value of that intelligence-as-property is captured largely by its developers and owners (witness Microsoft's Bill Gates), while fewer operators are required.

Economist Brian Arthur, Citibank Professor at the Santa Fe Institute, argues that the ever increasing role of knowledge makes the tenets of modern economics badly outdated, pointing out that high-tech products such as software are a form of "congealed knowledge." This contrasts with goods like coal, coke, iron and similar "congealed resources" that were scarce and, during an era of bulk manufacturing, subject to diminishing returns (the more you do something, the more expensive, harder or less interesting its gets). With the huge up-front R&D costs that go into software, pharmaceuticals, telecommunications and such, these get progressively cheaper as their congealed knowledge produces increasing returns. As he explains: "The first floppy disk to go out the door for Microsoft Windows cost the company $50 million. The second ten dollars—to copy the disk, print the manual, and whatnot."[26]

Therein lies another of our paradoxes. Without substantial public investment in education, the stock of useful intelligence will remain either confined to Reich's top 20 percent—the symbolic analysts—or claimed by those who own the products or processes that embody this congealed knowledge. Meanwhile, everyone else will be left increasingly disconnected. British Nobel laureate James Meade cautions that even those policies addressing economic ills through education, training and increased investment "are concerned basically with raising the output per head of those who are in employment rather than about the number of heads that will find suitable employment."

In *The End of Equality*, author Mickey Kaus warns that "when the reality of these trends begins to sink in, American society will be subject to terrific strains. Only a strong civic culture will be able to contain the potential insecurities, prejudices and outright animosities."[27] Likewise, Professor Peter Drucker predicts that "the acquisition and distribution of formal knowledge may come to occupy the place in the politics of the knowledge society which the acquisition and distribution of property and income have occupied in our politics over the two or three centuries that we have come to call the Age of Capitalism."[28]

In truth, we are midstream in another dramatic shift in the nature of production. Due to the ability of developing countries to leapfrog technological development that took two centuries to emerge elsewhere, this shift is also found worldwide. True, we will continue to see organizations in which special-purpose physical assets are organized and directed for mass production. However, we also now see new-style "knowledge companies," in which it is people alone rather than people and machines that comprise a firm's critical resource. This new form of capital resides in what are characterized as the "competence carriers" or the "cognitive elite,"[29] who work alongside products and processes that embody a culture's "congealed knowledge."

The Search for Organizational Competence

Drucker points to an emerging dichotomy. On the one hand, knowledge workers need the organization because "only the organization can provide the basic continuity that knowledge workers need in order to be effective." On the other hand, "the most probable assumption for organizations . . . is that they need knowledge workers far more than knowledge workers need them." As the high-tech entrepreneurs of California's Silicon Valley discovered long ago, retaining highly mobile human capital requires a reliable means for ensuring their long-term commitment to the organization. Ownership is the time-proven solution, typically stock options. Even the headhunters in Silicon Valley are now taking part of their search fee in options.[30]

Brookings Institution economist Margaret Blair suggests that this represents a return to the "craftsman" scenario of an earlier era, when skilled laborers worked in shops organized to make the best use of their specialized abilities. She urges a return to earlier notions of "proprietorship," where both work and the workplace are redesigned to ensure that these key workers think like owners. However, even as more people move into the ranks of symbolic analysts, there will continue to be work for which only modest skills are required. The United States employs 1.5 times as many janitors as it employs accountants, lawyers, stockbrokers, investment bankers and computer programmers combined. M.I.T. economist Paul Krugman wryly notes that "the time could well come when most tax lawyers are replaced with expert systems, but human beings are still needed for such truly difficult occupations as gardening and house cleaning."

Every economy will continue to have work that requires more common sense than complex training. The Bureau of Labor Statistics projects that 563,000 cashier jobs will be created by 2006. One of the key social challenges is how, in a system that values both free markets and political equality, a value should be placed on the services of those who serve, stoop, hoe and hammer. Are they of lesser worth because they are the "commonsense carriers" rather than the competence carriers or the cognitive elite?[31] Marvin Minsky, a founder of the artificial intelligence movement, observes: "What people vaguely call common sense is actually more intricate than most of the technical expertise we admire."

Added to this ever widening skills gap is the fact that employment itself has become ever more unstable and tenuous. President Clinton advises Americans that they should expect to change jobs seven times during a working lifetime. The Bureau of Labor Statistics reports that the median number of years someone has been with an employer is four years. Between 1983 and 1996, the median fell from 7.3 to 6.1 years for men ages thirty-five to forty-four and from 15.3 to 10.5 years for ages fifty-five to sixty-four. Former Labor Secretary Reich speaks of the "anxiety" workers feel in today's fast-changing, globally competitive environment. That anxiety has deep roots, in part because the psychic dominance of the work ethic and its policy manifestation—full employment—continues to mislead people about the economic context in which they live.

In truth, the widespread prevalence of productive, labor-saving technologies, including information technology, could provide a foundation of security and leisure for a broad base of those living in developed economies. Instead, the workweek continues to expand while incomes stagnate and baby boomers wonder why their lives have become progressively more devoid of those basic human activities their parents enjoyed: caregiving, community involvement, even relaxation and reflection. Today's fixation on jobs continues to erode the ability of people to orient themselves. In an age when the workplace reality is a twenty-first-century world of capital- and knowledge-intensive, information-processing, labor-saving technology, policymakers in both the public and private sectors continue to rely on an outdated, outmoded nineteenth-century interpretation of how to participate effectively in a modern economy.

Full Employment: A Clear and Present Danger

The resulting stress shows up not just in individuals,[32] families and communities but also in seemingly unrelated areas such as national defense and international arms sales. The Pentagon budget has long been an adjunct of national full-employment policy. A half century after the end of World War II and a decade after the fall of the Berlin Wall, weaning the U.S. economy off this job-creation machine still poses a major political barrier. In an unguarded moment during a July 1994 Senate debate on continued funding for the $44.4 billion B-2 Stealth bomber, Senator Dianne Feinstein of California (home to Northrup-Grumman, the primary contractor) justified her support by arguing that the B-2 "can deliver a large payroll." Only later was her revealing slip of the tongue corrected to read "payload" in the *Congressional Record*.

Congress approved $266 billion in 1997 defense spending, $11 billion more than the Pentagon requested. In early 1997, Business Leaders for Sensible Priorities launched a campaign decrying defense spending that remains at peak Cold War levels while massive cutbacks in education, training and health care pose a serious threat to economic and personal security. To reinforce their message Sensible Priorities founder Ben Cohen, cofounder of Ben & Jerry's, launched a new ice cream flavor called "Totally Nuts."

Whether liberal or conservative, the temptation of job-creation defense spending seems impossible to resist, even when the attendant dangers are clear and present. For instance, during the Bush administration, the Chinese agreed to comply with the provisions of the Missile Technology Control Regime, which restricts the export of technology to build missiles capable of carrying warheads at least 185 miles. However, during the 1992 election season in California, Bush allowed California-based General Dynamics to sell 150 F-16 fighter jets to Taiwan. Incensed, the Chinese reneged on their agreement and began the shipment of missile technology to Islamabad. They also sent specialized magnets for the enrichment of uranium, converting Pakistan into the first Islamic nation with nuclear weapons technology.[33] India, Pakistan's frequent antagonist, has now developed a similar missile. Since Pakistan's independence from India in 1947, the two nations have gone to war three times; their disputed border remains one of the globe's most troubled frontiers.

Arms sales are a hard-to-kick full-employment habit. In August 1997, President Clinton relaxed a twenty-year-old embargo on American arms sales to Latin America, a change lobbied hard by Lockheed Martin and Boeing, who want to sell fighter jets to Chile and others in the region. In truth, the U.S. stance was "a policy of restraint with the presumption of denial." But, in effect, few exceptions were allowed. The change outrages former Costa Rican president Oscar Arias, who sees little difference between pushing drugs and peddling arms, arguing that the region's grotesque inequalities call for devoting resources not to an arms race but to schools, health and infrastructure. Arias documents that 82 percent of conventional arms transfers are provided to governments that use them to block rather than advance democracy. Almost half are manufactured by U.S. firms who made more than $23 billion in conventional arms transfers in 1996.[34] Ironically, 85 percent of conventional arms sales are made by the five permanent members of the UN Security Council.

Overcoming Policy Hypnosis

The Greeks invented the concept of *nemesis* (literally, the goddess of divine retribution) to indicate how any virtue, if stubbornly maintained, can be transformed into a costly or destructive vice. The cost of relying so totally on this limited form of economic participation (i.e., jobs) continues to mount, particularly in market environments where productive technologies put steadily downward pressure on labor's contribution. However, the psychological appeal of the work ethic remains almost hypnotic. Psychologists have long known that the effect of hypnosis is real but also ephemeral, because it lacks a context capable of locking it in place. That's why the effort required to sustain a hypnotic suggestion puts so much stress on the nervous system.

The work ethic, along with its policy complement—full employment—takes a similar toll on the economic system. Lacking a market-based context capable of holding the work ethic in place, other ways must be found to connect Americans to their economy. Full employment will doubtless remain a central policy objective, and certainly knowledge workers will continue to gain in prominence and income. Economies worldwide will also continue to require large numbers of what Reich calls "routine operators and personal service providers," those essential commonsense carriers.

However, one barrier to sustained full employment is well entrenched: a job remains a cost, similar to any of the other three major expenses: capital, raw materials and energy. The cost of capital and raw materials is largely outside a company's control. That's also the case for energy, though with conservation and energy efficiency a company can restrain overall use.[35] It should come as no surprise that managers focus their cost-reduction efforts on those expenses over which they can exercise some control. That can only mean continued downward pressure on both job opportunities and labor incomes, leaving full employment an endangered form of economic participation under siege from all sides.

The impact that flows from this jobs myopia is partly dependent on the social and cultural environment in which people live. In the United States, with its intensely individualistic free-market culture, labor is seen as simply another factor of production. Four decades ago, the implied social compact was captured in William H. Whyte Jr.'s 1956 best-seller, *The Organization Man*: "Be loyal to the company and the company will be loyal to you." No longer. The company's chief loyalty is now to financial markets in which decision-making is dominated by cost-minimization and short-term return maximization.

Beyond the Job Ethic

In the working world of the future, British futurist Charles Handy predicts, people will have not a "job" but a "portfolio" of skills that they will market to various customers. Executive leasing is an early example of this trend. Companies hire, say, a chief financial officer to fill a short-term skills gap. Temporary-employment agencies are now all the rage in market economies, particularly in the United States. Though "temps" still comprise less than 3 percent of the U.S. workforce, their growth has been explosive, accounting for 26 percent of all job growth from the recession of March 1991 through December 1993.[36] That trend has continued since.

According to the Bureau of Labor Statistics, 23.2 million Americans—17.5 percent of the workforce—are employed part-time (a broader category than temps), up from 10.6 million in 1968, or 14 percent of total employment.[37] The issue of the "contingent" workforce surfaced dramatically in 1997's mid-summer Teamsters' strike at UPS, where part-timers account for 60 percent of the company's workforce and where thirty-eight thousand of the forty-six thousand jobs (83 percent) that the company has created since 1993 are part-time. Much of the employer appeal of part-timers stems from the ability to escape fringe-benefit costs. At UPS, for instance, the use of contingent workers saves about 35 percent in employee benefits.[38]

In *JobShift,* author William Bridges insists that the concept of the job is itself rapidly being eliminated through a combination of reengineering, self-managed work teams, project teams, flattened organizations and the computerization of routine work.[39] What is disappearing, Bridges clarifies, is not work but the notion of the job, what he describes as a "social artifact" that emerged during nineteenth-century industrialization as a way to package tasks that needed doing. In the place of standardized work hours, fixed workplaces and the notion of one-person-one-job, we are seeing the emergence of a market for work that is increasingly more open, part-time, freelance, temporary and outsourced. Bridges pans the notion of a worldwide jobs policy as an outmoded "rigid solution to an elastic problem." Jobs, he insists, "are no longer socially adaptive." His prediction: "By the year 2020 . . . we'll look back on jobs the way people look back on the family farm: a nice way of life that doesn't meet today's needs."

In this newly envisioned "post-job" environment, a person has neither a job nor a fixed position but, rather, a portfolio of capabilities and competencies. Careers—if they can be called that—become a succession of multiple and simultaneous commitments.[40] Access to information becomes crucial, particularly that formally controlled by increasingly superfluous managers. Hierarchy becomes less useful as work organizes around projects, rather than job classifications. Skills-based deployment rather than job-based employment becomes the norm. In the United States, the inability to see this newly emerging world of work stems from what Reich calls "vestigial thought"—a view of industry, the workforce and the social contract between them that ossified in the late 1950s. Viewed through the outdated, job-myopic imagery of the work ethic, today's de-jobbed environment fosters a trepidation, insecurity and even impotence, leading to the rise of what Reich calls the "anxious class."

The Emergence of the Deployed Worker-Capitalist

These trends are destined to have a far-reaching impact. For instance, the sources of competitive advantage, according to Michael Beer and his Harvard colleagues, are now the "three C's": competence, commitment and coordination—all of which are undermined by people continuously changing jobs. However, the de-jobbed corporation could coordinate work through networked computers. In that way, contract workers could contribute their competence and commitment to an organization that embraces a different notion of the corporate entity and what it means to work.

This emerging notion of the "virtual corporation" is largely a creature of new capabilities in computer databases and network technologies. "Delocalized" coworkers and even "dematerialized" operations become increasingly feasible as commercial relationships blossom in cyberspace—on the Internet, through electronic mail or via interactive television. MCI predicts that the volume of data traffic on global phone systems will supersede voice traffic by the year 2000. Previously, the location-specific nature of firms was due, in part, to the costly expense of negotiating with many different workers and contracting for and monitoring remote tasks, plus the need for the capital-intensive equipment associated with manufacturing.

Computerization means that transaction costs (negotiating, contracting) will continue to plummet, bringing directly into question a key rationale for the place-wedded firm as an organizational entity. Turning the real estate maxim on its head ("location, location, location"), cyber-job proponents claim that one of the key benefits of siteless work is "no location, no location, no location." Yet even in cyberspace, oddly enough, culture is key. In seventy-five interviews with members of physically distributed "virtual teams," author Jessica Lipnack found unanimous agreement that success is 90 percent culture or people, and only 10 percent technology.[41]

As cyber-careers become more common, compensation schemes will need to keep pace with these new, steadily shifting "value-adding relationships" (the search is on for a word to replace *work*). New training and communication programs will have to be devised. The notion of a "career" will need to be reconceptualized, as will the concept of career development in a world where employment is displaced by concerns about how individuals can continuously redeploy their skills portfolios on a series of projects (vs. jobs). In short, new forms of organization, including newly structured ownership systems, will need to reflect this new relationship with work, the changing nature of work and the entity through which (and for which) work is performed.

Compensation plans that include an ownership component could help ensure that the three C's are reflected. Competent people know that the potential upside in a project is an effort with which they should be associated. That's why top executives (and other symbolic analysts) routinely bargain for an ownership stake. Stock options, for example, are a proven means for soliciting long-term commitment from both contract employees and direct employees while also providing an incentive to ensure long-term coordination (the third of the three C's). An ownership solution could also ensure that productivity gains (reflected in share prices) are harvested, at least in part, by those who contribute to generating those gains. That would be immensely pleasing not only to John Locke and Karl Marx but also to Adam Smith and to the competence carriers themselves.

As for the *worker* (another word in need of an update), he or she will need to continue to assemble a portfolio of market-valued skills in which (typical of portfolios) diversification will play a part. A portion of that portfolio will need to be those labor-based "core competencies" to which Handy refers (literacy, facility with numbers and competence with information technology). In addition (and in return for contributing their skills), those laborers will need to assemble a property-based portfolio of income-generating assets. Two alternatives present themselves.

First is the traditional approach, in which an additional cash cost is built into a contract, enabling the worker to invest in other companies. That's the typical case today, where pensions are invested in a widely diversified portfolio. Or the worker could take an equity stake in each of the companies to which he temporarily leases his competencies, thereby assembling a diversified portfolio as he progresses through his working life. A combination of the two may be best. From the contracting employer's viewpoint, such noncash compensation (in the form of shares, share options, or other equity-based compensation) could provide a cost-effective, cash-efficient means to pay for quality work.[42] Where that compensation vests over a period of years, this ongoing ownership relationship could mimic the commitment that accompanies long-term employment, but without the accompanying commercial risk imposed by fixed labor costs.

Imagine Work

Buckminster Fuller, futurist, philosopher, engineer and author, coined a term that aptly describes what is happening to the world of work: he labeled this process "comprehensive ephemeralization, the process of doing more with less." As he explained: "Since World War I, the world has turned from the wire to the wireless, the track to the trackless, the visible structure to the invisible structure. In each instance, man is able to do more with less and less and less."[43] Information technology accelerates this trend so that, increasingly, we are living in an intangible economy in which amusement, beauty, pleasure, even spiritual fulfillment are becoming as real and as valuable as the steel beams and cotton bales of an earlier era.

In a social and political environment firmly wedded both to the work ethic and to political equality, the challenge lies in figuring out what a nation's people are to *do* as the "doing-ness" of production is done less and less with the involvement of human power and more and more with the productive power (and knowledge) embodied in their culture's tools, including its information and networking technologies and its remarkable array of congealed knowledge. This steady decoupling of productive output from human input has been ongoing at least since the dawn of the industrial revolution. However, even though our systems for *accomplishing* work have evolved in astonishing ways, we have yet to devise genuinely systems-wise means for *connecting* people to the work that is done.

While it is clearly time to focus on preparing people for a more global form of capitalism (through training, lifelong learning, computer networking, etc.), it is also clear that the time has arrived to prepare capitalism for people. Full-employment policies will continue to be essential, but they are no longer sufficient. The challenge lies in how to update the work ethic to make it relevant to the realities of modern production. A modern form of economic connectivity is long overdue.

CHAPTER **8**

Reinventing Labor Unions

What does labor want? We want more schoolhouses and less jails; more books and less arsenals; more learning and less vice; more leisure and less greed; more justice and less revenge; in fact, more of the opportunities to cultivate our better natures.

—Samuel Gompers, American labor leader 1850–1924
(carved on wall in lobby of AFL-CIO headquarters, Washington, D.C.)

One place where the work ethic is being reworked is in progressive labor unions, led by one of the largest, oldest and most militant of the industrial unions, the United Steelworkers of America. The steelworkers' embrace of an ownership strategy is rich in historic irony, as it was the miserable working conditions in Britain's mid-nineteenth-century steel mills that induced Marx to propose communism as an ownership prescription for what then ailed the worker.

The Steelworkers offer a particularly instructive story, due to the key role they played in America's industrialization. In September 1919, a nationwide strike of virtually every U.S. steel producer was organized by the American Federation of Labor. Over the ensuing three months, dozens of people were killed and thousands jailed. Often the most outspoken of all the federation's unions, steelworkers have long been in the thick of nationwide political action,[1] including serving as key fund-raisers for Bill Clinton's two presidential campaigns. Consequently, their leadership in the employee-ownership arena transcends their numbers (700,000, including many in nonsteel employment), particularly since the announcement of their pending merger with the United Autoworkers (800,000 members) and the International Association of Machinists (490,000).[2] A common denominator: all three unions have substantial experience negotiating ESOPs. A common goal: to gain more political clout for the labor movement—suggesting that ownership solutions may yet emerge as a means for putting some movement back in the labor movement.

Risk Without Ownership

Historically, American labor unions have resisted their members owning shares in companies where they work, fearful that would undermine collective bargaining and even the union movement itself. Instead of their steadfast commitment as adversaries, employee-owners would be "bargaining with themselves." They would be "co-opted." Some unionists also recalled when, during the Knights of Columbus era, unionists joined worker cooperatives in which early co-op members excluded from membership those who were hired later. In effect, the original members became the "capitalists," hiring their union brethren to work for them—not a high-water mark for worker solidarity.[3]

Nevertheless, the American labor movement included an early advocacy of employee ownership as "an alternative to the wage system," according to William Sylvis, president of the National Labor Union, in an 1872 speech to his membership. With an appeal that retains its resonance in today's globalizing labor markets, Sylvis argued: "So long as we continue to work for wages, so long will we be subjected to small pay, poverty and all of the evils of which we complain." That earlier employee-ownership movement, organized as industrial cooperatives, spread to more than two hundred workplaces covering some thirty-five trades before fading from the scene by the turn of the century, largely due to lack of access to the financial capital required to compete against larger employers organized as corporations.[4]

Other concerns also served as a barrier. Stock subjects workers to the risks of uncertain returns in the form of fluctuating dividends and share values. Economists insist it is more "efficient" for employees to draw fixed wages, letting this investment risk be shouldered by the well-to-do. Yet fixed wages, in turn, impose a risk on the company (a key reason for the steady growth in the contingent workforce). During the 1960s, legendary labor leader Walter Reuther, longtime president of the United Autoworkers, embraced the notion of employee share ownership as a risk-reducing form of profit sharing: "Profit sharing in the form of stock distributions to workers would help to democratize the ownership of America's vast corporate wealth. If workers had a definite assurance of equitable shares in the profits . . . , they would see less need to seek . . . increases in basic wages."[5]

By the early 1980s, the Steelworkers faced a dramatically changed environment with a high risk of substantial layoffs and the potential loss of pension benefits. The risks of ownership began to look less foreboding as they found themselves struggling against foreign producers armed with labor-saving continuous casting while at home they faced lax enforcement of antidumping laws,[6] rising costs of environmental compliance and the acceleration of costs associated with an aging membership in a declining smokestack industry (U.S. Steel then had five retirees for every active employee).[7]

After considerable soul-searching, the Steelworkers turned to ownership as a way to access information, participate in decision-making, and share in any upside gains. Their "investment bargaining" strategy soon altered the very nature of collective bargaining, confronting union leaders with the task of representing their members both as workers (fair wages, safe working conditions, etc.) and as owners.[8] Rather than being co-opted, however, the leadership soon found that this strategy strengthened the union because, once employees became owners, they became even more resistant to arbitrary treatment at the hands of management.[9] And because they were more willing to grant concessions *to themselves*, that newfound flexibility helped retain jobs, preserve pensions and sustain the union's membership rolls.[10]

The most dramatic aspect of this strategy may be its influence on the union's leadership. As worker-owners began to expect a more business-savvy leadership, the rhetoric of the class struggle gave way to debates about the need for quality control, financial literacy and work-rule flexibility. Though traditional union goals remained intact (decent wages, safe working conditions, etc.), the union found nontraditional ways to attain them. As changes in the company culture altered interactions between managers and workers, negotiations became ongoing and incremental rather than periodic and dramatic, while strikes became, in practice, an anachronism.

A New Way for Labor

At the outset, this strategy was based on a survival instinct. Nationwide, steel industry employment peaked in 1953 at 650,000 before beginning a steady decline to 163,000 in 1997. This also helped salvage jobs and pensions at a time when modernization mandated change (labor-saving continuous casting affected 20 percent of U.S. steel production in 1986 but 86 percent by 1996). Investment bargaining became one key component in a successful survival strategy (more than 60,000 steelworkers participate in ESOPs). In the steel industry as a whole, labor contracts are now longer, typically six rather than three years, lending more stability and certainty to strategic planning, while labor representatives serve on the board of all six major steel producers.

The Economic Strategy Institute reports that the labor portion of U.S. steel costs declined from $262 per ton in 1982 to $161 per ton in 1992, while overall costs declined from $650 to $525 per ton, converting the American steel industry into the world's most productive in terms of man-hours per finished ton of steel. By the end of 1994, the industry was operating at 96 percent of capacity and had earned over $1 billion for the year, compared with losses of $350 million in 1993. The resurgence of the U.S. auto industry may trace its roots to this change, as automakers built 1990s cars with steel provided at 1980s prices.

From Negotiation to Institutionalization

In evaluating the merits of a union-embraced investment strategy, it's important to recall that labor unions were founded as a moderating influence on the often dehumanizing aspects of primitive capitalism, with its long hours, meager wages and grisly accidents. It was not the dignity of labor but its drudgery that was at issue when America embraced a Faustian bargain, trading off the dignity (and the drudgery) of work on the family farm and in the specialty-skill guilds for the efficiency of bulk manufacturing, with its relentless search for what efficiency apostle Frederick Winslow Taylor called "the one best way."[11] Even Adam Smith, whose *Wealth of Nations* was founded on the division of labor, cautioned that

> in the progress of the division of labor, the employment of the far greater part of those who live by labor . . . comes to be confined to a very few operations, frequently one or two. . . . The man whose whole life is spent in performing a few simple operations . . . has no occasion to exert his understanding or to exercise his invention. . . . He naturally loses, therefore, the habit of such exertion, and generally becomes as stupid and ignorant as it is possible for a human creature to become.

It was with the hope of humanizing these dehumanizing features that notions of worker solidarity arose, along with the need for workers to band together to oppose the insensitive and monopolistic practices of those "finance capitalists" (Marx's term) who then wielded Adam Smith's invisible hand. Many of those early market-humanizing measures, often first conceived in union negotiations, are now viewed as a natural component of the social contract, including the prohibition against child labor, the minimum wage, time-and-a-half for work in excess of a forty-hour week, unemployment compensation, workplace health and safety and so on. This "institutionalized humanization" also includes such widely accepted practices as gender-equal pay, race-blind employment opportunities and federally mandated standards governing retirement income security. Those who suggest that the decline in union membership reflects the demise of organized labor overlook the fact that much of labor's agenda has found its way out of bargaining and into law.

Politics is a key arena where this shifting public/private balance is struck. However, because the reach of national law is only national, the downward pressure on U.S. labor costs is certain to continue so long as trade remains open to the outside world. In the labor environment in the United States, with only 15 percent of the total workforce unionized, including only one in ten in the private sector (down from an economy-wide peak of 35 percent of nonfarm workers in 1953),[12] union bargaining leverage has become steadily more difficult to muster. Yet those just entering the workforce and those with few market-valued skills will continue to be particularly needful of new ways to cope with an increasingly globalized labor market. A union facilitated ownership strategy could play a part. For example, a 1994 survey by the Gallup Organization and the Employee Benefits Research Institute found that younger Americans are more likely to prefer extra cash in their paychecks or company stock that could be cashed out when they leave their jobs, while older Americans are more likely to prefer pension benefits.

This suggests that union strategists should consider an idea historically viewed as contrary to union solidarity: the notion of "two-tiered" bargaining, with less experienced workers paid on a different basis than those more senior—similar to what Walter Reuther proposed, only targeted to those employees who voice a preference. This could provide a new tool for creating and maintaining jobs, particularly among younger workers, where union recruitment efforts are at their weakest. Research in Britain also confirms that the highly entrepreneurial Generation X gravitates toward the notion of employee stock ownership,[13] suggesting that entry-level employees might agree to more employer stock in their pay package while those closer to retirement opt for more pension benefits. Certainly that's the experience in the computer industry, where Silicon Valley employers even grant stock options to summer interns.

From Reaction to Relationship

The addition of investment bargaining to union bargaining is creating flexibility and adaptability in industries not known for those features. The deregulated U.S. airline industry offers several examples. The most dramatic is United Airlines (described in Chapter 5), where union leaders realized that labor-cost reductions were essential if the airline was to survive, particularly with the entry of nonunion, low-cost carriers. They also recognized that, without employee ownership, any labor-cost reductions inevitably would flow to remote shareholders who may not be inclined to follow a growth-oriented, job-preservation strategy. United's pilots' union figured they could either buy their way into a position of control or passively stand by as their jobs were contracted out.[14]

Thus, in July 1994, United's union leadership (absent the twenty thousand flight attendants) negotiated a $5 billion ESOP purchase of 55 percent of United's outstanding shares. Investment bargaining pay cuts of 8 to 15 percent are presently being applied to repay the ESOP loan. Employees swung their support behind this ownership solution once they were persuaded that the sacrifices were necessary, affordable and equitable. They also ensured that their investment was done without excessive debt, knowing that the only real job security comes from working for a financially healthy company.

United offers a study in how an ownership solution can create an entirely new set of challenges. To borrow the funds required, the three participating unions had to agreed to a sixty-nine-month no-strike clause. This could create a labor relations imbroglio should the flight attendants decide to strike—say over the company's hiring of overseas staff for international flights. That hot-button issue kept the flight attendants on the sidelines during the deal-making—and out of the ESOP. No one yet knows whether the members of one United union will cross the picket line of another.

Adjustment pains are apparent within the leadership of both the union and the company. Those with an adversarial background find it difficult to adapt to a more collaborative culture. Some unionists complain that their members think too much like owners. Others worry that the employees' stake is not "perpetual" because, as the ESOP loan is paid off and employees retire or leave, their shares are sold. Although such ownership-oriented strategic thinking is new to unions and to American business, it may yet become the norm as a way to cope with the emerging global labor market.

When ESOPs first gained popularity in the mid-1970s, the political Left viewed them as a right-wing union-busting ruse, while the political Right saw them as a left-wing notion akin to Marxism, or worse. The progressive and pragmatic wing of the American labor movement has since embraced investment bargaining as simply another way to save their members' jobs and, just possibly, the union movement. Likewise, progressive business leaders now view the idea as a proven catalyst in persuading workers to think more like businesspeople, realizing that the scope of bargaining now must be both internal (on the company) and external (on the global economy). Ownership is proving itself a powerful lens for sharpening that focus.

Winning the Map and Losing the Territory

Both business and labor are having to rethink their positions as the wage-leveling global labor pool grows ever more accessible and as financial capital becomes ever more mobile. America's free-trade policy has long allowed other nations to sell their goods here, enabling them to generate funds to finance their economic growth and modernization. Critics complain that Americans continue to stand idly by while their industrial base is steadily dismantled, only to show up in other, lower-cost countries. One symptom: U.S. imports of manufactured goods grew from 14 percent of total manufacturing output in 1977 to 36 percent in 1993. The establishment of free-trade zones is destined to accelerate that trend. For example, World Watch Institute reports that in the free-trade zone with Mexico the average hourly wage is $1.67 for workers at twenty-two hundred factories established by General Motors, General Electric, Ford, Sylvania, RCA, GTE, Westinghouse and other U.S. companies. Meanwhile, the average hourly wage is $16.17 for manufacturing workers employed by those companies inside U.S. borders.[15]

Although Americans are fond of their low-priced imports, the displacement of well-paid manufacturing jobs by work performed elsewhere at lower wages is destined to have an impact, both personal and national. The personal impact shows up as income stagnation, economic insecurity and fast-widening economic disparities. The national effect is more complex. In addition to the impact of slower economic growth, the economy is groaning under a foreign indebtedness that is expanding at a pace faster than the underlying economy. From 1980 to 1996, Americans imported $1.9 trillion more merchandise than they exported. That has to be paid for. Those payments were made with borrowings of various sorts. Most obviously, both companies and the government sold bonds abroad. Less obviously, foreigners brought their export earnings to the United States and bought assets, ranging from high-profile corporations (Columbia Studios) to buildings (Rockefeller Center) and golf courses (Pebble Beach).

Though Americans chuckled when some of those investments soured, the underlying trend has profound implications for labor. In 1994, the nation crossed a critical threshold when, for the first time since Woodrow Wilson was president, financial outflows paid to foreigners on their assets here (profits, dividends, interest) exceeded the inflows from Americans' holdings abroad. Since 1970, the United States has gone from being a net holder of foreign assets (equal to 30 percent of GDP) to a debtor position in 1995 of –8.5 percent,[16] reflecting America's shrinking balance sheet in the global economy. From labor's perspective, this trend means that the richest nation on earth is steadily redistributing its wealth to investors in other countries, the very wealth on which their members' standard of living ultimately depends.

Those who represent the interests of labor are awakening (albeit slowly) to the fact that the traditional nostrums no longer work. When U.S. budget deficits began to explode during the Reagan era, conventional wisdom predicted that the trade deficit would sort itself out as imports became too expensive. This mismatch between theory and reality became obvious when trade deficits persisted as the dollar slid from 250 yen in 1982 to 85 in mid-1995, while trade deficits set a new record ($173 billion). When that theory didn't pan out, purveyors of the conventional wisdom offered another, assuring policymakers that the *real* problem was America's low savings rate. That seemed logical enough: if people saved more, there would be less need to borrow. Yet during Bill Clinton's first term, federal deficits shrank at a steady rate while the trade deficit ballooned to a record $188 billion in 1996. Policymakers even lent their support to the notion of outlawing the *symptom* (i.e., budget deficits), proposing to amend the Constitution to mandate a balanced budget while simultaneously approving tax legislation projected to shrink revenues by $270 billion over the next ten years.

This failure of both diagnosis and prescription suggests the presence of a structural explanation that has yet to be identified. One little-understood element in this drama stems from the fact that Americans simply chose to absorb the costs of the shifting terms of trade, largely by ceding lower-cost production to other countries. Rather than defend the nation's production base (say, by imposing domestic content requirements on foreign imports), a choice was made to favor free trade and export growth. That policy was paid for by working Americans in shrunken pay packages and displaced jobs.

Who Pays and Who Plays?

To date, the ownership implications of this phenomenon have escaped the attention of policymakers. Some economists insist that trade deficits are no longer a significant problem because, on an ownership basis, a portion of that trade is generated on an intracompany basis as U.S. multinationals produce globally, with parts and supplies being both imported from and exported to their operations worldwide in a tangled web of corporate identities that a mere layman could never comprehend. This is certainly partly true. However, it begs the obvious point: just who reaps the benefits of this wage-leveling, global-trading regime? To say Americans are the beneficiaries glibly passes over the obvious: Which Americans? Ultimately the real winners are the owners.

Both common sense and social equity suggest that, if national policy is to be put at the service of the free trade in goods and capital, free-traders ought to ensure that this benefits their constituents with something more than just lower-cost products.* That's particularly the case if, in the bargain, their constituents lose the purchasing power with which to buy those products. On the other hand, if America's job base (and, over time, its wealth base) is to be traded away in order to boost the short-term financial value of U.S.-based multinationals (of course, this is never phrased so directly), what then should be demanded in return?

Yet even the ownership implications are confused by the fact that indirectly (through pension plans, mutual funds and so on), American workers own significant stakes in those multinationals. While on the one hand institutional investors prod these firms to scour the world for lower-cost production to boost investment returns, on the other hand their success may undermine the livelihoods of those whose funds they invest. The issue for labor is not how to resist this development. Globalization is here to stay. The challenge is how to ensure that labor's interests are served by it.

From the perspective of the corporation, even the most brilliant labor-saving advance counts for naught if there are not enough buyers for what is produced.

---

* Of course, the free trade debate is considerably more complex. However, a "collective choice" dilemma faces those who propose to loosen restraints on trade or approve broader trade-negotiating authority ("fast track") for the president, typically focused on a range of "greater good" arguments. That's because, while the benefits of free trade are diffused and deferred (cheaper goods, growing exports), those who have lost their jobs due to free trade (or believe they will) lobby vociferously for protection. The trade-offs are numerous, including the possibility that, with less ability to lower trade barriers overseas, U.S. manufacturers may have more incentive to relocate, to get access to those protected markets.

On that score, multinationals and labor share an interest in ensuring there are enough customers with enough cash to maintain market demand. Yet the evidence suggests that global overcapacity (in airplanes, appliances, autos, chemicals, film, drugs, paper, steel, tires) is putting downward pressure on labor costs which, in turn, shrinks consumer purchasing power as supply outpaces demand.* Though the U.S. inflation rate has fallen, in part due to worldwide overcapacity, the issue—for labor, for policymakers, for corporate strategists and for trade negotiators—is how to foster balance in this fast-changing equation.

An ownership strategy—as yet an overlooked component—holds great promise for addressing these interrelated concerns. As systems theorist Stuart Kauffman points out, economists have yet to construct a theory that incorporates "complementarities."[17] A car and gasoline are consumption complements; you need both to go anywhere. Likewise for hammer and nail; they're production complements—both are required to nail boards together. Of course, a screw and a screwdriver might do just as well for fastening boards, serving as production substitutes. It is these matching patterns of functional couplings that make up the web of transactions called economics. Yet economists have yet to consider (much less figure out) what role ownership patterns might play in helping maintain patterns of broad-based market demand. Production capacity and consumption capacity are complementaries; when it comes to production, there's no substitute for customers. If producers refuse to cure the mismatch, perhaps labor should.

Cross-border networks of employee-owners may yet provide the nucleus around which a new global labor movement could arise. At present, the market itself is all that connects employees. Yet its actions pit them against each other rather than providing a needed forum in which to discuss their shared reality and their mutual interests so that they might better weigh the trade-offs between their social values and their financial interests, their current interests and their interest in a secure retirement income, their local values and the values of free trade—all with an eye to creating a more humane, prosperous and sustainable global economy.[18]

Servicing an Atomized Workforce

Today's workers are increasingly nonunion and isolated. They work not in large industrial conglomerates but more often in widely dispersed and relatively small enterprises. This presents a daunting challenge for traditional worksite-oriented labor organizing. Charles Handy's descriptive term "portfolio

---

* "There is excess global capacity in almost every industry," according to Jack Welsh, chairman of General Electric. Louis Uchitelle, "Global Good Times, Meet the Global Glut," *The New York Times*, 16 November 1997, p. WK 3.

worker" aptly describes the condition of many postindustrial workers. In 1996, the Bureau of Labor Statistics documented 2.4 million temporary employees nationwide,[19] a threefold increase from 1978. Compared to 2 percent annual job growth since 1972, temp jobs have expanded almost six times as fast (11.8 percent per year).[20] If part-time workers (17.5 percent of the workforce) and the self-employed (11.8 percent) are included, these account for three of every ten jobs in the workforce.

The challenge faced by organized labor is clear: the secure, high-benefits union job in manufacturing is being replaced by the insecurity of the low-benefits service-sector job or the nonbenefits world of temps, part-timers and the self-employed. In addition, the one-earner family (with relatively high wages) is being replaced by the two-earner family with low to moderate wages.

If unions ever hope to recover the sense of "solidarity" on which the movement was founded, they will need to reinvent themselves in response to this fundamental shift in the nature of work and, more generally, to the shifting nature of economic participation. In *The Age of Paradox*, Handy suggests the usefulness of a "club" that would be available for portfolio workers. Rather than a "club for the unemployed" with notions of shared misery, he suggests a networking hub for workers to search not for jobs but for clients to whom they could market their "portfolio of competencies."

These competencies need not all be of the usual "trades" variety; they may well include not just job skills, but also those skills useful to the community. "If we want to reconcile our humanity with our economics," Handy suggests, "we have to find a way to give more influence to what is personal and local, so that we can each feel that we have a chance to make a difference, that we matter." Like people everywhere, unionists seek purpose, meaning and direction in their lives. While the economic domain is important, that comprises but one dimension of the total person that unionism is meant to serve. This more holistic view suggests a broad range of services that today's unions should provide—not only during their members' lifetimes but also after they retire, as well as during those periods when they are between paid positions.

Unions, Solidarity and Service

To serve tomorrow's "de-jobbed" environment, the union agenda needs to be broadened to focus not just on unionists' trade skills but also on that broader range of skills with which their members can make a contribution. Handy's "portfolio clubs" could become Internet-connected "skills banks" linking labor skills not only to employment needs but also to personal and community needs that might otherwise go unmet (tutoring, mentoring, scouting, coaching, environmental restoration, etc.). This broader agenda could also help offset local fiscal burdens otherwise associated with providing community services (librarian, teachers' assistant, etc.).

Much as not all of their members' skills and interests are job-related, so too not all of a union's goals are job-related. An increasingly de-jobbed environment offers an opportunity to refocus labor's varied competencies on the rebuilding of social solidarity, labor's original purpose. Some of those tasks may not be compensated in the usual sense of pay and benefits. However, this expanded agenda could help ease their members' transitory periods of personal dislocation (and depression) while also advancing labor's broader social purpose and filling an ever widening gap in community services. "I don't know what your destiny will be," Albert Schweitzer advised, "but one thing I do know: the only ones among you who will be happy are those who have sought and found how to serve." That sage counsel might feature prominently in articulating the mission statement in every portfolio club.

Those clubs could also become training centers for upgrading union members' skills portfolios—providing support for the lifelong learning of current members while offering skills training to potential members, an untapped recruiting tool.[21] The need for training and ongoing education is growing rapidly. In 1979, for example, male workers with college degrees earned 49 percent more than those who had completed only high school. By 1993, that differential had widened to 89 percent,[22] pushing more people to the bottom while undermining both union notions of social solidarity and democratic notions of a classless society. With employment a primary path to ownership, and job skills the entry fee to employment, the union agenda needs to embrace a far more fundamental mission, yet one with the potential to reinvigorate union membership, while also broadening labor's social commitment.

Employers and Deployers

If indeed the era of a permanent job with a single employer is over, along with its promise of lifelong benefits and a pension, there may well be a role for unions to play in filling that void. DEMOS, a London-based think tank, suggests the need for "deployers" (versus employers)—firms with a long-term relationship with individuals that contract (deploy) their labor to others. Similar in function to temp agencies, these firms could commit to filling the employer void by providing training, benefits, vacation, parental leave and holidays, and by offering labor representation that is portable throughout an individual's working life rather than being dependent on continuous employment with a single employer (or even a single union).[23]

With economic security shifting from employer to employability, such firms could play a key role in facilitating client (versus job) transitions while also providing a sense of career continuity. With modest initial capital requirements, these deployment firms could be established by the unions and owned by their members. Regular clients (previously known as employers) may find it wise to invest in such companies, with an agreement that the deployer would take over a portion of the training function. This may also provide a cost-effective means for providing employee benefits, the "fixed cost" component of labor compensation that is driving the trend toward contingent employment. Looking back to labor's roots, unions could form private-sector purchasing cooperatives for their members, using their massive memberships (far larger than those of employers) to negotiate group rates on everything from insurance and health care to adult education, financial planning, travel services, car rental, consumer protection and lifestyle consulting.

One such "demographic union" has already discovered this secret: the American Association of Retired Persons. Within three days of my fiftieth birthday, a membership card mysteriously appeared in my mailbox. For $8 per year, a new world of group discounts became available. Similar economies of scale could be organized for union members (and potential members) by entrepreneurial union leaders. Consider, for example, the fact that the average annual cost for administering a 401(k) plan for a small or midsize company is now $475 per year. Surely economies of scale could be realized there, using the cost savings to supplement retirement savings. Similarly, consider that practically every unionist carries at least one credit card, typically paying ludicrously high interest to a bank. Yet unions could sponsor those credit cards, allowing their members to borrow against the balance in their own 401(k) plans, paying interest (at a lower rate) to themselves and thereby letting their consumer purchases supplement their retirement savings.[24]

The scope of potential services that could be provided by union-established "deployers" is extraordinary. For example, they could sponsor mutual funds in which their members invest, and into which members "roll over" tax-deferred cash and noncash benefits. Thus, for example, where members are compensated partly in the form of client-company shares (or share options), members could transfer their shares to a deployer-managed mutual fund and then diversify through trading facilitated within the fund. Fund managers, in turn, could invest members' cash savings in labor-friendly firms that foster broad-based capital accumulation among union members. In return for their services, deployers could take warrants in client companies, dedicating the proceeds to the establishment of community-responsive networking clubs, or to other members' needs (such as education and training materials), or to funding pensions for union staff, thereby ensuring that their economic interests are aligned with those of their members.

In short, if today's union leaders hope to stem the decline in their members' economic security, including the loss of traditional benefits, they've got to become much more creative about how those benefits might be organized, accessed and financed. With the emergence of a very new sort of workforce that is much more independent of the employment relationship, unionists simply must get smarter about how benefits could be provided with less dependence on employers. To date, union leaders instead have focused most of their energies on protecting their members from foreign trade, pitting their members' interests as workers seeking high-paid jobs against their interests as consumers seeking low-priced goods.[25] That inherent conflict has long undermined support for organized labor's efforts to erect trade barriers. However, November 1997 saw an undercurrent of worker discontent bubble to the surface when congressional Republicans, allied with President Bill Clinton, failed in their attempt to enact "fast track" trade legislation granting the executive branch broader authority to negotiate trade agreements.

Union strategists continue their efforts to cement employment relationships so that jobs will not be "contingent" and benefits will be provided.[26] Certainly that's one tack worthy of pursuit, though it flies in the face of a clear trend away from fixed jobs that can be shielded and steadily augmented. Meanwhile, however, a full third of the workforce (a group more than three times as large as the private-sector union membership) is struggling with how best to cope with precisely the sort of needs for which unions were originally conceived.

With more Americans today owning a small business than holding a union card, the potential is enormous for labor unions to offer a range of services to a much underserved community. However, unionists need to realize, as ecologists discovered decades ago, that monocultures don't work very well. The world of work is now too diverse to depend on any one solution to a problem. As author Joel Garreau advises: "You want to create solutions with as much diversity as life itself."[27]

If You Build It, They Will Come

From the perspective of the unions' attempt to regain robustness in setting the national social agenda, one of the most intriguing aspects of this strategy is its potential to foster an allegiance to the union movement that is much stronger than now exists with any employer. In setting out what he calls the "New Rules for the New Economy," Kevin Kelly (editor of *Wired*) suggests: "We are headed into an era when both workers and consumers will feel more loyalty to a network than to any ordinary firm."[28] Labor's challenge in this new economy is to help build an empowering network that earns the loyalty of those now struggling to stay afloat in a turbulent sea of change and in a workaday world comprised of what Kelly calls "patchworks of vocations."

In computer parlance, the challenge lies in fashioning an open, integrated "platform"—a readily accessible network of relationships that deliver value to union members or potential members. In the computer world, a platform would be made up of software developers, hardware manufacturers, users and such. The platform in a "deployment" world would be made up of clients, benefits administrators, mutual-fund providers, health-care providers, retraining centers and a range of both deployment-related and personal services, including those dealing with mortgages, credit cards, tax preparation, business-plan-writing, travel, fitness, even bookkeeping and baby-sitting.

In essence, membership would offer access to a network of member-desired services. Not just a fixed job at a fixed location (though that constituency should also be served), but assistance with a broad range of locale-specific coping skills and services that add value in a real and tangible sense. Jobholders and portfolio carriers might change positions from time to time, much like academics now take sabbaticals. If union leaders hope to advance their members' prosperity (and expand their membership), not only will they need to reframe the challenge; they will need to let the scope of desired services be directed from the bottom up, with very little concern for what emerges.

Absent that member-directed, union-facilitated flexibility, this arrangement will lose its capacity to cope with what will continue to be a time of unsettling disequilibrium as globalization continues to work its will on the workplace. Labor unions, in turn, may find that the loyalty now lacking in the labor movement may be resurrected as newly empowered and well-served members (including new members) are drawn to a union-facilitated network of services that meet their needs. Esther Dyson, a well-regarded commentator on the computer community, offers a systems metaphor that fits the challenge facing labor leaders: "As routine is sucked out of our daily work lives, people who can create stability from chaos will be key."[29]

A New Covenant for a Maturing Capitalism

The political rhetoric of the mid-1990s called for a "New Covenant," and a "new social contract." In part, that phrasing was intended to prod the business community to take over more of the costs of closing the gap between low- and high-skilled employees, "the fundamental fault line running through the American workforce," according to former labor secretary Reich. "The Cold War ended dramatically," he notes. "We watched it on CNN. But America's middle class crumbled quietly. We watched it happen day by day, but somehow we never saw it. And now we confront its consequences."

A 1994 report by the Departments of Commerce and Labor characterized this development as the "bifurcation" of the American labor force, with an "upper tier of high-wage skilled workers and an increasing 'underclass' of low-paid labor." Reich insists, "We just can't go on as a society in this direction. At some point a society cannot be stable if it has two tiers of workers." However, due to America's overstrained fiscal capacity, the labor secretary could only address the concerns of this "anxious class" by going hat-in-hand to business leaders, imploring them to invest in upgrading the skills of a workforce whose mobility and ever-increasing contingency makes it unlikely that corporate managers could justify the expense of investing funds where their chances of recovery are slight.

Arguably, workers of all stripes have never needed unions more than they do now. But the need is not for yesterday's job-myopic labor agenda. The manufacturing sector, long the bastion of trade unionists, is certain to continue its steady decline in employment—at least absent some fundamental shift in the terms of trade and the pace of technological change. We are witnesses to a century-long evolution in production and politics that is finally fusing the forces of labor-saving technology, global capital markets and free trade. That combination, long seen as threatening to the interests of labor, could yet become the capstone of labor's century-long struggle.

However, that requires a labor movement willing to get smarter about ownership, including ensuring that its members gain a stake in those income-producing assets with which they are being displaced. Full employment is no longer sufficient as a goal—not for labor, not for business and certainly not for national policymakers. The need is for leaders—in labor, business and politics—with a broader view of economic participation and a more comprehensive vision of what solidarity really means. The consequences for social cohesion could be grave if labor's leadership fails to quickly fashion a vision and a plan in response to this fast-emerging commercial world in which trade and finance are reorganizing the globe into a unified marketplace. A vision is simply values projected into the future. Labor's challenge lies in ensuring that the future it envisions is engineered to reflect the values that it holds most dear.

The emerging global capitalism that confronts labor is still immature, animated by an internal logic that has succeeded in identifying the greatest possible returns precisely because it fails to account for the multidimensional consequences incurred in generating those returns. In evaluating its effect in certain areas, such as the environment, its performance seems akin to an oblivious child playing with razor blades and badly in need of parental guidance. A newly energized, owner-ized and visionary labor movement, informed and motivated by a broader frame of reference, and empowered by the rights and responsibilities attending ownership, may be just what's needed to restore a measure of prudence, care and foresight.

At present, the abstract and largely indifferent forces at work in the commercial domain are on the verge of creating a hierarchy of concentrated economic power that will define the nature of global commerce for the next century. A failure to act now could prove fateful as the atomizing nature of the marketplace further divorces people from responsibility for their actions, and as financial self-interest diverges ever more widely from the broader moral purpose.

A Capitalism That Works for Everyone

Modern civilization can survive only if it begins again to educate the heart, which is the source of wisdom, for modern man is now far too clever to survive without wisdom.

—*E. F. Schumacher*

This four-chapter section covers several of the "soft science" components of ownership engineering, including a review of the oftentimes bizarre "politics of ownership" that have amazed and amused me for more than two decades. Due to the dominant role that money plays as a signaling agent in free enterprise, it's essential that we first understand how money is created and why so much of it ends up in the hands of so few. Thus, we begin with a look at the sources of money and credit, along with the supporting role played by central banks in determining patterns of wealth accumulation and economic power. Our goal here is to consider how an ownership solution could help restore our atrophied civil society while also evoking a broader sense of responsibility for the environment.

Given the steady increase in transnational capital flows, it's essential to our purpose that we fully grasp the origins of that capital and the forces that drive it. To my knowledge, policymakers in both the public and the private realm have yet to consider the multidimensional impact of this very new phenomenon (i.e., global capital) or the implications of its reach into every aspect of life, including its little-understood effect on the natural world. For the first time in human history, we live in a world where global terms like *eco-sphere* and *biosphere* are bandied about with the same ease as *town* or *village* were in an earlier era.[1] The notion of a "global village" is now a reality—at least in the domains of money, the environment, civil society and politics—the four key subjects of our inquiry in this section. In searching for an organic metaphor to explain this emerging phenomenon, let's turn to physician-philosopher Lewis Thomas, who observed in his popular 1974 book, *Lives of a Cell,* "The degree to which we are all involved in the control of the Earth's life is just beginning to dawn on most of us, and it means another revolution for human thought. . . . We are becoming a grid, a circuitry around the earth."

Certainly this global interconnectedness is the case for money, as global capital encircles the world in a feeding frenzy of financial return-seeking. That may well seem terrific for those who own that capital and pocket those returns, and for those who collect the investment fees. What's often less than terrific is the impact this has on the environment, on civil society and on policymaking. If the impact in these key realms proves sufficiently unjust or unsustainable, a threat is posed to the very notion of global capitalism—at least in its current form.

Finance capitalism has about it an elegant simplicity, which may also be its principal weakness. In any system, a broad array of information and feedback is required to maintain long-term system health. For capitalism, the problem arises from the fact that finance filters out all save one source of feedback: money-denominated returns. The concerns of other constituencies—communities, watersheds, forests, a nation's fiscal condition, the rightful claims of the next generation—do not figure in. In theory, these concerns are addressed by government. But as laissez-faire economics once again surged to the foreground, those concerns faded to a faint murmur in the background.

It's important to recall that laissez-faire was a disaster in the last century. Its excesses evoked Marxist-Leninist thought, stimulated the emergence of the Soviet threat, elicited a foreign policy to contain Soviet expansionism, and led to the expenditure of $4 trillion (plus countless lives) during the Cold War—resources that might otherwise have been directed to economic, social and human development. The goal that continues to elude us is how best to advance the human community without resort to rabid individualism, naive communalism or totalitarian communism. This section suggests that a new synthesis is possible, one that goes beyond Left, Right or even centrist to embrace something very new and difficult to classify.

In the political arena, confusion reigns. The ultra-right governments of the 1980s are on the wane as they've steadily been replaced during the mid-1990s by left-of-center governments (such as in France and Britain). However, it's far from clear that today's Left has an agenda capable of addressing the ills that are of most concern to its constituents. For instance, when it comes to a willingness to address the dangers associated with today's emerging ownership patterns in the United States, the political choice is now between the Demopubs and the Republicrats—as both scurry to avoid any mention of this long-festering issue. Meanwhile, in Britain, though Prime Minister Tony Blair has long called for a "stakeholder society," he's struggling with how to put some meat on those bare rhetorical bones.

A shared capitalism has the potential to serve as a social cohesive, a societal binding agent that connects people to their communities, to their capitalist culture and to their natural surroundings. In other words, it has the potential to build "community without the communism." I find great cause for optimism. On the ownership front, we now have clear historical guidelines indicating what works and what doesn't. As we approach the next century, we are faced with a clear choice: whether we want an exclusive or an inclusive free enterprise capitalism. If we want the inclusive version, radical laissez-faire policies are simply inadequate to the task. Yet that raises the obvious question: What should be embraced in its stead? The first step in answering that question requires a clear understanding of the origins of money. It is to that which we now turn.

CHAPTER **9**

Making Money

When it comes to money, everybody is of the same religion!

—Voltaire

Karl Marx hoped communism would mean an end to money. He understood how crucial money is to the working of finance capitalism and to a market economy, which responds to pricing signals denominated in monetary units—dollars, pounds, pesos, and so on. He also knew that, notwithstanding Adam Smith's laudable moral sentiments, a market economy doesn't respond to people; it responds to people *with money*. Otherwise, as hunger expert Frances Moore Lappe reminds us, how can we explain a half billion people worldwide living in market economies and going hungry?

With increasing frequency, the possession of money requires possession of either (*a*) high-value human capital (such as that residing in "symbolic analysts") or (*b*) nonhuman capital—machinery and equipment, chemical processes, computer software and such. Nature takes care of the distribution of human capital at birth ("All men are created equal"), uniformly allotting each person one labor power. Of course, the skills required to make that human capital valuable in the marketplace may require decades of investment (for instance, my law degree culminated nineteen years of continuous schooling). For access to nonhuman capital, nature is not nearly so democratic. In that realm, wealth begets wealth and poverty begets poverty because investments in either physical or human capital depend on current income. For those not born to wealth . . . well, as an anonymous sage once advised, "If you're not born with it, you've got to borrow it."

As this chapter will show, access to credit is critical both to a nation's economic growth and to who will own that growth. That access, in turn, determines who will have access to the money created by a nation's central bank, the money-creating entity charged with facilitating that growth. Nonspecialists liken this obscure process to the divinations of alchemists. Indeed, in ancient times, the creation of money was left to the priests in their sanctuaries. Even the Latin root for *money* (*moneta*) denotes the goddess Juno, whose temple was the site for the minting of coins. The purpose of this chapter is to make those divinations accessible to us mere mortals. I do that so we can better see how to reverse the ownership-concentrating tendencies of modern finance and its unwitting handmaiden, central banking.

Moneysworth

In my experience, few in politics understand the origins of money and credit. Senator Russell Long was one of those few. He also had an uncommon knack for reducing complexity to a simple, often humorous image. For instance, he once wondered aloud about the difficulty Americans have in understanding either money or the government's role in its creation. While not objecting to those who prefer to feature "dead politicians" on their currency, he questioned whether it might prove more useful to feature tools and equipment as a way to illustrate that a nation's currency should be backed by productiveness, because that's what gives it value. For example, in place of George Washington, he suggested that the one-dollar bill feature a screwdriver; a wrench could go on the five and perhaps a power saw on the twenty.* (See figure on next page.)

Consider for a moment what happens when a nation neglects Long's humorous lesson and, instead, prints currency without the backing of that productiveness. History is full of examples. During the last few months of President Mobutu's corrupt rule in Zaire (now Congo), the central bank introduced 1 million, 500,000- and 100,000-zaire notes to make up for back pay due civil servants and soldiers. In 1993, the exchange rate was three zaires to the dollar; by April 1997, it was 340,000 to the dollar. Local money changers quickly labeled them "prostates" since their issuance coincided with Mobutu's operation for prostate cancer. A similar process unfolded in Russia when the central bank issued trillions of rubles of credits to state-owned enterprises at a time when everyone knew the Russian economy had not increased its productive capacity. When I first visited Moscow policymakers in the late 1980s, one dollar netted me 0.56 rubles. In July 1997, I could exchange my dollar for 5,600 rubles. Russians long ago coined a typically bleak phrase to describe this politically based (vs. productivity-backed) moneymaking process: "We pretend to work and they pretend to pay us."

Wealth versus Money

To understand the key role that central banking could play in facilitating an ownership solution, it's necessary to examine the origins of the Federal Reserve. Initially organized in 1913 as a consortium of twelve regional banks, its original

---

* Commencing with the 1995 Christmas season, a limited edition of U.S. Federal Reserve $1 notes have been printed each year with a picture of Santa Claus in place of George Washington. Each bill was sold for $2, with half the proceeds flowing to Easter Seals, a nationwide charity. A 1995 poll found that 35 percent of Americans favor placing advertising on the dollar bill to help cut the deficit or lower taxes.

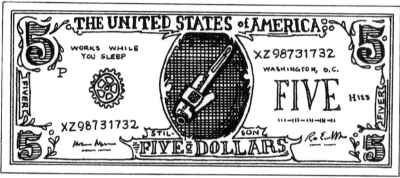

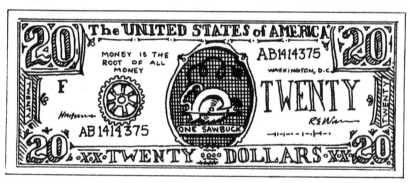

purpose was to ensure that money would be available to meet the seasonal liquidity needs of an agrarian economy at a time when the financial demands of the industrial revolution were also steadily increasing. The availability of credit and money was particularly crucial at harvest time when farmers expected to be paid in cash for their crops, and again in the spring when it was likewise essential that money be available to buy seed, fertilizer and farming implements.

Before delving into this intangible world where credit and money are created, it's useful to note that often we confuse "the map with the territory," a concern that philosopher Alan Watts had in mind when offering the following story to illustrate the difference between money and genuine wealth:

Remember the Great Depression of the Thirties? One day there was a flour-ishing consumer economy, with everyone on the up-and-up: and the next, un-employment, poverty and bread lines. What happened? The physical resources of the country—the brain, brawn and raw materials—were in no way depleted, but there was a sudden absence of money, a so-called financial slump. Com-plex reasons for this kind of disaster can be elaborated at length by experts on banking and high finance who cannot see the forest for the trees. But it was just as if someone had come to work on building a house and, on the morn-ing of the Depression, the boss had said, "Sorry, baby, but we can't build to-day. No inches." "Wha-d'ya mean, no inches? We got wood. We got metal. We even got tape measures." "Yeah, but you don't understand business. We've been using too many inches and there's just no more to go around."

A few years later, people were saying that Germany couldn't possibly equip a vast army and wage a war, because it didn't have enough gold.

What wasn't understood then, and still isn't understood today, is that the reality of money is of the same type as the reality of centimeters, grams, hours or lines of longitude. Money is a way of measuring wealth but is not wealth in itself.[1]

Elastic Money

John Maynard Keynes held a similar view of money, comparing the money supply to water in a reservoir. In his *Treatise on Money* (1930), Keynes likens the role of a central banker to that of a caretaker of a reservoir, filling or drain-ing the water level as circumstances warrant. The goal of ensuring liquidity (a sufficient supply of money) is the origin of central or "reserve" banking, which traces its roots to seventeenth-century Great Britain and Sweden and the need to have a lender of last resort for the private sector banking system. Origi-nally, a bank's reserves were held as gold, silver or some scarce commodity. Thus, the supply of money ("inches") was limited by the amount of precious metals on hand, clearly an artificial limitation.

Before establishment of the Federal Reserve as America's "lender of last resort" (i.e., once bank reserves were exhausted), the only alternative was Wall Street's despised "money trust" of vintage capitalists such as J. P. Morgan and National City Bank (now Citibank). The primary issue then, as now, was how rapidly the economy could grow and how the supply of money (and credit) could facilitate that growth—without setting off a bout of inflation that would undermine money's value. That requires a constant balancing act between overly bright exuberance and unduly bleak pessimism. From the outset, flexibil-ity was viewed as desirable lest economic expansion be unnecessarily stymied. Too loose and the flushing of excess liquidity into the system may support not the real, wealth-generating economy but, instead, the "finance economy," ar-tificially bidding up prices, including the prices of stocks—one popular theory for the stock market crash of 1929, when the Fed was only a teenager.

Originally, the primary moneymaking tool was the Fed's "discount rate"—the interest rate at which the twelve regional banks loaned funds to commercial banks in their regions. The discount system initially relied on the Fed buying short-term IOUs that local banks took as security when they lent to businesses. Those were typically IOUs of merchants or farmers whose loans were backed by physical assets—real estate, farming equipment and such—what Alan Watts would call real wealth. The Fed could dampen monetary expansion by raising the price (the "discount rate") at which it exchanged money (Federal Reserve notes) for those "real bills" (IOUs) presented to it by member banks. That gave the money supply some elasticity.

Populist Response to the Money Trusts

The original design of the Fed had behind it a populist-inspired purpose. In Woodrow Wilson's speech accepting the Democratic Party's nomination in 1912, he warned against "a concentration of the control of credit" and how it could "at any time become infinitely dangerous." However, it was the money trusts themselves who recommended what became (and remains) the heart of the Federal Reserve's structure. They originally proposed a private network of regional banks authorized to create money (Federal Reserve notes) by lending reserves to private banks. As with many of the European central banks at the time, this network of lenders would be owned by the member banks.

Though the basic structure was retained, Wilson partially foiled the bankers' plans by adding a national coordinating council, the Federal Reserve Board located in Washington, D.C. However, the system continued to rely on the commercial banks as the government's hands-on operating partner to ensure that the money supply was set "with a view of accommodating commerce and business" (as the legislation phrased it). Commercial feasibility (can the loans be repaid) and monetary stability (noninflationary growth) became the compass by which this collaborative effort was to set its course.

This account is intended only to show that the creation of money is not some inscrutable mystery. Reserve banking retains its original function: facilitating the availability of credit through member banks who (quite literally) are granted a franchise to print money. Operating in coordination with the Treasury and the Bureau of Engraving and Printing (where money is *physically* made), the politically independent Fed has enormous latitude and profound power. The twelve member banks soon formed an investment committee so that the commercial banks could purchase government bonds for their own portfolios. Initially, the impact of this arrangement was not well understood, even though their bond purchases expanded the amount of money in circulation as the federal government found it could easily raise money (to build dams, levies, etc.) by selling its bonds to the banks.

From Passive to Active Player

It soon became clear that the discounting of "real bills" was altogether too passive. Though it worked well for expanding credit (and money) when people wanted to borrow, it was wholly ineffective as a means for turning the economic tide rather than floating along with it. On the other hand, the member banks *could* stimulate activity even during an economic contraction, by purchasing government bonds. Policymakers caught on when they saw how this money had a stimulative "multiplier effect." Proceeds from the sale of government bonds could do more than just fund a construction project; that project's payroll and purchases, in turn, provided cash to other merchants who could then hire more employees who made other purchases and so on. As a rule of thumb, each of these "high-powered" dollars rippled through the economy five to six times, multiplying the stimulative impact.

This "multiplier" phenomenon was the key attraction of Keynesian "demand-side" economics when Roosevelt turned to this strategy to pay for government-subsidized jobs during the New Deal era. This policy lever became even more accessible after 1935 when FDR stripped the twelve regional banks of their autonomy, shifting control of monetary policy to the board of governors and shifting control over the sale and purchase of government securities to the Fed's Open Market Committee made up of the governors (who serve by presidential appointment) plus a rotation of representatives from the regional banks (with New York retaining a permanent seat).

The money supply (more accurately the "credit supply") continues to be set largely by this committee. One of the oddest (and most stimulative) elements in this arrangement is the fact that the federal government can write a check on itself. For instance, suppose the U.S. Treasury makes a payment of $50 million to a government contractor, writing a check on its account at the Federal Reserve. The contractor would then deposit that check in its bank, and the check would be presented for payment to the Federal Reserve, which would credit the bank for $50 million. Nobel laureate economist Paul Samuelson calls the Federal Reserve "a legal counterfeiter." As Peter Drucker notes: "When the government talks about 'raising capital' it means printing it. That's not very creative, but it's what we're going to do." A similar "monetization" process was utilized in the early 1980s to pay for Reagan-era deficits. Though much of this debt was sold abroad, the financing of those deficits would have been impossible without help from the Fed.

The De-Linkage Continues

Modern central banking is no longer linked either to "real bills" or to commodities such as precious metals. Even the ability to convert U.S. money into gold ended in 1933. As it now states clearly on all U.S. currency, Federal

Reserve notes are "legal tender for all debts, public and private." Try to redeem a dollar bill and you will be given not gold or silver ("real money") but another Federal Reserve note. The progression has been slow but steady as the national currency shifted from "real money" (gold and silver dollars with intrinsic value) to "real bills" (backed by productive assets) to "fiat money" (greenbacks)—backed by the confidence of those willing to accept it.

This de-linkage of money has made it impossible to "run out of inches," because there is no longer any *physical* limit to the credit (and money) the Federal Reserve can create. Linking the money supply to private sector IOUs ("real bills") once served as a restraining influence.[2] But once policymakers grasped the stimulative potential of government bond purchases and the direct printing of money, control of the money supply shifted from the private to the public sector and to the deliberations of the Fed's Federal Open Market Committee.[3]

But I am getting ahead of my story. The point in chronicling this development is to bring us back full circle to Chapter 3 ("Why Does Capitalism Create So Few Capitalists?") and to Russell Long's point that "credit is already allocated"—to those who have collateral. That's a key reason central banking is such a crucial accomplice in today's ownership-concentrating closed system of finance. This, in turn, takes us back to the invention of Louis Kelso's ESOP financing concept and the role that ownership-expanding self-financing might play in this monetization process.

Past versus Future Credit

The Depression presented the youthful Kelso with a puzzling phenomenon: factories standing idle yet people wanting to work and needing what those factories could produce. Kelso argued that "we are preoccupied with the monetary shadows of reality, rather then reality itself." Where money is allowed to become the factor limiting production, he insisted, we are treating the institutional structure as though it were the reality, allowing it to determine the feasibility of activities whose limits should instead be decided by the physical capacities of the natural world and the business judgments of the commercial world. If the social contract is written such that a carpenter can indeed be laid off (or not get a job) due to a lack of inches, then it's time to take policymakers out back, point out the lumber and the nails, and provide them another tape measure.

The tape measure Kelso recommends is intimately related to the function of central banking. Traditionally, economists have insisted that investment is limited by the amount of savings. There can be no money to lend unless money is accumulated for that purpose. Thus the emphasis on household thrift and the current debate about the merits of shifting to consumption taxes as a way to stimulate savings and investment.[4] In Kelso's view, personal saving is an artificial constraint of limited relevance in a world populated by reserve banks whose goal is to ensure that an economy does *not* run short of money. He recommends that commercial finance be reengineered to focus not on accumulated "past saving" but on what he calls "future saving"—pledging the future earnings of productive assets to repay debt used to bring those assets online.[5]

To recap: at present, the limits to commercial lending are threefold. First, there must be adequate collateral for the loan. Typically that's a lien against assets—either the assets being financed or other security.[6] Second, the enterprise must be able to generate sufficient revenue to repay the loan. Lastly, there must be sufficient accumulated savings that the loan can be made with a feasible interest rate. Kelso agrees that the first two requirements should be retained; they form the basic building blocks of business feasibility that underlie all commercial finance. But the third requirement (accumulated savings) he urges be scrapped as an artificial monetary barrier to tapping an economy's physical productive potential.

Lord Keynes held a similar view of savings orthodoxy. He felt that capitalism was ripe for unprecedented abundance, widely distributed, if only policymakers would leave behind the Calvinist ethic that views self-denial and suffering as essential to the human spirit. In his conclusion to *The General Theory of Employment, Interest and Money*, Keynes cautioned that, up to conditions of full employment, every dollar of household saving was depriving a merchant of a potential sale. Challenging the conventional view of savings and interest, Keynes advocated steps designed (over one to two generations) to decouple investment from savings. This, he suggested,

> *would mean the euthanasia of the rentier, and, consequently, the euthanasia of the cumulative oppressive power of the capitalist to exploit the scarcity-value of capital. Interest today rewards no genuine sacrifice, any more than does the rent of land itself. The ownership of capital can obtain interest because capital is scarce, just as the owner of land can obtain rent because land is scarce. But whilst there may be intrinsic reasons for the scarcity of land, there are no intrinsic reasons for the scarcity of capital. . . .*
>
> *Thus we might aim in practice (there being nothing in this which is unattainable) at an increase in the volume of capital until it ceases to be scarce. . . .*
>
> *Only experience can show how far the common will, embodied in the policy of the State, ought to be directed to increasing and supplementing the inducement to invest; and how far it is safe to stimulate the average propensity to consume, without forgoing our aim of depriving capital of its scarcity value within one or two generations.*[7]

To this observation, Kelso and Russell Long add the additional concern that, regardless how scarce or plentiful the financial capital, the conventional closed system of finance will concentrate wealth and income by restricting credit to those with a preexisting asset base that only they can pledge as collateral. Thus, even if current saving posed *no* limit to investment, access to *ownership* of those investments would continue to be limited because credit would still be allocated according to Russell Long's first rule of finance: to those who have collateral.*

Matching the Map to the Territory

In short, Kelso insists (as Keynes implies), that the Fed could be a more potent stimulus to prosperity that would be more broadly shared. This would require, for example, that the Fed's discount function be limited to private-sector loans (i.e., "real bills") that private-sector bankers appraise as being both self-liquidating and ownership-broadening.[8] Though others anticipated Kelso's notion of "pure credit" (i.e., credit not backed by accumulated saving),[9] Kelso is the first to advocate the linkage of expanded credit to expanded ownership and to do so for the explicit purpose of stimulating consumer demand.

Kelso's approach suggests the creation of a two-tiered "real bills" discounting system that favors the use of ownership-expanding financing techniques. Rather than allocating the nation's available bank credit solely to those with collateral (per Russell Long), credit would flow to its best-perceived economic use based on conventional business feasibility, but with a key, ownership pattern–sensitive difference.[10] This conscious coupling of income-producing capital to broad-based ownership lies at the heart of this unconventional view of reserve banking.[11†]

---

* By limiting tomorrow's productive capacity to yesterday's savings, upward pressure is put on interest rates by making "money" a scarce commodity and creating an artificial shortage of what, with reserve banking, is essentially a social good: credit. The fact that financial credit is available at all is, in part, due to the contribution made by a broad base of citizens living in harmony, maintaining trust in their commercial environment, and helping build and maintain the nation's "social capital" (such as business confidence). That provides the essential context in which all financial commitments are made. The swiftness with which this crucial social glue can come undone is legendary (witness the impact on Mexico when the Zapatista guerrillas made their presence known on New Year's Day 1994). To a very real extent, financial credit is built on a foundation of trust secured by a nation's social capital, lending support to the notion that those who contribute to maintaining this social capital have a legitimate stake in its fruits.

† In pointing out the historical irony that a well-to-do Republican lawyer and investment banker should advocate such a populist vision, William Greider explains:

If everyone owned capital, each would be more free—less dependent on both concentrated wealth and the liberal welfare state. Kelso's vision resonated with the same principles (and the same distrusts) that had motivated the original Populism, but his mechanics were adapted to the terms of corporate capitalism. Owning stock had replaced owning farmland as the primary source of wealth and independence, but access to credit was still the heart of the matter. . . .

Instead of only buying government securities when it created money, the Fed would also buy the debt paper of employee-owned or community-owned trusts, which financed new capital formation. When the new ventures paid off the debts on their new machines and

If this approach to monetization can be made to work (the technical and transition challenges are daunting), then an economy's *productive* capacity would no longer be constrained by its *money* capacity (i.e., accumulated savings). Instead, the "map" (money and credit) would be brought more closely in line with the "territory"—the world of physical productive potential. Also, by making money and credit more transparent to the general public, the financial domain would become more subordinate and accountable to democratic forces than is presently the case. In addition, the voting public might finally understand just what it means, for instance, for the U.S. government to service each year more than $5.5 trillion in debt.[12]

An analogy might be drawn to a 1916 experiment by Eddie Stinson, a pilot who found himself caught in a dangerous spin and discovered that, no matter how hard he tried to pull up the nose of his plane, the aircraft would not respond. In desperation, he pushed the nose down, gained speed and pulled out of the spin. It was his pulling back on the controls that caused the problem; pushing the plane forward to flying speed was the key to recovery. His discovery has since saved the lives of countless pilots. Rather than lengthy periods of monetary restraint, prudent expansion (combined with expanded ownership) may be just the monetary medicine needed.[13]

Creating a Constituency for Constraint

The impact of monetary policy is widely felt—on the affordability of home mortgages, the feasibility of business expansion, job creation and so forth. This creates an ongoing dilemma for central bankers who are in constant need of a supportive constituency, particularly during times when credit constraint—never popular—is essential to long-term monetary stability. An ownership pattern–sensitive reserve-banking policy could help build that constituency. That's because, as a group, capital owners are the most consistently vocal in their opposition to inflation, the bane of central bankers worldwide. A reserve banking policy aimed at consciously broadening the base of those with a direct stake in the conduct of monetary affairs could only help central bankers in their role of insisting on prudence when others are pushing for expansion.

Any initiative in this area would also need to be adjusted to account for the revolution ongoing in the financial world. Many banks now routinely sell their loans, either to other financial institutions or to investors by way of the securities market. Eighty percent of all mortgages, 50 percent of college loans and 15 percent of car loans are now sold via a debt "securitization" process whose pace continues to accelerate. This is transforming banks from money

---

factories, the loan paper would be retired, and ordinary citizens would hold title to the new capital stock. Over a generation or longer, without confiscating or nationalizing anyone's property, the ownership of wealth would become more broadly distributed. Greider, *One World, Ready or Not* (1997).

lenders to middlemen and brokers, as they become a securities-originating adjunct to the capital markets. Whereas thirty years ago banks provided three-quarters of all short- and medium-term business credit in the United States, that share is now barely half, largely because funds can now be raised directly from capital markets.[14] Banks still retain certain key advantages, including the ability to offer government-backed deposit insurance.

Communities and Credit

Community is the purpose of politics. However, money and credit, with their overarching influence, can undermine the best of community-building intentions. With increasing frequency, globalization means that local, regional and even national governments are under pressure to put aside policies designed for the common good—of local people, local businesses, local cultures, and local environments.[15]

The conventional wisdom suggests that money is equivalent to any other good that flows across borders, and, thus, the unrestricted and unconditioned flow of return-maximizing capital should be not only allowed and encouraged but even mandated by international treaty. On 13 December 1997, the United States and more than one hundred other countries signed in Geneva the Multilateral Agreement on Investment committing to the dismantling of hundreds of financial barriers and admitting foreign banks, insurance companies and investment firms to their markets, including granting foreigners more freedom to own and operate companies in the financial services industry.[16]

To conclude where we began: money is a medium through which the economic system communicates with its participants. With no will of its own, it simply responds to the values of those who own or have access to it—or those to whom it is entrusted. Our current money-dominated feedback mechanism is failing us because it fails to signal us that something is fundamentally amiss. As we shall see in the next two chapters, in the absence of a redesign of current financing techniques, the ever freer flow of financial capital is unlikely to contribute to the building of community, either within or among nations. And sustainability—by whatever measure—will continue to lie beyond our grasp.

CHAPTER 10

Capitalism as if Our Children Mattered

> Man, according to the Stoics, ought to regard himself, not as something separated and detached, but as a citizen of the world, a member of the vast commonwealth of nature . . . and to the interest of this great community, he ought at all times to be willing that his own little interest should be sacrificed.
>
> *—Adam Smith*

This book began as an effort to suggest a model of economic and environmental sustainability that would be replicable across today's dazzling variety of nations, cultures and economies. Because of the central role that private property plays in free enterprise, ownership patterns are destined to play a role in that model. That point was brought home to me in April 1996 when I participated in a program in Prague with the Czech minister of environmental affairs. In evaluating the Czech Republic's Soviet-imposed, centrally administered economy, his conclusion was frank: "Nothing could be worse."

The Soviet Union offers a harrowing tale of what can happen when an economic system fails to address the causes of environmental degradation. According to a 1995 World Health Organization report, life expectancy for Russian men plummeted since 1990 from an already low sixty-four years to just fifty-seven years—lower even than Egypt, India or Bolivia—the first country in history to experience such a sustained reversal in human welfare. At first, health experts blamed economic stress, psychological damage and a health care system in ruins. But with a catastrophic rise in congenital abnormalities and fatal birth defects (four times the U.S. rate), scientists now point to environmental factors, including chemical plants that dumped toxins into lakes and rivers; farmers and factory workers exposed to dangerous pesticides and chemicals; and decades of open testing of nuclear weapons. With their genetic heritage now in jeopardy, the culprit is clear: the Soviet system itself.

The situation is equally perilous in Asia, home to thirteen of the fifteen cities with the world's worst air pollution. The World Bank calculates that

2.03 million Chinese die each year from the effects of water and air pollution, 50 percent more than died in the Indochina wars over a twenty-year period. Not only does Asia have 60 percent of the earth's population, twelve times as many people as North America; its industrialization is taking place at triple the pace of the West's industrial revolution.[1] Sixty-five percent of Shanghai children have lead levels higher than the point considered dangerous to mental development. The average Asian river has fifty times more bacteria from human feces than World Health Organization guidelines allow. Continent-wide deforestation means that Asia is losing 1 percent of its forests each year. This chapter examines the relationship between ownership systems and natural systems and explores how ownership patterns may affect the environment.

The pursuit of sustainability must begin with a definition of just what sustainability means. A popular definition stems from *Our Common Future*, a 1987 report by the World Commission on Environment and Development:[2] "Sustainable development meets the needs of the present without compromising the ability of future generations to meet their own needs." The question then becomes, to how many generations is this obligation owed? The "Great Law of the Iroquois Confederation" has a standard that I urge we adopt for our purposes: "In our every deliberation, we must consider the impact of our decisions on the next seven generations." We'll return to that tough standard as we ponder how to create a capitalism that nurtures rather than endangers our children and our children's children.

As ecologist David Brower points out, it was "a new kind of foresight that brought us Yosemite and Yellowstone." Writing in 1995, Brower notes that "In just the twenty-five years since the first Earth Day, we have reduced enough forests around the world to cover the United States from the Mississippi to the Atlantic seaboard, north to south. We've lost enough soil by other means—pavement and condominiums, wind and water erosion, inundation, and poorly informed application of chemicals—to equal all the cropland in India. That's one-seventh of the world's productive land lost since Earth Day began. And in that time our population has doubled. The enormity of what we are doing must come to pervade our thinking. Our religions haven't quite prepared us for our current situation."[3]

From Self-Interest to Self in Relationship

Murray Gell-Mann, Nobel laureate in physics and a founder of the Santa Fe Institute (specialists in the study of complex adaptive systems), argues that we must include in our decision-making more "collective foresight."[4] Otherwise, mankind's relationship with today's environment may well degrade the quality of those relationships available to future generations. That presents a huge challenge in a world where remorseless capital markets are geared to produce returns every calendar quarter. Results are more often measured in months than in years, decades or centuries. In the world of money managers and stock option-sensitive corporate managers, the next quarter century (one generation) seems impossibly remote, while concerns that reach well into the next century (seven generations) are viewed as a utopian fantasy.

Americans relate to their environment largely through their wallets and through signals from the marketplace. At present, those signals are simply incapable of guiding us toward sustainability. Pricing alone—whether for products or for property (such as share value)—cannot convey the complex information required, in Adam Smith's words, to "self-design" a sustainable future. Yet pricing is seldom challenged, because no one has yet proposed a complementary signaling system other than government control or government regulation, the world's most prevalent (and most reviled) feedback system. If we return to core principles, we find that Adam Smith viewed humankind as fundamentally a moral force whose "invisible hand" of personal preference would act collectively with a discernment honed by the inner voice of conscience. The sustainability challenge, I believe, lies in determining how best to bring that moral force into play in those commercial entities that pose an environmental threat, because it is *there* that collective foresight is most needed.

Home Economics

The very existence of the "G-7 plus 1" group of industrial nations (Britain, Canada, France, Germany, Italy, Japan and the United States—plus Russia) is an acknowledgment of the comprehensive, cross-border forces at work within the global economy, now known as the "ecosphere." Similarly, the 1992 Rio "Earth Summit" and its 1997 sequel in Kyoto brought an acknowledgment of what summit organizer Maurice Strong characterized as "the transcending sovereignty of nature"—now known as the "biosphere." The ecosphere and the fate of the biosphere are closely related: G-7 nations produce 45 percent of the world's greenhouse gases and, with 25 percent of the world's population, consume 70 percent of its resources. The United States, with 4 percent of the world's population, produces more than 20 percent of all greenhouse gases. An average American is responsible for eight times as much greenhouse-gas emissions as a typical Chinese.

The notions of ecosphere and biosphere both reflect the relatively recent admission that just as by-products of economic activity cross the borders of politically sovereign nations, so too must efforts to deal with them. However, short of a world government or the emergence of strengthened and well-funded international institutions (such as the United Nations), mankind lacks both an institutional structure and a comprehensive economic theory capable of addressing today's environmental challenges.

Current notions of market economics, like shallow notions of ecology, are decidedly anthropocentric. The resources we've inherited, whether renewable or nonrenewable, are viewed as essentially free goods with little or no value until transformed into some consumer-useful product or service. Both man and nature are seen simply as "factors" of production, reflected in the use of such terms as "human capital" and "natural resources." A deeper understanding of the forces at work recognizes that the world is not simply a collection of isolated objects but a complex network of natural phenomena that are inescapably interdependent.[5]

The scope and duration of potential environmental damage are astounding, and, to some extent, there is no going back. Even if industrial production and chemical-intensive agriculture were halted tomorrow, their environmental effects would remain. The impact of certain refrigerants on the Earth's protective ozone layer are still only dimly understood. In 1992, over sixteen hundred senior scientists, including a majority of the living Nobel laureates in the sciences, endorsed a document titled *Warning to Humanity*, in which they concluded that "human beings and the natural world are on a collision course . . . that may so alter the living world that it will be unable to sustain life in the manner that we know." Their terse conclusion: "We, the undersigned senior members of the world's scientific community, hereby warn all humanity of what lies ahead. A great change in our stewardship of the earth and the life on it is required, if vast human misery is to be avoided and our global home on this planet is not to be irretrievably mutilated."[6]

Despite widespread denial about environmental strains, at least the *threat* of climate change is now widely accepted within the scientific community[7] and the political community[8]—and increasingly so in the fossil fuel community.[9] The U.S. Department of Energy estimates that from 1995 to 2015 the demand for energy will grow 54 percent worldwide and by 129 percent in developing Asia, where China and India are expected to meet their exploding demand for energy by tapping their huge reserves of coal, among the very dirtiest of the fossil fuels and the primary source of both atmospheric sulfur (i.e., acid rain) and carbon dioxide (i.e., the primary heat-trapping greenhouse gas). In December 1997, more than 150 nations convened in Kyoto, Japan to reach global consensus on a coordinated series of steps to reduce greenhouse gas emissions.[10] Under the tentative agreement, the United States would need to reduce emissions by 7 percent below 1990 levels during a period between 2008 and 2012. That would require a cut of as much as 30 percent from the energy use levels projected over that period based on current trends. With developing countries refusing to act until they see developed countries succeed in cutting their own emissions, approval of the accord could prove politically difficult.[11] Even the envisioned reductions are not enough to prevent overall atmospheric concentrations of greenhouse gases from continuing to rise. Those risks are now raising concerns in the financial community as well.[12]

The sulfur dioxide released by coal-fired generators produces acid rain that can damage forests hundreds of miles from the source. Fishery experts agree that the limits to sustainable landings of wild fish have already been exceeded, and that fishers are now living off capital by hauling in today the fish that should produce *tomorrow's* catch.[13] The UN Food and Agriculture Organization found that eleven of the world's fifteen main fishing grounds are seriously depleted. As the global fishing fleet continues to expand, more than one hundred countries have become embroiled in fishing disputes.[14] As with many other areas of replenishable resources (such as forests), the limitation is no longer a lack of financial capital or manmade capital (such as sawmills), but a shortage of natural capital (fishes and trees).[15]

In certain areas, the challenge is immediate, the cost of delay difficult to discern, and the potential danger frightening to contemplate. For instance, population experts predict that if worldwide resources devoted to reproductive health do not grow to $17.2 billion annually by the end of the 1990s,[16] the opportunity will be lost to reduce family size in this century, a delay that could make a difference of up to 4 billion by the year 2050—equal to the whole of Earth's population in 1975. International assistance is well off the pace required, with only $5.7 billion committed in 1996.[17]

Timeless Capitalism

Corporations operate largely on the basis of "timebound" concerns, with a financial orientation toward relatively short-term returns. That is poised to change. Increased scrutiny by stakeholders and regulators; the rise of public concerns about sustainability; the widening circle of influences (governments, employees, independent directors); the growing influence of the media; and the growth of large, practically "permanent" shareholders (institutional investors)—all are hastening the time when financial calculations alone will no longer suffice as the standard for measuring acceptable corporate performance. The issue then becomes what are the bearings the corporation will use to set its course. I suggest that the trend will be to embrace criteria that strike a balance between traditional "timebound" concerns (such as financial results) and those that might best be described as "timeless." Sustainability must embrace both—meeting the needs of both the present and the future.

How does a business operating within severe constraints imposed by timebound capital markets begin to evaluate its responsibility in this long-term, even timeless context? The opening of commercial decision-making to embrace the concerns of a multigenerational, universe of stakeholders implies a fundamental reordering of conventional commercial priority-setting and decision-making. For instance, when radioactive isotopes have known harmful effects that span twenty thousand years (more than eight hundred generations), how does an investor compute the "net present value" of an investment in nuclear energy? Or calculate the "economic value added" from the use of ozone-depleting refrigerants? Or the "market value added" from the use of agricultural chemicals that endanger underlying aquifers?

The answer is found not in economics but in its predecessor science: ethics. Adam Smith reasoned in his day that our ingrained "natural sympathies" for our fellow human beings would hold us in check, along with that "impartial spectator that resides within our breasts." It was impossible for Smith to foresee that the dominant force in free enterprise would become not people but an amoral entity—the capital market—in which personal virtues of empathy, conscience, concern and self-restraint are a poor match for the countervailing and abstract power of financial markets to nurture, rationalize, reward and even exalt our most selfish tendencies. It is here that "self-interest" displays its most anthropocentric face. Paradoxically, the damage is often done collectively through investments in the name of individuals who, if they knew, would oppose the damage done in pursuit of their financial interests.

If, indeed, this aspect of free enterprise is allowed to undermine the values that comprise its very foundation, then modern-day capitalism risks becoming unmanageable. The current owners of capitalism's primary actor, the corporation, need quickly to recognize, as UCLA professor James Q. Wilson points out, "that, while free markets will ruthlessly eliminate inefficient firms, the moral sentiments of man will only gradually and uncertainly penalize immoral ones. But, while the quick destruction of inefficient corporations threatens only individual firms, the slow anger at immoral ones threatens capitalism—and thus freedom itself."[18]

If we are to evoke a genuinely sustainable capitalism, tomorrow's corporations must embrace multiple bottom lines. Fortunately, business will be drawn in this direction by the same three market forces that presently discipline corporate managers: product markets, capital markets and boards of directors. Increasingly well-attuned consumers will demand products with more sustainability content. "Green and clean" are product features already touted by astute marketers. Similarly, financial markets will raise the cost of capital to those firms perceived as higher risk because they fail to measure up to prevailing community standards. The "precautionary principle"[19] is fast becoming the norm as more expansive theories of legal liability become commonplace, a development that asbestos, breast implant and tobacco industry executives (and their shareholders) discovered to their chagrin. In the 1980s, federal "Super Fund" rules imposed on firms the costs of hazardous waste cleanup even though their activity was not illegal when the hazards were created. That served notice that shareholders can be exposed to substantial liabilities by retroactive legislation or by court judgments.

A Question of Policy Focus

Once persuaded that sustainability is an appropriate standard for decision-making, the question then becomes where corporate and public policy might best be focused. In its call for a shift toward sustainable business practices, the World Business Council for Sustainable Development (made up of the Chairs/CEOs of 125 large multinational companies) argued that "clean, equitable growth remains the greatest problem within the larger challenge of sustainable development."[20]

That suggests a policy focus on two fronts. The first is how best to ensure that the market values genuinely clean growth, particularly in a pricing environment (product pricing, share pricing) that largely ignores environmental costs. The second is how to open free enterprise to broader, more equitable participation. I suggest that these concerns are related in ways we are only just beginning to understand. We may find that both concerns can be addressed by ensuring that a component of economic growth is owned by those whose lives will be most directly affected if that growth is not undertaken in an environmentally sound fashion. Sustainability has local roots. Acid rain is not an abstraction; it begins with a specific facility in a specific location emitting identifiable toxins that travel in highly predictable patterns. Similarly, when solvents show up in an aquifer, it is because of a particular producer at a specific locale manufacturing explicit products for specific clients.

Though we can often identify the immediate physical cause of environmental damage, little attention has been paid to identifying the underlying *institutional* cause, particularly the economic and social conditions that evoke, mask, condone or even reward such behavior. One of the key challenges to sustainability is the notion that every environmental problem can be tackled by a technical or regulatory fix—cleaner refrigerants, a better smokestack scrubber, stiffer penalties, quicker clean-up and so forth. Though technical, regulatory and after-the-fact remedies are all helpful, a *contextual* solution is also required. Sustainability also involves prevention, knowing that it is better to build a fence at the top of the cliff than station ambulances below.

For example, imagine an annual shareholders' meeting of an electric power company at which a question is raised about the potential effect on the community from the disposal of the utility's effluents. Imagine further that there is potential for long-term damage to the health of that community's children depending on the choice of waste-disposal method. There's nothing quite like a contingent of concerned, vocal and *empowered* parents showing up at a shareholders' meeting *as shareholders*. That change in context would change both the tone and the content of that meeting, transforming what is typically an impersonal, financially oriented, detached discussion into a forum in which emotional, nonfinancial, personal and moral concerns all would play a part.

Broadening the range of opinions presented (and feedback solicited) could result in a very different decision-making process, particularly where the environmental effects are local but uncertain or difficult to quantify.

As Matthew Connelly and Paul Kennedy point out, this preference for personalized, community-focused feedback finds ample support in anthropology:

> *The human capacity for adaptive response evolved in face-to-face interactions. Humanity's strong suit is quick response to environmental cues—a response more likely to be appropriate when the relevant environment is immediate and local. The mind's horizon is here and now. Our ancestors evolved and had to succeed in small groups that moved around relatively small territories. They had to succeed one day at a time—or not be anyone's ancestors. So, unsurprisingly, signals that come from the local environment are powerfully motivating.*
>
> *Let the globalists step aside. One-world solutions do not work. Local solutions will. Everywhere people act in accord with their perception of their best interests. People are adept at interpreting local signs to find the next move needed.[21]*

Feedback-Enhanced Capitalism

A key hypothesis of *The Ownership Solution* is the very Adam Smith notion that, given an opportunity to do so, people will act in their own best interest, and this will include sound environmental practices. The challenge lies in ensuring they are given that chance. Here I examine just such an opportunity provided by the management of Michigan-based furniture manufacturer Herman Miller, Inc.

Beginning in 1950, Herman Miller introduced participative management practices at a time when the company had 120 employees and annual sales of less than $2 million. In the mid-1970s, the introduction of "open plan" office systems (where work space is defined by modular panels) pushed the company into a growth spurt. Sales grew to $175 million by 1979 and its worldwide workforce to twenty-five hundred. Beginning in 1983, every full-time employee became a shareholder, providing a foundation for their participative management style. The company has since become the second largest furniture company in the United States (ranked by revenue) and 869th on the "*Fortune* 1000" list of industrial and service companies, with 1997 sales of $1.5 billion and a global workforce of seventy-five hundred.

Out of this feedback-intensive environment emerged a national leader in sustainable business practices—a particularly challenging task for a company that relies on a wide range of both natural products (woods, paper, cardboard, fibers) and synthetic chemicals (paints, plastics, varnishes, solvents). Yet, since 1992, Herman Miller's primary production facility has cut by 85 percent the trash it hauls to landfills. Reflecting its commitment to cyclical production (completely eliminating waste from production), in 1997 the company shipped 2 million pounds of scrap fabric to North Carolina, where it was reused as insulation for car-roof linings and dashboard padding, saving the company $50,000 in dumping fees while generating revenue of $100,000. Luggage makers buy its leather scraps for attaché cases. Its "AsNew" program repurchases its used office partitions and refurbishes them for resale. Concluding that it wasn't practical to recycle the eight hundred thousand Styrofoam cups it used each year, the company distributed reusable plastic mugs bearing Buckminster Fuller's slogan "On spaceship earth, there are no passengers . . . only crew."

In pursuit of its "waste-to-energy" philosophy, the heating and air conditioning needs of its headquarters complex are met by a cogeneration facility that converts wood scraps into energy, saving $350,000 in annual gas bills. It also joined the U.S. Environmental Protection Agency's "Green Lights" program, installing energy-saving lighting systems. As with each of their cost-benefit-screened activities, this one also saved money ($100,000 each year since joining in 1991). Realizing that buildings consume some 40 percent of all energy, the company helped establish the U.S. Green Building Council to integrate environmental features into building design and operation. In 1990 Herman Miller realized that its appetite for rosewood, featured in its award-winning Charles Eames lounge chair, was endangering tropical rain forests. Until the company is persuaded it has access to a sustainable source of rosewood, the chair will feature veneers crafted from walnut and cherry.

The company's environmental initiatives fall into three categories: reduce, reuse and recycle. Reusable blanket wrapping has become a preferred shipping method, cutting $250,000 a year from materials and shipping costs by eliminating 70 percent of Styrofoam and cardboard packaging. A supplier of plastic shells for office chairs helped design returnable bins to facilitate the reuse of cardboard and plastic shipping wrap, saving $300,000 a year. Scrap foam rubber is sold to a firm for use in low-grade carpet backing, while large plastic bags are transformed into trash bags. From 1994 to 1997, Herman Miller reduced landfill from 10,000 tons to less than 4,000 tons and increased recycling from 2,500 to 10,700 tons.

Its commitment also affects others with whom it does business. With its focus on "closing the recycling loop," the company announced its preference for environmentally friendly suppliers, using recycled inputs whenever feasible (its corrugated box specifications require 40 percent recycled content). With a "vision statement" describing both the company and its employee-owners as "corporate stewards" of the environment, Herman Miller has succeeded in infusing its operations with a commitment to sustainability. In 1997, *Fortune* magazine ranked Herman Miller second nationwide for corporate and environmental sustainability. The National Wildlife Federation earlier awarded the company its Environmental Achievement Award for its "commitment to earth stewardship," while in 1996 the State of California conferred its Waste

Reduction Award. *Fortune* consistently lists Herman Miller among the top twenty-five most admired American companies, ranking it first in the furniture industry in 1997 for the ninth straight year.

Although other companies have sustainability programs, most are directed from the top, typically pushed along by a top executive with a green streak. What makes Herman Miller unusual is the bottom-up nature of its program. By creating a workplace environment that embraces both financial and workplace participation, and with support for both from within the management ranks, Herman Miller succeeded in creating a corporate environment in which sustainability counts. This story merits telling because the "invisible hand" that drives Herman Miller's sustainability initiatives is largely "on automatic" (which is just what Adam Smith hoped for)—but only because the company was *consciously engineered* so that employees would have not only a voice in how company operations are managed but also a personal "at risk" financial stake in the company through its programs for employee stock ownership. With that dual stake, Herman Miller's empowered insider-owners opted for sustainability—not because it was forced from the outside (or dictated from the top), but because it seemed to them the sensible thing to do.

Such company environments do not emerge spontaneously. That would be like expecting an office building to construct itself without the aid of an architect, engineer or construction company. Participative systems require ongoing organizational and financial engineering, along with a leadership corps committed both to the goals (profitability *and* sustainability) and to the means chosen to achieve those goals—i.e., feedback systems that include both a financial and a workplace culture component.

Built to Last

Herman Miller's story is consistent with recent research showing that America's most successful companies do not remain successful because of their leadership or because they were founded on some terrific idea. Rather, they remain top performers over the long term because they instill employee commitment capable of surviving no matter who is CEO or how the market shifts. According to *Built to Last* by Stanford professors James Collins and Jerry Porras, in those companies with strong company cultures, employees share such a strong vision and mission that they know in their hearts what is right for the company.[22] Paradoxically, that requires managers with enough foresight (and humility) to make companies "management proof."

Herman Miller's success in evoking sustainable business practices is helping it on other fronts as well. Because many of today's most pressing issues are *systems* problems (economic, environmental, social) requiring systems solutions, it should come as no surprise that savvy customers are demanding more systems-savvy goods and services. The early evidence suggests that firms catering to this new sensitivity will prosper compared to those that don't. Tomorrow's successful products are likely to have a much higher "sustainability content"—appealing not only to the self-interest of consumers but also to their broader interests, including a cleaner environment.

Astute marketers realize that consumers are no longer "sold" products; they now need to be instructed, even trained, regarding why and how to buy. This implies more information-intensive marketing, designed both to educate and to differentiate. Such marketing is becoming easier (and more effective) as ecological literacy rates rise, which, in turn, will generate more sustainability-branded companies. Herman Miller's rigorous cost-benefit screening (green projects must also save money) suggests that such companies will also push their competitors in this direction.

As sustainability consultant Paul Hawken, an adviser to Herman Miller, points out: "Companies that create more elegant ways of doing things, that create material and energy flows that are exponentially more efficient will become inefficiency arbitrageurs. They'll force internalization [of costs] onto their competitors because these companies will achieve efficiency at negative or nearly negative costs, which will set the standards for the rest of the industry. This will be the wedge, the foot in the door."[23]

Toward a System of Up-Close Capitalism

One ongoing concern among environmentalists is how to prevent a potentially irreversible "tragedy of the commons." Aristotle was among the first to note that "What is common to the greatest number has the least care bestowed upon it." However, as Hawken reminds us in *The Ecology of Commerce*, "commons" have historically been extremely well regulated by the communities to which they belong. Therein lies the problem. Many of today's commons no longer "belong" to any one community or even any one nation. It is no longer just the town square or local pastureland that is at risk but entire natural systems, including forests that stretch across national borders, fishing beds that underlie the Earth's oceans, and aquifers relied on by hundreds, even thousands of communities.

One clue to the answer lies in the most fundamental assumptions on which present free-enterprise systems are built. Without exception, money managers seek the highest financial return. Financial analysts have an array of yardsticks for measuring that return, including profitability, return on investment, earnings per share, capitalized earnings and the latest entries in the financial sweepstakes: economic value added, market value added and total shareholder return.[24] However, none of these measures includes the expense of dumping or "externalizing" certain "spillover" costs onto the environment, such as acidic emissions released into the air or toxic chemicals leached into rivers and oceans. Today's accounting systems are not designed to score these costs.

In short, the market's primary feedback mechanisms fail to signal the true costs of production. Consequently, when inaccurately priced sales show up in company revenues (and, in turn, are reflected in share prices), the result is at best misleading and at worst deceptive. Even the beguiling notion of profit can be a seductive misrepresentation if it attracts more investment into an activity that treats as private gain the consumption or destruction of public goods—irreplaceable natural resources, clean air, water. Though price signals are clearly essential to a market economy, it's equally clear that price signals alone are insufficient. Complementary forms of feedback are required.

In my opinion, that needed signaling system awaits a political and commercial climate adept at evoking forms of ownership that are more personalized, more human-sized and more attuned to the needs of the immediate environs. Paradoxically, it is precisely by involving more "selves" in the "self-design" of free enterprise that capitalism will become less imperiled by rampant self-interest. By my reckoning, it is partly the detached and disconnected nature of today's capitalism that fosters such self-centeredness. If I limit my interest in my mutual fund solely to the financial return it generates, there's very little reason for me to shift from a human-centered to a more biocentric worldview.[25] Experience suggests that a sustainability-sensitive perspective is more likely to emerge where I own a stake in something nearby.

Needed: Distributed Ownership and Networked Operations

This up-close signaling strategy for sustaining both communities and the environment is not so far-fetched as it may first sound. On an operational basis, the Fortune 100 largest industrial companies are often small to mid-sized companies. A survey by Barry Stein at Boston's Goodmeasure, Inc. found that even as far back as the mid-1970s, the average number of employees per production site was less than three hundred.[26] Stein concludes that the *diseconomies* of scale, those costs that increase with size, are largely the result of huge aggregations of ownership and control, including (at the time) large numbers of middle managers required for coordination. Corporate size also often reflects managerial empire-building along with the cross-subsidization of poorly performing units by other operations.

Even after the recent reengineering movement reduced the ranks of mid-level managers, the ownership point remains: these corporate giants are combinations of, in most cases, relatively small operations linked by common ownership. What, then, are the limits to useful and efficient reductions in firm size? And what might be the effect if, along with this de-conglomeratization, their workforces, suppliers, distributors and community residents became partial owners? The sustainability benefits of such change could be substantial— as could a range of other more conventional effects: efficiency, productivity, and so forth. For instance, the generation of new ideas and their applications are far more common in small than in large firms. Smaller firms also tend to be more flexible and more responsive to change (economic, social, environmental) because they can perceive the need for change more accurately (being less insulated) and, just as a small ship can maneuver more easily, smaller firms respond more rapidly, including making changes required to respond to signals from the local environment.

Kevin Kelly, editor of *Wired*, argues from a systems perspective that the organizational issue lies in how best to coordinate "networked intelligence."

> *One can imagine the future shapes of companies by stretching them until they are pure network. A company that was pure network would have the following traits:* distributed, decentralized, collaborative, and adaptive. . . .
>
> *Where does the company end and the supplier start? Customers are being roped into the* distributed company *just as fast. Ubiquitous 800 numbers just about ring on the factory floor, as the feedback of users shapes how and what the assembly line makes. . . .*
>
> *We'll coordinate as a network,* sharing information and control, *decentralizing functions between us. It will be hard at times to tell who is working for whom.*[27]

The analysis of Stein and Kelly suggests the obvious: sustainability could be enhanced by a more distributed and decentralized form of ownership—to match what are already relatively small, distributed and decentralized operations. The goal would be to rely less on common corporate control as the means to coordinate activities and instead rely on collaborative (networked) intelligence and information. Properly understood, information technology is less about replacing people than it is about connecting them to each other and to their customers, suppliers, distributors—that network of which they are already an inescapable part. The network technology required to support that vision is fast becoming a reality. In May 1997, Microsoft announced a major shift in its paradigm whereby it will compete head-on with IBM, Oracle, Sun Microsystems and others to popularize network computers, combining centralized computing capacity with decentralized terminals.*

Technology-wise, this is poised to be the next logical step in organizational development. Looking back, we can see that 1980 was the decade we officially entered the information age. Prior to 1981, capital expenditures for industrial equipment surpassed amounts spent on information-processing equipment. The crossover year was 1981. By 1996, only $129 billion was spent on industrial equipment while $212 billion was spent on information-processing

---

* As this book was going to press, five major companies were working collaboratively on the development of common standards for a new Internet-based "platform" that could function with any type of operating system or hardware much as different brands of telephones work when plugged into the telephone network. See Elizabeth Corcoran, "Joining Forces Against Microsoft," *Washington Post,* National Weekly Edition, 24 November 1997, p. 18.

and related equipment.[28] In 1997, *The New York Times* reports that total information technology spending in the United States was an estimated $454.5 billion, including $154.2 billion for technology problem-solving (up from $61.4 billion in 1992). Business spending represents 88 percent of the total.[29]

Deconcentration could also sharpen corporate focus by accelerating the trend toward "corporate clarity," responding to an investor preference for firms that stick to their "core competence." Frederic Escherich, a corporate finance manager at J. P. Morgan, evaluated the "business clarity" of 830 U.S. firms, each with a market capitalization of more than $500 million at the end of 1994. When firms narrow their focus, he found that their shares outperform the market by an average of 11 percent, whereas broadly diversified firms underperform the market by 4 percent.[30]

At the same time that mergers and acquisitions grew in size and popularity during the 1990s,[31] so too did corporate spin-offs.[32] During 1995, 25 major spin-offs totaling $27 billion were completed.[33] During 1996, twenty-six major deals totaled almost $50 billion. Westinghouse, Monsanto, General Instruments, AT&T—all have done major spin-offs driven by the push to generate shareholder value through corporate "focus." According to a study by professors at Penn State University, the spun-off entities typically thrived, with stocks of spin-offs outperforming both the market and their peers by 25 to 30 percent over the three years following the spin-off: they invested more, their sales rose faster and their operating income expanded more rapidly.

That trend continues. 3M's data storage and medical imaging division was spun off in 1996, creating Imation, a $2.3 billion publicly traded company. Its 12,700 employees are involved in a profit-sharing plan and a plan designed to enable them to share in up to 5 percent of the company.[34] With the prodding of a supportive policy environment, this process could ensure that a significant employee share scheme is made a part of each spun-off enterprise, thereby simultaneously "localizing" and "ownerizing" these entities.

Rest assured: policy input is *essential*. Without it, the ownership of these divested operations is certain to follow conventional investment banking practice, whereby divestitures are structured to benefit either another corporation or a group of absentee investors (typically organized by the investment bankers) while the employee ownership component (if any) is limited to those employed as senior executives. For example, in February 1997 Lockheed Martin announced a $650 million spin-off of ten "noncore" divisions with five thousand employees to a newly created company. Who are the new owners? The company will be jointly owned, 50 percent by a Lehman Brothers Holdings Inc. partnership, 35 percent by Lockheed Martin and 15 percent by a team of senior managers.

America's "cognitive elite" (its investment bankers, lawyers and accountants) would welcome the opportunity to split these conglomerates into smaller entities so that their scale of ownership better matches their scale of operations.

Investment capital should be readily available, especially if the institutional investor community is persuaded of the enhanced returns (financial and otherwise) available from a decentralization/ownerization strategy. That's a real possibility judging from the research documenting the benefits that accompany corporate "focus," particularly when employee financial participation is introduced alongside employee participation in workplace decision-making.[35] This "localization" of ownership should also attract the financial support of community banks, further facilitating transactions.*

Much as Adam Smith extolled the market's invisible hand as a disembodied entity operating through the collective will of countless individual decision-makers, so too could an "invisible network" of up-close owners (employees, suppliers, consumers, community residents) advance the environmental agenda by ensuring that the views of those physically closest to corporate operations are taken into account. The locally attuned "networked intelligence" that could emerge to inform corporate decision-making is one of the key missing ingredients in today's detached, disconnected and dangerously aloof capitalism. As Kelly suggests, the goal should be to create companies that are "distributed, decentralized, collaborative, and adaptive."

Needed: Posterity-Focused Production

There's another key element to be considered in reengineering free enterprise for sustainability. Carl Hahn, chairman of Volkswagen AG, suggests: "If we think of the future—a central part of the obligation to rising generations—we must adopt the *cyclical approach* on which the whole of nature is based." If that sentiment is carried to its logical end, we reach the same conclusion as Paul Hawken in *The Ecology of Commerce* where he argues that we must "rearrange our relationship to resources from a linear to a cyclical one" by *completely eliminating waste from production*. Rather than try to dispose of, store or recycle toxic by-products, he advises, "we need to design systems of production that have little or no waste to begin with."[38]

Hawken collaborator William McDonough insists that this does not mean conventional recycling, which he lampoons as a dangerous form of "down-cycling"—the conversion of waste into other, less usable products. McDonough

---

* To finance the employee-ownership component of these newly independent firms, companies selling off units could agree to accept ESOP notes (IOUs) from the divested operations. Those notes, in turn, could be bundled into marketable securities ("securitized") and sold to institutional investors, including the pension plans of other companies.[36] In cases where an ESOP is combined with other ownership-broadening strategies (such as ownership by those employed by a company's suppliers or distributors),[37] this decentralization strategy could also help narrow the gap between the concentrated power typically found in corporate entities and the dispersed power represented by consumers and communities, resurrecting a theme that animated the nation's original antitrust legislation.

recommends instead "cradle-to-cradle" design, offering as an example Interface, Inc., an Atlanta-based carpet-tile manufacturer that leases carpet. Instead of replacing the carpet every seven years or so, Interface offers to maintain it indefinitely through an "Evergreen Lease," periodically replacing the 20 percent of carpet tiles that get 80 percent of the wear. Interface is developing technology that will use recovered carpet as a technical nutrient for rendering into another carpet. Along with Amory Lovins of Colorado's Rocky Mountain Institute, Hawken and McDonough suggest a similar ownership solution to reduce the waste associated with the production of consumer durables—proposing that cars, ovens, refrigerators, computers and the like be leased rather than sold. Manufacturers would retain ownership as a way to ensure a return of their products for refabrication into the next generation of consumer durables. Mitsubishi Electric is setting up "take-back centers" throughout Japan to receive appliances manufactured by both Mitsubishi and its competitors, disassemble them, and reprocess the materials into new products. Information learned in the disassembly will be linked to product design teams who will design new products that can be disassembled and remanufactured.

McDonough and German chemist Michael Braungart suggest that we think of products as *services* rather than as *things* to be used and then discarded. Thus "products of service" would include cars (transportation services), refrigerators (cooling our food) and so on. The user would lease the service, while ownership would remain with the manufacturer who, in turn, would be obliged to design products so that they have value when they are returned (as in nature), not just when they leave the factory. Customers (versus "consumers") could keep a product indefinitely. Or they could sell it to someone else. Or return it to a "de-shopping center," where it would be returned to the manufacturer for reuse and remanufacturing.

That would be accompanied by a design science dedicated to reducing material intensity per unit of service. Scandic Hotel's new rooms (servicing the traveler's sleeping needs) are 97 percent reusable and recyclable. They cost 15 percent more today but will save enormous sums down the road. As Interface CEO Ray Anderson sees it, the company delivers the benefits of carpet tile— color, texture, warmth, beauty, acoustics, comfort under foot—but continues to own the means of delivery, theoretically for as long as the building stands, with Interface retaining the "landfill liability."[39] Cochair of the President's Council on Sustainable Development, Anderson calls this approach the science of "EcoMetrics"—the search for a scale that weighs such diverse factors as toxic waste, aquifer depletion, CO_2 emission and nonrenewable resource depletion. The goal, he insists, is not to make companies merely sustainable but restorative—putting back more then they take from the earth. His goal is to see Interface (1997 sales exceeded $1 billion) become the first name in industrial ecology worldwide.

Despite the best of corporate intentions, certain services show up as "unmarketables"—compounds like persistent toxins, radioactive isotopes and bioaccumulative chemicals. In a creative use of ownership, McDonough and Braungart suggest that these "products as service" should belong to the manufacturer in perpetuity and be "molecularly tagged" with the maker's mark. Thus, legal liability would be traceable to the manufacturer if, say, a toxic chemical shows up in my well water or a bioaccumulative chemical in my liver. McDonough, the "green dean" of architecture at Thomas Jefferson's University of Virginia, puts a historical spin on environmental responsibility, suggesting in a "Declaration of Interdependence" that we have an obligation to leave to our descendants an environment free from "remote intergenerational tyranny"— much as America's founding fathers left their descendants free of the remote *political* tyranny of England's King George III: "The question is no longer what are we going to leave behind for our children," McDonough argues, "but what are we *not* leaving behind? . . . If we permanently destroy genetic information and don't leave that as a resource, and we persistently toxify the planet, what we have left is a poisoned place, devoid of valuable information."[40]

The U.S. Constitution implies that sustainability is a legal obligation, committing its citizens not only to preserve liberty (which implies free markets) but also to "promote the general welfare, and secure the blessings of liberty to ourselves *and our posterity*" (emphasis added). The question is one of balance. To allow free enterprise such free rein that we bequeath the next generation a depleted, ravaged or endangered environment is a clear breach not only of that express social contract but also of an implied intergenerational covenant.

Eco-pioneer Gunter Pauli makes the case for what he calls "zero emission economics," arguing in *Breakthrough* that "waste from one industry, in whatever form, must become an input factor for another business."[41] As director of the Zero Emissions Research Initiative at the United Nations University in Tokyo, he suggests that "clusters" will begin to shape corporate site strategies as companies locate near each other because they *need* each others' waste. Cities and counties will target specific investments because they realize that by attracting one company, they are likely to attract another while at the same time solving an environmental problem. "For the first time," Pauli suggests, "improving industrial efficiency, securing investments, implementing inner city development, and enhancing sustainable social and economic development can go hand in hand."

A Key Barrier: Ecological Illiteracy

While zero-emission economics, cradle-to-cradle design and products-as-service may serve well as an ideal, conversion could be an economically wrenching and politically difficult task if implemented too rapidly. More fundamentally, conversion requires a level of ecological literacy now widely lacking. Ask the average American the source of heat in his home and he is likely to point to his furnace. Inquire where his human waste goes and he may well show you his toilet. To a surprising extent, even well-educated people are profoundly ignorant of the extent to which their patterns of consumption and elimination are part of a larger, natural system.

If ever we hope to achieve cyclical production, there will need to be both a constituency for change and a constituency empowered to effect that change. However, most people remain connected to their economy by only the most tenuous of threads: a job. Imposing environmental charges on corporations (such as requiring the internalizing of environmental costs) forces a difficult choice, particularly where the cost of labor may already be the firm's most controllable expense. The uncomfortable truth is that a new round of environmental costs or regulations may be accompanied by yet another round of layoffs and labor retrenchments.

It's difficult to argue with the science suggesting that production systems must evolve into "closed systems," with a rigorous redesign of both inputs and outputs. That laudable goal, I submit, is more likely to be achieved as our organizational systems become increasingly "open"—incorporating feedback from those whose lives the firm affects. In my ownership "systems" view of the world, I see that happening most naturally (as at Herman Miller) as we succeed in transforming a company's stakeholders into property-empowered shareowners. As a firm's "natural owners" become *genuine* owners, the needed "greening" of production will gain acceptability, adaptability and hands-on support.

The silver lining in the challenge of sustainability lies in the potential it holds for awakening mankind to a more holistic way of thinking, and to the necessity of reflecting this thinking in the reengineering of his laws and institutions. This awakening could come remarkably quickly, particularly as communications reach ever more broadly into the world community and shape the very image that man has of himself and his place in the web of life. Ecologists recommend a very simple personal standard for people to keep in mind whenever contemplating an action that may have environmental consequences: "What if everyone did it?" I recommend that same standard when contemplating the consequences of up-close ownership patterns: "What if everyone did it?"

CHAPTER **11**

Community Without the Communism

What life have you if you have not life together?
There is no life that is not in community,
And no community not lived in praise of God....

When the Stranger says:"What is the meaning of this city?
Do you huddle close together because you love each other?"
What will you answer? "We all dwell together
To make money from each other"? or "This is a community"?

T.S. Eliot, Choruses from "The Rock"

Never in recorded history have such systemic changes been under way in so many nations at one time—whether in the unwinding of the Soviet Union, the emergence of Asia as an economic powerhouse or the uniting of America's Western allies into a European Union. In this ongoing search for new paradigms, neither collective-oriented socialism nor myopically individualist capitalism is likely to prove satisfactory. That's because neither system accounts for the full array of linkages that weave a people into a community, whether that community is defined culturally, geographically or by common economic concerns. Something new is required that can reconcile the overlapping moralities of individuals, the community and the marketplace.

This chapter suggests that a new synthesis is emerging, one that views ownership matter-of-factly as a social tool for linking people not only to things (productive assets) but also to each other, to their community and (importantly) to their endangered environment. With the benefit of hindsight, policymakers in both the public and private sector can sort through history's dustbin of failed ownership solutions (collectivization, plutocratization, etc.) and construct a political and commercial environment that evokes the best features of those that flourished, while avoiding those that failed. Where successful, this ownership engineering will succeed in incorporating the best features of capitalism while answering the charges of capitalism's harshest critics. This is not meant to suggest that other components of a nation's social capital are unimportant—families, civic associations and such. However, I contend that a poorly conceived ownership policy (or none at all) is certain to undermine attempts to strengthen civil society.

Francis Fukuyama, former deputy director of policy planning at the State Department, argues that the United States has been living off its social capital.[1] Replenishing that capital is a complicated and in many ways a mysterious process. "While governments can enact policies that have the effect of depleting social capital," Fukuyama notes, "they have great difficulties understanding how to build it up again."[2] The difficulty stems from the fact that social capital arises not out of rules and regulations but instead "out of a set of ethical habits and reciprocal moral obligations internalized by each of the community's members."

Research on the component of civil society that most affects people's waking lives (i.e., work), suggests the time is ripe for some creative paradigm-shifting to restore depleted social capital in the work environment. Managers know that their best employees expect more from their jobs than just monetary income. The high-performance, high-retention companies are those that operate with values-based management systems that generate both monetary and psychic income.[3] "Values are like organizational DNA," according to *Healthy Companies* author Bob Rosen. "They also set the first stage for helping employees decide if a company is the right place for them."[4] A company is no longer just about making money, it's also got to make meaning.

Similarly, today's effective corporate leader is no longer just a manager; he or she must also be able to set out a broad vision and create a culture of commitment. Today's high-impact management practices include not only the standard, contractual issues of pay and benefits but also how to create a workplace environment where employees have an opportunity to develop their full human potential. Generation X is particularly emphatic that interesting work, not just money and position, is a key motivator.[5]

From Contract to Covenant

Economists have long professed, and managers have often believed, that people will perform well only if they see something in it for themselves. This narrow interpretation of Adam Smith's notion of self-interest is the bedrock upon which much of modern economic science is built. It also serves as a core assumption of market-based economic analysis.[6] Like most conventional wisdom, it is partly true. However, corporate managers have discovered another powerful motivating force: the potential inherent in making it possible for people to give of themselves to one another.

Managers at the Herman Miller Company were taught this commonsense lesson decades ago by the company's founder, D. J. DePree, a lesson kept alive by his son, Max DePree, recently retired chairman of the board.[7] The genesis of Herman Miller's management style dates from the 1920s, when DePree's father became the company's major shareholder and, shortly thereafter, was faced with the death of a key employee, the millwright. When the elder DePree stopped by the millwright's home, the widow inquired if he would like to hear some poetry. He replied yes and soon found himself genuinely touched by the beauty of the poems.

When DePree asked the name of the poet, the widow replied that the poet was her late husband. To this day, managers at Herman Miller are reminded to ask themselves: Was this employee a millwright who occasionally wrote poetry? Or was he a poet who also worked as a millwright? That insight evolved over the years into the Herman Miller management philosophy that companies, like the people who comprise them, are always in a state of becoming. Much as a faculty and staff *are* a university, a company can never become something that its people are not. Thus, they concluded that the firm's leaders serve best by helping make the workplace a place of *realized potential*, a place where people can become their very best.

Herman Miller managers (called "leaders") are reminded that they have not just a commercial *contract* with those employed there but also a personal *covenant*—to provide a workplace environment designed with the goal of self-realization in mind. To reach that ambitious goal, DePree realized that the workplace must become an environment characterized by high-quality relationships. That, in turn, calls for a particular type of leadership. In formulating that leadership, DePree, a devout Christian, drew for his inspiration from the Book of Luke, which advises that a leader is "one who serves."[8]

DePree argues that corporate leaders serve best by transforming their companies into communities—in the knowledge that relationships are more important than management structures. He concludes that Herman Miller succeeds in creating this culture because the company also created a corporate architecture consistent with that theme. How? By ensuring that each position is staffed by someone who is both an employee *and* an owner. A telling remark in DePree's 1989 best-seller, *Leadership Is an Art,* captures the essence of what this management philosophy is about: company managers report that when someone visits their company they want them to say, "Those folks are a gift to the Spirit."

People-based Performance

Does this person-oriented, relationship-based management philosophy really work? All we know for certain is that it has worked for Herman Miller over an extended period. For instance, over the 1977–1986 period, the company ranked seventh nationwide in total return to investors, realizing a 41 percent annual compound return. Herman Miller shares bought in 1986 at $19 were selling for $53 in January 1998 after a 2:1 stock split, ranking it sixth among the NASDAQ's one hundred fastest appreciating stocks for 1997, with a one-year increase of 92.7 percent. It is also the most productive company in its industry in terms of net income per employee, even while outspending its competition two to one on research and development. As for nonfinancial indicators, the company has been prominently featured in each edition of *The 100 Best Companies to Work for in America*. In addition, two prominent women's magazines, *Ms.* and *Working Women,* have repeatedly given the company high marks for addressing issues of particular concern to women in the workforce.[9]

The psychological insights of DePree's father have since become mainstream. As yet, however, few companies have embraced them as their operating philosophy. That may be because corporate managers find it disconcerting to discover the full extent of the duties they are now expected to perform and the interpersonal skills they need to possess. Psychiatrist and author Scott Peck (best known for the successful self-help book *The Road Less Traveled*) sums up today's management challenge thus: "Managers create the environment in which people can flourish or shrink. . . . I think management is the highest spiritual calling there is." The late Jonas Salk, inventor of the polio vaccine, put today's management challenge in historical perspective:

> *Major developments in the realm of human relations are as important today as was the advent of agriculture 10,000 years ago or the understanding of microbes and machines in the past couple of centuries. The challenge of evoking the best in us may seem utterly forbidding but, surely, no more so than previously "impossible" challenges—heavier-than-air flight, electricity, space travel.*

It should come as no surprise to find that people-oriented corporate cultures are fast becoming an essential ingredient in evoking superior performance, particularly in retaining top-performing "knowledge" workers.

Corporation as Community

Over the past few decades, the corporate entity has proven itself sufficiently adaptable, flexible and successful that it has emerged as the world's most common task-oriented organization, supplanting all but the nation-state as an embodiment of the human will. As a creature of contract, it is endowed with immortality. Though its shareholders may die, the entity lives on. The term *company* stems from the same Latin root as *companion*—someone with whom you break bread—suggesting that a company is a collection of companions bound together for a common purpose. What more natural setting for the emergence of nonfinancial, noncommercial values than where people spend the bulk of their waking hours?

The corporate entity is destined to become even more prevalent. Visionary corporate leaders may yet emerge as our first true global leaders. The steady spread of this relatively new organizational entity suggests the gradual emergence of a new notion of community, one very different from its original connotation as a geographically specific "place." Today's large companies often have production and service sites spread across the globe. Asea Brown Boveri, the Swiss/Swedish engineering giant, employs more than two hundred thousand people in over five thousand profit centers worldwide. It's not unusual for a multinational corporation to operate in several dozen countries with more than one hundred work sites.

To create a sense of community around such a dispersed workforce suggests the need for mechanisms capable of fostering a place-transcendent notion of belonging. Where successful, the payoffs can be quite substantial. "Introduce genuine community into your business," Peck advises, "and you will guarantee its ethical integrity." In a similar vein, Marjorie Kelly, editor and publisher of *Business Ethics*, suggests that this unique era in human history represents the emergence of "a higher organizational life form." Dr. Peck agrees, arguing: "We're on the end of an industrial/technological revolution, and at the beginning of an organizational evolution in group consciousness."

As an organizational tool, the corporation can be used either to advance or impede a range of social objectives. Social philosopher and theologian Ivan Illich offers a novel way of looking at the various tools, whether physical or organizational, that can enrich or impoverish life, including life within an enterprise. In his 1973 classic, *Tools for Conviviality*, he points out that

> *People need new tools to work with rather than tools that "work" for them. . . . Tools are intrinsic to social relationships. An individual relates himself in action to his society through the use of tools that he actively masters, or by which he is passively acted upon. To the degree that he masters his tools, he can invest the world with his meaning; to the degree that he is mastered by his tools, the shape of the tool determines his own self-image. Convivial tools are those which give each person who uses them the greatest opportunity to enrich the environment with the fruits of his or her vision.*

With the corporate entity now the world's most prevalent organizational tool, it is essential that this tool become as convivial as possible. The evidence suggests that efforts to enhance conviviality can have dramatic payoffs, not only in enhanced performance (in the traditional sense of productivity, profitability, etc.) but also in protecting the natural world while nurturing the human spirit. Though that may not be nirvana, surely it reflects a major advancement in the human condition.

New Frontiers of Community

Notwithstanding the myopia of radical free-market theorists, a nation is more than a collection of customers, clients and consumers. A nation's well-being can be measured by its success at building and sustaining a sense of community, a role that typically requires organizational input from the state. In the future, we are certain to see a continuation of this ever shifting balance between state and market, public and private. Governments have the potential to do substantial good, yet they can be oppressive and horrifically inefficient. Markets can be extremely useful, advancing the human condition in ways that are unimaginable in centrally run economies. But they can also be harmful and oppressive, generating human and environmental horrors in their relentless search for financial returns.

Similarly, private property can be brutal, even inhumane, excluding vast numbers from even a modest standard of living when concentrated in the hands of a few. Yet private property can also protect essential political rights, providing security, even sanctuary. Both markets and property are human tools that can be engineered either to advance or degrade the human condition. Convivial or not, in combination such tools form the institutional skeleton of all advanced economies. No one suggests that we go backward. The challenge lies in how best to proceed forward.

Theorists ranging from theologians to politicians have spent the past century struggling with the friction between markets and Marx, capitalism and community, private and public property, and practicality and ideology. Pope John Paul II suggests that the challenge is to focus on the "social ecology of work" in order to create "more authentic forms of living in community" as an antidote to the alienation that permeates both socialist and capitalist economies. "Human work," he insists, "by its nature is meant to unite peoples, not divide them."[10] As Harvard Business School professor Michael Jensen puts it: "Companies will understand the need to rebind the corporation and create a sense of community again. The ones that do that will be the winners in the next stage of competition."[11]

The Search for Societal Glue

People once lived in genuine communities. In the developing world, many still do. Certain aspects of economic development are clearly an improvement on life in lesser developed countries. However, if the notion of community is abandoned in the name of development, what will replace it? This longing for a sense of belonging is palpable and real. The erosion of community in developed countries has come slowly, much like the Oriental notion of "death by a thousand cuts." Some of the changes have been subtle, often related to small links in the chain of economic efficiency. For instance, automated bank-teller machines eliminate the small talk that previously accompanied routine banking transactions. The gas station self-service pump does the same, as do drive-through fast-food eateries, postage stamp machines and other labor-saving conveniences common to modern-day life. The human element in such everyday transactions is part of the social adhesive that helps bind a community. This sense of connection and continuity contributes to social cohesion, social concern and the robustness of civil society.

As communitarian philosopher Amitai Etzioni phrases it, "What we need is a new concept that explicitly recognizes that every mosaic requires some framework and glue."[12] This glue is coming undone in the siege mentality that grips parts of the United States. A key symptom: by 1995, the U.S. prison population had grown to 1.4 million from 350,000 since 1973. America's rate of imprisonment rose at five times that of Western Europe, with 519 people in prison per 100,000; Western European nations average from 60 to 100 per 100,000.[13]

This is not meant to suggest that, in the name of community, we resurrect low-paying, routine service jobs. However, the modern world's daily diet of isolation and abstraction is taking its toll in ways both obvious and subtle. The epidemic of drug use and alcoholism (each day Americans swallow 76 million Valium; 10 million take Prozac or other antidepressants) is partly the reflection of a culture that provides so few opportunities for connection and community, the essential soil in which human concern, social solidarity and democracy have always grown.

The expanding breadth and depth of this disconnectedness is associated with a broad range of social pathologies from which we may yet learn. For example, the United States was once home to hundreds of orphanages, a trend that has since been reversed as research found it far better for children to grow up connected to real families and real communities than to live apart. In an analogous finding, 1994 research by Brett Brown of Child Trends found that more than 10 percent of young Americans are "disconnected" for at least an entire year between the ages of sixteen and twenty-three: they are not in school, working, in the military or married to someone who is. The rate is 23 percent for black males. One sign of the "pathology of disconnectedness": young men who were disconnected for at least twenty-six weeks in three or more years had, by the time they reached their late twenties, less than 50 percent the annual family income of those who had never been disconnected.

The Economics of Place

This theme of disconnectedness runs deep in the psyche of those who live in modern market economies. A sense of being left out and left behind is reflected in a host of nationwide surveys. This suggests the need for organizations that nurture a sense of "place," the foundation on which communities have traditionally been built. Fritz Schumacher once noted, by way of illustration, that it is possible to become protein self-sufficient by relying on silvaculture, the harvesting of protein-rich nuts (walnuts, hazelnuts, almonds, pecans, etc.).[14] The problem: establishing tree stock takes time—and an allegiance to place. The impermanence and literal "uprootedness" fostered by modern notions of economic participation—such as labor mobility—erode both the incentive and the means to stay put. As with the disincentive to plant tree stock, today's transience undermines the long-term commitment and caring required to put stock in our communities.

The Ownership Solution urges that we not lose any more time in ensuring that people become both connected to their economy and rooted in their community. The alternative is too costly. Consider just one example: a homeowner cannot realize a return on the energy-saving cost of retrofitting his residence for energy efficiency unless he remains in place for at least four to five years, never mind the twenty years required for trees. As yet, no one has attempted to identify and quantify the *diseconomies* that accompany transience, including the intangible costs such as the forgone stewardship, the unformed friendships, or that nagging sense of alienation and aloneness that so often pervades the modern world.

Ethnobiologist Gary Paul Nabhan brings to this analysis a fresh perspective on the important role played by culture and community. Writing in *Cultures of Habitat,* he examines, side by side, two color-coded, county-by-county maps of the United States. The first displays the relative duration of human residency within each county. The second tallies the endangered species. In overlapping the two maps, he finds a near-perfect alignment: where people stayed put longer, fewer plants and animals had becomed endangered. From that he suggests a relationship between community stability and biological diversity or, by extension, between human culture and ecological well-being.[15]

Although mobility has its place (indeed, labor mobility is the Rosetta stone of labor economists), the high value placed on that aspect often undervalues the importance of place and stability. Those institutions that foster a bit *less* mobility could make a major contribution to raising the quality of living and just possibly, the sustainability of all life. More permanence could also enhance values that conventionally trained economists find altogether too imprecise for their financial tastes—values like conviviality, continuity, stability, remembrance, affection, family ties and, yes, community.

Fuzzy Capitalism

This ongoing evolution in organizations is difficult to describe and impossible to categorize, in part because the change is affected by so many factors—financial, social, demographic, cultural and so on. To assist my own thinking, I look to a systems-engineering concept known as "fuzzy logic." Ever since Aristotle, Western thought has decreed that something is either on or off, either an apple or an orange. Fuzzy logicians recognize that in reality things are often a blend—shades of gray rather than black or white.

Fuzzy logic traces its roots to the Orient. I first encountered it in Japan, where farmers are known for such hybrids as the Noshi, a delectable blend of an apple and a pear—not one or the other, but both. Such fuzzy thinking permeates systems engineering. For example, by incorporating fuzzy logic into heating and cooling systems, engineers can save energy with an internal feedback mechanism that anticipates changes in the ambient air (the system's context) so that a climate-control system neither overshoots nor undershoots the intended temperature target.

Emerging developments in the corporate world (and in economics more generally) suggest that a fuzzier logic may yet provide free enterprise with a useful new yardstick by which to measure organizational performance. Ownership lends itself particularly well to fuzzy logic. In determining whether someone is an "owner" or whether an economy is "capitalist," the answer may well lie in the realm of fuzzy logic. For instance, Argentina "privatized" its state-owned telephone company by selling it to a Spanish state-owned telephone company. While that is not quite "capitalism," neither is it the usual brand of socialism.

Consider the classic "fuzzy" question: If from a pile of sand you remove one grain at a time, when does it cease to be a pile of sand? The classic fuzzy answer: it becomes less and less a pile of sand as each grain is removed. Both ownership and capitalism evoke similar answers, socialism too. Consider a real-world situation in which the United Steelworkers of America negotiated for employees a junior lien (a second mortgage) on a specific building until such time as an employer (the building's owner) fully funded its retiree health benefits. Is that "employee ownership"? Well, sort of. I mean it's certainly not NOT ownership. When the health plan became fully funded, the lien expired. So what *was* that? "Fuzzy" ownership?

Property is itself becoming fuzzier. Today's trustee-dominated "institutional capitalism" is a new and decidedly fuzzy form of ownership that is far from fully jelled, particularly when compared with the simple certainties of turn-of-the-century proprietor capitalism. In this decidedly fuzzy era of modern "disconnected" ownership, corporate leaders are likely to experience increasing levels of anxiety due to continuous and often inconclusive negotiations for precise boundaries between rights that are private and clearly shareholder based and those that are more ambiguously stakeholder based.[16]

Such ambiguity is also likely to blur the comfortable certainty of today's financially dominated corporate decision-making. Longer time horizons and broader return criteria, including nonfinancial returns, will become commonplace. Consciously engineered, highly participative ownership strategies—including a steady growth in insider ownership—will continue to make corporate agendas more complex. A certain element of fuzziness should be expected while the search continues for how best to strike a proper balance between those responsibilities that should reside with government and those that rightly belong to the individual, the family, the community or the enterprise.

Needed: An Opportunity to Give

The search is on for an ownership solution that is equitable and efficient, market responsive and consumer empowering, and an economic system in which power (both political and economic) is more proximate and personal. The answer lies in a design solution. This need not mean a solution mandated by government. However, it's naive to expect a solution to emerge *uncoaxed* from the unbridled operations of current capitalism.

What's missing is an appropriately scaled sense of personal "connectivity." A nation-state is simply too vast and too abstract. Citizenship is a fine start, even an essential prerequisite. But that connectivity needs also to take form in a more individualized and community-ized fashion. The opportunities for such connections are widespread. Though doing more with less labor is the hallmark of industrial- and information-age development, it is labor that is most needed to do much of the most important work now required at the community level, including restoring the environment, teaching basic skills (and values), caring for the sick and the infirm,[17] retraining those whose skills have been made technologically obsolete—in short, creating, rejuvenating and preserving local communities and their resources.[18]

With an ownership system that systematically empowers more people, more people could *afford* to volunteer their services on a nonpaid basis. Portions of this work could be partially compensated with vouchers for other services, much like college tuition credits can be earned through service in the U.S. military. At present, much of the work that was previously performed as part of being a member of a family or a community is instead pushed into the marketplace, where it is priced and then financed, often showing up as a rising fiscal burden. That burden, in turn, crowds out other government services (health, education, environmental restoration).

A more sustainable balance must be struck among the diverse needs that underlie human motivation. People want to give to each other—to their spouses, their children, to others in their community. Yet their lives are frequently so consumed with subsistence toil and other demands that they cannot afford to give either of their time or their money. That not only erodes marriages, families and the bonds that comprise community; it also eats away at one's sense of self-worth, reinforcing feelings of inadequacy, isolation, alienation and impotence. In combination, the result is an intensely personal poverty that is both financial and civic, a perverse sort of poverty in which people feel deprived of their capacity to give.[19]

Commentators point to the dearth of great art as a sign that people can no longer afford to create. Others suggest that the fragmentation of the family is due to the fact that people cannot afford to spend more time on relationships. Still others worry that those lacking a relatively secure situation in the present often are little motivated to care for their longer-term future, including the environment. *The Ownership Solution* is a call to the financial leaders of this finance-dominant era to devise ways to finance the future in such a way that a steadily broadening base of Americans can afford to participate in what has long been hailed as the uniquely "human work" of mankind: caring for others, literature, music, the arts, politics, spiritual practices, raising children and so forth.[20] The very human need for such participation, for a sense of *being in community*, is a primary theme underlying this work. Fundamentally, it is this need to which attention must be directed if national leaders hope to contribute to the restoration of civil society and the strengthening of community. Absent that support, Americans are beginning to turn elsewhere for help. In closing this chapter, I'll describe two examples—the use of local currency and community-based lending.

Community-Responsive Money

While serving as special counsel to the New York investment banking firm of Kelso & Company, I often heard a familiar Wall Street refrain, "Money is smarter than people," confirming money's tendency to seek its highest rate of return. Like most such aphorisms, it has a ring of truth. For those who own that money, that process ensures a steady increase in their wealth, particularly if they allow those funds to seek that return without regard to the consequences of their investment, as capital markets routinely do. For others, the impact is decidedly more mixed, particularly as large money-center banks and mutual funds extract savings out of communities (and community banks) and into pools of institutionalized (and globalized) capital—all chasing those same financially denominated returns. Add to that the recent phenomenon of megastores (Wal-Mart, Home Depot, Toys "R" Us) that drain funds from local merchants and customers to distant corporate headquarters, fostering little or no wealth for locals.

Societies become economically and socially stratified in large part according to their citizens' ability to access credit and thereby create and accumulate wealth. Economically depressed communities are invariably net exporters of financial capital, including otherwise resource-rich communities (rich in timber, minerals, petrochemicals) that lack local means for extracting those resources on behalf of local residents. The response to this money-is-smarter phenomenon has been mixed. Oftentimes people have simply followed the money, flocking to urban centers where much of the "value-added" component of production has traditionally clustered, whether for the milling of grain, the production of metals or the manufacture of automobiles.[21]

One of the more innovative responses to this community-corrosive trend is emerging from the New England region of the United States, long known for its "Yankee ingenuity," where locally sensitive currencies (scrip) are gaining in popularity as residents cope with the modern challenges of accessing credit locally.[22] Cut off from conventional sources of money, community residents turned to the logical alternative: they printed their own. For instance, in 1990, delicatessen owner Frank Tortoriello printed five hundred "Deli Dollars" in his close-knit community of Great Barrington, Massachusetts. By selling them for $8 each, he raised the $4,000 he needed to move his shop across the street where his homegrown currency could be redeemed for $10 in deli food. To prevent counterfeiting, he signed each note. This provided him a way to raise the funds that local banks wouldn't lend but local residents would.

This community-backed scrip soon began to circulate. Knowing that the local pastor was a regular deli diner, parishioners dropped Deli Dollars in the offering plate. Secure in the knowledge that its employees liked to eat there, a local construction firm paid its crew partly in Deli Dollars. Much like the original idea behind Federal Reserve notes, these homemade "real bills" were retired from circulation as they were redeemed over a three- to six-month period following the deli's move, with Tortoriello repaying the loan not in Federal Reserve notes but with sandwiches, sodas and the heartfelt thanks of a newly relocated owner.[23] Each Deli Dollar depicts Frank (still cooking) being moved by his customers to his new location.

Community Preserve Notes

Commodity-based scrip is nothing new to the United States, where currencies have been based on everything from land to livestock to lumber. A national currency first became commonplace when President Lincoln issued federal notes to raise funds for the Union's war against the Confederacy. Until then, local banks commonly issued their own currency, backed largely by the confidence of local residents. Scrip again became prevalent during the Depression as a way to mobilize local resources when community residents lacked access to the national currency—a key reason, I expect, that its popularity is returning. It was FDR's New Deal policies and his infusion of Keynes-inspired, demand-stimulating greenbacks that displaced local scrip redeemable only in the surrounding community.

The Schumacher Society describes a typical circumstance surrounding an early issuance of scrip:

> A former editor of the Springfield Union in Massachusetts told us the story of a scrip issued by his newspaper. He was just a copyboy at the paper during the bank failures of the 1930s; he remembers that the publisher, Samuel Bowles, paid his newspaper employees in scrip. It could be spent in the stores which advertised in the paper, and the stores would then pay for ads with the scrip, thus closing the circle. The scrip was so popular that customers began to ask for change in scrip—they saw Bowles every day and had more confidence in his local money than in the federal dollars. Newspaper money kept the Springfield economy flowing during a period of bank closures, facilitating commercial transactions that went well beyond the original intent of the issue.[24]

Since local scrip can only be used locally, residents are encouraged to shop in their community instead of, say, shopping from a mail-order catalog. That often translates into trying new products and services—providing a new market for local businesses that accept the scrip. As part of an initiative to support local farmers, locally minted "greensbacks" were purchased by the federally funded Berkshire Women with Infants and Children (WIC) program to distribute to local families, allowing them to escape the welfare stigma of government-issued food stamps.

Traditional economists may scoff at the homespun nature of this experimentation, pointing to the inefficiency and high transaction costs and the fact that much of this currency is nothing more than a simplified futures contract. Others sense there may be a lesson here for financiers to learn about how to build and preserve community while also giving definition and identity to local cultures. As Wendell Berry points out in *The Work of Local Culture*:

> A human community, if it is to last long, must exert a sort of centripetal force, holding local soil and local memory in place. Practically speaking, human society has no work more important than this. . . . The loss of local knowledge and local memory—that is of local culture—has been ignored, or written off as one of the cheaper "pieces of progress," or made the business of folklorists. Nevertheless, local culture has a value, and part of its value is economic.[25]

Those involved in creating these new financial models, including homemade currencies, view money as a social tool capable of doing more than just seeking its highest return. Local currencies provide a means for a community's residents to "vote" for the kind of small independent businesses that help to make a local economy more self-reliant and personal by encouraging more face-to-face transactions. The widespread loss of *community* in a community is seldom dramatic or even obvious; the change is usually gradual, like quarter turns on a screw.

For example, in 1993 a Washington appeals court threw out a thirty-year-old licensing requirement of the Federal Communications Commission that had long given preference to local over absentee owners to encourage community involvement in the daily management of radio stations. That ruling allowed small stations with community ties to be acquired by distant investors. By further relaxing the ownership rules, Congress kicked off a gold rush, as broadcasting became yet another financial property open to passive investors rather than retaining a preference for hands-on, locally engaged proprietors.

More than one thousand stations changed hands in 1996 in deals totaling $25 billion, up from $8 billion in 1995.[26] Again, the impact is invisible to conventional economic analysis, even though music may now be run by a computer programmed weeks in advance by an out-of-town "time broker" or contract operator offering standard playlists. Financial analysts dismiss as quaint, outdated and irrelevant the notion of local broadcasters who host community-building events by using airtime to honor the teacher of the month, interview the high school sports star, endorse local charitable events or broadcast lost-pet announcements.

This loss of the local and the personal involves costs that conventional finance has no way to measure. Yet that loss is real to those who experience it. All too often, a mismatch of financial value and community values accompanies the workings of conventional capitalism with its incapacity to reflect the valuable in what it values.

Capital Without the Capitalism

Other versions of local scrip are also gaining in popularity, often facilitating the barter-exchange of personal services. For instance, in the Upstate New York town of Ithaca, one "Ithaca Hour" can be used to purchase local services valued at ten dollars, the average hourly wage in Tompkins County, home to Cornell University. A local "penny saver" newspaper lists all Ithaca Hour traders (more than 1,200 individuals and stores trade in the scrip). Local retailers calculate their dollar-denominated overhead and periodically adjust their Ithaca Hour redemption policy in the knowledge that there is only so much of this local currency they can use to pay their bills.[27]

Since local scrip can only be used locally, this feature helps direct more of the community's commercial energy into the community rather than seeing it diverted into New York City. According to Ithaca Hour organizer Paul Glover,

"We're making a community while making a living." For instance, a cash-strapped farmer borrowed Ithaca Hours from a customer who had accumulated an excess, enabling the farmer's family to pay for child care, movie tickets and other local services, repaying the loan with produce from their next harvest. A local credit union accepts scrip in partial payment of mortgage loans because the credit union's employees have agreed to accept a portion of their pay in scrip, secure in the knowledge that they, in turn, can exchange the scrip for local goods and services.

The expanding lack of access to the national currency has resulted in a steady expansion of community currencies nationwide. Several banks in North Dakota cooperated with local chambers of commerce to issue no-interest loans in local scrip during the winter holidays. With that stamp of approval, trade that would normally flow to catalog sales and national chain stores flowed instead to small, locally owned stores that accepted the scrip, providing seasonal jobs and community revenue while also boosting local tax collections. The State of California even issued scrip to public sector workers in 1992 as a short-term loan to bridge a temporary fiscal crisis.

Other communities have also found it useful to use the hour as a unit of account. However, rather than use a labor-backed "fiat" currency, they rely on "time dollars" as a mutual credit system in which credits can be earned for hours worked in services like child care, tutoring or assisting the elderly. The provider can later claim services when he or she needs help. In a Miami day-care center, a single paid professional is supplemented by a staff of time-dollar volunteers, largely grandmothers, who provide the attention, discipline, teaching and hands-on care that is often missing in homes with two working parents. A health clinic in El Paso allows the partial payment of patients' bills with time-dollars earned staffing a teen-pregnancy program, assisting with a nutrition program and helping out with a transport pool run by the clinic.

Bernard Lietaer documents the steady spread of such local currency and time-denominated mutual credit systems worldwide, finding more than fourteen hundred in operation as of June 1997.[28] Variations on this theme are commonplace. For instance, when interest rates soared to 20 percent in Canada in the early 1980s, Michael Linton founded Canada's first "local exchange trading system" (LETS), which has since grown to assist people in some thirty Canadian communities barter the exchange of their personal services. In France, 350 such networks specialize in trading knowledge and information (a 1994 survey found that 10 percent of the French now trade regularly). More than four hundred LETS systems were operational in Britain in mid-1997. In 1992, there were fewer than one hundred.

In Japan, with its large elderly population, a coordinated time-based credit and exchange system enables volunteers to credit their donations of service time toward a "time saving account" against which they can draw in the future for elderly care. Different values are assigned to different tasks while a national clearing house assists in enabling a volunteer, say, in Tokyo to earn time credits for use by his elderly parents in Nagoya. Others bank the time like a supplemental old-age insurance plan while some give their accounts to those they perceive as more needy, raising the possibility of "double giving."

Lietaer also describes what may be the first genuinely "complementary currency system" in the form of a smart debit card encoded with the information required for merchants to record transactions in both U.S. dollars and in local currency. The test marketing of this notion by Commonweal of Minneapolis allows, for instance, a restaurant to accept in payment a blend of U.S. dollars and "community service dollars" (C$D). It is expected that merchants will adjust their C$D acceptance policy based on when spare capacity might be available, whether it be unfilled seats for a movie theater matinee or vacant weekday rooms at a resort. For instance, an eatery might accept C$D for 40 percent of a dinner bill before 7 P.M. and 20 percent afterward. Or a movie theater could accept, say, 80 percent of the ticket price in C$D for off-peak shows.

From the commercial perspective, this "currency exchange network" provides merchants a way to get paid something rather than nothing for idle capacity while also building a customer base without detracting from their usual dollar-paying clients and, in the process, assisting local nonprofits. Nonprofits, in turn, can stretch their budgets by paying social workers with a mix of dollars and C$D. With popular "cause-related marketing," they also earn referral fees whenever one of their members pays with their Commonweal HeroCard. The cardholder, in turn, can choose the nonprofit to whom an agreed-to percentage of the value of any card transaction is credited—much like a credit card where a small portion of each purchase is paid over to a social cause.

An appealing element of discretion also accompanies these new community-strengthening strategies (i.e., local currencies, time dollars, time saving systems, local exchange trading systems, mutual exchange credit systems and currency exchange networks). For instance, by enabling the unemployed and poorer people to convert their time into money, they can more fully participate in the economy. When someone pays with a smart debit card (with its embedded microchip of account information), no one need know whether he is paying with U.S. dollars or C$D. These systems also finesse what can be an awkward issue for those who need care but may be embarrassed to ask (such as Japan's elderly). Given the emerging nonaffordability of elderly care for many of America's vast and rapidly aging baby-boom generation, this complementary care system has potentially enormous relevance in the United States.

Geoff Mulgan, director of DEMOS, a London-based think tank, suggests that these complementary currencies and local exchange systems could help create jobs in a "parallel economy" for those lacking the wherewithal to participate in the national currency-based "first economy." Lietaer compares the effect to that of a dam: "it enables us to irrigate and re-circulate the nutrient-carrying means of exchange within a controlled area."[29]

A Return to Personal Economies

Similar in tone to the ESOP notion of up-close capitalism, community-sensitive "bioregionalism" seeks to create systems in which wealth generated in a region is retained for the benefit of those who live there. Bioregionalism resists the tendency of national currencies to concentrate investment (and wealth) in urban financial centers, draining outlying areas of needed financial resources and undermining their capacity to respond to changing economic conditions. Local currency, for example, is seen as not just an economic tool but as a way to promote and preserve local culture. In *Cities and the Wealth of Nations,* Jane Jacobs captures the dilemma facing communities due to their reliance on a common currency in today's increasingly globalized economy:

> *Currencies are powerful carriers of feedback information . . . and potent triggers of adjustments, but on their own terms. A national currency registers, above all, consolidated information on a nation's international trade. Imagine a group of people who are all properly equipped with diaphragms and lungs but who share among them only one brainstem breathing center. In this goofy arrangement, the breathing center would receive consolidated feedback on the carbon dioxide level of the whole group and would be unable to discriminate among the individuals producing it. Everybody's diaphragm would be triggered to contract at the same time. But suppose some of those people were sleeping while others were playing tennis? Suppose some were reading about feedback controls while others were chopping wood?*[30]

Bioregionalism questions whether it is sensible for all regions and communities to adjust their economies to the same financial standard, regardless of local conditions, allowing stagnant local pockets to go unaided in an otherwise seemingly prosperous economy. Bioregionalism also questions whether small businesses in rural areas can realistically compete with multinational corporations or with the federal government, especially in a policy environment in which real interest rates are impacted by the need to service a huge national debt. "Money should never be separated from values," argues Professor Rosabeth Moss Kanter of Harvard Business School. "Detached from values it may indeed be the root of all evil. Linked effectively to social purpose it can be the root of opportunity."

The Human Dimension of Moneymaking

The bioregional concept strives to reach well beyond the usual boundaries of economics to address concerns now described as "deep ecology." The scope of this concern is illustrated by another Berkshires financing program called SHARE (Self Help Association for a Regional Economy), coordinated by the E. F. Schumacher Society in Great Barrington, Massachusetts. SHARE assists community residents in securing loans for small enterprises by directly addressing the catch-22 that confronts all would-be borrowers: the need for collateral. SHARE members make modest deposits at local banks, where they are issued a passbook savings account in which SHARE becomes a joint account holder, agreeing that SHARE can pledge the savings account to collateralize small loans meeting financial, social and environmental criteria. Typically loans are for those with no credit history or for people who need funds for commercially feasible projects that are unfamiliar to local bankers. Once SHARE approves the project, passbook savings books are delivered to the lending bank as collateral for the loan.

One of SHARE's first loans was for the production of goat cheese. Sue Sellew, a local entrepreneur, needed access to Federal Reserve notes to purchase construction materials (cement, stainless steel tanks, windows, etc.) required to build a state-licensed milking room. SHARE provided the collateral. Importantly, SHARE members are kept informed about how and with whom their money is invested so that they know precisely where their money is each day: it's invested locally, helping someone they know build a business that has local relevance.

In this case, SHARE members visit the goat farm; they take their children to pet the goats; they recommend the goat cheese to their friends and neighbors. I suggest that, in this case, people are smarter than money, because that loan does more than earn returns for detached investors; it also builds community by encouraging social interactions that give shape, tone and texture to local culture. The goat cheese becomes more than simply a commercial product; it's now identified with a local way of life. It even takes on a different ambiance sitting on the kitchen table. As SHARE administrator and deep ecologist Susan Witt explains: "You expect it to weave a web deep into other aspects of life, and knit it together."[31] What SHARE discovered with its connecting of local lenders (and local collateral-izers) to local borrowers is that those connections *themselves* become the best insurer of success, because those people then buy the products and recommend them to others, providing a local network of personal support and simple human concern that is often as valuable as the money itself.

In a recent interview, Schumacher Society Executive Director Witt provides a sense of why it is that the Society has such an affinity for issues of appropriate scale: "It strengthens the whole web of relationships and connections that form a community. Can we picture the carpenter who made our kitchen table or her children who were fed by its purchase? Have we walked the forest which was the source of its wood? The associations and connections go on and on. And they continue to build into a much larger social and cultural fabric which defines our place and makes it unique. At the Schumacher Society we say that our quality of life is dependent on the number of stories we know about the items we use in our daily life."[32]

The Politics of Ownership

The realm of politics is a twilight zone where ethical and technical issues meet.

—Reinhold Niebuhr

After working for more than two decades in this policy-sensitive area, I am often reminded of the counsel offered a young legislator by a more seasoned colleague. When asked how to oppose a matter without being seen as doing so, the old pol advised: "Just remember, never oppose a church—just oppose its location." That's often my experience in advocating broad-based ownership. It's notorious for long-winded words of support (who could oppose it?) accompanied by precious little action.

The prevailing political paradigm is reflected in the maxim: That government is best which governs least. Yet by granting dominance to the domain of dollars while simultaneously insisting on a minimalist role for the state, inequality has expanded dramatically while civil society has been seriously eroded. While governing less, the financial burden of government has grown. Compared with two decades ago, Washington now consumes more, borrows more ($5,500 billion in 1997 vs. $900 billion in 1980) and employs more (19.5 million in 1996 compared with 16.2 million in 1980).

Despite the many flaws of the neoclassical model (which replaced a flawed neoliberal model), American politics still seems to require a major dilemma to force political realignment. I see at least three such possibilities. The first stems from capitalism's proven ability to push aside the old in the process of embracing the new. On the one hand, economic conservatives admire the dynamism of the marketplace. On the other hand, social conservatives deplore the devastating impact this disruption works on families and on social and community stability, the bedrock of conservative values. The American Right also harbors a sensible contempt for the nanny state. However, this sentiment often shows up as disdain for government and the good it can do. A classic policy paradox arose during the Reagan era, when conservatives rushed to defend the Panama Canal, a project they never would have built. Conservatives know that local civic life cannot be strong unless America is strong nationally and internationally, yet they can see no way to concede the need for a proactive government without relaxing their laissez-faire beliefs.

The second dilemma emerges in the environmental area. Conservative Republican presidential candidate Pat Buchanan posed the question thus: "Conservatives who worship at the altar of an endlessly rising GNP should tell us: What is it they any longer wish to conserve?" Today's market-obsessed model of free enterprise is clearly at odds with environmental sustainability. But, again, policy intervention runs contrary to faith in the all-knowing wisdom of unfettered free enterprise.

Third is the entitlement dilemma. A frightening fiscal future is fast rushing toward us as the gap steadily widens between the ability of baby boomers to support themselves and the ability of their children to afford their support. Yet both liberals and conservatives dodge the dilemma while acknowledging that continued avoidance amounts to fiscal malpractice. Voters are of two minds on the matter, neither of them friendly. A 1995 poll found that 79 percent favor a constitutional amendment requiring the government to balance its books by the year 2002. But only 32 percent favor the amendment if it requires cuts in Social Security, the single largest budget item.[1]

These three dilemmas, in turn, suggest four key challenges—one conceptual and three that raise very practical political concerns. The conceptual challenge: how to modernize the role of the state. In the old model, governments determined what needed to be done and then did it. Modern policymakers realize that what the public needs is structures and institutions that guide, coax and encourage rather than administrators who mandate, regulate and dominate. All too often, the state has tried to be the horse rather than the jockey. That's why policy intervention is now often characterized as unconscionable rather than unavoidable.

The first political challenge finds its roots in the fact that democracies are intended to be feedback-intensive, people-responsive systems. Politicians typically get reelected by looking after those who elect them. With political participation on the wane among low-income Americans and on the rise among the well-to-do,[2] any significant change in ownership patterns may require an alliance between the middle class and the poor. Progressive/populist candidates may yet emerge who speak for that disenchanted, disempowered and disconnected constituency, enticing them back into politics. Either that or candid appeals to fiscal foresight and social equity may yet persuade the well-to-do to cooperate in improving economic conditions for others.

The second political challenge arises from the fact that policies advancing long-term change can be difficult for those who run for office on a short-term basis. Significant capital accumulation takes time. Plus, useful prescriptions don't lend themselves well to fifteen-second sound bites. Yet there's also potential for considerable political payoff as leadership in this arena is likely to be rewarded with enthusiastic support from newly empowered constituents. In addition, if an outspoken leader were to take a strong stand in favor of broad-based ownership—and propose a feasible program to back it up—how could a subsequent leader do anything other than agree to improve on it?

Lastly, today's leaders and wanna-be leaders must be willing to advance a new paradigm even while the old one limps along in a bruised, battered but not yet broken manner. That's an inherent challenge for anyone proposing a genuinely new approach. That's further complicated by the fact that there was a time early on in this century (during the era of Huey Long) when anyone advocating a change in ownership would be portrayed as decidedly Left of center—or worse. Things are no longer so simple. As I indicate below, the political genealogy of support for widespread ownership cuts across the political spectrum. This chapter provides a feel for the politics of an ownership solution—in the hope that it will enhance the confidence of those who agree that the time is ripe for action.

Politics and Ownership Policy

At the beginning of the industrial age, what saved American-style capitalism from a Marxist fate was its democratic reform movements that succeeded in humanizing the market, introducing a measure of social responsibility in the form of an economic safety net along with other market interventions that narrowed the gap between the haves and the have-nots. Historian Arthur Schlesinger argues that this intervention was crucial in "rescuing capitalism from the capitalists."[3] As I indicate in earlier chapters, another rescue effort is now needed.

The average American is fast being drawn into a web of economic insecurity last seen in the 1930s. However, this time around there's much less of a sense of "we're all in this together," because not everyone is. Yet despite the many shortcomings of the current neoclassical paradigm, opponents have yet to offer a feasible framework of persuasive big ideas. Nor have they proposed a way to shrink the size of government. The result is policy stalemate, with both camps exhibiting a curious agnosticism about ownership patterns while devoting valuable legislative time debating an array of "bread and circus" social issues as a litmus test of politically correct social values: reproductive rights, same-sex marriage, flag burning, even the legislative process itself (the line-item veto, a balanced budget amendment to the Constitution, etc.).[4]

Because political support in this area is so broad-based, there's very little either side can do to politicize the issue, although the rich-get-richer legacy of the Reagan-Bush era may come back to haunt the Republicans. Though both parties have voiced interest in broadening ownership, the political capital required to genuinely move the idea forward has yet to be committed. The best way to describe the sometimes puzzling politics in the ownership arena is to provide a sampling of comments dating back more than two decades. Of necessity, the bulk of those comments focus on ESOPs, America's first fledgling attempt to effect an ownership solution. In addition to conservative Democrat Russell Long, other early supporters at the national level included conservative Republicans Ronald Reagan and Jack Kemp, along with moderate Republican Senator Mark Hatfield of Oregon.

Political activity at the state level provided an early indication that ownership could prove a focal point for harmonizing divergent political views. In 1974, in populist-inclined Minnesota, state senator George Pillsbury, a director of the Pillsbury Company, introduced legislation to encourage ESOPs. After retiring from management at the age of forty-eight, Pillsbury watched as his substantial personal wealth grew at an even faster rate. That proved to him that his law-school-age son, Charlie, was correct when he insisted that increasing the size of the economic pie is not enough; people must also own "a piece of the pie-making machinery."[5] The elder Pillsbury, a lifelong Republican, soon forged a political bond with his Democrats-for-McGovern son based on their shared passion for Louis Kelso's notion of "universal capitalism."

The political potential in this area became obvious to me when, over the span of a two-week period in 1986, I was asked to provide speech material for both Republican senator Jesse Helms and Democratic presidential candidate Jesse Jackson. A harbinger of this political eclecticism appeared in *Barron's*, when the newsweekly argued in 1975: "The Kelso doctrine is the only economic doctrine introduced in generations that could become a plank in either the Democratic or Republican platform."[6] *Forbes* also sensed its broad political appeal: "One of the great things that ESOPs have going for them is that they are such a natural from a political viewpoint: Who in populist Washington, whether liberal or conservative, would knock the idea of spreading corporate ownership?"[7]

Carl Madden, then chief economist of the U.S. Chamber of Commerce, favorably cast the idea as "a quiet evolution in wealth ownership rather than the unquiet revolutions wealth owners have faced too often in the past."[8] Former Oklahoma senator Fred Harris, a onetime Democratic presidential candidate, included in his 1973 book, *The New Populism*, a chapter titled "If a Little Capitalism Is Good, What's Wrong with a Lot?" A year later, conservative Republican Ronald Reagan proposed the ESOP as a modern counterpart to an earlier ownership solution:

> *Over one hundred years ago Abraham Lincoln signed the Homestead Act. There was a wide distribution of land and they didn't confiscate anyone's already privately owned land. They did not take from those who owned to give to others who did not own. It set the pattern for the American capitalistic system. We need an Industrial Homestead Act. . . . It is time to formulate a plan to accelerate economic growth and production at the same time we broaden*

the ownership of productive capital. The American dream has always been to have a piece of the action.[9]

Winnett Boyd, then president of Arthur D. Little (Canada), went well out on a professional limb, declaring: "Kelso's ideas will have as big an impact on the world in the next 100 years as those [competing Communist ideas] of Marx and Engels in the past century."[10] *San Francisco Business* reported, "Some brokers are saying that the ESOP trend may be exercising as much influence on the future as the computer."[11] New York's *Village Voice* questioned whether Kelso was the "Marshall McLuhan of economics," and quipped, "It sounded like Huey Long with good grammar."[12] Media guru McLuhan conceded, "I had a ball reading [this] metaphoric tale." Meanwhile, *The Whole Earth Catalog* praised Kelso by poking fun at its counterculture readers, noting:

> *There is a conspicuous void in the arguments and the programs of the counter-culture groups of this country, in that they have produced no well-formulated economic theories. Unfortunately, and ironically, Lou Kelso, who has some very imaginative economic proposals, has been offering them for many years to the establishment, the dinosaur culture. . . . So either Kelso is a lousy sales-man or the dinosaurs are convinced their own designs will see them through.*[13]

In a review of Adler and Kelso's 1958 book, *The Capitalist Manifesto*, Caspar Weinberger, head of Bechtel Corporation's legal department and later Reagan's secretary of defense, suggested: "Kelso and Adler's book could start a revolution." Conservative commentator William F. Buckley embraced Kelso's prescriptions, calling them a "radical answer," while the liberal *Berkeley Daily Gazette* characterized Kelso as "possibly the only genuine revolutionary in the United States."[14] Sterling Clements, writing for the staid *Saturday Review,* noted: "The proposals . . . will strike the economic establishment as revolutionary and even impossible—but are they?" Writing in *The Washington Post,* columnist James J. Kilpatrick mused that "Kelso's formula sounds like Lydia Pinkham's Vegetable Compound. . . . The whole theory sounds crazy. But, then, one may recall, they said all that of Copernicus too." Similarly, *Fortune* commented: "Like the case for acupuncture, it sounds bizarre, even alarming— but a suspicion remains that there may be something to it." After a lengthy interview with Kelso, *The Washington Post*'s Nicholas von Hoffman concluded:

> *In America, the greatest, most famous capitalist country in the world, there are almost no capitalists. The largest majority, silent and noisy, are job serfs, wage villeins, dependent on salaries for all the money they'll ever see.*
>
> *The great, lazy, anti-Calvinist, hedonistic Kelsonian truth is that you can't get rich through labor because it doesn't produce enough wealth.*
>
> *Kelso's idea won't solve all our problems; it can't possibly work out as nicely as he thinks, but it can move us from this barren repetition of fifty-year-old disputes.*[15]

Mainstream economists have never known quite what to say about Kelso.[16] Free enterprise guru Milton Friedman complained: "Instead of saying labor's exploited, as Marx did, Kelso says capital's exploited. It's worse than Marx. It's Marx stood on its head." In apparent agreement, *Pravda*, the Soviet Union's Communist Party–controlled newspaper, charged: "In those discussions, there is as much of the wanderings of a madman as there is of cannibalism." Challenging both Friedman and *Pravda*, Federal Reserve Board Chairman Paul Volcker wondered why more companies weren't embracing what he saw as a helpful component in price stability (one of Friedman's mainstays), telling the American Economics Association in 1983:

> I welcome the new interest in profit-sharing arrangements or other ways of rewarding workers when things are good, without building in an inexorably rising floor on costs. The concept of quality circles, experimentation with worker representation on boards of directors, and methods of encouraging employee stock ownership and other initiatives—often born in adversity—carry promise for changing the confrontational nature and brinkmanship characteristic of so much of our industrial relations.[17]

Though even now commentators routinely begin their articles with some trite version of "ESOP's Foibles" or "ESOP's Fables," the concept has become very serious for politicians regardless of their ideological persuasion. In 1989, New York governor Mario Cuomo characterized ESOPs as "supply side for workers," urging that employee ownership should become "the basis of a new relationship between corporations and their employees. It can spread the pride of ownership and encourage the self-esteem that comes with being a master of one's own destiny."[18] Likewise, a campaigning George Bush declared that "employee stock ownership plans work."[19] Sensing the appeal to conservatives, George Will lauded employee ownership as a hopeful new way to help "produce a nation with a propertied middle class and hence a conservative temperament," arguing in 1997 that ESOPs "will diminish some of the forms of social strife that have fueled modern liberalism."[20]

Soon after the 1994 midterm congressional elections in which both houses came under Republican control, the Clinton White House moved quickly to outflank the Republicans on certain hot issues, directing the General Services Administration to use an ESOP to privatize its operations. Similarly, the Office of Personnel Management soon announced that an ESOP would enable eight hundred employees to buy the Office of Investigative Services, which conducts background checks on new government employees and officials in sensitive jobs.[21]

There's something about ESOPs that just seems to resonate with seasoned campaigners; they sense that ownership solutions can enhance both their political appeal on the stump and their survivability once in office. Nicholas von Hoffman captured the odd allure of Kelso's provocative message: "He isn't going to solve all our problems . . . , but we desperately need new problems. What makes his ideas appealing is that they'll liberate us from our old problems which are now exhausted, as sources of creativity."[22]

Step-by-Step Solution

A few cautionary notes merit a brief mention. Sociologist Gregory Bateson warns that "there is always an optimum value beyond which anything is toxic." That is clearly the case for today's concentrated ownership patterns. An overengineered ownership solution is a temptation I urge policymakers to resist, as I do its opposite—no ownership engineering. Hesitancy should also accompany any policy proposal that unduly forces financial capital into particular *types* of investments. Regardless of investment type, the goal should be to err on the side of broad- versus narrow-based ownership.

The Ownership Solution is not a panacea. Ownership as simply one component of the social contract that can be written either to divide or to unite. Properly engineered, ownership patterns have the potential to be a powerful agent of social cohesion. The challenge lies in how best to ensure that capitalism gains in strength and robustness from an ever widening circle of interdependent yet self-sufficient capitalists. History offers ample proof that where societies encourage free enterprise, people become more prosperous and where they don't, people don't.

The political sphere already includes a preference for broad-based participation, reckoning that decisions derived from an informed, engaged and concerned citizenry are preferable to those reached by isolated government officials, however well intentioned. The Japanese coined an appropriate aphorism: All of us are smarter than any of us. Experience suggests that both economic and political systems gain in vitality, robustness and moral legitimacy as they gain in active participants. Instead, today's wealth gap may itself be a cause of declining participation in the democratic process. Declining voter participation, alienation and apathy mirror the tenuous nature of participation in the economic domain. In addition, growing uncertainty and economic insecurity provide fertile ground for those who would make minorities or the poor scapegoats for a variety of social problems.[23]

The Progressive Paradox

We've been here before. Back at the turn of the century, American progressives struggled with a similar set of issues in their attempt to seek balance between the power of concentrated economic forces and the appeal of locally attuned democratic forces. This challenge traces its roots at least as far back as Thomas Jefferson, who cautioned against the social and political perils of large-scale manufacturing, fearful it would lead to propertyless citizens lacking the personal independence and civic capacity required of a system of self-government.

This predicament continues to bedevil democratic society as people experience in their lives a steady erosion of life based on self reliance and community—the traditional site of democratic governance—alongside a scale of economic life that is both disempowering and disorienting. In particular, the appearance on the local scene of highly impersonal firms along with the emergence of mega-millionaires and even multi-billionaires brings with it a sea change in the nature of self-rule and our aspirations to live in a genuinely classless society. Also, we see accompanying this phenomenon the re-emergence of intolerance, racism, jingoism, nationalism and other symptoms of a society that seems to have forgotten the innate value of inclusion.

Yet the search for a solution is wrought with paradox. Either a movement can be launched to decentralize economic power, or the capacity of government can be enlarged to regulate that power. To date, the latter route has been the one chosen, commencing with President Teddy Roosevelt's "New Nationalism" that set out to combine centralized power over interstate commerce with civic education aimed at enhancing Americans' sense of national identity.[24] That approach, in turn, raised the specter of how to preserve democratic government while also mustering government muscle sufficient to counter concentrated economic power. As political events transpired, New Deal politics shifted the debate to issues of economic growth and distributive justice as Keynesian demand-stimulative spending provided a handy way to avoid resolution of what remains a crucial issue in crafting an ownership solution.

Ronald Reagan's emergence on the scene provides a study in what might be done, as well as how what might be done could go badly awry. As author Michael Sandel points out, Reagan's genius lay in "his ability to identify with Americans' yearnings for a common life of larger meanings on a smaller, less impersonal scale."[25] Blaming big government for disempowering Americans, he proposed a "new federalism" in which the "bigness is badness" villain was government alone, ignoring the impact of global capital flows and the emergence of corporate and personal economic power on a vast and unprecedented scale. Though he rightly sensed the national mood of discontent, his prescriptions missed the real anxiety: the erosion of those social structures between citizen and state—families, neighborhoods, workplaces, schools, towns, congregations, civic clubs—the real center of self-governance.

Plus, as Sandel points out, these "intermediate communities" were situated in "a global economy whose frenzied flow of money and goods, information and images, pays little heed to nations, much less neighborhoods." Reagan's combination of nostalgia and market conservatism played well politically but did little to repair the social fabric of communities. Indeed, some suggest he did much to undermine *civic* conservatism, putting communities and families at risk by choosing to ignore circumstances with which they continue to struggle.

The remedy required may well be found in an observation first offered by Alexis de Tocqueville, who wrote eloquently about "the slow and quiet action of society upon itself." By that he meant the array of public institutions that both bring people together and separate them—athletic leagues, schools, civic clubs, religions and the various occupations (law, the clergy, medicine) that give moral texture to those multilayered relationships that comprise both civic education and civic participation. Good citizenship and moral behavior emerge not by force but by a complex blend of persuasion and practice that eventually emerge in society as what theologians call the "habits of the heart."

At the same time that Americans find they are losing control over the forces that govern their economic lives, their image of who they are is also changing. The loss of personal mastery and erosion of community calls for a form of self-governance that evokes a more expansive civic identity. While clearly that involves the emergence of more global institutions designed to address issues of shared concern to the world community (global warming, acid rain, terrorism, AIDS, weapons, etc.), it also means the need to cultivate richer and more complex relationships within the local community. The development of an ownership stake—both locally and in multinational corporations that operate locally—could be one key form of "connectivity" that evokes a more expansive identity while also advancing a broader sense of personal responsibility, both local and global.

While "Think Globally, Act Locally" makes for a nice bumper sticker, today's citizens need both to "Think Globally, Act Globally" *and* "Think Locally, Act Locally." Recycling is a personal obligation not just for our local communities but for the sake of the global community; likewise the use of energy, water, paper goods, what we eat and so forth. Yet citizenship must also now include involvement in global politics, such as commitment to a personal lifestyle that supports meeting the objectives in the Kyoto accord on global warming. The relevant focus must change to one based both on local identity and on a greater sense of identity with (and responsibility for) those global forces that now confirm humankind's interdependence.

The solution to the progressive paradox lies in ensuring *both* (a) that governments are more powerful *and* (b) that political and economic power is more dispersed. Politically, that means power is both more diffused (among those acting globally, nationally, regionally, locally) and more personal, including, I suggest, a component of personal economic power evidenced in an element of local ownership. An analogy might be drawn to the emergence in information technology of networked computers. Rather than replicating immense amounts of personal computer capacity for every user, the trend is toward a system architecture where each operator has a less-sophisticated PC that draws on more sophisticated capacity at a centralized location. Individuals, dispersed and independent, are empowered by access to more centralized and more powerful computing power which, in turn, is dispersed through a coordinated network of server sites engineered to meet on-site needs.

They're independent, dependent and interdependent. That rich overlay of relationships is precisely the "stuff" of community. We'll soon see a similar paradigm emerging in the energy sector as advances in microturbine technology make it feasible to put the source of power closer to the user.[26] Although that suggests a shift from large-scale, capital-intensive energy distribution to small-scale *distributed* energy production, the microturbine's low output (like the PC) is likely to ensure that large-scale energy production remains a part of the economic pattern, pressured by the microturbine to become cleaner and more efficient. As with the PC/network combination, the microturbine will be embedded in a larger system, fostering independence while allowing for dependence (I may not want to be dependent on the microturbine to meet all my energy needs) and acknowledging the notion of interdependence (the microturbine's chief feature is energy efficiency and low pollution).

Leadership in the Age of Paradox

One key purpose of government is to cultivate a shared national identity grounded in social solidarity and mutual obligation. Yet the notion of a place-dependent politics (the *polis* of Aristotle's time) needs now to be complemented with a multi-place, transnational, even transcendent sense of allegiance, one that crosses not only national borders but also dimensions of time—as reflected in concerns about the multigenerational impact of global warming.

With globalization comes a fundamental shift in how we see our world, how we see our relationship to the world and how we make commitments and assign our allegiances. In short, we are rapidly changing our sense of who we are—irreversibly. Though the pace of change may seem unnerving, keep in mind it's been less than three decades since mankind first saw a photograph of our entire habitat from outer space. From that perspective (i.e., the earth from space), We the People takes on a *very* different connotation. Yes, we're a nation state but not just that. That very new image of ourselves makes for a far more ambiguous political environment, one where nostalgia for a bygone era is embraced only at our (and our children's) peril.

We now have a generation raised on "post-Sputnik" imagery, for whom the notion of an alone and aloof, rough-and-ready brand of American individualism seems not only quaint and outdated but hackneyed, even trite and dangerous. Today's politics require a more mature vision, one more relevant to and grounded in today's reality of overlapping, conflicting and oftentimes confusing obligations, and one where traditional notions of national sovereignty and political allegiance are certain to suffer further erosion by a steady increase in the cross-border flow of goods, capital, people, information, images, entertainment, pollution, disease, drugs, crime, and so forth.

That, in turn, makes leadership particularly challenging—both politically and within the corporate entity. As pointed out by Ronald Heifetz, director of the Leadership Education Project at Harvard's John F. Kennedy School of Government, the need for constant adaptation in a broad range of very different settings means that leadership can no longer be some combination of "having a vision and aligning people with that vision" or what he calls "grand knowing and salesmanship."[27] Instead, it's about setting the stage and creating a context in which constant learning and adapting can occur and in which people are genuinely engaged "in confronting the challenge, adjusting their values, changing perspectives, and learning new habits."[28]

That, in turn, requires that members of an organization take responsibility for the situations that confront them. "Leadership has to take place every day," Heifetz argues. "It cannot be the responsibility of the few, a rare event, or a once-in-a-lifetime opportunity. . . . We face adaptive challenges all the time. . . . Learning, as seen in this light, requires a learning strategy. . . . The adaptive demands of our time require leaders who take responsibility without waiting for revelation or request."[29]

In his attempt to grasp the implications of this new environment, author and leadership scholar Joseph Jaworski takes his cue from the new physics, arguing that "a true leader sets the stage" for the unfolding of order, secure in the knowledge that "everything in the universe affects everything else because they are all part of the same unbroken whole."[30] The challenge for the United States (and, indeed, for political and corporate leaders everywhere) is to organize around guiding principles and to set the stage for "a collective form of leadership that simply cannot be provided by a single individual."[31] Part of that process involves deliberative dialogue, the ultimate source of organizational learning. Even the sense of ceremony that so often surrounds politics is an integral part of how that dialogue (and learning) is taken out into the world to engage others in facilitating the emergence of a new order.

"Just as a melody is not made up of notes," Martin Buber reflected, "nor the verse of words nor the statue of lines," the exercise of leadership means nothing less than ensuring that a *process* is in place that engages people in the act of both discovering and influencing an unfolding future. The complex challenge of constant adaptive change requires, in essence, a return to a brand of economics that evokes the resources of character, insight, passion and compassion that reside in each of us. To the extent that we can yield to the design of this "implicate order," we will better find our way.

Futurist Duane Elgin puts a name to this process in an October 1997 report titled "Collective Consciousness and Cultural Healing" in which he points out: "It was our ability to communicate among ourselves that has enabled *Homo sapiens sapiens* to travel an enormous evolutionary distance and to now stand at the edge of establishing a planetary civilization. In turn, it will be our ability to communicate that will determine whether we are able to cope with the systems challenge posed by unprecedented human numbers, dwindling natural resources, and mounting ecological devastation."[32]

Among physicists, it is said that we live and operate within "fields" of thought and perception—nonmaterial, invisible forces that structure both space and behavior within it. Gravitational fields, magnetic fields, electron fields and other vibratory patterns make up the invisible, intangible world of quantum theory, the very building blocks of the universe. The challenge for leaders is to evoke the forces—to set an organizational field, if you will—with the capacity to evoke social cohesion along with optimum, sustainable performance. It is in that broader context it seems to me that ownership patterns—an invisible field—work their influence for good or ill.

Back to a Sense of Place

My suggested theme of "connectivity" is both new and old. The idea is old in the sense that agrarian cultures had a definite sense of "place" to which their people were connected by common inhabitation and a common web of relationships. That remains largely the case. Worldwide, the dominant form of ownership remains family and community oriented, centered on the land. Those bonds are often nurtured by cross-generational linkages based on a place-defined sense of belonging. In traditional cultures, the worst form of punishment is not jails (which are largely nonexistent), but banishment—the denial of a person's natural longing to be part of the community. In that sense, what I propose as a modern political theme is quite ancient.

However, this theme is also new in the sense that modern man (particularly in the more developed countries) is increasingly uprooted and cut off from traditional means for weaving past and future into each day's work. Along with a commitment to constantly update those channels of communication and persuasion through which we cope with and manage change. Overcoming this uniquely modern lack of *place* requires continuous innovation. Broad-based ownership, I believe, is one component. While that alone is not a complete solution, it's also unlikely that a fully satisfactory solution can be devised without it. As Paul Kennedy notes in *Preparing for the Twenty-First Century:*

> *The internationalization of manufacturing and finance erodes a people's capacity to control its own affairs. . . . The real logic of the borderless world is that nobody is in control—except, perhaps, the managers of multinational corporations, whose responsibility is to their shareholders, who, one might argue, have become the new sovereigns, investing in whatever company gives the highest returns. . . . The people of the earth seem to be discovering that*

their lives are ever more affected by forces which are, in the full meaning of the word, irresponsible."[33]

Today's complex political challenge calls for a combination of both forecasting and "backcasting." Politically, we need to envision a societal design that starts from where we want to be and then design our way back to what must be done *today* to get us there. With that in mind, Section 3 provides an overview of potential policy initiatives meant to take us in the direction of a more fully connected populace. As you read through these initiatives I urge that you keep in mind an observation by nature historian and biologist Jay Gould, who documents that natural systems tend to change slowly, interspersed with periodic bursts of "punctuated equilibrium" during which dramatic change occurs before the system settles back into a more familiar state of gradual evolution. With the proper vision, committed leadership and popular support, it would be quite possible to enact a sweeping legislative scheme that could quickly put the U.S. economy (or practically any economy) on the road toward an ownership solution.

The potential for dramatic change is particularly keen in this area. We know from modern physics that changes in large systems tend to accompany many changes in smaller systems. This interdependence between part and whole suggests that even modest, incremental improvements in the "connectivity" in local systems could lead to a quantum leap in the larger system of which they are a part. That, in turn, could lead to slow and quiet improvements in society's capacity for vision and collective foresight.

Toward a Twenty-First-Century Capitalism

> Relation is the essence of everything that exists.
>
> *—Meister Eckhart*

Legend has it that the sun and the wind made a wager about which could persuade a horseman to remove his coat. The more the wind blew, the tighter the rider held his coat close to him. Then the sun began to smile and, as it got warmer, the rider loosened and then happily removed his coat. Moral: there are two ways to go about influencing change; one is by force and the other by creating an environment that evokes change.

Readers persuaded of the merits of a more inclusive capitalism may wonder if such a system is feasible or whether it is destined to remain only an interesting theory. That question is answered in this section with a three-chapter overview of initiatives that, over time, could make an ownership solution quite real—provided the will exists in both the corporate world and among legislators to build a significant ownership stake for more than a privileged few.[1] We turn in the final section to a global overview of how ownership solutions could be applied abroad to address an array of foreign-policy issues.

Let me begin by conceding that fairness and simplicity are not natural allies in the fashioning of prescriptions for broading ownership. During my seven years as counsel to the Senate Finance Committee, I discovered time and again that the simplest solutions were generally the least equitable (the "flat tax" being the most obvious). A capitalism that fosters less inequality is destined to include elements of both complexity and inefficiency. Arthur Okun, chairman of President Lyndon Johnson's Council of Economic Advisers, captured the essence of this natural trade-off in a treatise titled *Equality and Efficiency:*

> *A democratic capitalist society will keep searching for better ways of drawing the boundary lines between the domain of rights and the domain of dollars. And it can make progress. To be sure, it will never solve the problem, for the conflict between equality and efficiency is inescapable. In that sense, capitalism and democracy are really a most improbable mixture. Maybe that is why they need each other—to put some rationality into equality and some humanity into efficiency.*[2]

Measuring Quantities, Missing Qualities

Economists study those things that are measurable (capital investment, household income), often ignoring patterns that lie behind the numbers. Imagine, for example, dunking a wire-frame bird cage in soapy water. When pulled out, the cage is covered with a soapy film. Economists do a bang-up job analyzing and describing the film. But the film takes its shape because of the connective properties of the wire frame, and only secondarily due to the properties of the soap. The wire frame is the stuff of social and political science, while economists are trained largely in the science of the soap.

That's why the social architects in any nation are its corporate leaders and its policymakers, those elected and appointed societal engineers who design the wire frame. Frank Lloyd Wright characterized architects as the "pattern-givers of civilization" and the "way-showers." That they are. The best of our social architects view themselves as public servants charged with oversight of society's key institutions. Despite today's widespread cynicism about politicians, most of them, in my experience, take their charge seriously, as do most corporate managers and directors. The genuinely great pattern-givers see themselves as stewards of the nation's welfare, and their job as building a better, more humane society. To measure to that high standard requires that we reengineer the wire frame so that the soap assumes a different shape.

Until recently, the ownership patterns generated by conventional capitalism have changed only dramatically and, typically, quite violently (Russia in 1917, China in 1949, Cuba in 1959). However, the rapid institutionalization of capital in the United States over the past two decades[3] provides ample evidence that ownership patterns can change both profoundly and peacefully in response to a reconfiguration of the legal framework. The goal of the changes I propose is not to maximize efficiency but to enhance economic and social *effectiveness.* Much as computer software is engineered with less speed and efficiency in favor of dependability, robustness and long-term effectiveness, I view ownership as a "societal software" that could be drawn upon to strengthen both free enterprise and democratic society.

Coaxing Capitalism to Become Consistent with Itself

Anyone who proposes to change current economic patterns had best be prepared to encounter staunch resistance from laissez-faire, level-playing-field policy gurus who stand ready to assure us that *any* situation—no matter how dire—will eventually right itself if only meddlers like myself will stay out of the way. In my experience, that's invariably a roundabout way of saying that we should instead embrace *their* prescriptions.

It often disturbs my right-of-center colleagues to find that I propose changes in policy. Indeed, some of the changes I recommend assume a purposeful federal government willing to take chances to transform an ownership-concentrating system that, by all accounts, no longer serves its constituencies. University of Maryland professor William Galston captures the policy paradox, noting simply: "A government too weak to threaten our liberties may by that very fact be too weak to secure our rights, let alone advance our shared purposes."[4] It is in that spirit that I offer a broad range of initiatives designed to transform ownership patterns. Although I focus much of this section on policy initiatives, there is no reason why foresighted corporate leaders need await the passage of legislation to act.

I divide my "solutions" into three broad categories. In the first chapter I describe how ownership patterns could play a key role in the formulation of national economic policy. I then demonstrate how the government's pervasive presence in the economy could influence those ownership patterns. The foreign policy implications are addressed in Chapter 14 and again in Chapter 16 ("The Development Dilemma"). In Chapter 15, I show the many ways that tax policy could broaden ownership. Though most of my prescriptions focus on national policymaking, that does not deny the clear interdependence of national, regional, state and local politics. Nor is this an attempt to disavow or discredit what has gone before. My goal is not to dismiss but to make sense of free enterprise by fashioning a new institutional environment—a social contract, if you will—that fosters a more inclusive capitalism.

To date, the financial component of free enterprise has been perceived as operating largely free of government direction. However, when that freedom has unintended effects, as I argue it did throughout much of the 1980s and beyond, responsible policymakers must act. The policy challenge lies in how best to evoke a more equitable and sustainable result. To foster a property system that favors more than a privileged few requires not a level playing field but a field designed to ensure that more players have a chance to get on the field. To that end, I offer not a definitive list of initiatives but a menu of illustrative options. Lastly, in my experience, success in this area requires three key ingredients: (1) imaginative and committed leadership from both the public and the private sector, (2) an understanding that significant change requires institutional change, and (3) time.

Reinventing Capitalism

> Public sentiment is everything. With public sentiment,
> nothing can fail. Without it, nothing can succeed.
>
> —*Abraham Lincoln*

Much of what policymakers can do is accomplished not by legislation but by exhortation—relying on the stature, visibility and credibility of their office to advance a goal through a combination of moral suasion and the bully pulpit. President Franklin D. Roosevelt was a master of the art. Though he pushed for the enactment of sweeping legislative changes, it was his leadership, not just his legislation, that helped lift the nation's spirits during the Depression. Not since the Progressive and Populist era of the 1930s have we seen a national leader willing to speak out either against greed or in favor of inclusiveness. Absent that candor, an ownership strategy may be difficult to advance on a nationwide basis. By way of illustration, here are six potential opportunities to inject ownership into policymaking.

❶ **Public Opinion Poll.** One key reason policymakers continue to enact ownership pattern–insensitive legislation is that they continue to ask ownership-insensitive questions. As I point out in Chapter 7, the Employment Act of 1946, still the centerpiece of national economic policy, gained political credibility with a public opinion poll conducted near the end of World War II, when pollsters inquired whether Congress should enact policies fostering full employment. To no one's surprise, the answer was yes. We will never know what the answer might have been had the questionnaire been broadened to ask if public policy should promote broad-based capital ownership. Certainly the opportunities were there. Huge sums of taxpayer money were funneled to private business through the Reconstruction Finance Corporation, including financing for what became America's privately owned aluminum industry. Taxpayers also funded the Marshall Plan, which helped to rebuild war-ravaged Europe ($13 billion in grants and loans, about $88 billion in current dollars). Both the Marshall Plan and the Dodge plan (for Japan) also had the welcome and intended benefit of providing customers for American companies as they converted from wartime production, updated their operations and expanded their facilities.[1]

Nor did anyone ask whether they'd like to own a stake in those wartime fortunes built with revenues generated by war bonds and record levels of government debt. Given the notoriously concentrated ownership patterns that prevailed at the peak of the Depression, the answer to that question almost assuredly would have been a resounding yes. To date, however, the question has yet to be asked, in the United States or in any country.[2] Such a poll could, for instance, inquire whether Americans are happy with a national economic policy that focuses on jobs but not ownership. Are they happy being workers, or would they like to be capitalists too? Sounds pretty obvious when it's put like that. Yet the inquiry would also need to determine whether the public supports policy intervention, and to what extent. Without such a display of support, policymakers may not be willing to expend their scarce political capital to pursue an ownership agenda.

The political potential is enormous. In the United States, for instance, business expenditures for new plants and equipment totaled more than $800 billion in 1996. Another $659 billion in assets changed hands through mergers and acquisitions ($1 trillion in 1997). Between 1998 and 2011, when the first baby boomers begin to retire, we can reasonably predict an outlay of some $12 trillion in capital expenditures to purchase new or replacement machinery plus office buildings, information-processing equipment and such. None of that income-producing capital is yet owned by anyone.

However, today's closed system of finance dictates that, of those assets held by individuals, roughly half will be owned by the already-wealthiest top 3 to 5 percent of households. Do American voters support that? If not, what means would they embrace to encourage more widespread ownership? What (if anything) would they be willing to give up to ensure widespread ownership? What responsibilities and risks would they be willing to take on? Given the sensitive and complex nature of the issue, combined with a widespread lack of financial literacy, such polling would need to be supplemented by focus group discussions and in-depth interviews. The moral legitimacy of democracy rests on its success in sustaining a robust feedback system capable of determining just what it is the citizenry really wants. On the sensitive and crucial topic of ownership, no one can confidently say just what it is that Americans want—because no one has ever taken the time to ask.

❷ **National Economic Policy.** Odd though it may seem, the United States, bastion of free-enterprise capitalism, has yet to declare widespread ownership a specific goal of national economic policy. That's a glaring oversight for a nation to whom many postsocialist countries look for guidance. Senator Hubert H. Humphrey III chaired the Joint Economic Committee in the mid-1970s when he convened the first-ever congressional hearings on broadened ownership.

The popular Humphrey proposed in the most general of terms the inclusion of widespread ownership as an element of national economic policy:

> *Capital, and the question of who owns it and therefore reaps the benefit of its productiveness, is an extremely important issue that is complementary to the issue of full employment. . . . I see these as twin pillars of our economy: full employment of our labor resources and widespread ownership of our capital resources. Such twin pillars would go a long way in providing a firm underlying support for future economic growth that would be equitably shared.[3]*

Even this modest, clearly innocuous statement never found its way into legislation.

❸ **Bipartisan Commission on Economic Empowerment.** A broader inquiry is needed. One of the few political terms that is widely acceptable across today's political spectrum is *empowerment*. This may provide just the sort of diffused focus required to convene a genuinely bipartisan commission charged with evaluating broad-based capital ownership as a national goal. From the perspective of simple fiscal responsibility, I expect the commission will conclude that we cannot do without widespread prosperity. Yet if broad-based ownership becomes a national goal, unfettered free-market forces will not suffice to reach it. At the same time, however, overly intrusive policy initiatives are inconsistent with the goal of strengthening free enterprise. A bipartisan effort to identify common ground would provide an opportunity to devise a range of ownership solutions.

❹ **An Office of Asset Ownership.** Those living in a private-property economy can earn income through the ownership of their labor, the ownership of capital, or some combination of the two. Every nation has a department (or ministry) of labor. However, no nation yet has an office to recommend and oversee policies designed to broaden ownership. The Employment Act of 1946 established the President's Council of Economic Advisers, requiring that it publish an annual report appraising the condition of the U.S. economy—with the glaring exception of any requirement to appraise the condition of the nation's ownership. An amendment to the 1946 act could create, say, an Office of Asset Ownership that, working with the council, could include in each year's *Economic Report of the President* a survey of current ownership patterns, an appraisal of progress made toward expanded capital ownership, an overview of challenges faced and an assessment of prospects for the future, including an analysis of pending legislative initiatives. What gets measured gets managed—or at least is not ignored.

❺ **Ownership Impact Reports.** Environmental-impact assessments are commonplace, particularly among governmental agencies. The World Bank mandates an environmental assessment for its projects. As yet, however, no nation (or international financial institution) has a requirement to assess the ownership impact of its policies and programs, even though the ownership environment is a key factor in determining quality of life. Most Americans have only a vague notion of America's ownership patterns, and an even dimmer understanding of how public policy and corporate practices affect those patterns. Such reporting could help. For instance, any authorization of government expenditures, including both direct expenditures (such as government contracts) and "tax expenditures," could be required to include an "ownership impact report" identifying both the short-term and projected long-term effect on ownership patterns.[4]

Similar reporting could accompany the granting of licenses (such as broadcast licenses), the opening of public areas to resource extraction (minerals, oil, timber), or government financial assistance (loan guarantees, export/import assistance). International financial institutions (World Bank, Inter-American Development Bank) could provide an ongoing "ownership audit" assessing the impact of their activities on the alleviation of poverty.

On a periodic basis, an Office of Asset Ownership could review reports and projections to assess their accuracy and improve reporting. For example, it is difficult to imagine that the U.S. Congress in 1981 would have approved $872.6 billion in deficit-financed "supply-side" tax incentives if they had come with a report projecting their (quite predictable) impact on ownership patterns.[5] Similarly, Reagan's trillion-dollar defense industry buildup may have faced closer scrutiny had his appropriations requests come with an assessment of the (again, quite predictable) impact of those defense contracts on ownership.

❻ **An Ownership Survey.** The best-known survey of American ownership patterns is the annual publication of *Forbes* magazine's "Forbes 400" list of richest Americans, along with its annual listing of the world's billionaires. The technical capacity is now available to support a nationwide—even a worldwide—ownership survey.[6] This capacity—combining satellite mapping with an examination of land title registries and corporate shareholder registries—could go a long way toward enabling policymakers worldwide to gain an accurate accounting of just who owns what.[7] In developed countries, ownership surveys have typically relied on secondary sources, particularly examinations of estate-tax returns and random surveys. Despite the key role played by private property in free-enterprise economies, no free-enterprise nation has ever undertaken an ownership census on a genuinely systematic and comprehensive basis.

The United States has a $26.6 billion annual intelligence budget in search of a post–Cold War mission.[8] Approximately a third of that is spent on photo reconnaissance and electronic eavesdropping. A major focus of the Cold War was its protection of private property systems from Marxist-Leninist systems intent on their destruction. It seems only fitting that the victorious West undertake a survey to assess worldwide progress in *expanding* participation in private-

property environments, both in the former socialist countries and in traditional free-enterprise economies.

When it comes to the natural environment, that need has already been recognized: a portion of U.S. intelligence capacity has been converted to environmental monitoring. American spy satellites regularly observe 260 environmental
sites around the world, from the high slopes of Mount Kilamanjaro to the low-
land tropical rain forests of Costa Rica. This expanded reconnaissance mission
reflects an enlarged definition of national security and a recognition that environmental changes can play an important role in regional conflict.[9]

Various forms of monitoring have long proved a useful adjunct to American foreign policy. For example, Manhattan-based Freedom House monitors
indices of freedom worldwide, publishing an annual ranking of nations according to the extent they reflect agreed-to notions of freedom.

As history has proven time and again, trends in ownership patterns can
have an enormous bearing on political stability. Thus the need for monitoring. For instance, although privatization efforts are now well advanced in
many of the former socialist countries, Western policymakers have only the
faintest notion of just *whose* privatization that has now become—with the
advice and counsel of American experts. As we shall see in later chapters, the
evidence to date is not encouraging, particularly in Russia.

With more than $4 trillion in taxpayer funds invested in Cold War expen-
ditures over the past half century, that intelligence could help policymakers
better evaluate American foreign policy, including the costs and the benefits of
today's ownership-pattern agnosticism. A steady monitoring of the global ownership environment is a natural extension of national security in a post–Cold
War world where private property free enterprise is a dominant theme of
America's presence abroad.[10]

CHAPTER ⓮

Reengineering Capitalism for Inclusion

Monological thinking looks for single answers—and there are none.

—*Buckminster Fuller*

I describe here twelve areas where the government's presence could be re-tooled to broaden ownership, particularly for businesses either dealing directly with the government or benefiting from governmental assistance. To put this in context, understand that the dollars spent each year by federal, state and local governments total about one-sixth of GDP. Understand too that governments often have their thumb on the economic scale.* Washington has intervened in private industry for decades through programs ranging from the deductibility of the interest on home mortgages to agricultural support programs.† Subsidies can be found at every turn.

For instance, for each year through 2005, owners of the 320 ships in the nation's merchant marine fleet will receive a payment of $2.1 million *per ship*.[1] During the 1960s, large-scale purchases of computers by the Pentagon and the space program were instrumental in lowering unit costs and cinching that industry's takeoff as a consumer giant.[2] A similar boost was granted the recycling industry when the Clinton administration ordered a shift from virgin

---

* For example, Richard Pratt, a Reagan appointee to the Federal Home Loan Bank Board, revoked a regulation requiring that savings-and-loan associations have no less than four hundred stockholders, thereby allowing single-owner S&Ls. The Congress then raised the limits on Federal deposit insurance (from $40,000 to $100,000 per account) and agreed to allow S&Ls to make loans of virtually any sort instead of being limited to their original purpose: home loans. The result: $150 billion in government-guaranteed bad debts.

† For instance, the U.S. government's sugar price support program costs American taxpayers $1.4 billion each year. Approximately 40 percent of that amount benefits the largest 1 percent of sugar farms; the thirty-three largest sugarcane plantations in the United States receive more than $1 million each. It is estimated that one Florida family alone pockets $60 million a year in artificial profits from price supports and import quotas. Stephen Moore and Dean Stansel, *Ending Corporate Welfare As We Know It* (Washington, D.C.: Cato Institute, March 6, 1995).

to recycled paper. A comparable boost may yet kick-start the solar power industry.[3] By spending not more but more wisely, governments the world over could have a dramatic impact on ownership patterns.

❶ **Government Contracts.** Simply put, government contracts help finance assets for the owners of firms awarded those contracts. A government contract can be pledged as security to borrow funds. Those funds can then be used to acquire the assets (and hire the personnel) to perform under the contract. In less-developed countries, kinship plus political and military affiliation have long been the chief qualification for receiving government contracts. The encouragement in government contracts of employee stock ownership would ensure that the benefits of the public purse are spread more broadly.

For example, during the 1992 presidential elections, Ross Perot used his fortune (estimated at $3.3 billion in 1997) to buy television time touting his case for a smaller, leaner, more efficient, less debt-laden government. Perot made the bulk of his fortune from government contracts, initially performing data processing for the Social Security Administration. He could have played a personal role in reducing the size and cost of government by financially structuring his company (Electronic Data Systems, now EDS) so that, as it grew, it built a capital estate for a broad base of those who worked for him, thereby anticipating their need for entitlements (Social Security, Medicare, Medicaid, etc.), the largest and fastest growing area of government spending. Instead, "populist" Perot elected to keep $3.3 billion for himself, most of which reportedly is now invested in government debt.[4]

The Defense Department's $45 billion procurement budget (for 1997) offers recurring opportunities to link taxpayer expenditures to broad-based ownership.[5] Three examples should suffice. In November 1996, the Pentagon announced two finalists (Boeing Company and Lockheed Martin Corp.) in the competition to build a new joint strike fighter airplane for use by the Air Force, Navy and Marines. Experts value the final development-and-production contract at between $200 and $750 *billion*.[6] The Pentagon awarded a 1996 shipbuilding contract to Louisiana-based Avondale Industries with an initial value of $641 million but a potential value of billions more, both for shipbuilding and for maintenance and refitting during the ships' expected forty-year lifespans (the chairman of the House Appropriations Committee is Louisiana Congressman Bob Livingston).[7]

In 1997, $736 million was added to the Pentagon budget by Senate Majority leader Trent Lott for the production of an Aegis class destroyer in shipyards in his home state of Mississippi while House Speaker Newt Gingrich of Georgia secured $470 million more for C-130 air transports built by Lockheed Martin Corporation in his home state of Georgia.[8]

This is an international phenomenon with wide-ranging implications. For example, China has successfully used government contract competition between

Europe's Airbus and America's Boeing as a means of muting both European and American critics of China's record on human rights.[9] The $66 billion cost of the "Eurofighter" (a new job-creating military jet under development for European armed forces and for sale around the world) has a per-job cost of about $15 million shared among Britain, Germany, Italy and Spain.[10] Whether in the United States or abroad, taxpayers would realize more value for their money if contract awards enhanced the economic self-sufficiency of a broad rather than a narrow base of their fellow taxpayers. That such contract awards do otherwise (as in the case of Ross Perot's company) amounts to fiscal folly because it ignores widespread capital accumulation as the only possible private-sector solution to the skyrocketing costs of entitlements.*

❷ **Government Spending Leverage.** The government's purchasing power, for items ranging from hammers and toilet seats to aircraft and aircraft carriers, could be directed to corporations with certifiably broad-based ownership. The value of these firms is often largely dependent on taxpayer-funded purchases. Government employees could also be required to limit their work-related purchases to such companies (for office supplies, transportation, food services, telecommunications). Other ownership opportunities abound.

In an effort to contain health care costs (14 percent of GDP and rising), nonprofit medical facilities are converting to for-profit operations. This could be combined with employee ownership, perhaps with workers exchanging some portion of their benefits for a combination of stock and profit-sharing. Such a move could also help retain motivated employees and improve employee morale and service. An ownership solution might also boost pride, purpose and professionalism in an industry struggling with the conflict between the dedication required of altruistic human care and the dictates imposed by return-seeking private capital.[11] Taxpayer-subsidized health care and drug prescriptions, such as those paid through Medicare and Medicaid, could be limited to those health-care providers and pharmaceutical companies maintaining a minimum level of employee ownership.†

---

* The relationship between political activism, government contracts and wealth accumulation is one that economic historians have not yet fully explored. For instance, during the Civil War, Andrew Carnegie served as a senior military officer organizing transportation and communication for the Union Army at Bull Run. He then began his legendary career as a steel magnate, establishing one of the first companies to replace wooden bridges with bridges made of steel, aided by a combination of government contracts and favorable tariffs, before selling out to J. P. Morgan for $480 million in 1901. Government contracts to build America's highways, including its interstate highway system, offered another opportunity (also forgone) to combine taxpayer-financed economic progress with widespread economic prosperity.

† Examples abound of opportunities, both obvious and obscure, where government spending affects capital accumulation. Often the amounts involved are staggering, even for seemingly small programs. For instance, participants in the U.S. government's Women, Infants and Children (WIC) program buy $285 million of dry cereal each year, setting off periodic political infighting among cereal manufacturers.

❸ **Government Licensing.** Governments have broad discretion to grant licenses and otherwise allocate access to scarce resources.* For example, the limited availability of wavelength spectrum makes it essential that this resource be allocated among vendors of broadcasting services (TV, radio) or communications (cellular telephones, pagers). Governments also have discretion in the granting of access to other limited resources, such as international air routes and airport landing slots. Because development of these resources (such as digital broadcasting or high-definition television) often requires large commitments of money, access to the wavelength spectrum has typically been closed to those without access to substantial capital. The allocation of these scarce resources has generally been accomplished through an "open" auction process (i.e., open to those with access to capital).[12] The confluence of politics and broadcasting is legendary.[13] For example, former U.S. congressman, senator, and president Lyndon B. Johnson amassed a family fortune through broadcast licenses acquired in his wife's name.

Beginning in 1993, the Federal Communications Commission held thirteen auctions, raising nearly $23 billion. In 1995, the FCC made a splash by raising $7.7 billion for personal communication services (PCS) from corporations like AT&T, Sprint and Bell Atlantic.[14] From an ownership-pattern perspective, what was missing here was any concern for how this crucial high-growth industry could be encouraged to promote broad-based American ownership. That would have gained a double victory: immediate cash from the sale plus a deferred bonus as more Americans became economically self-sufficient through their accumulation of equity in this key industry.

In truth, the Congress tried to broaden ownership through a set-aside of licenses for small businesses, rural phone companies and businesses owned by minorities and women. When a 1995 Supreme Court ruling scuttled the special treatment for minorities and women, the FCC redesigned the auction to favor companies with annual revenues of less than $40 million, allowing qualified bidders to pay over ten years at below-market interest rates, with interest-only payments for the first six years. When the auction garnered $10.2 billion in bids, it initially appeared that this policy succeeded. However, the easy payment plan enticed the winners to bid an average $40 per customer, well above the $10 to $15 paid by the established players just a year earlier. The combination of high prices, a glut of players and a downturn in the market made financing unavailable. As this book was being completed, Congress

---

* The conditions imposed on private access to scarce public resources take many forms. For example, since 1920, the Jones Act has required that companies use U.S.-built ships to transport passengers or goods between U.S. ports. Because most ships in the rapidly growing cruise ship industry are built in foreign countries that have long subsidized their shipyards, cruise ships operated by these companies often bypass Jones Act restrictions by stopping at a foreign port between stops at U.S. ports.

and the FCC were trying to sort out whether to grant the bidders more generous terms, or require that they forfeit all or a portion of the licenses (to be auctioned again), or allow the licenses to be tied up in bankruptcy litigation. From a fiscal perspective, this auction fiasco means that the Congress has counted as revenue funds that will likely not be forthcoming—at least not soon.

In retrospect, it's clear that this scheme's ownership broadening would have been modest at best, because there was no requirement for broad-based ownership within those small companies. In addition, many bidders were backed by foreign investors who may well have stepped in. A more viable ownership-broadening, revenue-generating alternative would be either to require these smaller bidders to establish ESOP/CSOP-like mechanisms (perhaps incentivized with a reduced price) or to allow the big players into the bidding, provided they compete on the basis of a combination of cash payments and an enforceable commitment to an ownership-broadening capital structure.

The allocation of this invisible real estate is similar in many ways to a bygone era when the government granted strips of land across the United States to encourage the development of nationwide rail transport. Several famous family fortunes were built around these subsidies, including those of Cornelius Vanderbilt, Leland Stanford, and Averell Harriman. For example, the last leg of the original transcontinental railroad was built eastward from Sacramento by the Central Pacific Railroad and westward from Omaha by the government-chartered Union Pacific Railroad. From the outset (1862), each railroad received loan subsidies ranging from $16,000 to $48,000 per mile depending on the difficulty of the terrain, plus ten land sections for each mile of track laid (one section = one square mile). A second Railroad Act of 1864 doubled the land subsidies, though little progress was made until labor and supplies were freed at the end of the Civil War, when the competition to lay track (and claim real estate) became heated. The two companies eventually laid 1,776 miles of track, joining at Promontory Summit, Utah, in May 1869. At only ten sections per mile of track (though much of the track qualified for twice that), the land subsidy element alone was 17,760 square miles, or 11,366,400 acres.

❹ **Private Access to Public Assets.** The public ownership of natural resources provides another opportunity for an ownership solution. Under a series of nineteenth-century variations on the Homestead Act, mineral-rich government-owned land is still being sold for as little as $2.50 per acre. In 1994, Interior Secretary Bruce Babbitt was forced under the Mining Law of 1872 to turn over title to public land containing more than $100 billion in gold. In return, a Canadian-based company paid less than $10,000, prompting Babbitt to call it "the greatest gold heist since the days of Butch Cassidy."[15] Over the past 125 years, ownership to more than 3.2 million acres of government land has been conveyed on a similar basis.

The Homestead Act was originally intended for small-scale hard rock miners as a way to encourage family-sized homesteading in the American West,[16] twenty-three of the top forty companies now extracting minerals from public lands are either subsidiaries of, or largely controlled by, foreign corporations.* Though justified on the basis of jobs, mining employment is now at its lowest level ever. Nationwide, employment in the metal-extracting industries has plummeted 50 percent since 1980. As capital- and chemical-intensive mineral extraction becomes more widespread, job losses will continue while the value of minerals produced will grow—as it did in twenty-nine of the years from 1960 to 1994.[17]

Timber offers another classic case. In exchange for logging fees, the U.S. Forest Service builds and maintains roads to access the timber. Only rarely do the fees cover the costs. In 1995, the Forest Service spent $234 million more in services to private logging companies than it made from the sale of timber cut on public lands.[18] In effect, taxpayers pay private timber companies to remove the public's trees. Again, the political trade-off is private access to public assets in exchange for jobs—accompanied by no concern whatsoever for who owns the logging companies. Since 1975, the Forest Service has built 340,000 miles of logging roads, more than eight times the length of the interstate highway system.[19]

An ownership perspective suggests two possible strategies. First, if a nation's public resources are to be converted into private fortunes, then (at a minimum) this conversion should benefit a broad rather than a narrow group of citizens. Second, if ownership is at least partially vested in those physically closest to and most directly affected by these assets, it is more likely that those assets will be managed in a sustainable fashion. The historical experience with Native Americans suggests that a modern counterpart to such "indigenization" could improve a system that, as currently structured, is inequitable, dysfunctional and unsustainable. For example, if both the jobs of those employed in extractive industries and some portion of the pensions were directly linked to sustainable yields, then where those assets are renewable (timber, fishing), the likelihood of overharvesting is apt to be reduced. Also, with their families living nearby, the influence of local, up-close ownership could also lessen the incidence of extraction-induced environmental damage.

This sort of analysis lies behind "fishery-share system" legislation enacted in January 1995 by Australia's New South Wales government. In an attempt to encourage efficient and sustainable fishing while also reducing the costs of

---

* Major U.S. corporations are also key beneficiaries. For example, environmentalist David Brower bemoans both the social and the environmental implications of Chevron's purchase of the 2,036 acres that make up the Stillwater mine that sits over the Beartooth-Absaroka Wilderness forty miles from Yellowstone Park, for a total of $10,180 (i.e., $5 an acre). The value of the mine's reserves of palladium and platinum are estimated at $30 billion. David Brower, *Let the Mountains Talk, Let the Rivers Run* (New York: Harper Collins, 1995), p. 164.

government regulation, the government is phasing out its annual fishing licenses with a self-enforcement mechanism whose unit of management is no longer the fisher but the natural resource: the fish. In return for the security of their right to the fish (as opposed to a right to fish), fishers pay for their private access to this public resource. Through a transferable share system granting them exclusive access to the allowable catch, fishers have a way to link personal value to the future value of the fisheries.[20] The architects of this ownership solution view it as adaptable to rights of access to other natural resources, including rights to water for irrigation, to take timber from native forests, to emit greenhouse gases, and to dispose of industrial wastes.

❺ **Public Service Providers.** Policymakers have spirited debates about which services (power, water, sewage, phone, trash removal, fire protection, etc.) should be provided by the public sector and which by private and, indeed, where one sector ends and the other begins. The balance has shifted to private, for-profit businesses, largely for reasons of efficiency and responsiveness. For instance, since 1986 the two thousand employee-owners of Norcal Waste Systems have provided trash-hauling services to residents in the San Francisco Bay Area. Even more unusual is the provision of fire, ambulance and other services by Rural/Metro Company of Scottsdale, Arizona. Founded in 1948 to provide fire-fighting services to an unincorporated rural community, this ESOP company has since grown to eight thousand employees in more than 350 communities in twenty states, diversifying into home health care and security monitoring, while generating revenues of $171 million in 1995 and $250 million in 1996.

Privatization of public services is growing. The issue is often not so much public versus private, but whether services are provided on a competitive basis. The use of private firms to provide public services dates from the turn of the century. However, in the 1920s and 1930s, communities found themselves abused as firms charged monopolistic rates, leading progressives to bring the services back under public control. The issue of abuse has arisen again, only this time in public-sector monopolies.

Since taking office in 1992, Mayor Stephen Goldsmith of Indianapolis, the nation's twelfth largest city, has insisted that more than sixty city services be opened to competitive bidding, reducing multiyear fiscal outlays for this city of eight hundred thousand by more than $400 million and shrinking its non–public safety workforce by 45 percent. After joining a different crew of city employees one day each week, he found such bureaucratic overstaffing in middle management that no rank and file employees were dismissed. He solicits worker support with profit sharing, returning a portion of the savings they identify. He also pledged $70 million in savings to develop seven of the city's poorest neighborhoods.[21] The balance are pledged to support a (previously unaffordable) $700 million bond issue to upgrade local infrastructure in order to attract more businesses and more private-sector jobs.

It comes as a surprise to most that the capitalist United States has a privatization policy. Crafted in the mid-1980s by the Office of Personnel Management (formerly the Civil Service Commission), this initiative took as its name an acronym only a bureaucrat could love: FED CO-OP (Federal Employee Direct Corporate Ownership Opportunity Plan). Politically, the goal is to use ESOPs to enlist employee support for privatization.* One hope is that America's 761,000 postal workers may someday decide to support an ESOP buyout. Faced with competition for both mail (faxes, e-mail, electronic payments) and packages (UPS, Federal Express), CEO Marvin Runyon must seek either higher taxpayer subsidies or continue to seek higher postage rates.[22] The time may be ripe to revisit how employee ownership could play a role in a restructured Postal Service. Under FED CO-OP, postal employees would gain a major stake in the Postal Service through an ESOP, while redundant employees would be given a stock bonus as part of their severance.

In Britain, a "Citizen's Charter" movement emerged in response to the concerns of those who depend on public services, whether they be patients, passengers, parents, pupils or benefit claimants. Public services in Britain are now required to publish standards of expected service along with accessible means of redress, with the goal of ensuring better quality service and greater customer choice. Thus, for instance, if the train from Oxford to Picadilly Station arrives more than twenty minutes late, passengers are told the reason for the delay and given a complimentary ticket for a subsequent trip. As of January 1998, forty charters had been published. Each year the government presents "Charter Marks" to those service providers who improve their standards. The program acknowledges that citizens are the ultimate "owners" of these services and it is to them that the services should be responsive. From a "systems" perspective, this institutionalized feedback provides an innovative monitoring mechanism normally lacking in the public sector.[23]

❻ **Trade Assistance.** With the end of the Cold War, free trade has emerged as the first genuinely global ideology.[24] Nevertheless, governments continue their aggressive practices to spur domestic business (and jobs), with government-financed trade assistance often offered openly. In 1996 the Export-Import Bank, a key instrument of U.S. trade policy, supported $11.5 billion in loans, loan guarantees and credit insurance to finance purchases of American exports. The political rationale: the creation of jobs in the United States.[25] The awkward ownership issue: Should such financial support include a requirement that applicant companies embrace an expanded ownership program?[26] To keep pace with the worldwide movement to privatize infrastructure—telecommunications, power generation, and such—the Ex-Im Bank projects a sixfold

---

* Investment adviser John M. Templeton suggests that those businesses now owned by the federal government be put into a holding company, with free shares distributed to every American adult that applies. John Templeton, personal communication, 13 July 1996.

increase in project financing, particularly in politically risky countries where the bank's assistance is most often sought, such as China.

Other subsidies could also be conditioned. For example, America's 162 embassies maintain commercial offices whose primary mission is to assist American exporters.* The State Department awards $5,000 cash bonuses to ambassadors and foreign service officers who help out. John Wolf, ambassador to Malaysia, was a 1993 winner for helping McDonnell Douglas secure a $700 million order for F-18 jet fighters. When Dow Chemical proposed to buy a run-down chemical complex in former East Germany, the Treuhand, Germany's privatization agency, balked, preferring to sell it instead to a German firm. After the U.S. embassy intervened, the purchase not only proceeded; it included $6 *billion* of Treuhand subsidies.

Reflecting the increasingly dominant commercial content of U.S. foreign policy, President George Bush issued a "Bill of Rights for U.S. Business" instructing embassy staff what businesspeople could expect, including not only the right to have their views considered in the formulation of foreign policy but also the right to assistance in contacting foreign government officials and business executives. At her 1997 Senate confirmation hearing before the Senate Foreign Relations Committee, then secretary of state designate Madeleine Albright conceded this commercial focus: "I think that one of the major goals of our administration is to make sure American economic interests can be pursued globally."

The ownership issue is straightforward: when granting public subsidies and providing taxpayer-funded commercial services, should Washington give preference to companies that use their foreign sales to accumulate capital assets for a broad (vs. narrow) group of American taxpayers? For instance, an ownership-oriented screening process could set priorities for the use of commercial officers' time and resources, or to qualify companies to be invited along on official government trade missions. During 1994, then commerce secretary Ron Brown jetted off, with corporate chief executives in tow, to Argentina, Brazil, Chile, China, Hong Kong and Northern Ireland. The trip to China alone is credited with helping U.S. companies seal $6 billion in deals. In early 1997, a trip to Beijing by Vice President Gore netted a $685 million order for Boeing passenger jets and a $1.3 billion agreement with General Motors to build one hundred thousand Buicks a year there.

The U.S. Department of Commerce maintains a "war room" where, with the help of officials from nineteen government agencies, it tracks (and offers assistance to) the one hundred largest business deals around the world for which U.S. companies are competing.[27] As of mid-1995, the department was taking credit for $19.45 billion in "successful advocacy projects." With not

---

* The exposure in February 1995 of a Central Intelligence Agency–staffed industrial- and trade-focused spy operation in France made apparent what trade strategists have known for years: American foreign policy has long had a major commercial focus.

so much as a hint of the impact this program has on private-sector capital accumulation (or the impact on share values of companies receiving this taxpayer assistance), Secretary Brown noted only that there was "a very simple equation: American exports equal American jobs."[28]

The granting of ambassadorships to those who contribute money to presidential campaigns is a well-known political favor. The 1997 release of transcribed tapes from Richard Nixon's presidency document how calculated and direct this long-suspected quid pro quo really is. During the Nixon era, $250,000 was the "going rate" for an ambassadorship.[29] This long-honored, highly opaque tradition could be made transparent and given some redeeming social value if conditioned on the source of the funds. For instance, in the granting of ambassadorships to those from the world of business (few else can afford the cost), a minimum percentage of appointees (say half) could be drawn from those who contribute proceeds realized from the sale of their shares to the employees whose efforts helped generate the funds contributed.[30]

One of the lesser-known trade assistance programs is the Agriculture Department's Market Access Program, under which U.S. taxpayers spend about $100 million per year underwriting the costs of advertising American products abroad. In 1991, for example, $465,000 was spent advertising McDonald's Chicken McNuggets, $2.9 million promoting Pillsbury muffins and pies and $10 million touting Sunkist oranges.[31] Taxpayers have paid for ads for Gallo wine, Miller beer, Campbell's soup and Mars candy bars. At one point, U.S. raisin growers received $4 million to advertise in Japan, an amount that exceeded the Commerce Department's entire Japan budget.[32]

A 1995 study by the Congressional Budget Office concluded that Washington spends $28 billion a year promoting commerce and business. In his Senate confirmation hearings in January 1997, then commerce secretary designate William Daley conceded that $250 million of Commerce Department export promotion in the previous four years resulted in over $40 billion in overseas sales. While such initiatives may reflect a genuine need for public support of the commercial interests of U.S. business abroad (as most nations have done for decades), the delicate issue remains: Just who should reap the private benefits, particularly the ownership benefits, of this public assistance?

Should policymakers become less enamored of unrestricted free trade, a range of community-strengthening measures could be considered that would add an ownership-engineering element to current international trade agreements.[33] For instance, access to U.S. markets could be conditioned on a "site here to sell here" policy designed to ensure that America's domestic purchasing power creates jobs for Americans.[34] Importers of manufactured goods (such as autos) could be required to ensure that part of their production (auto assembly) is performed in the United States utilizing American labor. Carrying that notion a step further, U.S. law could mandate a "site here, own here to sell here" policy whereby an element of employee ownership becomes part of the "toll charge" for access not only to American markets but also to valuable infrastructure, including many property-protecting, value-enhancing features—such as police, courts, and a tax system that allows use of depreciation allowances to shield U.S. revenues from U.S. tax.

❼ Loans and Loan Guarantees. Governments worldwide create contingent liabilities that never appear on their accounts unless the contingency occurs. Loan guarantees are among the most common. These guarantees typically fuel traditional closed-system financing, though a few exceptions can be found. For instance, in the mid-1970s three U.S. government agencies extended fifteen separate economic development loans to struggling businesses contingent on their willingness to establish ESOPs.[35] Without such an ownership-sharing proviso, the risk of loan default is spread broadly among all taxpayers while the primary benefit (ownership) is harvested by a few.

Homes (and home building) provide another potential opportunity. The U.S. government-backed Federal National Mortgage Association ("Fannie Mae") is a New Deal–era banking facility created in 1938 to ensure a steady flow of mortgage funds to middle-class Americans in the belief that widespread home ownership is a public good. From the outset, Fannie Mae has purchased home loans from local lenders and resold them to investors, freeing up local money for new mortgages.[36] Fannie Mae's $800-plus billion in mortgages makes it certain soon to become a trillion-dollar financial company. The sums that flow through it, $5 trillion per year, exceed the GDP of Germany. Though publicly chartered, its shares ("Fannie Mae's") trade on the New York Stock Exchange. Operating as a for-profit corporation yet exempt from state and local income taxes, Fannie Mae is a unique ownership hybrid that combines the strengths of both public policy and private enterprise.

The firm is "the equivalent of a Federal Reserve for housing," according to former Fannie Mae vice chairman Frank Raines (since May 1996, Clinton administration director of the Office of Management and Budget). With the exception of the U.S. Treasury, Fannie Mae is Wall Street's largest client, generating more than $100 million per year in fees as brokers bundle Fannie Mae–qualified mortgages and sell them as mortgage-backed securities. The balance of its mortgages are held in Fannie Mae's own portfolio, generating interest and principal payments to the tune of more than $2.1 billion in annual profit.

Fannie Mae's most valuable asset is its special government-conferred status and Wall Street's belief that Washington will not let it fail. With only thirty-five hundred employees, Fannie Mae is America's most profitable company per employee. Its stock value grew by 27 percent a year during the past decade, which raises the obvious question: Why doesn't Fannie Mae have an ESOP?*

---

* A departing Fannie Mae chief executive reportedly was paid $27 million in severance in 1994, suggesting that a very *exclusive* form of employee ownership is already in place.

As a publicly sponsored conduit for such huge amounts of private-sector cash flow, other "ripple effect" ownership strategies also should be considered. For example, Fannie Mae could purchase mortgages only of lenders that sponsor a substantial ESOP; it could also limit its securities dealings to those firms in which a broad base of employees own shares.*

❽ **Development Banks.** Numerous countries have development banks chartered specifically to provide long-term capital at preferential rates. Germany has its reconstruction bank; South Korea its state development bank; Japan its Industrial Bank of Japan; France the Credit National; Mexico has Nafinsa; and so on. Often tax concessions enable them to offer preferred interest rates to attract depositors. As in other areas where public policy boosts private fortunes, the missing ingredient is an effort to ensure that these subsidies underwrite ownership patterns that are highly participatory.

❾ **Antitrust Policy.** A robust antitrust policy is crucial to the fair and efficient operation of a market economy. Economic history is a study of the lengths to which producers will go to exclude others. Trustbusters operate with a political charter founded on hard-earned experience, namely that no entity in a democracy should become too powerful. In an earlier era, antitrust enforcement occasionally required a company to sell off a subsidiary or a division. Those mandated divestitures could have required that the spun-off entity establish an ESOP whose financing would be partially guaranteed by the divesting company as part of the legal remedy.[37] To date, however, it is not ownership concentration but market concentration that has consumed the interest of antitrust regulators.

Antitrust policy began with the trustbusting fervor of the 1890s and extended well into the Populist-inspired 1930s. Over the past twenty-five years, antitrust sentiment has change dramatically. The rationale has also evolved from its origins in policies designed to ensure market access and a doctrine grounded in big-is-badness. Starting in the mid-1970s, the focus shifted to combating market concentration beyond a predetermined limit. Since the 1990s and the emergence of a more globally integrated economy, the focus has shifted again, this time to competitiveness: an antitrust complaint must show that a company's conduct would raise consumer prices. Thus, rather than antitrust orders requiring bust-ups of companies, we entered a "fix it" era, with lots of market analysis and negotiated settlements and few court cases (until 1997, the U.S. Supreme Court had not heard a merger case in twenty years).[38]

---

* One step further removed: Fannie Mae–qualified mortgage lenders could be required to generate a minimum percentage of mortgages from homes built by construction companies maintaining a prescribed level of employee ownership. The ripple effect of this financing becomes obvious when one realizes that this requirement could also be extended to companies supplying materials to those construction companies.

There is considerably more at stake here than first meets the eye. Current capitalism shows a tendency toward a new form of monopoly—not just monopolistic behavior in the marketplace but also monopolistic patterns of ownership. For example, the free and independent media so essential to democracy is disappearing. Fifty years ago, four hundred U.S. cities supported two daily newspapers. Today, that's true for only twenty-four cities, while more than 90 percent of newspaper circulation is controlled by corporate chains with headquarters far from the cities they serve. Two companies, Barnes & Noble and Borders, control 45 percent of the retail book market. In Canada, 58 of the nation's 104 dailies are controlled by a single person (Conrad Black).

Previously, one company was allowed to own no more than five AM and five FM radio stations. Today, one corporation owns 102 and another 82, as many as 12 in one market. Two cable companies control 47 percent of the cable audience. Three movie studios account for 57 percent of that market. Mergers have steadily concentrated the communication system underlying democracy (Disney/ABC, Westinghouse/CBS, General Electric/NBC, Time Warner/Turner Broadcasting).[39] The danger is that the nation grows ever less likely to hear an opposing view as information merges with entertainment to become infotainment. That's why media critic Danny Schechter titled his new book *The More You Watch the Less You Know*.[40]

Now that the trust-busters have endorsed the concentration of ever-larger shares of economic activity into fewer and fewer hands, it may be difficult to get the dual genies of corporate giantism and concentrated ownership back into the bottle. A handful of corporate behemoths now dominate several key sectors, with each week bringing word of yet another consolidation (Bell Atlantic/Nynex, Compaq/Digital, ITT/Sheraton and Westin). "Bulk up to keep up" has become the corporate credo, advanced with tacit government approval. A similar trend is emerging in banking and professional services where the "Big Six" (previously the " Big Eight") accounting firms recently consolidated (with the merger of Price Waterhouse and Coopers & Lybrand) to become the "Big Five."

Microsoft offers an unusually challenging case that illustrates how these twin aspects (monopolistic behavior and monopolistic ownership) can operate in tandem, raising anew historical concerns about the distinctly American ideal of checks and balances. If Microsoft has its way, it may soon be poised to collect a charge from every airline ticket bought, every credit card purchase made, every fax sent, every Web site visited on the Internet. This scenario flows from Microsoft's dominance in an abstract arena: the architecture ("operating systems") and the emerging standards controlling software design. This industry was unheard of when Americans decided, with adoption of the Sherman and Clayton Acts (of 1890 and 1914 respectively), to forgo some short-run efficiency that accompanies bigness in favor of the openness and competitiveness that comes only when a few firms *don't* dominate the market. From the outset, the tricky part has been where to draw the line.[41]

Most personal computers run on Microsoft's Windows operating-system environment—estimates range from a low of 80 percent to more than 90 percent, including a lock on the Macintosh office applications market. A form of intellectual property that Microsoft developed and owns enables it to exploit the scale and momentum of these network-access advantages. In a dramatic example of the market power accompanying such technological "lock-ins," Microsoft, virtually unknown in the early 1980s, stands poised to dominate the information age, including controlling many of the technical specifications of the global Internet that determine whether and how well various computer hardware and software work together.[42] On the other hand, the uniformity of those specifications and access to an integrated platform make it possible for software developers to invent programs that can be distributed around the world by minimizing problems of communication and systemwide coordination.[43]

The effect of a 1995 Justice Department antitrust consent decree was summed up in one word by Microsoft chairman Bill Gates: "Nothing."[44] On October 20, 1997, Attorney General Janet Reno filed a petition in federal court charging that Microsoft was unlawfully taking advantage of its market position and asking that the company be ordered to stop forcing makers of personal computers to include its Internet browser when they install its Windows 95 operating system. Claiming that Microsoft violated the earlier decree, the Justice Department sought a fine of $1 million a day in contempt-of-court charges if the company failed to change its policy—which Microsoft agreed to do three months later, but only after damaging itself in the court of public opinion by mounting an aggressive and arrogant defense. Reno's position follows an earlier stance when decades ago a more aggressive Justice Department halted AT&T from using its position in mainframe computers to expand into the computer business, notwithstanding its considerable computer research. Absent those earlier restraints, the market may not have been left open for the likes of Microsoft.

Historically, the dominant theme of antitrust legislation has been how best to maintain a fair and open economic *and political* system. In these market-myopic times, that second part is often overlooked. It was not just pricing power but also political and social power that was viewed as unseemly and dangerously undemocratic when accumulated in excess. Ohio Senator John Sherman, America's first antitrust champion, routinely railed against the economic royalists of his era with their "kingly perogatives."

From an ownership-pattern perspective, the crafting of a solution is challenging. Microsoft offers a classic conundrum: How can capitalism's own "operating-system environment" (including its standards reflected in antitrust legislation, corporate codes, tax laws, labor standards and such) maintain an open and competitive marketplace alongside a relatively classless society that encourages Microsoft-style entrepreneurship (which has created some 3,000 "Microsoft millionaires") while also ensuring that the wealth generated is not monopolized by a few? With the spread throughout the world of well-capitalized multinational companies along with a wave of global mergers, we are certain to see the emergence of more immense accumulations of personal wealth. Until modern capitalism is reengineered so that it meshes more effectively with financial systems designed to expand ownership, tomorrow's capitalism is destined to become populated by fewer (though ever richer) capitalists.

Microsoft also offers an opportunity to consider how the nature of wealth creation is changing. With the advent of the information age and the "dematerialization" of production (i.e., doing more with less units of energy, raw materials, labor, etc.), those positioned at the gateways of information exchange stand to reap many of the financial benefits of this historic transformation. However, as with railroads, power lines, water pipes and other natural monopolies, there are only so many gateway providers that make sense. Antitrust legislation, developed in the era of rail barons, steel magnates and oil monopolists needs to be updated to meet the new realities of the information age, where technology and its standards can determine access to the electronic environment.

Ownership-pattern-wise, the 1990s are reminiscent of the 1890s—except the dollar amounts are greater, the mergers are now global and the deals far larger: Chase/Chemical; Sandoz/Ciba-Geigy; Boeing/McDonnell Douglas; Morgan Stanley/Dean Witter; Banc One/First USA. Globally, 1997 saw more than $1 trillion in mergers in the United States alone, 50 percent higher than in 1996, itself a record year, including 156 transactions valued at $1 billion or more. When some companies merge, others come under pressure to do the same to remain competive. During the 1995–1997 period, more than 27,600 companies joined hands, completing more mergers than in the entire 1980s. An ownership pattern-busting strategy may be the only recourse.*

⑩ Public Pension Plan Investments. One of the most contentious areas in the ownership arena involves what role governments should play in providing pensions. To the extent that governments set funds aside to provide for pension obligations, the question arises as to how those funds should be invested. The United States initially chose a pay-as-you-go Social Security system, collecting funds only as needed to pay retirees. In the mid-1980s, the Reagan-era Greenspan Commission proposed a steady buildup in the system's financial reserves.

---

* When the original trustbusters moved against the cartels of separate companies that conspired to control markets, they inadvertently triggered some to cooperate through merger. In the midst of a booming stock market not unlike today's, there emerged the likes of DuPont, U.S. Steel, General Electric and International Harvester.

However, this commission did not advise that Social Security invest its payroll tax collections in the stock market, fearful this would place Washington in the position of picking winners and losers, and might well lead to political interference either in markets or in the companies themselves. Instead, the commission recommended that the Social Security trust fund apply its reserves to buy U.S. government bonds. Though the Social Security system remains largely on a pay-as-you-go basis (84 percent of current revenues pay for current benefits), it is accumulating government bonds at the rate of about $65 billion per year.[45] That excess is due largely to higher Social Security payroll taxes enacted in 1983, along with an expanding workforce.[46]

I suggest that these taxpayer dollars be invested in a way that aggressively begins to open the traditional ownership-concentrating closed system of finance. For instance, reserves could be used to buy securities in an index that mirrors the market as a whole. However, rather than blindly "index-investing" those reserves (thereby bidding up the prices of stocks held by the already well-to-do), the index could be restricted to companies that maintain at least a minimum level of broad-based employee ownership. A rating system could provide a preference for those companies that combine employee equity participation with participative management practices, a potentially fruitful strategy for enhancing portfolio returns.[47] This index could also include securities backed by pools of commercial loans made to such companies. A Fannie Mae–like financial intermediary could purchase those loans from local lenders and bundle them for resale, thereby (as with Fannie Mae's support for home mortgages) freeing up additional private-sector capital. The index could also include investments in mutual funds that, in turn, invest primarily in such ownership-broadening securities.

The long-term fiscal goal should be to attract these taxpayer funds into private investments only where they foster genuinely widespread economic self-reliance, thereby reducing the need for government-funded entitlements. Fiscal foresight requires that tomorrow's capitalism be financed in a more inclusive way. This will never happen so long as those reserves are circulated within the public sector (through the buying of government bonds) or invested through the conventional closed system of finance—the only two options offered to date.

Another alternative would be for employees themselves to invest all or a portion of their Social Security contributions, instead of turning them over to Washington to be invested. Advocates for the privatization of public pensions often point to Chile, whose government "privatized" its public pension system in 1981. Within a few years, 90 percent of Chile's workers opted into the new system, in which they pay 10 percent of their wages to private investment firms, with their pension based on the eventual value of their portfolio (it is too early yet to identify who fared best—workers, investment firms, insurance companies,

Chilean taxpayers or the Chilean government). American conservatives are intrigued by the Chilean system, even though Santiago strictly regulates the permissible scope of investments.[48]

A 1994 Bipartisan Commission on Entitlement and Tax Reform recommended a private investment option for 2 percent of the Social Security payroll tax as one of thirty-two options it outlined for system solvency.[49] A two-year study by a Clinton administration Advisory Council on Social Security also recommended alternatives to the current system. Though the thirteen members split into three differing groups in their January 1997 report,[50] each looked to stock market investments as a way to generate higher returns. A key difference among the groups: whether the government or individuals should do the investing. The option that attracted support from six of the thirteen panelists (including labor's representatives) called for a study of what would happen if the government invested 40 percent of Social Security's tax collections in the stock market. The second plan, supported by five members, urged a "personal security account" that would apply 5 percentage points of the 12.4 percent payroll tax to a personal retirement plan where individuals could invest as they wish (stocks, stamps, gold, guns, antiques, art, etc.).* The third option would raise the payroll tax to fund a new savings account in which workers would choose from investment options identified by the government to lessen the risks of bad investments or financial scams.

From the perspective of an ownership solution, this privatization initiative is news both good and bad: good in that these funds would begin to flow into private investment,[51] but possibly bad if these funds are, as presently proposed, invested in a conventionally indexed fund, such as Standard & Poor's. The effect on ownership patterns is clear: it would reinforce today's closed system of finance by ensuring a huge (and growing) market for those securities, including a virtually assured market for any new stock offerings by companies on the government-approved index. For example, the proposal for personal security accounts is projected to pump $140 billion in new funds into the stock market at the outset, more than the record $125 billion invested in mutual funds in 1995.† The use of such substantial funds to purchase securities that have the government's stamp of approval assures a buoyant market for those securities

---

* This "personal security account" proposal represents a fundamental philosophical shift because it would move the Social Security system to a private, albeit mandatory, "defined contribution" system operating much like Individual Retirement Accounts (IRAs) or 401(k) plans, in which all investment risk is borne by the individual. Under this proposal, remaining Social Security funds would finance a minimal benefit, initially up to $410 per month. This would be a radical break with the origins of Social Security as a "defined benefit" social insurance system where the risk is borne by the system itself (i.e., all taxpayers).

† One unresolved issue is whether these funds would create new investment capital or simply transfer to the stock market those Social Security taxes now being used to buy Treasury bonds. If the latter, the U.S. Treasury may find itself siphoning out of the private sector a matching

while also potentially denying this capital to small- and mid-sized companies that fail to gain the government's imprimatur.* Indeed, if one goal of this strategy is to strengthen communities, some portion of funds should be invested within the locality or region where these payroll levies originate.

❶ Tapping into the Bewildering Variety of Government-Facilitated Roads to Riches. The history of tycoons in developed countries is a veritable "Who's Who" of fortunes built on a foundation of government-assisted access to assets (or credit), particularly in the construction of essential infrastructure (railroads, highways, power, telecommunications, etc.) and in providing transportation and services (such as the data-processing services that Ross Perot's company, EDS, provided to the U.S. government). Those fortunes continue to accumulate, in both developed and developing countries. The following story from Brazil illustrates how a savvy policy entrepreneur can exploit a broad range of government subsidies to amass a private fortune.

Taking advantage of a series of government concessions stretching over four decades, Olacyr de Moraes accumulated a $2 billion personal fortune. Beginning with a São Paulo city contract to transport paving stones from a quarry, de Moraes won government contracts to help build São Paulo's bus station, its subway and then its international airport, the largest in the Southern Hemisphere. In the 1970s, he used tax concessions and government-provided low-interest loans to help open the Amazon basin to soybean farming. In the 1980s, he used agricultural subsidies to plant sugarcane. The 1990s found de Moraes expanding his holdings to include a bank (Banco Itamarati, one of Brazil's larger private banks), gaining him easier access to the capital required to continue expansion. In 1995, he opened one of the world's largest sugar mills. His latest venture is a ninety-year government concession to build a 1,072-mile railroad line deep into the Amazon interior. His concession includes a government commitment assuring him profitable freight tariffs, a financial subsidy that finds a precedent in the nineteenth-century fortunes accumulated by America's rail barons.[†]

---

amount of funds in order to finance ongoing deficits—driving up interest rates in the process. Absent an ownership-pattern investment policy, the most well-to-do are certain to be the primary beneficiaries of any scheme to direct payroll tax receipts into the stock market. For example, because Microsoft is a certain candidate for any index, the result would be more investment dollars chasing a limited amount of Microsoft shares, with a foreseeable impact on Microsoft shareholders such as Bill Gates and Paul Allen who already saw the value of their Microsoft shares double during the bull market of 1996 and 1997 to approach $60 billion.

* In March 1997, Dow Jones & Company announced it would replace four of the thirty stocks that make up the Dow Jones industrial index, reflecting the growing role of technology, health care and financial services. Leaving the index are Bethlehem Steel, Texaco, Westinghouse Electric and Woolworth, replaced by Hewlett-Packard, Johnson & Johnson, the Travelers Group and Wal-Mart Stores.

† A variant on this practice continues under U.S. law. For example, in January 1997, the Surface Transportation Board, which replaced the Interstate Commerce Commission, ruled that railroads

In Latin America, where key services have traditionally been a government monopoly (power, telecom, water), the opening of such activities to private investment virtually assures the creation of massive private fortunes, particularly where monopolies remain intact as privatization proceeds, or where a quasi-governmental entity sets rates at a level guaranteed to ensure profitability.[52]

⓬ **Ownership and Political Corruption.** The relationship between money and politics needs no documentation. Hardly a month goes by in any country without a scandal, typically followed by an indignant public reaction and accompanied by further erosion in public confidence. Politically based personal fortunes are the worldwide norm. In the United States, the practice reaches well back into history, from tariffs on imported steel to government purchases of agricultural surpluses, from land grants for rail barons to wartime munitions and shipping contracts, from Marshall Plan–financed export markets to the private ownership of the taxpayer-capitalized aluminum industry.*

The list of U.S. beneficiaries continues to grow, both in number and notoriety. Many of them are among the largest and most consistent contributors to political campaigns,[53] regardless of whether the subsidies they receive are direct and obvious (such as defense procurement[54] and ethanol,[55] maritime,[56] tobacco,[57] and sugar subsidies) or indirect, even obscure (school textbook purchases, government-reimbursed travel, Ex-Im Bank loan guarantees,[58] access to airport gates,[59] timber rights on public land, tax allowances for accelerated depreciation, etc.).

---

have the right to set their own rates in three cases where utilities complained that they were served by just one railroad in receiving shipments of coal. The Association of Railroads estimates that a ruling adverse to the railroads could have affected $2.4 billion in annual profits. Since deregulation in 1980, the number of U.S. railroads has declined from forty-two to just five megasystems, with only two railroads controlling most freight movements west of the Mississippi. As this book went to press, the CSX Corporation and Norfolk Southern Corporation were splitting up Conrail, leaving just two major railroads east of the Mississippi. Much of the improvement in railroads that accompanied deregulation was financed by $2 billion in new cash that flowed from 1981's supply-side tax legislation. Known as "retirement-replacement-betterment," this taxpayer subsidy was included as part of President Reagan's overhaul of the tax rules governing allowable depreciation. See *Joint Committee on Taxation, General Explanation of the Economic Recovery Tax Act of 1981* (Washington, D.C.: GPO, 1981), p. 92.

* The Reconstruction Finance Corporation was established by Congress in January 1932 "to provide emergency financing facilities for financial institutions, to aid in financing agriculture, commerce and industry." It was envisioned that the RFC would operate as an independent agency, making loans where private funds were unavailable and where the public's interest would be served. Political influence became an issue beginning with congressional hearings in 1948. When Republicans came to power in 1953, the lending powers of the RFC were terminated. The private fortunes that emerged from the establishment of both Alcoa (originally the Aluminum Corporation of America) and Reynolds Aluminum trace their financial roots to the RFC. The financial assistance provided to both was justified, in part, on the basis of the need for the United States to have a strong aluminum manufacturing capability, particularly for military aircraft required by the Department of Defense, a principal customer. During its lifetime the RFC lent more than $13 billion (approximately $88 billion in 1998 dollars).

The government subsidy allowed ethanol producers provides a revealing picture of what the critics call "corporate welfare." Tax subsidies for ethanol and price supports for sugar reportedly helped Archer Daniels Midland Co. (ADM) earn profits of $300 million in 1995 alone, about 40 percent of its overall profits for the year. ADM's ethanol profits ($75 million in 1995) come directly at the expense of the federal highway trust fund—to which the tax proceeds are dedicated. Trust fund officials claim they have lost approximately $7 billion in tax revenue since 1980 due to the ethanol tax exemption, money that could have helped repair and maintain the nation's roads and bridges.[60]

Political Campaigns and Public Finance

One of the most contentious and recurring issues facing the Congress is the reform of campaign financing. The clamor continues to grow for some alternative to the corrupting influence of private political contributions. However, what many of those outside the beltway fail to realize is that we already *have* publicly financed elections—at least that's my appraisal as someone formerly "inside the beltway." That's because many of these so-called private political contributions are really recycled taxpayer funds that flow back into campaign coffers from the grateful few who benefit from the government's largesse. Rest assured, you are already paying for much of the cost of federal elections.

Though the connection between public subsidy and political contribution is never direct (that would be bribery), the correlation is clear to anyone who has ever worked in Washington in any position of influence. George Washington Plunkett, the turn-of-the-century Tammany Hall boss, called it "honest graft."[61] The 1996 election season saw the candidates for president and Congress and their advocates raise a record $2 billion, almost twice what had ever before been spent on an election.[62] This honest graft comes in many forms. Ron Brown, Mr. Clinton's 1992 campaign chairman, was rewarded with an appointment as commerce secretary, in which office he reportedly raised public favors to political donors to new heights with his use of trade missions to steer multimillion-dollar contracts to Democratic contributors.[63] One way to limit these corrupting financial flows, or at least to redirect them toward a more productive end, is to ensure that the ownership benefits flowing from government subsidies are spread more broadly.

America's founders as well understood full well that political accommodation would always be an essential lubricant in a system with such enormous diversity. Absent such horse-trading, UCLA professor James Q. Wilson cautions, "all coalitions would have to rest on ideology, a weak and slender reed." Rather than a system where ideology, experts or a monarch determine what is in the public interest, Wilson argues, "Our Constitution is based on the opposite belief. It assumes that majority coalitions will be formed by bargaining among local representatives."[64]

Even Washington's current location is partly the product of pork. Virginians Thomas Jefferson and James Madison initially objected to Alexander Hamilton's plan for the federal government to assume old state debts from the Revolutionary War, particularly when some of the states (including the largest, Virginia) had already repaid their debts and were reluctant to be taxed again. However, they agreed to go along when Hamilton supported their plan to relocate the nation's capital not in Hamilton's New York but on the banks of the Potomac River in northern Virginia.

Needed: Global Leadership for a Global Economy

The scope of government subsidies for wealth accumulation is so vast that I can in this chapter only point to several of the more glaring examples and propose a few responses from the perspective of an ownership engineer. The next chapter continues this exercise, with a focus on the use of tax policy to give shape to a domestic ownership strategy.

It's my belief that, in a step-by-step fashion, ownership pattern–sensitive development should also become the subject of international treaty. Much as the geophysical environment is now the subject of international agreements, the ownership environment could become the focus of ongoing multilateral collaboration. The Framework Convention on Climate Change, signed in Rio de Janeiro in 1992 as part of the "Earth Summit," entered into force in March 1994. One reason for its broad appeal is its deliberately ambiguous language urging (though not requiring) nations to hold greenhouse gases to 1990 levels by the year 2000, a goal that was subsequently amended in Kyoto, Japan, in December 1997. The convention obliges all signatory nations to conduct inventories of emissions, to submit reports of national actions taken under the convention, and to take climate change into account in their policymaking.

An analogous convention could focus policymakers on the important role played by the ownership environment, both within and among nations. A global commission could propose international policy initiatives and coordinate action to foster participatory ownership systems with the goal of negotiating a similar framework convention. In the case of the Climate Convention, the United Nations Development Program is entrusted with the mission of promoting "capacity building" for sustainable development.[65] Here, too, an ownership analog makes sense. A UN-coordinated effort could propose and promote the institutional tools (laws, regulations, financial reforms and such) needed to advance participatory patterns of ownership. Much as nations are moving closer to adopting international and financial accounting standards, policymakers (in both the public and private sector) should, at a minimum, endorse international "best practices" for ownership—public vs. private, concentrated vs. broad-based, foreign vs. domestic, institutional vs. personal, distant vs. up close, etc.

Ownership Standards Required

More than two centuries have elapsed since publication of *The Wealth of Nations* (1776) and more than a century since *The Communist Manifesto* (1848). Three centuries of experience should suffice in drawing some conclusions about what works and what doesn't in the ownership arena. The adoption of baseline international standards on ownership, even if ambiguous at the outset, could do much to focus attention on this crucial subject. Ideally those standards would evoke a combination of private-sector leadership and public-sector legislation advancing more participatory patterns. Again, a precedent in the environmental area could be adapted to this purpose. The North American Free Trade Agreement (NAFTA) includes a clause forbidding signatory nations from lowering their national environmental standards (or their enforcement) to attract investment.[66] As in the environmental area, unless international standards are agreed to and maintained, there will be a tendency for financial capital to flow where standards are least restrictive.

What's also needed is a watchdog and an ownership-pattern "conscience" created by international convention. A precedent can be found in the International Labour Organization (ILO), which has long issued standards on such issues as child labor and workplace safety. Though it lacks enforcement powers, its investigatory powers, its ability to convene high-profile public hearings, and its capacity to showcase both best and worst practices provide the ILO with an international moral presence that has proven quite useful in steadily improving workplace practices worldwide.[67] An analogous organization could help advance worldwide improvements in ownership practices.

On the environmental sustainability front, a global initiative to advance up-close ownership could prove crucial in providing a way to supplement current market signals. At present, there's no international agreement or mechanism to ensure that the prices of things reflect their full environmental costs.[68] Consequently, the liberalization of trade is certain to advance ecologically unwise practices as today's market-pricing model seeks out inputs that appear to be lower cost. That's destined to accelerate not only the depletion of natural resources, but also the creation of lower-cost "pollution havens" where environmental laws are lax or nonexistent. This phenomenon has already surfaced as one of the most perplexing components of current trade agreements. That's because *domestic* environmental laws may be found to violate *international* trade agreements. One high-profile example: the first major ruling of the World Trade Organization (in 1996) charged that the U.S. Clean Air Act discriminated against foreign oil refiners because American clean-air standards disallowed the import of "dirty" Venezuelan Oil.[69] The result: the WTO directed the United States to amend the Clean Air Act.

Empowering and Protecting Systems Within Systems

Futurist Arthur Koestler invented terminology to describe how the individual, the community, the nation and all of human society are interrelated living systems embedded within each other, like Chinese boxes or a set of Russian nested dolls. Consequently, he cautioned, the interests of embedded "holons" (individual and community interests) can be overridden by the interests of "holarchies" in which they are embedded (interests that are national or global in scope).[70] As evidence of that phenomenon, consumer-activist Ralph Nader points out that WTO rules forbid domestic legislatures from advancing a broad range of community objectives, such as significant subsidies to promote energy conservation or sustainable farming.[71]

In our search for ways to evoke a social framework to address these overlapping and competing interests, evolution biologist Elisabet Sahtouris, a consultant to the UN on indigenous peoples, suggests that we look for guidance to the evolution of living systems. In nature's domain, we find continuous negotiation to achieve that dynamic equilibrium we call balance. As an example of failed negotiation, she points to cancer as a symptom of what happens when the proliferation and appetites of individual cells overtake the needs of the whole body.[72]

This notion of self-interest operating simultaneously at several levels suggests a need for ongoing negotiation among individual parts and levels of an organization—among the holons within a holarchy. This self-interest–energized dance needs to take place in an environment where it's acknowledged that no part or level can be sacrificed without damaging the whole, any more than a village would starve three families in order to overfeed a fourth. Commenting on the "biology of globalization," Sahtouris notes that one can discern in evolution "a repeating pattern in which aggressive competition leads to the threat of extinction, which is then avoided by the formation of cooperative alliances."[73]

The Ownership Solution embraces this living-system analysis to argue by analogy that we must evoke social systems, including ownership systems, that enable life's multisystem, multilevel negotiations to become cooperative and life-advancing rather than antagonistic and potentially life-threatening. Because of the dominance presently granted property rights worldwide, I find great hope in the notion that ownership patterns could evolve into a locally attuned force for resolving competing interests and smoothing the adaptations required in response to today's rapid change.

In his search for the common factors that led to the failure of twenty-one past civilizations, historian Arnold Toynbee identified two: concentrated ownership and inflexibility in light of changing conditions. I see those as two sides of the same coin (i.e., concentration and inflexibility). In that context, it's important to note that the change called "globalization" is not on the way here, it's already here—in communication, entertainment, food, money, transport, pollution, disease, weapons. What American civilization requires to "negotiate" with this phenomenon is a web of human relationships that facilitate a high degree of flexibility, cooperation, and locale-specific sensitivity. In other words, the answer to Toynbee's challenge lies latent in his findings: the route to the flexibility we require will be found in addressing history's most enduring danger: concentrated ownership.

The Policy of Living Systems

Yesteryear's mechanical metaphor of a well-oiled international system is a relic of the past. Healthy human and natural systems are inherently alive, interactive, complex and constantly evolving. What's now needed are human-constructed, law and ethics-based guidelines for commercial behavior so that these multi-evel, multisystem negotiations can become ongoing and flexible without becoming unduly one-sided—either at any one level: community, national, global—or in any one domain: personal, commercial, ecological, etc.

Sahtouris suggests a solution when she points out that "in nature living holons promote their own health, the health of their embedding holons (e.g., ecosystems) *and* the health of their embedded holons (e.g., cells) in this improvisational dance of negotiating interests."[74] Drawing on that imagery, it seems to me foolish to think we can have a healthy free enterprise without private property and the self-empowering notion of self-interest. But the health of private property as an embedding system is undermined, even endangered, where it fails to make fully engaged, self-interest-motivated owners of those who are inextricably embedded in it. If private enterprise is likened to a dance, it's essential to system health that we have more people on the dance floor.

In the formulation of both domestic and foreign policy, legislators and business leaders alike must become more attuned to the sensitive balancing of economic, social, cultural and environmental goals. To the extent that there is imbalance in any one area, stability is put at risk. As a threshold condition, healthy development requires that prosperity be shared, not hoarded—both within and among nations. Leadership in this key area is one of the ingredients presently missing in international affairs.* In his famous 1947 article in *Foreign Affairs* proposing containment as the strategy for dealing with Soviet expansionism, George Kennan (who later became ambassador to the USSR) offered a vision of American leadership that retains its relevance a half century later:[75]

---

* Reflecting the sort of creativity that may be required, State Street Chairman and Chief Executive Officer Marshall Carter suggests that early retirees be utilized as a volunteer staff for aid agencies, with pension funds thereby effectively contributing to the cost of a country's aid effort.

It is rather a question of the degree to which the United States can create among the peoples of the world generally the impression of a country which knows what it wants, which is coping successfully with the problems of its internal life and with the responsibilities of a World Power, and which has a spiritual vitality capable of holding its own among the major ideological currents of the time. . . . The United States need only measure up to its own best traditions and prove itself worthy of preservation as a great nation.

Yankee Stay Home

America's recent accumulation of political, economic and cultural clout has been accompanied not by a penchant for world leadership but by a curious combination of arrogance and isolation. Though American values of openness and meritocracy have global appeal, the nation that developed them seems oddly bereft of any vision of what's required to bring others into the fold. Our shortcomings are readily apparent to other nations, including America's oldest Western allies, where globalization's "Made in the USA" label appears paradoxical, contradictory and sometimes bullying.

With 5 percent of the world's population, the United States accounts for nearly a quarter of the world's greenhouse gases. How, the Germans ask, can this imbalance be continued? When the United States continued to resist paying its past dues to the UN, both the British and the Germans leveled withering comments. Others question America's engagement with China but its isolation of Cuba; or its tolerance of human rights abuses by Israel and Saudi Arabia but its criticism of Iran; or its preaching the virtues of disarmament while promoting weapons sales worldwide. Even the legendary equanimity of South African President Nelson Mandela was put to the test when the United States tried to derail his visit with Libyan leader Muammar Qadafi, even though Qadafi was one of the few to stand by the Mandela-led African National Congress liberation movement while the United States opposed the ANC as a socialist-led band of insurgents.[76]

Yet the fact remains that the United States is the only nation with a military force able to act anywhere in the world. Its culture—its movies, MTV, McDonald's—is a worldwide phenomenon, both reflecting and setting the spirit of the times, for good and ill. However, without the coalescing tendency of an outside threat (such as the Soviet Union), U.S. dominance does not always translate into persuasive influence, as President Bill Clinton found in his early 1998 attempt to rally an international show of force against Iraq's Saddam Hussein. Similarly, the French took clear delight in ignoring American objections as a French energy company signed a $2 billion contract to develop Iran's natural gas fields. Other countries have also grown wary of America's oftentimes self-serving stridency on the merits of free trade. Knowing the U.S. dominance in electronics in this hemisphere, South American electronics manufacturers resist American attempts to build a massive hemispheric free trade zone.

Whereas eight decades ago Woodrow Wilson proposed that "The world must be safe for democracy,"[77] observers now question whether the current push for free markets has less to do with shoring up democracy than carving up market share. Worried about the lack of accountability in "a world economy without a world polity," historian Arthur Schlesinger Jr. suggests we pause to consider the disruptive consequences accompanying the onrush of a global capitalism: "Let us understand the relationship between capitalism and democracy. Democracy is impossible without private ownership because private property—resources beyond the arbitrary reach of the state—provides the only secure basis for political oppression and intellectual freedom. But the capitalist market is no guarantee of democracy, as Deng Xiaoping, Lee Kuan Yew, Pinochet, and Franco, not to mention Hitler and Mussolini, have amply demonstrated. Democracy requires capitalism, but capitalism does not require democracy, at least in the short term."[78]

Schlesinger gives voice to the concerns of many who worry that capitalism's preference for short-term plans and profits is at variance with the need for long-term perspectives that require public leadership and affirmative government. His concern is one that this book attempts to address, namely: "In the world at large, can capitalism, once loose from national moorings, be held to social accountability?"[79] It seems clear that nation-states, including the United States, will continue to decline in effectiveness because, in the comment made famous by sociologist Daniel Bell, they are "too small for the big problems and too big for the small problems."

Leadership, Foreign Policy and the Science of Service

Democracy's strength has long been its capacity for self-reflection and self-correction. It is this self-organizing notion that continues as its core appeal. Yet quoting British diplomat Lord Bryce, Schlesinger points to a key paradox of our times: "Perhaps no form of government needs great leaders so much as democracy." With the emergence of an array of global forces now at work in the world—some democratic, many not—what does that imply for leadership? With the recent emergence of systems analysts and artificial intelligence, along with the "new physics" that animates them both, we are beginning to realize that organizations have imbedded within them an intelligence, even a consciousness of sorts that emerges when a certain level of organization is reached.

Global capital markets offer an example, where a multinational, multicultural army of analysts are able to translate into discounted present value myriad inputs worldwide: the effect of El Niño on the citrus harvest, the release of IBM's performance projections, the import of Alan Greenspan's latest remark. All these various relationships are distilled into a set of financial figures that show up as stock prices, interest rates, exchange rates and so on. A classic joke in these circles: how many stock analysts does it take to change a lightbulb? None, because the change has already been discounted.

Writing in the bestseller *Leadership and the New Science*, Margaret Wheatley concludes that such complex adaptive systems are "kept in harmony by a force we are just beginning to appreciate: the capacity for self-reference. . . . everywhere in nature, order is maintained in the midst of change because autonomy exists at local levels."[80] That self-reflecting, self-correcting aspect of systems—whether human or natural—lies at the core of successful change and adaptation. From that "systems perspective," capital markets offer a *type* of leadership ("money is smarter than people"). Yet this aspect of private property—despite its inherent intelligence, even consciousness—is too concentrated in form and too disconnected in operation either to fully reflect local information or to promote local autonomy. It's clearly important as one essential component in a global signaling system, but it's proving woefully insufficient. That's not an attack on either capital markets or private property; rather that's to suggest we need to consider how private property might be better dispersed and "reconnected" in order to tap the creative intelligence embedded in a private enterprise system. "Life opens to more possibilities," Wheatley argues, "through new patterns of connection."[81]

Anything that better secures the realm of democracy is likely to serve the interests of the United States. That's a primary reason for the emergence of the alphabet soup of self-referencing, self-correcting international institutions and agreements that have emerged on the scene: from the UN to NATO and the WTO, from the OECD and the IFC to GATT, NAFTA and others. Josef Joffe, editorial page editor of *Foreign Affairs*, points out that "no alliance has ever survived history."[82] But the institutions left in their wake often *do* survive and go on to foster stability while providing a broad range of services. That, Joffe suggests, is the direction of leadership in the future: "power exacts responsibility and responsibility requires vision that transcends niggardly self-interest. . . . Great powers remain great if they promote their own interests by serving those of others."[83] Thus, it seems that the foreign policy of the post superpower standoff requires a power (with a lowercase "p") willing to adopt a leadership style that is more attuned to what House Speaker Newt Gingrich calls "learning and listening."[84] Certainly that coincides with what ssystem cience has identified in nature as the essential building blocks of seccessful adaptation and change—and the "dynamic equilibrium" certain to typify the formulation of foreign policy.

If that systemic learning and listening were also informed by a private property capitalism that was genuinely participatory, then a new world order would emerge from a more broadly based personal autonomy (the democratic ideal). In addition that property-empowering strategy—necessarily global in scope—could, in Schlesinger's words, help "cope with the spiritual frustrations and yearnings generated in the vast anonymity of global society."[85] Neither private property capitalism nor participatory democracy can afford to operate uninformed by its constituents. "Participation, seriously done, is a way out," Wheatley argues. "We need a broad distribution of information, viewpoints, and interpretations if we are to make sense of the world. . . . The more participants we engage in this participative universe, the more we can access its potentials and the wiser we can become."[86]

As free trade and technology continue to drive countries toward greater integration and cooperation, that is certain to spawn more transgovernmental organizations and nongovernmental networks established to address mutual concerns. This interplay of independence and interdependence—at the personal, community, national and international level—typifies the challenge that public- and private-sector policymakers will face in the twenty-first century.

CHAPTER 15

Creating a Capitalism That Creates More Capitalists

> The avoidance of taxes is the only intellectual pursuit that
> carries any reward.
>
> —*John Maynard Keynes*

Policymakers influence financing in the private sector in many ways, most notoriously through tax policy. It's not by chance that the Senate committee in charge of tax policy is called the Committee on Finance, while the allowable ways and means of finance are determined in the other chamber by the House Committee on Ways and Means. Because any government policy affecting finance is certain to have an impact on who becomes a capitalist, ownership policies are a natural adjunct to tax policy. To date, however, tax policies affecting corporate finance have been largely indifferent in their effect on ownership patterns.

Every cell in the body is replaced every seven years, blood cells every six months. Capitalism's assets are likewise constantly being renewed and replaced. The capitalism we had yesterday is not the same capitalism we have today. With political will and business leadership, the capital-ownership pattern we have today need not be the pattern we have tomorrow. The key to an effective ownership solution lies in achieving a "critical mass" of encouragement so that the current closed system of finance (which concentrates ownership) becomes less attractive than financial techniques that broaden ownership.

Given the slow-paced spread of ESOPs in the United States,* it is clear that the current array of tax incentives does not provide that needed critical mass. Additional encouragement is required if today's closed system of finance is to be pried open to employees as a preferred category of up-close capitalists.[1] For example, a preferred corporate income tax rate might be allowed companies that maintain a prescribed level of broad-based ownership, including

---

* The ESOP Association's financing advisory committee reports that its professional members tallied 1996 ESOP transactions totaling only $618 million. *ESOP Report,* October/November 1997 (Washington, D.C.: The ESOP Association).

broad employee ownership.[2] Or more favorable depreciation could be allowed ownership-broadening firms. For instance, when Ronald Reagan proposed rich depreciation incentives as part of his supply-side tax cuts, those could have been linked to ownership-broadening techniques (such as ESOPs) so that companies wishing to expand the nation's capital base could do so while also expanding the capital ownership base.[3]

The investment tax credit (ITC) offers another possibility. The ITC has been around since 1962 when John F. Kennedy allowed companies a $3 credit against their taxes for every $100 they invested in equipment and machinery. As a direct dollar-for-dollar reduction in tax liability, the ITC is a 100 percent subsidy from taxpayers to shareholders.[4] During the 1970s, the ITC was raised to 10 percent,[5] with an eleventh percent allowed where companies used that extra 1 percent to fund an ESOP. This proved an irresistible incentive to capital-intensive firms such as utilities and mining companies (Con Edison, 3M), who rushed to establish "tax credit ESOPs." Later, this was changed to payroll-based tax credit ESOPs equal to 0.5 percent of payroll, making "PAYSOPS" attractive to labor-intensive firms (Sears, J. C. Penney, etc.).

Economists routinely ignore the impact of policy on ownership patterns. In March 1992, one hundred distinguished economists proposed $50 billion in deficit-financed spending for private and public investment, split between investment tax credits for private investment and government spending for public infrastructure (roads, bridges and so on). This was an unusual hybrid of Keynesian demand-side pump-priming (for public works) and 1980s-style supply-side incentives. Conspicuous by its absence was any mention of the proposal's impact on ownership. None.

Here are ten different ways by which commonly discussed tax policies could be reengineered to foster broad-based capital accumulation.

❶ Conditional Tax Relief on Capital Gains. Many countries have capital gain taxes, including fifteen of the twenty-four OECD countries. Others have them under consideration.[6] Relief from capital gain tax could be based on (*a*) the use of the proceeds, (*b*) the nature of the buyer, or (*c*) the nature of the shares sold.[7] For instance, a lower tax rate could apply where proceeds are reinvested in companies that maintain a minimum threshold of employee ownership. Or a tax deferral could be allowed where the shares are bought by an ESOP (as under current law in Britain and the United States). Or a tax break could apply where the shares sold are in an employee ownership company.[8] Rather than conditioning capital gain tax breaks on ownership, 1997's tax bill cut the capital gain taxes from 28 percent to 20 percent, conditioned only on whether the assets were first held for a year. For assets held five years, the rate is 18 percent.[9]

The challenge lies in making this type of sale at least as attractive as the "tax-free exchange" that presently allows business owners to swap their shares for those of another company and postpone tax until those shares are sold. Craig McCaw, a pioneer in cellular telephones, exchanged his stake in McCaw Communications for AT&T shares in 1994, instantly making him a billionaire in a tax-free stock swap valued at $11.5 billion.[10] Shareholders looking to convert their stock into cash provide a key opportunity for converting a company into broad-based ownership. Even a deferral of tax can be attractive (as in America and the United Kingdom) because, as tax attorneys routinely advise their clients, "a tax delayed is a tax unpaid."[11]

❷ **Opening Bank Credit to Those Without Collateral.** The fiscal health of free enterprise requires a thorough reappraisal of the role played by financial institutions in the accumulation of wealth. This includes the tax treatment allowed lenders on loans that further concentrate ownership. With capital markets now encroaching on territory once dominated by banks,[12] tax policy could provide a new investment medium where, for example, a mutual fund holds securities backed by ESOP loans—providing a means for attracting capital into ownership-expanding investments. A lender could also be allowed lower income tax rates based on the percentage of its loan portfolio comprised of loans that expand ownership. A similar incentive could be aimed at bank reserve requirements, those funds a bank is required to set aside to protect against loan default.[13] For example, 25 percent of the balance of ownership-expanding loans could be credited toward those requirements. In combination, these two provisions (reduced tax rates and lower reserve requirements) would grant banks the financial feature they most cherish: the ability to generate more interest-paying business from their funds on deposit.

❸ **Death and Taxes.** A variety of strategies could be used to reengineer estate taxes to advance broad-based ownership.[14] For example, a reduction in the estate tax could be allowed for those shares an estate holds in companies with a minimum threshold of broad-based employee ownership. This would encourage wealthy investors to anticipate (and avoid) this tax by investing in employee ownership companies, thereby providing a source of capital for such companies while also encouraging today's high-growth companies to become more broadly owned. Or a deduction could be allowed, say, for half the proceeds realized on an estate's sale of stock to an ESOP. That would encourage heirs to sell shares to the company's "natural" owners.[15] The continuity of family businesses is often jeopardized by the death of a major shareholder. In extreme cases, a company has to be liquidated (or sold on a distressed basis) to generate funds to pay estate taxes. Estate tax relief could enhance both business and job continuity in a way that also promotes ownership by those who helped shareholders build their companies.[16]

By law, capital gains are typically excludable from tax at death because heirs are entitled to inherit stocks at their current appraised value (using a "stepped-up basis") rather than at the value when acquired by the deceased.

If the shares had been sold preceding death, a capital gain tax would have applied. The Congressional Joint Committee on Taxation estimates the five-year cost of this tax break at $91.5 billion.[17] This break could, for example, be limited to securities in companies with a verifiably broad ownership structure.[18] Rather than an ownership pattern–sensitive cut in inheritance taxes, Washington instead decided in 1997 to raise the estate-tax exemption.[19]

❹ **More Bang for the Fiscal Buck.** A bit less than half the $12 trillion held in institutional hands in the United States is held in plans to pay employees deferred compensation (pensions, 401(k) plans, etc.).[20] When those funds were set aside, employers were allowed a tax deduction for that expense. Until paid out, the funds grow tax-free.[21] The five-year cost of these plans totals $453.4 billion in forgone tax receipts.[22] Tax relief is allowed these funds regardless of how or where they invest. At the very least, some portion should be invested to motivate those whose efforts are relevant to performance of the U.S. economy.[23] While that obviously includes employees, it could also include those employed by suppliers and distributors of those companies.[24] The "systemic" goal should be to create a "virtuous circle" of wealth expansion to relieve tomorrow's fiscal pressures. Thus, for example, where 25 percent of a pension plan's assets are invested in the securities of ownership-expanding companies, the pension plan could retain its full tax exemption; otherwise, the current benefit of 100 percent tax-free growth could be cut, say, to 50 percent.

Today's lack of widespread economic self-reliance makes Americans desperate for an array of fiscally debilitating expenditures, including public-sector jobs (such as those in the defense sector). In addition, the huge cost of tax benefits for pension plans crowds out the fiscal capacity needed for other public services, ranging from health and education to environmental cleanup and restoration. Fiscal foresight mandates that policymakers no longer be indifferent to how and where these funds are invested. Similar fiscal leverage could be gained by ensuring the high-impact investment of the vast sums now accumulating tax-free in foundations, university endowments, religious organizations and charitable trusts. Although those institutions already play a vital role in the economy's dynamism, diversity and vitality, they could also be investing a portion of their funds in an ownership-expanding, fiscally responsible manner in return for their continued tax-free status.

❺ **Every Person an Owner.** Tax relief is commonplace for individuals buying shares through their employer, typically by investing in a 401(k) plan. Often an employer will make a "matching" contribution of, say, fifty cents for each dollar contributed by an employee.[25] Tax relief is allowed for these plans because they are required to ensure broad-based employee participation. In the mid-1970s, President Gerald Ford proposed a personal tax deduction for 15 percent of the expense incurred by anyone buying shares in U.S. corporations.

Noting that Ford's ownership solution would simply reward the well-to-do for what they would do in any case, his proposal was quickly labeled the "Stockbrokers Relief Act" and ignored by the Congress.[26] Ford's insensitivity to the need for "democratic" participation doomed it. More can be done with tax policy to encourage personal investment in U.S. companies, but it should be done with sensitivity to the resulting ownership pattern—not only among savers but also within those companies where their savings are invested.

❻ Creating Indigenous Investors from Foreign Investment. By treaty, U.S. companies are allowed a domestic credit for taxes paid abroad so that they are not taxed twice on the same income. That tax credit could be made conditional, linked to verification that the income was generated through enterprises that maintain a prescribed threshold of broad-based ownership.[27] Such a tax policy would encourage multinationals to foster ownership patterns abroad that are more appropriate to the development of robust and equitable private enterprise democracies. As the primary repositories of the world's productive capital and the principal agents of economic development in developing countries, transnational corporations are the conveyors of the ethics of private property and free enterprise. All too often, when these commercial giants enter developing countries, the local benefits are harvested either by a few already well-to-do families or by well-connected politicians and their cronies, whether it be the Coca-Cola bottling plant, the McDonald's franchise, the Fuji film-processing facility, or a local company supplying DuPont, 3M, or Archer Daniels Midland.

❼ Time for a Limit on Greed? Although a wealth tax has many well-documented drawbacks, some limitation may be appropriate now that these accumulations have reached what anyone would agree has no conceivable purpose other than to preclude others from the modest accumulations essential to economic self-sufficiency.[28] Today's disparities in wealth mock the moral and ethical foundation on which free-enterprise democracies are built. Yet progressive income taxes are simply inadequate, because they address only the symptom, not the cause.[29]

Writing at a time (1927) when wealth disparities (and wealth concentrations) were remarkably similar to those of today, John Maynard Keynes penned an essay in which he looked forward to a time when "We shall be able to afford to assess the money-motive at its true value. The love of money as a possession—as distinguished from the love of money as a means to the enjoyments and realities of life—will be recognized for what it is, a somewhat disgusting morbidity, one of those semi-criminal, semi-pathological propensities which one hands over with a shudder to the specialists in mental disease."[30] Rather than cast this levy as a tax on wealth (or on greed)—with all its negative connotations, perhaps this policy might best be thought of as a "user fee" charged for the privilege of utilizing the nation's private property tradition as a vehicle for accumulating assets totally disproportionate to any conceivable notion of need.

As of 1990, eleven of the twenty-four OECD countries taxed household wealth on an annual basis. Most have been doing so for decades. Twenty-two of them have death and/or gift taxes.[31] An annual tax (say 3 percent) could be levied on personal accumulations that exceed a threshold of, say, $10 million.[32] Public debate could establish an appropriate threshold, exclusions, tax rates, valuation procedures, and so on. In the OECD countries, both the thresholds and the rates tend to be quite low.[33] Exclusions could exempt a portion of proceeds realized on sales to ESOPs or similar ownership-expanding mechanisms.

The Swiss have a modest wealth tax with rates ranging from 0.05 percent to 0.30 percent, with a family exclusion of about $56,000. If the Swiss system were in place in the United States, New York University professor Edward Wolff estimates it would annually raise approximately $45 billion,[34] enough to fund the entire defense procurement budget. Although a wealth tax is an indirect and, at best, a hindsight policy, the certainty that traditional closed-system financing techniques will continue to concentrate wealth confronts policymakers with the challenge of how else to respond to the phenomenon of steadily increasing disparities in wealth and income.[35]

❽ **But Where Will I Get the Money?** Preferred access to the U.S. Federal Reserve's discounting of commercial loans could provide a strong incentive for the use of ownership-broadening financing techniques. Worldwide, central banks play a central role in maintaining the closed nature of current corporate finance. Chapter 9 ("Making Money") includes a more detailed description of central bank operations and how they might be reengineered to support an ownership solution.

❾ **Taxing the Foreign Freeloaders.** Federal law generously allows foreign citizens to spend up to one-third of their time in the United States without paying income tax, even if their income is generated by U.S. companies. With sophisticated tax planning and the capacity to travel constantly, it becomes possible, in effect, to pay no federal taxes while having full access to the public infrastructure those taxes support: the judicial system, airports, highways, clean water, clean air, along with America's culture, scenery, weather, and so on. In effect, current tax policy allows a major shareholder of a major U.S. corporation to be a freeloader, benefiting from most of the advantages of U.S. citizenship while bearing none of the costs. The annual *Forbes 400* listing of America's richest families provides a roadmap to identify many of these freeloaders. Such circumstances merit a remedy.

Other situations can be even more egregious. Media tycoon Rupert Murdoch offers a case in point. A company official acknowledges that Mr. Murdoch pays almost no taxes on his U.S. businesses, though they account for 70 percent of his News Corporation's operating profit. Here's how the *Wall Street Journal* explained his ownership solution:

> One tax-efficient ploy: In 1985, the News Corporation acquired Ziff-Davis travel publications for $350 million. However, the purchase was made by a News Corporation division based in the Netherland Antilles, a tax haven with virtually no income taxes. That subsidiary also held New York, Seventeen, Soap Opera Digest *and other magazines.*
>
> A big percentage of publishing profits—close to an estimated $100 million in 1989—was siphoned off to the Netherlands Antilles company in the form of a royalty, thus reducing United States taxable income. Meanwhile, in 1986, after paying $1.8 billion for United States TV stations, the company began writing off most of that purchase price against profits, further reducing taxable income. And, when the Netherlands Antilles company sold the Ziff-Davis magazine for a $325 million profit, it avoided most United States capital gains taxes by keeping much of the profit offshore. Mr. Murdoch's view: "If you can move assets around like that, isn't that one of the advantages of being global?"

🔟 Ownership-Oriented Financial Services. As I said early on, finance is a type of technology—invisible and intangible, yet every bit as real as the physical assets its operations bring into being. Finance is poorly understood, particularly the intricacies of corporate finance, including mergers and acquisitions.[36] That's why investment bankers and corporate lawyers manage to extract such large fees for their services. An ownership solution will require the services of an extended family of financial service providers, including investment bankers, commercial bankers, lawyers, accountants and appraisal experts. It will also require a major education and communication campaign to better school citizens about finance, business and the various paths to ownership.

To date, the most promising response to business illiteracy is a series of "Open-Book Management" forums and videotapes produced by Jack Stack, based on his best-seller, *The Great Game of Business.*[37] The government could assist this effort by funding the production of educational materials on financial subjects, or more generally by supporting business literacy programs in the nation's education system. For example, school accreditation criteria could be expanded to include a range of financial and business subjects. An earlier era offers a precedent. For more than a century, the U.S. government has provided American farmers with a network of agricultural extension services designed to help them utilize the most up-to-date farming techniques, including crop rotation, erosion-control plowing techniques, irrigation methods and the use of hybrid seeds. Unfortunately, policymakers did not foresee the need to provide analogous services to industrial workers. Instead, as Americans moved off the farm, they became a nation of employees rather than proprietors, becoming wage earners and modern-day sharecroppers rather than equity-empowered stakeowners. That must change.

A modern counterpart to the agricultural extension service could provide the educational and technical assistance required to enable American households to gain an ownership stake in their nation's next wave of income-producing assets. That effort could also help them learn how not to be left out when ownership is transferred from one set of hands to another. Several of the states have active employee-ownership efforts.[38] Their impact can be substantial. Researchers found that the efforts of New York's Center for Employee Ownership and Participation gave the state a big advantage in kick-starting and sustaining that state's employee ownership agenda.

The most useful aspect of New York's program involves funds to help managers, owners and employees understand how ESOP-type financing works. To prime the pump, "pre-feasibility" grants are allowed that convert to a loan once a transaction goes forward. Federal support for a nationwide network of such centers would provide a useful stimulus. In many states, such centers assist at the information-gathering stage, serving as a repository of information and a clearinghouse for professional service-providers.

The disturbing truth is that the current ownership-concentrating, closed system of finance is "on automatic." Without a proactive, countervailing effort, financial techniques that broaden ownership simply will not be utilized, as recent history has proven. Also, experience suggests that changes in the business world happen most quickly when experienced managers share their personal, hands-on experience with other managers, a process that could be supported by regional, state and local efforts. Support is needed for ownership participation centers that provide education, information and networking opportunities, along with technical support.

S E C T I O N **4**

Coping with Global Capitalism

To subdue the enemy without fighting is the acme of skill.

—Sun Tzu

Those residing in "capitalist" economies often think there is only one way to "do" capitalism (usually *their* way). However, the free enterprise found in the United States or in Britain is dramatically different from that of Germany, which differs radically from that found in Japan, Scandinavia or in newly industrialized Asia. Cultural, historical, economic and political influences all play a part in determining capitalism's shape, texture and tone. The differences among national systems are sufficiently distinct that it's impossible to characterize any version as "typical."

The same holds true for socialism. In part this is because, from the outset, socialism included an incoherent compromise between the "orthodox" socialists led by Karl Kautsky (who believed in the irredeemable nature of capitalism and the certainty of its eventual collapse) and the "revisionists," who knew that capitalism could be reformed and felt that socialism should be considered an ethical orientation, not a panacea or a how-to guide for reforming economies. This conflict crystallized when, at a seminal 1891 Socialist International Congress held in Erfurt, Germany, Kautsky's theoretical stance was combined with a more practical position crafted by Eduard Bernstein. The congress then endorsed both.[1] The result was that socialism became ever less coherent in matters of doctrine, while in practice it ran the gamut, with the more clever and successful socialists rejecting orthodoxy in favor of practicality, including the Swedes in the 1930s and the German Social Democrats in 1959. This split continues today. The British Labor Party only abandoned its call for a nationalized economy in 1996.

Combine socialism's muddled political origins with the fact that "capitalism" initially was described in the most scathing way by Karl Marx, its primary detractor and the person who coined the term, and you have a formula for certain confusion, confrontation and intellectual chaos. With that as background, and in light of the collapse of the world's largest socialist economy (the USSR), it should come as no surprise that we see emerging on the global scene dramatically new and wildly hybridized versions of both socialism and capitalism. Many are making their debut among the in-transition economies of the former Soviet Union and its satellites, where policymakers are engineering an extraordinary variety of ownership patterns, including widespread use of employee ownership and an array of broad-based ownership schemes, often resorting to novel means for matching assets to people and marking the first time in history that policymakers have reversed nationalization on a massive scale.

Lest anyone conclude from this that the global community has unanimously agreed that markets are the last possible word in revealed wisdom, it should be noted that Socialist International affiliates recently won elections in France and Britain, and Socialist parties of one stripe or another hold the reins of government in most of the countries of Europe (as of early 1998). One key reason: the change of ownership from government to individuals raises a host of complex and sensitive issues, though perhaps none more volatile than the issue of just who are a nation's natural owners.

In Russia, for example, "grabification," "mafia-ization," "klepto-fication" and "nomenklatura capitalism" are among the terms heard to describe the cozy deals that have transferred state assets not to "the people" (to whom the people had long been told they belonged) but to the politically well-connected, to their cronies and to foreigners and *their* well-connected cronies. One of the jokes making the rounds in Moscow: Question: "Is there any system worse than communism?" Answer: "Yes, post-communism." Though that may be an exaggeration, it also reflects a bitter reality. One of privatization's many paradoxes is that it succeeds best as an *equitable* mechanism for shrinking the state when the state is at its most attentive.

Property Formalization—The Bedrock Requirement

Before turning to the role that ownership patterns are destined to play in the post–Cold War world, it's helpful first to step back in time to understand the role played by the ownership of land—and how that provides a foundation for today's capital markets, a key tool on which reformers are relying in making this historic transition from socialism to an as-yet-unnamed successor.

Though this may seem like an odd segue, it's essential that we grasp why emerging global capital markets must become a phenomenon whose benefits are broadly dispersed, particularly in light of the fact that we are certain to see a continued trend toward securitization (the packaging and sale of tradable claims on income-producing properties). While it's easy to understand that some of humankind is hard at work in steamy rice paddies while others toil atop luxury office buildings structuring mergers and acquisitions, it's not as easy to see how the economic disparity between these two is certain to widen if present-day capitalism is left to its own devices.

At present, the huge and rapidly increasing funds flowing into capital markets are creating massive windfall gains for the owners of securities. For example, even though the face amount of U.S. Treasury securities skyrocketed from less than $1 trillion in 1980 to more than $5.5 trillion in 1997, the market value of each bond rose, indicating that even this huge supply of bonds was too small to satisfy worldwide demand, driving prices upward. Finance experts insist this is only the beginning. As Babson College Professor John C. Edmunds points out, "The total dollar value of all investment-grade securities worldwide that could potentially be issued is upward of $150 trillion, roughly five times the value of annual world output."[2] By his computations, only 40 percent of these securities have been issued so far.*

In other words, financial prosperity—*for someone*—is engineered into the system that Marx derisively labeled "finance capitalism." The issue we address in this section is whether we have the foresight to evoke a capitalism that is broadly inclusive, or whether historical forces will continue to work their will, dividing nations and peoples into haves and have-nots. Because securitization is a worldwide trend, it will he helpful to our inquiry if we briefly examine the origins of this phenomenon, commencing with the securing of title to land.

In *The Other Path,* Peruvian economist Hernando De Soto chronicles the emergence of "informal economies," documenting how the lack of secure title to land inhibits economic development.[3] That lack of title means a lack of access to credit due to the lack of collateral. In the United States, for instance, 70 percent of the credit extended to new businesses stems from pledging property titles as collateral for mortgages. Lack of title also undermines incentives. For instance, De Soto found that investment in home improvements increased ninefold when Peruvian squatters gained title to their homes.

From a political perspective, De Soto offers the example of Peru's notorious Maoist guerrillas (the "Shining Path") who made inroads with farmers

---

* "The dollar value of unsecuritized income-producing assets is approximately $90 trillion. If securitized, the value of these assets could approach $150 trillion. Thus, an income-producing asset is worth about three times the value of its annual gross output if it is not securitized and five times the value if it is securitized. . . . Securitized assets are worth more than the 'lumpy' assets that collateralize them, partly because they are more liquid." John C. Edmundson, Ibid., p. 126.

by settling boundary disputes on untitled land and protecting them from ex-propriation. Yet without access to secure title, the poor are left dependent either on the benign neglect of rightful owners or on armed leftists. De Soto's office is reportedly the most-bombed private-sector building in Peru. Why? He surmises it's because his titling initiatives free Peru's poor from the pro-tection of the Maoists, undermining their support.

Lack of proper title also shortens planning horizons, eroding incentives to protect land, water and other natural resources. Without secure title, land is frequently overworked rather than being stewarded in a way that preserves its long-term capacity to yield healthy crops. Brazil offers a dramatic example, where squatters clear and farm Amazon acreage for only a season or two before pushing ever deeper into threatened rain forests.[4] Land registration also enables local governments to levy taxes required to fund key services such as primary education.

The High Costs of Informality

Secure title, in turn, is closely linked to the origins of financial markets. An owner's stake must be clear; otherwise property rights cannot facilitate the transfer of resources to their highest valued use. When secure, property rights can enter the marketplace in a form adapted to exchange, whether as mortgages, contracts, warehouse receipts, promissory notes or share certificates. Com-mercial legal codes are built on a foundation of such standardized instruments. Many of those instruments, such as land titles and corporate securities, are entered in a land registry or in a corporate share registry governed by legally enforceable rules. Indeed, much of their value derives from this formalization and institutionalization.

Modern capital markets generate economic growth in part because formal-ized property rights remove uncertainty, which lowers transaction costs—facilitat-ing low-cost exchange, fostering specialization and enhancing productivity. "Without formal property," De Soto insists, "a modern social market economy cannot exist." This link between formalized property and economic progress has been overlooked due largely to historical circumstances and the long pe-riod of time over which this subtle transition occurred. As he explains:

> *The appearance of widespread property ownership in France is remembered as the triumph over feudalism rather than the beginning of a formalization process. The concessions on property extended to German peasants at the beginning of the 19th century are recalled as a tactic for enlisting their sup-port against Napoleon and insulating them from the effects of the French Revo-lution rather than as the official initiation of awarding title to common folk. The granting of formal property rights to homesteaders and squatters in North America is recounted as a political strategy for expanding territory by push-ing back Indians, Mexicans and European colonialists. In Japan, Korea and*

Taiwan after the Second World War, the campaign to massively formalize the property of farmers is fixed in memory as a policy to contain communism and to weaken local elites, rather than as one of the most important measures taken for social market economy systems to flourish in those countries.

Widespread urban and rural squatting in developing countries (the barrios of Mexico, the bidonvilles in former French colonies, the shantytowns in former British colonies) is the spontaneous, unbridled emergence of informal property systems. To direct that natural energy into a process that creates formalized, secure and bankable property rights, De Soto proposes a mechanism for rapidly titling many parcels of land. With a combination of high-tech aerial reconnaissance (including satellite mapping) and low-tech community networks (for mobilization and support), De Soto's experience suggests that this formalization process can proceed rapidly and at remarkably low cost. The need for such property formalization services is enormous. The UN's Universal Declaration on Human Rights includes "equal access to property rights" as a key component of the fundamental rights of mankind. Over the next twenty-five years, the World Bank looks to assist Indonesians in registering more than 50 million parcels of land. At its most basic level, any ownership solution requires secure property rights on which other development efforts can be built.

From Formal Title to Formidable Development

In this final section, we explore the peculiar ownership dilemma that confronts those who live in the "transition" and developing countries as well as those who advise them and those with an interest in investing there. We will then examine some of the hopeful ownership solutions that may yet emerge in a wide range of countries, including those now reversing their decades-long experiment with socialist-style ownership solutions.

Although free-enterprise capitalism is presently sweeping the world, celebration is, I submit, premature. In many countries, political leaders seem oblivious to the danger that their policies are re-creating social and political environments hauntingly similar to those that preceded nationalization. If this trend continues, as presently seems likely, movements can be expected to arise that will challenge privatization and other market-based reforms. This trend can already be seen in the resurgence of socialist parties in Europe and in the populist backlash in Mexico and elsewhere.

The current insensitivity to ownership patterns is understandable but inexcusable. Oligarchies, plutocracies and outright thievery have long been common features of ownership patterns worldwide, particularly in those lesser-developed countries where the rule of law has yet to take root. But now those plutocratic patterns have gone global. Concentration is the fast-emerging norm in economies of every sort: transition, developing and developed. Its most disturbing aspect stems not from corruption and chicanery. That much we have learned to expect. What makes the blood boil is when a people struggling to escape from an unworkable and poverty-plagued past are offered ownership pattern–insensitive advice by experts who should know better, including those employed by international financial institutions.[5] In his ongoing struggle to craft a new course for the World Bank, President James Wolfensohn insists that "we begin to recognize that ultimately we will not have substainable prosperity unless we have inclusion."[6] In the last chapters of *The Ownership Solution*, we will take a closer look at a diverse collection of countries and consider how what we've covered earlier can be used to craft more sustainable ownership patterns.

CHAPTER 16

The Development Dilemma

Policy emerges when concept meets opportunity.

—*Henry Kissinger*

Though industrialized countries have funded development efforts for a full half-century, 60 percent of the world's population live on less than $2 per day.[1] In many countries, living standards have fallen steadily. In Central and South America, general poverty now afflicts 200 million people, 60 percent of the population, almost double the number of twenty years ago.[2] Sub-Saharan Africa has lost wealth every year since the mid-1970s.[3] Twenty sub-Saharan African countries remain below their per capita incomes of twenty years ago.[4] The World Bank predicts it will take another four decades for the people in these countries to reach the living standards they enjoyed two decades ago.[5]

On the other hand, although Indonesia had a gross national product (GNP) lower than Nigeria in 1965, it now boasts a GNP three times that of this struggling African country. Similarly, Thailand, with a GNP lower than that of Ghana thirty years ago, became one of the fastest-growing Southeast Asian economies. At every turn, however, we are faced not only with the question of what causes development but also how to measure it. Indonesia, for instance, has been a Southeast Asian success story for more than twenty years, its economy (until recently) the envy of countries throughout the region.[6] However, much of that success was generated by selling off its nonrenewable mineral wealth, clear-cutting its tropical forests and exhausting its topsoil with overly intensive farming.

Measuring the Wealth of Nations

With increasing regularity, development experts challenge not only the measurement but even the very concept of development. Dr. Mahbub ul Haq, former head of policy planning at the World Bank and now president of Pakistan's Human Development Centre, argues that for developing countries to reach the GDP of developed countries would require ten times the known reserves of fossil fuels and two hundred times the known mineral wealth.[7] To

227

further confound matters, during the 1980s, GNP was changed to GDP (gross domestic product).[8] Previously, the earnings of a multinational company were reflected in the national accounts (GNP) of the nation where the company was owned and to which the earnings would eventually flow. Now GDP attributes those earnings to the country where the operations are *located*. Foreign owners (or creditors) could be draining a nation's resources while a rising GDP signals that the country is booming.

Because numbers drive development policies ("what gets measured gets managed"), it is essential that development scorecards "measure what we treasure."[9] After years of prodding, the World Bank proposed in 1995 a new system for measuring national wealth,[10] assigning numbers to the costs of resource depletion and environmental degradation by, for instance, debiting each nation's "wealth account" as mineral resources are extracted. By the bank's accounting, Australia leads 192 economies in national wealth ($835,000 per person), with Canada second ($704,000), Japan fifth ($565,000), Qatar eighth ($473,000) and the United States twelfth (at $421,000). Russia has an estimated per capita wealth of $98,000 compared with Mexico's $74,000, China's $6,600 and Ethiopia's $1,400. With this new measuring system, countries can also be identified in which development amounts to eating their seed corn, such as Kenya, Libya, Nigeria and Venezuela, nations where wealth accumulation is offset by a measurable depletion of raw materials and fertile land.

The study measures wealth in three primary categories: produced assets (machinery, factories, roadways, etc.); natural capital (subsoil deposits, water, timber, protected natural habitat); and human resources (literacy, skills, nutrition). A fourth category, not yet separately measured, embraces "social capital," a fledgling attempt to estimate the contribution of organizations and institutions such as families, communities and civic associations—a nation's wealth embodied in its "collective processes." Aptly subtitled "A Work in Progress," the report validates those who have long argued that sustainable development depends on more than investment in bricks, mortar and machines.

Its most surprising finding: in the world's twenty-nine high-income countries, produced assets (typically called "the means of production") account for only 16 percent of total per capita wealth and natural capital just 17 percent. Worldwide, produced assets make up only 20 percent or less of the wealth of nations.[11] "Human resources make up a much larger share of real wealth," the report found, "and richer countries are generally those that invest more in human resources—in education, nutrition, and health care."[12] The world's total wealth was estimated at $390 trillion.

Yet even this rudimentary attempt to measure wealth and its sources provides no insight into how that wealth is distributed. For example, the natural resources of Central and South America are far superior to those found in Japan, Taiwan, Hong Kong or Singapore. However, Latin America has chosen to develop in a way that provides prosperity principally for a privileged few. For instance, though resource-rich Brazil has enjoyed an annual growth of 7 to 8 percent, it has one of the world's most dramatic income inequalities, with more than 40 percent mired in poverty. In 1960, the top 20 percent of Brazilians received thirty times more income than the bottom 20 percent. By 1989, that gap had grown to sixty times.[13]

The determination of who reaps the rewards of development depends, in part, on who owns that development. To date, this politically sensitive question has routinely been avoided. I submit that a key component of the social capital of a nation is the "institutional capital" (laws, regulations) that determine whether development results in broad- or narrow-based ownership of produced assets and natural capital. Even the development of human resources is affected by who owns these other resources, in the same way that a more well-to-do family can afford better schooling for its children.[14]

Development Designed as a Unifying Force

The development challenge lies in determining how best to empower a nation's people to engage in value-adding production and to capture that value *for themselves* rather than for foreign investors or for locals who are already well-to-do. Development agencies are not yet organized with *both* those goals in mind. Moreover, during the 1980s, the World Bank became less a traditional capital-provider and more a "capital catalyst" as it focused on fostering market mechanisms (especially capital markets) to advance development.[15] "Financial markets don't just oil the wheels of economic growth," claims former World Bank chief economist Lawrence Summers. "They *are* the wheels."[16] Even the rhetoric of development has changed to reflect the ascendancy of financial capital: nations in need are no longer described as developing countries, they are now "emerging markets." However, as Nobel economist Douglass North argues, you can't simply leave development to markets alone, as we shall see.

In part, this focus on financial markets reflects the reality of global capitalism. In 1990, for instance, official development assistance totaled $56.3 billion. That compares with $44.4 billion in private capital sent to emerging markets that year. By 1996, private capital flows had grown to $243.8 billion—nearly a sixfold increase—while funds from development agencies dropped to $40.8 billion, almost half that from the World Bank. Thus the bank's emphasis on fostering investor-friendly environments. However, faith in markets has its limits. Three-quarters of that private capital flows to a dozen countries; nearly one-quarter goes to China. That leaves vast regions of the world untouched. Also, in addition to fostering an environment that is investor-friendly and politically stable, Professor North points out that policymakers must also develop the institutions, legal and otherwise, that support development.

Free markets are not really free. They come with a price. For instance, without a (costly) legal system that reliably enforces property rights and contracts, people are understandably reluctant to do business with strangers. Thus, despite the emergence in Russia of market-based exchange (vs. a system based on state control), investors remained wary until key institutional reforms began to jell. Also, it's important to note that democracy is of only incidental concern to financial capital. Though its presence may be important for *noncommercial* reasons, capital inflows correlate closely with the confidence investors have in the political environment, regardless of whether that environment is democratic, plutocratic, autocratic or even totalitarian—witness the remarkable capital inflows to Singapore and China.[17]

Internally generated personal savings are also a factor. However, Hugh Peyman, managing director of Kleinwort Benson Research Asia, confirms Professor North's point regarding the key role played by institutional capital, cautioning that "An obsession with (personal) savings is like an obsession with making bricks. They are essential to building a house, but so are many other tangible inputs from glass to wooden beams, not to mention intangibles like skilled labor and efficient infrastructure."[18]

More significant is the presence of a collective mix of intangibles such as the quality of primary school education, computer ownership, the social environment (such as press freedom) and access to information exchange technology because, he argues, "they determine how efficiently and creatively the savings are used." Pointing to the high savings generated during the heyday of the Soviet Union, Peyman notes that many of those savings turned out to be "like water flowing into sand."

The increasingly important role played by information exchange has now been documented in an innovative "Wealth of Nations" index developed by Boston-based World Times Money Matters Institute. In a survey of thirty-five emerging nations, the Institute's "triangle index" evaluates economies across sixty-three equally weighted factors grouped into three primary categories: economic environment, information exchange and social environment. Though 1997 marked only its second survey year, the conclusions add significantly to Professor North's thesis that it is often the invisible and intangible dimensions that make all the difference in a nation's development. Thus, for example, although China ranks high in its economic environment (eleventh of the thirty-five nations in domestic savings, GDP growth rate, foreign reserves, etc.), it ranks only twenty-fourth in the overall index because of low scores in its social environment (twenty-eighth in political rights, daily calorie supply, access to clean water, etc.) and information exchange (twenty-seventh in literacy, telephone accessibility, Internet service hosts, press freedom, etc.).

Though the full implications for long-term development are still being plumbed, Crocker Snow, editor-in-chief of *The World Paper*, cautions against the extremely high costs likely to accompany policies that block developing nations from fully participating in the information age. That's because it's not just the flow of goods and capital that now drive development; it's also the flow of technology and information. Also, as Alison Sander, president of Cambridge Transnational Associates points out, as prices continue to plummet, "The net effect of all the competing technologies being offered (phone, fax, courier, air mail, e-mail) is that communications will move from an age of scarcity to an age of abundance."[19]

The confluence of the forces fueling development with those essential to democracy is inescapable. It's not a coincidence that the most closed societies continue to have more one-way sources of communication (television) than two-way sources that undermine central authority (telephones, faxes, Internet host providers, etc.). The interactive, self-organizing forces that fuel both markets and democracies share many of the same principles. Margaret Wheatley insists that "networks and conversations are what matter"[20] and that "participation and democracy are not choices, they simply are the way systems operate. . . . Democracy is the only path that life accepts."[21] Suggestive of the emerging role yet to be played by a combination of telecommunication and information technologies, she insists that "systems can change dramatically by amplifying one element of feedback."[22]

Institutional Capital as a Unifier or Divider

Douglass North's insight about institutional capital needs to be taken one step further. Yes, investor confidence and market mechanisms are essential, financial markets are helpful, and the availability of key institutions (contract law, an honest court system) is a genuine plus. But these alone are insufficient, even in combination. For development to take root and for prosperity to be enjoyed by more than a financially savvy few, the financial value of that development must not only be captured for those *residing* in the developing country; it also must be captured for a *broad base* of those residents.

Even where an investment results in increased efficiency and profits, Nobel laureate economist Robert Solow cautions that "efficiency *alone* cannot sustain economic growth. There must also be robust market demand for goods and services and that demand must show up not abroad but *in that country*." What he neglects to mention is that this demand must also be *broadly dispersed*. Wages alone, history suggests, are not enough to ensure broad-based prosperity-sharing. That traditional approach becomes steadily more deficient as a development strategy as labor costs become steadily more arbitraged worldwide—as global production flows to low-wage countries.

Transforming Foreign Capital

Every investor has a time period over which an investment is projected to earn a return *of* his capital plus a return *on* his capital (his profit). In developing countries, this "investment horizon" is typically three to five years. Even in the most stable of developed countries, it is seldom longer than seven to ten years, except for infrastructure. Five to seven years is the norm. Often a host country gives up more than required to attract foreign investment. For instance, when an investor makes a decision on an investment horizon of only three to five years, why should he be offered *permanent* ownership? "It is neither efficient nor equitable," Shann Turnbull argues, "for investors to obtain profits in excess of the incentive required to invest."[23] Turnbull suggests that a gradual change in ownership be built into the initial capital structure so that, as investors approach their investment horizon, that foreign capital transforms into domestic ownership. Such "time-limited" property rights are already a well-known feature of patents, copyrights, bonds, mortgages, leases and other commercial concepts widely used in the financial world.

The appeal of ownership-transforming financing techniques (and dynamic ownership rights) will become steadily more apparent as cross-border investment flows continue to increase from mature, slow-growing industrial countries to faster-growing developing countries—in response both to their lower-cost production and to generally higher returns. Additional factors will also play a part as global trade becomes more free; investors seek new means for diversifying their portfolios; the social capital in developing countries becomes more investor-friendly and political stability becomes more widespread.

In a multivolume 1993 study of this capital-flow phenomenon, Michael Bruno, then the World Bank's chief economist, found "convincing evidence on the benefits of portfolio flows, *particularly from the perspective of industrial countries' investors*."[24] In other words, although global capital markets are a clear boon to developed countries, the impact on developing countries is decidedly mixed. I submit that the impact will not become clearly beneficial until these capital flows are transformed into broad-based *domestic* ownership that supports broad-based *domestic* purchasing power—per Robert Solow's recommendation.[25]

Steadily rising cross-border capital flows will also be pushed along by a confluence of other developments, including the fact that well-funded pension plans continue to be the exception in Western Europe. German companies, for instance, have long been allowed to claim a tax deduction when creating a "book reserve" promising to pay retirement benefits without fully funding that promise. As a consequence, pension-fund assets in Germany total only about 6 percent of GDP (though pension promises are often reinsured). That compares with some 20 percent of GDP in Japan, more than 60 percent in Britain and fully 68 percent in the United States (as of 1995). France (at 3 percent) and Italy (1 percent) are even less well funded. This suggests an aging workforce in the developed world whose members will grow increasingly hungry for the high-return investment opportunities that are more likely to be found in the developing world.

A Call for Financial Creativity

The Economist poses a provocative scenario: what if the percentage of pension assets invested abroad were to increase to 20 percent, a figure roughly in line with developing countries' projected share of world stock market capitalization by the year 2000? Modern portfolio theory suggests that this level of diversification would be prudent. *The Economist* projects that the enhanced return and reduced risk could generate an additional $120 billion in investment returns compared with a pension portfolio invested solely in developed countries. "That could make for a neat symmetry," *Economist* editors suggest. "Both tomorrow's pensioners in the aging rich countries and the young recipient countries will gain as first-world pension funds buy a stake in the faster growth of these more dynamic economies." The challenge for both private- and public-sector policymakers in these developing countries (and in the development banks) is how to get the most "bang for the buck" from these vast capital flows. As I see it, the goal is to provide attractive returns for capital-providers while also structuring in-country investments for eventual broad-based domestic ownership.

The development task is complicated by the fact that the globalization of capital markets has largely bypassed the poorest countries. With 20 percent of the world's people, these countries receive a meager 0.2 percent of the world's commercial lending. In addition, their share of world trade fell between 1960 and 1990—from an already low 4 percent to less than 1 percent.[26]

These circumstances make development banking's poverty-reduction agenda ripe for financial creativity. It's also a key reason why the development banks are turning to microcredit and microenterprise development as a newly hopeful development strategy (discussed below). The spread of grotesque global inequities also enhances the appeal of proposals designed to raise funds by taxing the world's financial "commons." For example, Mahbub ul Haq proposes a 0.25 percent levy on foreign exchange transactions. With more than a trillion dollars traded daily in the world's various currency exchanges (largely to hedge currency risk), that would yield $250 billion each year for development purposes, including funding for microcredit programs. Futurists Hazel Henderson and Alan Kay propose directing proceeds to the UN.[27]

That brings us full circle back to three interrelated dilemmas facing the development banks. First is the simple fact that the cost of evaluating, monitoring and lending is roughly the same for large as for small projects, creating a bias toward project approval.[28] Second, because loans are typically made to sovereign governments, the banks are always repaid.[29] That is not the case for private lenders, who suffer a loss if the money is poorly utilized. This lack of market discipline ensures a less-disciplined loan-approval process. Lastly, as a practical matter, development loans are often negotiated by personnel drawn from the well-to-do in developing countries because it is primarily they who can afford the education and training required to operate in this sophisticated environment.

It should come as no surprise that it is largely in the former Soviet Union and its satellites that we find the keenest taste for development that results in broad-based private ownership. This contrasts, for example, with Latin America and the Caribbean, where ownership patterns remain remarkably plutocratic. Development financing has long had a telltale tendency to either (a) feed into megaprojects (dams, power projects, etc.) that spin off lucrative contracts for private companies owned by local elites, or (b) fuel the widely prevalent closed system of finance, further concentrating ownership.

People-ized Development = Sustainable Development

Development banks routinely require that projects include an environmental-impact assessment. As yet none require an ownership-impact assessment. On a forward-looking basis, this requirement alone could add needed focus to the development agenda. On a hindsight basis, it would be revealing (though doubtless embarrassing) to undertake an ownership assessment of projects financed, say, over the past twenty years, including an assessment of who accumulated wealth based on contracts that accompanied the many concrete artifacts for which development banking is so famous, such as dams, power plants, water projects and such.[30]

Inhabitants of developing countries are understandably skeptical about development-bank lending when they see their governments borrow funds to further empower local elites, belying World Bank president James Wolfensohn's well-intentioned claim, "We're in the poverty reduction business." Development assistance would be much more appreciated by those whose plight it is intended to address if a broader base of the "addressees" gained a palpable personal stake in that development. Also, reluctant donor countries (such as the current U.S. Congress) would be much more supportive of development-bank efforts if they could see proof of a development model with real potential to reduce poverty. As history has shown, the current model's "agnosticism" about ownership patterns often aggravates the division between the haves and the have-nots, while poverty deepens.[31]

Development bankers need not ascribe to the social justice concerns implied by the ownership pattern–sensitive model I propose. They need only keep in mind a well-worn Wall Street maxim that applies worldwide, namely: Don't walk in the front door until you can see the back door. In other words, don't put money into something without knowing how you'll get it out. The lack of an investment exit is a major disincentive for any investor contemplating the developing world, where reliably liquid capital markets remain a rarity (a key reason they're called "emerging" markets). To compensate for that risk, investors require higher financial returns. That, in turn, shrinks the range of attractive investments, slowing capital inflows and development.[32]

To succeed, development strategies must focus on both capital inflow and capital's exit; ownership solutions can play a key supporting role. The development of capital markets can help, but that requires considerable time. Plus, participation in fledgling stock exchanges is rarely broad-based, particularly at the outset. The use of ownership-expanding, ESOP-like exit mechanisms could address both social justice concerns and the "back door" issue by providing a way to transform capital (whether foreign, domestic or development bank capital) into broad-based domestic ownership. That, in turn, would create a broader base of citizens with a stake in capital market development. That contrasts with more traditional "top-down" capital market strategies that typically enhance liquidity for the well-to-do without addressing how to involve the grassroots. So, even if social justice is rejected and poverty reduction too, the appeal of lower investment risk should make converts of even the most people-insensitive and radically laissez-faire of the development economists.

Ownership Pattern–Sensitive Development

The effectiveness of two key instruments of the World Bank Group could be much improved with more sensitivity to ownership patterns. First is the International Finance Corporation (IFC), which provides investment capital in the form of both debt and equity. The IFC operates as a donor country–funded merchant bank, acquiring stakes in private companies worldwide (1996 saw $6.7 billion in approvals in 276 projects). Because of the IFC's successful investment record, its participation is widely viewed by other investors as a "seal of approval." That, in turn, reduces those investors' up-front costs, because they often can rely on the IFC's investment appraisal.

The IFC's investment portfolio includes substantial sums in the form of illiquid shares in unlisted companies. This creates two challenges. First, by locking their equity capital into old projects, the IFC is constrained in its ability to invest in new projects. Second, its "back door" is not designed to improve local ownership patterns.* An ownership-sensitive exit strategy could both address the IFC's liquidity needs and improve its impact on poverty reduction.

Second, an ownership-sensitive strategy could enhance the political risk insurance provided by the bank's Multilateral Investment Guarantee Agency

---

* Historically, the IFC's equity exit mechanisms have been concentrated in four channels: (1) sell the stake to another investor in the project (typically a foreigner or an already-well-to-do local investor); (2) sell to a foreign investor; (3) sell into a fledgling stock exchange (where participation is typically dominated by local elites); or (4) sell to an institutional investor such as an insurance company or a pension plan (typically the poor in developing countries can neither afford insurance nor participate in pension plans).

(MIGA), which in 1996 provided seventy guarantee projects in twenty-five countries. The principal political risk has long been expropriation. Yet historically, that risk emerges in countries where Marxist movements nationalize private assets on behalf of *nonowning* workers. Both experience and common sense suggest that a component of worker ownership should become a standard component in MIGA's risk management.

The ripple effects of such ownership-pattern sensitivity could also be felt in other areas of concern to development. For instance, capital markets are a high-priority goal because of their ability not only to mobilize savings but to swiftly transform them into capital formation. Experience in the United States suggests that here too a focus on ownership patterns could help. For instance, San Diego–headquartered Science Applications International Corporation (SAIC) established an in-house broker-dealer to help make an internal market in its shares for its employee-owners. For one day once every three months, the company facilitates an in-house stock exchange (called "Bull, Inc.") so that SAIC's thirty thousand employee-shareholders can trade shares among themselves, a practice they began when they had only a few hundred employees. An adaptation of this model could help kick-start capital markets in developing countries.

Imagine, for instance, if one hundred companies around Shanghai sponsored such mini–stock exchanges. I see at least three advantages. First, by providing an investment vehicle (their employer) with which grassroots investors are familiar, savings may well increase, particularly if employers are urged to encourage employee participation. Second, intracompany trading among employee-owners (say through an Internet linkup) would reduce the risk of both nondiversification and illiquidity while also setting a traded value on the shares—often a highly conjectural exercise in emerging markets.[33] Third and perhaps most importantly, this could address the difficulty encountered in providing a "bottom-up" stimulus for companies to list their shares.

Such a strategy could also help advance the public's understanding of the important role that securitization and financial markets can play in development. Fledgling stock exchanges are often caricatured as casinos for the rich because participation initially often seems to benefit only the well-to-do.[34] Broader, grassroots participation could do much to build support for the development of this "social capital." In addition, ownership-pattern sensitivity is crucial to advancing development in those policy environments (such as China and Cuba) where capital markets encounter ideological opposition because they epitomize the worst element of "finance capitalism."

Positive experiences in other areas of development financing (such as microlending to microenterprises) confirm the importance of such bottom-up initiatives. Where local people help organize a process, and where they and others they know gain a palpable stake, development has a much higher likelihood of success. An institutional design is required that consciously and directly involves more people if development experts hope to build confidence in financial markets and enthusiasm for what they can deliver. Indirectly, this ownership participation strategy could also have a positive impact on population control, if a credible ownership initiative succeeds in persuading people that asset accumulation is a feasible alternative to children as a source of social status and economic security.

An Ownership Strategy for Stability

Stable exchange rates (the original goal of the World Bank Group's International Monetary Fund) may also be advanced by such an ownership pattern–sensitive strategy. By relying on traditional closed-system financing techniques, foreign investors frequently gain a permanent stake in developing countries—witness Firestone's (now Bridgestone's) stake in Liberian rubber. That ensures a perpetual claim on the country's foreign-exchange earnings as offshore investors repatriate their export earnings in hard currency. As a consequence, less foreign exchange is available to purchase components for the local manufacture of goods that otherwise must be purchased abroad, requiring the generation of even more foreign exchange. For commodities-based, export-dependent economies, this vicious cycle accelerates the drawdown of nonrenewable resources (such as selling minerals to buy machinery and parts for local manufacturing) in an attempt to generate ever more foreign exchange.

At present, there is no formalized, systematic process for dealing with exchange-rate issues, excepting sporadic G-7 meetings dominated by the industrial economies. Other than the rigors of politically unpopular structural adjustment (whereby an economy's fiscal and monetary affairs are put in order), the IMF/World Bank Group has few available tools to advance local economic environments supportive of exchange-rate stability. If, indeed, a relationship exists between exchange-rate stability and ownership patterns (domestic vs. foreign, concentrated vs. broad-based), then development efforts should insist on those ownership patterns that best support stability along with the developing nation's ability to sustain an attractive current account balance.

As suggested in earlier chapters, such an ownership pattern–sensitive development strategy could also assist countries in addressing future fiscal strains, an oft-overlooked component of structural adjustment. Absent an asset-accumulation strategy, traditional capital market-funded development will continue to be accompanied by widespread assetlessness, leaving populations dependent on a government-funded safety net—a priority target for structural adjustment. Where democracies become robust (a key goal of development) while ownership remains concentrated, that shows up as a deteriorating fiscal condition along with a steady erosion in property rights as voters demand redistributive and fiscally debilitating "entitlements." As the current fiscal condition of the United States suggests, emerging markets cannot afford to be agnostic when it comes to emerging ownership patterns. Broad-based asset-accumulation can also free up fiscal resources to focus on the development of human resources (education, health, training)—the key to any nation's long-term development. Never again should development efforts be deployed in support of ownership patterns such as those that emerged in Indonesia under the Suharto clan (CIA estimates their wealth at $35 billion).

Making Banks People-Worthy

Crafting a response to the needs of the abject poor in developing countries presents a particularly vexing challenge. Under Wolfensohn's leadership, the World Bank has shifted its focus from megaprojects (dams and such) toward human and social development, capacity building, and sustainability-focused endeavors (literacy, clean water, sanitation). In Africa, for example, he urged a new generation of leaders to come up with their own ideas, which are serving as the blueprint for the bank's activities. Projects are now typically smaller in scale and closer in proximity to those they're designed to help, whether it's buying textbooks for Moldova, supporting an irrigation project in Mali, helping fishermen on the shores of Lake Victoria or assisting Ecuador in reforming its judicial system.

To reach the abject poor, a major new trend in finance has emerged that originated with a microcredit program initiated by the Grameen ("Rural") Bank in Bangladesh. Grameen Bank became famous not only for its success in using small business loans to lift the poor out of poverty but also for its commercial success reflected in its high rate of loan repayment (in excess of 98 percent) on 2.2 million loans of more than $1.8 billion in thirty-seven thousand rural villages in the very poorest of the poor countries.[35]

Dr. Muhammad Yunus, Grameen Bank's founder and managing director, reports that he first realized the need for small, very personalized loans during the 1974 famine in Bangladesh when he met a woman who was making only two cents profit on her handmade bamboo stools because she didn't have the money to buy raw material. Instead she had to borrow from a trader who required that she sell the stools to him at a price he determined, making her virtually bonded labor. With the assistance of a colleague, Dr. Yunus identified forty-two women in his neighborhood facing similar circumstances who together needed to borrow a *total* of $27.

Embarrassed that, as a Ph.D. in economics, he had "eyes blinded by knowledge," he provided the first loan himself and then personally guaranteed a series of loans until a microcredit program could be put in place. Initial loans remain quite modest, typically less than $100. In response to those who question whether the poor are creditworthy, he responds that the loan repayment record of the well-to-do is not nearly so good. He turns the question on its head, asking, "Are the banks people-worthy?" Based on his in-the-trenches experience, he insists: "Poverty is not created by poor people. Poverty is created by the institutions we have built around us. We have to go back to the drawing board and redesign those institutions so that they do not discriminate against the poor as the present ones do." The denial of credit to the poor, he argues, amounts to "financial apartheid."[36]

At the first-ever "Microcredit Summit" convened in Washington in February 1997, global leaders and heads of development banks pledged to reach 100 million families with microcredit by the year 2005 at an estimated cost of $21.6 billion (microcredit programs presently reach some 8 million people on six continents).[37] As of late 1996, 223 Grameen Bank–like lending programs had been established in fifty-eight countries. Several dozen programs operate in the United States, many of them for Native Americans.

Much like the "small is beautiful" notion popularized by Fritz Schumacher in the 1970s in his book by that title, the Grameen Bank's people-centered notion of finance has a distinctly human face. One key element is its emphasis on self-esteem, particularly among Muslim women, who are often denied economic and social status. As it turns out, lending to women makes good sense, both as a matter of prudent banking and as a focus of sound development policy. Women not only have greater respect for their financial commitments than men; they also take more responsibility for advancing the development agenda. Family planning, for instance, is twice as high among microcredit borrowers, and child mortality 34 percent lower. The independence women gained through microcredit doubtless played a role in a drop in Bangladesh's fertility rate from 6.2 children per woman to 3.4 over the past ten years. Practices also improve in other key areas, including sanitation, nutrition and water quality. When coupled with improved access to education, health care and social services, microcredit has proven effective in reducing extreme poverty.[38]

Doers or Ditherers?

Never in the half-century history of development banks has there been such a worldwide need for their services. Yet never has there been such "donor fatigue," as developed countries have cut back rather than expanded their input of expertise and support. Overall levels of aid declined by nearly a quarter between 1995 and 1996 alone. The United States, historically an aid leader (dating back to the Marshall Plan), has instead become the leader in cutbacks. The State Department's modestly funded Agency for International Development is under siege and America's contributions to the World Bank Group under attack, even while the U.S. economy has enjoyed an unprecedented seven consecutive years of a booming stock market.

Yet Americans are grossly ill-informed about what they spend on foreign aid. Nearly 60 percent believe Washington spends more on foreign aid than on Medicare, when in reality Medicare accounts for 13 percent of the federal budget while foreign aid amounts to less than 2 percent (survey respondents thought that aid consumed 26 percent). "Ironically, when survey respondents were asked how much of the budget *should be* allocated to foreign aid, the average response was 13 percent, fully six times more than what the government actually spends."[39] If the United States hopes to retain its leadership as a moral voice abroad, it need only do what its citizens think it already does: devote more resources to improving living standards in other countries.

Foreign policy experts are only just beginning to understand the relationship between economic development and efforts to advance democratic reforms. "People do not love democracy if it does not bring improvement in their economic conditions," insists Michael Novak, resident scholar at the American Enterprise Institute. "They will not be satisfied with democracy if all it means is the opportunity to vote every two years. Typically, they do not ask for utopia but would like to see the possibility of solid economic progress for their families over the next three to four years. This is the psychological mechanism which makes capitalism, or at least a dynamic economy, indispensable to the success of democracy. *Capitalism delivers the goods that democracy holds out as one of its promises*"[40] (emphasis added).

Therein lies both the promise and the peril. Experience has confirmed time and again that capitalism, unless engineered to do otherwise, will create ownership patterns that are patently inequitable, fiscally unworkable and, I maintain, politically, socially, culturally and environmentally unsustainable. As the world's leader in the use (and abuse) of creative financing techniques, the United States has the capacity to show how free-enterprise democracies can be engineered to improve the economic conditions of everyone. My fear as an American is that, in the cautionary words of Secretary of State Madeleine Albright, "we will be known as world-class ditherers, who stood by while the seeds of renewed global conflict were sown."[41]

Reinventing Capitalism in Europe

> Ownership is not a vice, not something to be ashamed of, but rather a commitment, and an instrument by which the general good can be served.
>
> —*Václav Havel*

H istory's most dramatic change in ownership since the Russian Revolution of 1917 is now under way in the former Soviet Union and its onetime satellites, including Poland, Hungary, the Czech Republic and the Baltic republics (Estonia, Latvia and Lithuania). Here we visit the path these countries are treading in their attempt to craft a response to the ruin left behind by the Marxist-Leninist version of an ownership solution.[1] We'll also look at how the lessons learned could be adapted to key Western European economies, including France and Germany, in their struggle to adapt to the new realities of an emerging global capitalism.

Though Poland was the first of the satellites to break away from the USSR, it was the slowest to implement an ownership strategy. The Poles decided to begin their privatization program with a combination of negotiated sales and public offerings on the fledgling Warsaw stock exchange. By early 1995, however, they had seen only a few dozen public offerings in addition to two hundred negotiated sales, mostly to foreigners. Largely as a legislative afterthought, small- and medium-sized companies were allowed to be liquidated and their assets sold to employees, but only if the employees could first raise 20 percent of the purchase price. Because employees lacked the cash, the government agreed to a leasing arrangement, with employees' payments credited toward the purchase price.[2] To the surprise of policymakers, this led to the privatization of more than twelve hundred state-owned enterprises, making this "afterthought" privatization's most successful component, characterized by the *Warsaw Voice* as "Capitalism with a human face."

The Czech Solution

During the late 1980s, many Czechs feared that the Communist nomenklatura would join forces with the multinational corporate community to buy its state-owned enterprises at bargain-basement prices. That was a justifiable fear. Potential investors knew the nation was an industrial power prior to World War II with a per capita GDP equal to that of Belgium. Yet by the 1980s when playwright Václav Havel led the successful Velvet Revolution ending Soviet domination, fully 97 percent of Czech production was under state control.

In an ultra-right reaction to that ultra-leftist era, Finance Minister Václav Klaus proposed Eastern Europe's most dramatic ownership solution with the virtually free distribution of shares in state-owned enterprises through a mass privatization scheme. Drawing directly from University of Chicago economist Milton Friedman's 1962 book, *Capitalism and Freedom* (advocating school tuition vouchers), Klaus proposed that any citizen over age eighteen would be entitled to buy a coupon (for a nominal sum) that could be used to bid for shares in privatizing companies.[3] By late 1991, 487 Slovak companies and 943 Czech firms were chosen for the first of two waves of "voucher privatization."

Despite the government's promotional efforts, the voucher privatization scheme generated little interest until Viktor Kozeny, a U.S.-educated entrepreneur, launched a massive ad campaign promising a 1,000 percent return within a year and a day to all those who invested their vouchers in his "Harvard Capital" investment fund in which he proposed to use those vouchers to bid at auction for blocks of shares in privatizing companies. As some four hundred funds entered this melee, participation jumped from 2 million Czechs in January 1992 to 8.5 million by the March 1992 deadline. Fully two-thirds of those eligible chose to participate. The six largest funds soon controlled some 30 percent of all shares. Harvard Capital became the third largest in terms of asset values with a stake in more than fifty companies.

As subsequent events have shown, Klaus's path to privatization had several foreseeable flaws. Many of the funds were undercapitalized, leading to concerns about a possible collapse in share prices should they need to sell shares to pay their hyped-up returns. That, in turn, could lead to the feared foreign control if multinationals were to snap up shares at distressed prices. More commonly, Czech speculators bought companies cheaply and sent their profits abroad.

Many of the funds were sponsored by state-owned banks, thereby undermining the hoped-for motivation for enterprise restructuring, a key rationale for privatization. The banks were keen to avoid politically awkward layoffs or costly bankruptcies. Thus, rather than the "invisible hand" of the market, the state's quite visible hand remained in place, as lax loans continued to prop up loss-making firms. Even in late 1997, tens of thousands of Czech workers were receiving paychecks from money-losing companies, allowing Klaus to tout his country's low rate of unemployment (under 4 percent).

Even that fails to tell the full story of the Klaus debacle. By mid-1996, more than half of the seventeen-hundred-odd companies subject to the shares-for-vouchers scheme had shifted control out of the hands of the state. At that point, mass privatization quickly gave way to what *The Wall Street Journal* characterized as a "mass asset grab" as the Czech post-privatization landscape was besieged by corporate predators. For instance, Chemapol, a cash-rich communist-era trading company, became the chief player in the Czech chemical industry, using its cash and financial leverage to go on a $250-million buyout binge.

Many of the investment funds converted into holding companies, enabling fund managers to control companies outright and escape what little regulation Klaus allowed. That, in turn, made them better able to defraud minority shareholders. According to a mid-1997 capital market review by outside experts, diversions by Czech fund managers were seen as "tunneling" a remarkable 40 to 80 percent of the funds' value.[4] The highly touted Prague securities market is contracting as companies now owned by a single shareholder withdraw from trading. Only a few dozen blue-chip firms are likely to retain their listings, with a second tier of smaller companies trading over the counter. The balance are unlikely to trade at all now that the Czechs have completed the Klaus-led transition, moving from public ownership "by the people" through a temporary phase of broad-based ownership by many people, to what has since become ownership dominated by just a few people. The Czech economy now finds itself in a confused muddle, with rising deficits (both trade and fiscal) and a depressed stock market. Meanwhile, the Harvard Fund's Mr. Kozeny resides in the Bahamas, where he carries an Irish passport.

Perhaps most tragically, the resulting lack of confidence in the capital market has undermined confidence in democratic institutions more generally, inhibiting investment, both domestic and foreign. Because the Klaus government often condoned unfair and abusive practices, the restoration of confidence will consume valuable time that could have been directed to creating a stronger economy and rebuilding civil society. Though other transition economies have suffered setbacks due to naive adherence to neoclassical nostrums, none have been so enthusiastically misdirected.

Klaus's well-known reputation as an arrogant and caustic ideologue was confirmed during my one brief encounter with him in the early 1990s when he was Václav Havel's finance minister. The Czech embassy's political counselor in Washington introduced me to him as an expert on ESOPs. Before I could say a word, he replied, "I know everything there is to know about ESOPs. We are not interested in a 'third way.'" With that, he turned his back, terminating our "discussion." I later found that he issued a regulation that privatization plans would be declined if they proposed more than a 10 percent stake for employees. President Havel, no fan of Klaus, summarizes his sanguine view of the Klaus-orchestrated policy environment: "No vision, no concepts."

From a distance, the Czech Republic looked terrific. Up close, the view is quite different. In mid-1997, the Finance Ministry released a report documenting fifteen techniques that investment funds and their managers are using to enrich themselves at the expense of the companies and the capital markets, including widespread asset-stripping, insider trading and stock manipulation.[5] With apparent disregard for who got hurt in building Czech-style capitalism, Klaus argued to a U.S. fund manager: "Jay Gould and Vanderbilt were robber barons, but one generation later they were respected people."[6] In the wake of revelations of a political party slush fund in a Swiss bank (holding cash donated by privatization beneficiaries), Klaus agreed to popular demands—and Mr. Havel's request—that he and his government resign, ending his reign in November 1997.[7]

The Yugoslavian Dilemma

When Poland's Finance Ministry first began its study of employee ownership in late 1989, its privatization team knew about U.S. ESOPs and was inclined to include ESOPs in its program. However, ministry officials told me that each time they raised the idea, their colleagues in Warsaw would object—"It sounds like Yugoslavia and we don't want that here." Thus, one early component of Polish privatization involved distinguishing American-style ESOPs from Yugoslavian-style worker ownership.

In neighboring Hungary, policymakers voiced similar concerns. In Budapest, politicians told me they feared that employees were not culturally prepared to become owners, that their inclusion required time-consuming education and training, and that they brought nothing new or useful to the privatization process: no new capital and no management expertise. Initially, employee ownership was viewed as a distracting detour, a way station until the arrival of the "real owners," who would bring the money, management and expertise that would lead both the companies and the nation into a bright new era of productivity and prosperity. That naive notion soon collided with the practical political challenge of kick-starting privatization in an environment where worker support was critical. However, as elsewhere in Eastern Europe, Yugoslavia's failed experiment initially soured the views of those with their hands on Hungary's policy levers—and with good reason.

In the Yugoslavia of the 1960s, company-dominant workers' councils (operating much like boards of directors) were granted considerable control over the revenues of Yugoslavian companies. With few restrictions, they could direct those revenues to wages or even to workers' vacation spas—a popular and oft-used option. If the company then ran short of cash, say for capital investment, they simply turned to the government for additional funds. That easy option was often chosen in lieu of setting funds aside for depreciation. In political and fiscal terms, there was no "hard budget constraint"—the government was happy to extend more cash or credit. This arrangement encouraged firms to live well beyond their means, secure in the knowledge they could turn to the government to bail them out. It's difficult for me to think of that as "ownership." In effect, the firms operated as quasi-independent, worker-managed units of the state. Polish and Hungarian legislators were rightly concerned that this poorly conceived ownership solution not find its way into their new paradigm for a post-Soviet economy.

The Path to Private Ownership—An Ideological Conundrum

Polish interest in worker ownership may have been a key reason the Soviets found the Solidarity-led uprising so threatening because, ideologically, worker ownership cuts to the very heart of the rationale for Soviet-style socialism—which was founded on a bloody workers' revolution. The Communist Party, in whom ownership formally resided in the USSR, was formed to manage the means of production in the name of the workers and for their benefit. Yet decades later, here were Polish workers in the Lenin Shipyard in Gdansk rejecting that version of worker ownership and proclaiming, in effect, "Thanks but no thanks, we'd rather own it ourselves."

However, once Solidarity took over the reins of government, worker ownership presented a policy conundrum. As finance ministry officals explained to me, those companies belonged (at least rhetorically) *to the people*, not just to those who happened to be on the premises at that particular moment in history. They worried that if they sold a company to its workers and the company did poorly (as some doubtless would), the workers would be upset, claiming they should have been given an opportunity to own shares in a broad base of companies, not just in their struggling employer.[8] Conversely, if the government sold companies solely to the workers and those companies did well (as some would), other Poles would be upset, claiming that they too should be allowed to own shares in companies that belong to *all* the people. While Polish policymakers saw no way they could exclude the workers, nor could they justify restricting ownership solely to the workers.

This political balancing act drove policymakers in Warsaw, Budapest, Moscow and elsewhere toward a blend of both employee ownership and mass privatization. At the same time, however, because each of these beleaguered economies sought access to foreign capital, their ownership solutions also reflect considerable sensitivity to the concerns of foreign investors. For instance, Hungary's early privatizations were widely criticized for being far too generous to foreign investors and for limiting employee ownership to those employed as senior managers. In addition, proceeds from early "spontaneous privatizations" were often retained by the company rather than being paid over to the government, often with hints of offical collusion.

Hungary initially embraced a highly optimistic "market-based" privatization policy, figuring all they had to do was throw a privatization party and investors would show up. They didn't. Policymakers then shifted to more realistic (and more politically driven) techniques designed to stimulate demand for shares, with privatization proceeds taking a decidedly secondary role to that of ensuring broad-based Hungarian participation. Based on the dogged persistence of employee-ownership activist Janos Lukacs, the government enacted a set of ESOP incentives that helped breathe life into what was then a stalled privatization program.[9]

Russia's Worker-Focused Ownership Solution

In Russia, both the managers and the workers were put in the driver's seat (at least initially) through a privatization policy that offered both parties a chance to buy substantial blocks of shares, with the balance sold to the general public, to voucher-type privatization funds and to other investors. Employees were given two options. The first included an outright gift to employees of 25 percent of a company's shares along with the right to purchase an additional 10 percent at a 30 percent discount.[10] The second option allowed employees to purchase up to 51 percent of the shares at 1.7 times book value (reflecting a "control premium"). In addition, every Russian worker received a 10,000-ruble voucher that could be used to purchase shares in any privatized enterprise through a privatization investment fund.

Three-quarters of eligible firms have since been privatized with option two, the balance with option one. Researchers discovered, however, that regardless of which option is used, 91 percent of the privatized companies became majority employee-owned at the outset, as employees acquired additional shares through voucher auctions, investment tenders and over-the-counter sales. Russia's voucher process expired in July 1994, with the transfer to private hands of fourteen thousand firms employing two-thirds of the industrial labor force.

Enormous problems remain, including a lack of financial capital, ill-trained managers, primitive accounting systems, manager-dominated boards and a difficult market plagued by both recession and inflation that keeps companies operating at reduced levels. Further, managers often are intent on becoming majority owners, not an unrealistic goal in an environment where cash-strapped employees are tempted to sell their shares at the first opportunity, and in which their jobs may be in jeopardy if they refuse.[11]

By 1996, more than one hundred thousand state companies had been transferred to private ownership. Approximately two-thirds of industrial firms had been privatized, along with eighty-five thousand shops representing 70 percent of the nation's total. Approximately 138 million vouchers have been invested, many through more than six hundred registered voucher investment funds with 40 million shareholders. Another 1 million people own small businesses. Reformers insist that this transition is now irreversible, even though the concept of property is not yet fully worked out.

Both the Russian firm and the Russian psyche will continue to undergo dramatic change in the search for ways to make companies productive, efficient, competitive and market-responsive—while also reflecting fundamental notions of economic and social justice. Therein lies the rub, because in Moscow the Chicago school of economics is more akin to Al Capone than Milton Friedman.

Cowboy Capitalism

A four-year study by the Department of Elite Studies at the Russian Academy of Sciences found that 60 percent of the wealthiest millionaires in Russia, about 580 individuals, have reaped enormous profits by leveraging their influence as high-level government or Communist Party officials.[12] Other reports suggest that these officials have exploited their connections in an array of state enterprises, banks, factories and government departments to amass an average net worth of $19 million each, plus further millions of undeclared and untaxed income.[13] Most of those early private fortunes came from one of three sources: trading, finance and raw materials. For example, massive imbalances in the pricing system meant that the well-placed could buy raw materials from the government at fixed prices and sell them abroad at world market prices, offering enormous opportunities for bribery. Similarly, banks could borrow from the central bank at subsidized rates and re-lend at higher rates.

Examples of what disturbs the average Russian abound. Let me describe just three. Beginning in 1991, shares in three large oil companies were sold to Russian citizens in return for their privatization vouchers. By buying these vouchers cheaply from a cash-starved population, a small coterie of oil company executives accumulated sufficient vouchers to gain control of these companies, paying prices that were artificially low because of the general lack of financial capital. For example, Yukos has estimated oil reserves of 6.6 billion barrels, equivalent to Exxon. However, whereas Exxon was valued at $76 billion at the time, the oil-producing arm of Yukos was valued at $80 million when most of its shares were acquired by a group of managers. In September 1995, Atlantic Richfield paid $250 million for a 6 percent stake in Lukoil, Russia's largest oil company. Three months later, 5 percent was sold for $35 million to a group that included Lukoil management.[14]

Another example: Russia's RAO Gazprom has long been viewed as one of the crown jewels of Russian privatization. Gazprom produces one-fifth of the world's natural gas. With one-third of the world's known gas reserves and supplier of 21 percent of Western Europe's natural gas, its privatization has long been awaited by the global financial community. Some investors did not wait. When Gazprom sold just over 1 percent of its shares in October 1996, investors found that several non-Russian investors, reportedly in cahoots with Gazprom managers, had already acquired a stake, paying one-twentieth the issue price. Their $16 million investment bought them shares that were quickly worth more than $300 million.[15]

Capital in Control

In a dramatic about-face that must have Marx spinning in his grave, financial capital has now assumed a position of stunning influence in Russia, epitomized by President Boris Yeltsin's mid-1996 appointment of industrialist and financier Boris Berezovsky as deputy secretary of the Security Council (in July 1997, *Forbes* estimated his net worth at $3 billion; Berezovsky countered that *Forbes* exaggerated his wealth by a factor of seventy-five thousand). At the center of his commercial empire lies the powerful Russian television channel ORT along with a newspaper and a magazine. Their full editorial and advertising power was applied to assist Yeltsin in his successful 1996 reelection campaign. Berezovsky's appointment followed soon thereafter. With a handful of other powerful businessmen, he played a key role in persuading Yeltsin to rehire Anatoly Chubais, the privatization czar, to run his campaign,[16] and to recruit as Security Council chief the charismatic General Alexander Lebed, a brief political union that helped shore up Yeltsin's conservative support. Lebed was dismissed after the election.

Berezovsky is frank in his opinion of the dramatic shift in the nature of power in post–Cold War Russia: "I think two types of power are possible. Either a power of ideology, or a power of capital. Ideology is now dead, and today we have a period of transition, from the power of ideology to the power of capital. I think that if something is advantageous to capital, it goes without saying that it's advantageous to the nation. It's capital that is in a condition, to the greatest extent, to express the interests of the nation."[17]

One of the challenges of the Soviet transition is summed up by Adam B. Ulam, director of the Russian Research Center at Harvard University: "Russians, along with other nationalities, wanted to get rid of the oppressive and demeaning system without any clear ideas of what was likely to follow it. And, as we know, what has followed has hardly brought better lives—certainly not in the economic sense—to the mass of Russian people."[18] The replacement of a Communist-era elite by one of corrupt bureaucrats, shady businessmen and Moscow's version of the Mafia isn't what Western reformers had in mind. Yet their silence lends tacit endorsement, particularly when those reformers, now safely back home in Chicago and Cambridge, offer no alternative. In mid-1997, the director of the FBI testified before Congress that "highly sophisticated" Russian mafia groups were establishing bases in Europe and the United States and posed a threat to the authority of the Kremlin itself.

Grigory Yavlinsky, a former senior policymaker and disillusioned pro-reformer, laments the naive, superficial and often shortsighted advice offered by the Americans: "Stabilize your budget and all will be well."[19] He says the more relevant issue is, "How did you deal with the robber barons and cartels during the Progressive Era?" Despite the widespread discontent with Russia's deal-making oligarchy and its criminalized form of capitalism, protest is undercut not only by the lack of civil society (its leaders remain notoriously aloof and unresponsive) but also by the fact that there is a crisis of ideas. Against whom and *for what* would they protest? What, if not unbridled free enterprise, is the unifying ideology? It's much easier for Russians to point out what they dislike than to articulate what they would put in its place.

One of the earliest champions of post-Soviet reform is financier-philanthropist George Soros, a Hungarian-born billionaire who established an Open Society Foundation in Budapest in 1984 and in Moscow in 1988. As an on-the-scene observer, walk-your-talk reformer, and legendary investor ($100,000 invested in a Soros hedge fund in 1969 would be worth $300 million today), Soros echoes the unspoken fears of others: "The system of robber capitalism that has taken hold in Russia is so iniquitous that people may well turn to a charismatic leader promising national revival at the cost of civil liberties."[20] What most concerns this consummate capitalist is the pervasive penetration of market values in society:

> *Although I have made a fortune in the financial markets, I now fear that the untrammeled intensification of laissez-faire capitalism and the spread of market values into all areas of life is endangering our open and democratic society. The main enemy of the open society, I believe, is no longer the communist but the capitalist threat.*

Reconstructed West European Capitalism

To close this European chapter, we turn to a consideration of how ownership engineering could address an array of difficulties emerging in Western Europe. The entirety of the European Union could find "ownership patterning" as a useful theme around which to converge, particularly in light of the corporate consolidation that is certain to accompany the coming of the euro.[21] Germany and France offer two illustrative environments with unique challanges. Germany faces a major ownership succession challenge as owners of many *Mittelstand* (medium-sized companies established after World War II) look to pass them on. In the United States, this postwar generation became an early source of employee ownership in the 1970s and 1980s when ESOP financing first became an attractive means for exiting an investment.

With a supportive legal and regulatory environment, Germany could quickly become broadly populated by stockholders despite what has historically been only modest public interest in shares.[22] Chancellor Helmut Kohl, the longest-serving Rhine leader since Bismarck, has been urging Germans to become less equity shy, in part because that presents a barrier to the multiphase partial privatization of Deutsche Telekom through what he vows will result in a "people's share."[23]

An ESOP-like ownership strategy could fit well the German culture where founders traditionally fade away slowly. In the United States, it is common for a founder to sell to an ESOP successive blocks of shares, accepting a series of company-guaranteed notes from the ESOP rather than involving a bank in financing the buyout.[24] Quite frequently, the original owner stays on as a consultant until the successor learns the ropes.[25] This ownership solution could be attractive for other reasons as well. The greater pay flexibility sought by the Bundesbank (the central bank) is a response to record-high unemployment (10 percent in mid-1997). Policy encouragement of "investment bargaining" (shares in lieu of cash) could lower labor's high fixed cash costs, stimulating employment.[26]

A nationwide ownerization strategy might also help ease reunification efforts. Germans living in the former East Germany are paid only two-thirds of what their Western brethren are paid for comparable work, leading many to complain. However, without that wage differential, businesses would locate even further east—in Poland, Hungary or the Czech Republic, where labor costs are lower yet. Granting them an opportunity to own a stake in the companies where they work could provide capital accumulation and dividend income to make up for their lower cash compensation.

The greatest challenge of reunification may be psychological. After five decades under a dictatorship, many East Germans have forgotten what it means to take responsibility for their own future. A sense of ownership could help rekindle that spark while also restoring a longed-for sense of community. At present, depression, uncertainty, insecurity and even impotence are palpable and widespread—reflected in a 50 percent drop in the birth rate and a 62 percent plunge in marriages. Former East Germans need a policy initiative that promotes a better sense of being more fully connected not only to their new economic order but also to each other.

They may embrace this paradigm even more quickly than their countrymen to the West. In a development that surprised (and heartened) companies that opened manufacturing facilities there, managers found that workforce traditions left over from the Communist era enabled workers to adapt quickly to modern management methods—not in spite of but *because of* their former experience and their lingering ideals. For instance, a General Motors manufacturing plant in Eisenach has steadily increased volume and quality as East German workers embraced work teams and continuous improvement techniques that GM is still struggling to adopt elsewhere in Europe.

Eisenach workers find it natural to labor in teams, similar to the "workers' brigades" common during the Communist era. And they are happy to strengthen team bonds with company-encouraged after-hours socializing, much as Japanese "company men" long have done. Likewise, the indistinct borders between manager and managed are of little concern. Moreover, their familiarity with manual skills—honed in scraping by with few cars and even fewer parts—has spawned a workforce that makes suggestions to save material and labor at ten times the average of GM workers elsewhere in Europe.[27]

With the date fast-approaching (1999) for Japanese automakers to gain access to the European market, car manufacturers continent-wide are anxiously focusing on cost-saving measures. This East German receptivity to collaborative work practices reflects, in part, the attitude of a workforce desperate for jobs. Plus, GM was able to test thousands of job applicants to select the best and the brightest for its new "greenfield" site. Despite these distinctions, however, the lessons learned here risk being lost on those anxious to find new ways to organize in response to a newly competitive environment.

A targeted ownership strategy could also prove useful in the ongoing attempt to weaken the grip that German banks have on industry through the equity stakes they hold in companies and through their presence on supervisory boards.[28] Long viewed as a model of European-style "corporate capitalism," a string of failures, scandals and outright theft has shaken confidence in this widely admired system.[29] Also, smaller companies and entrepreneurs complain that banks routinely deny them needed capital and that lenders are slow to bring new companies to market where, arguably, capital markets could help plug the financing gap now filled by bank loans.

If banks swapped their shares for ESOP loans, those shares could be distributed to employees as the loans are repaid, boosting stock trading on Germany's equity-scarce stock exchange. This combination of broad-based rank-and-file ownership and widespread stock market participation, in turn, would increase the public's familiarity with equity ownership. In combination with a policy stimulus for employers to establish funded pension plans, this ownership solution could prod the maturing of Germany's fledgling institutional investor community, a key ingredient inhibiting the privatization of Deutsche Telekom.

In a nation where social contributions devour 40 percent of gross salaries, competitiveness is on the line as Germans continue to avoid the daunting task of crafting an acceptable successor to their "social market economy." Though its long-fabled "capitalism with a human face" has brought some five decades of post–World War II prosperity, today's Germany needs less state and more private initiative as it alters the way it runs itself.

An ownership-focused theme might be just what's needed to engage not only the newly resurgent Left but also Kohl's coalition from center-right. Leaders from the sixteen politically powerful regional states (*Lander*) could be natural allies in identifying those companies that could be prime candidates for advancing an initiative that, over the span of a single generation, could transform Germany into a nation of risk-sharing stakeholders.

French-Style Capitalism

France offers another economic environment in which an "ownerization" strategy could stir the political pot with beneficial results. To date, France's privatization program has built a web of cross ownership among some of the country's most powerful financial and industrial companies, creating a core of stable corporate shareholders (a *noyau dur*). For instance, in the 1994 privatization of oil giant Elf Aquitaine, a combined 10 percent stake was acquired by automobile group Renault, Banque Nationale de Paris (one of the largest banks), and Union des Assurances de Paris, the nation's largest insurer.

French capitalism hovers somewhere between the German and Japanese models—with their cross-corporate ownership and management linkages among industry, banks and insurers—and the more market-dependent model of the United States and Britain. It also reflects the French government's desire to protect French companies from takeovers by non-French investors. Even more fundamentally, France's largely unfunded pay-as-you-earn pension system means that it too lacks large accumulations of domestic capital. Thus, when privatizing, the French must turn for investors to local banks, insurance companies and industrial companies.

However, there is no reason why these investments need to be owned by the corporations themselves. With a supportive legal structure, some portion of these shares could be purchased on behalf of the employees of these large corporations, with the shares held in pension-like plans. In addition to blunting union opposition to privatization, this approach may also help restrain labor costs as employees shift their demands from cash to capital accumulation. This strategy could also stimulate France's private pension system while strengthening its fledgling institutional investor community. Its appeal should be enhanced by the May 1997 election of a Socialist government led by Premier Lionel Jospin who, in his first speech to the National Assembly, revealed his opposition to privatization "without justification in the national interest."

Faced with a government pension system rapidly approaching the breaking point, French policymakers would do well to consider any opportunity to move private-sector assets into employees' hands, particularly given the minimum fifteen to twenty years it takes to create a fully funded pension system.

The election of Lionel Jospin, as the polls made clear, reflects the appeal of his promise of *concertation* (consultation) in an attempt to reach a new balance between market and society. A more broadly shared ownership stake could provide a commercial focus for that consultation and for what Jospin promises will be programs that master "the evolutions that are going on" around them.

Indeed, that phrase serves as a good capsulation of the concerns that swirl around Europe as it slouches its way toward integration. Germany and France are not alone in the challenges they confront. Throughout Western Europe, a shortage of personal capital accumulation threatens to create an intolerable fiscal environment in which the financial demands of a retirement-age population begin to crowd out the fiscal resources required to sustain the region's key comparative advantage—its infrastructure, including its transport system, its energy production and its education system.

While it's clear that no one has a one-size-fits-all answer for Europe's economic malaise, most everyone is persuaded that things must change. Some suggest a look at the Netherlands, where a "third way" combines a relatively open and vigorous market with generous social benefits. The Dutch have long been methodical in their consensus building, proving themselves masterful at avoiding the ideological divides so common in Britain, France and now Germany. In essence, labor accepts a measure of financial discipline and business accepts a relatively pricey welfare state. Yet rumblings can be heard there too, not only about a steady rise in inequality but also about the pending threat of an aging population whose care will be funded by proportionately fewer workers. Like their neighbors, the Dutch will also find themselves caught in the wage-leveling logic of globalization as noncompetitive labor costs drive industry and jobs abroad, leaving those behind to pay higher taxes to support the elderly.

Community-Strengthening Ownership Solutions

In the ongoing search for a workable hybrid, European leaders in both corporate and policymaking circles might do well to look southward and consider an adaptation of ownership solotions and civil society–building strategies that have worked well in Italy and Spain. The Basque region of Northern Spain, for instance, has gained world renown for its much-studied Mondragon group of cooperatives employing thirty thousand people and generating more than $5 billion in 1996 sales, nearly half of that in exports.

It also has a financial group with $6 billion in assets and over 250 branch banks around the Basque country. Originally conceived by a charismatic priest steeped in Catholic social teachings, Mondragon has long been a Mecca for fans of worker ownership, its ongoing success the subject of a steady stream of studies, books and films. Nearby Italy also has a lengthy record of successful cooperatives—more than seven thousand nationwide, along with a steadily expanding body of supportive legislation.

What began in 1956 in Mondragon with one firm and twenty-five people is now a major international business group comprised of nearly one hundred employee-owned firms and support organizations, including a self-contained social security and insurance organization, a vocational school, three research and development centers and a university. Key characteristics include pay solidarity (wage ratios are between 4.5:1 and 6:1) and democratic property rights (one-person, one-vote). Mondragon is also known for its creative blend of financial and organizational sophistication, particularly its penchant for financing the start-up of new firms whenever an old one grows to more than five hundred employees, thereby ensuring that companies remain relatively small, flexible, decentralized and personal.

With the onslaught of globalization and the integration of Spain into the more competitive environment of the European Union, all of Mondragon's various operational and support organizations were brought under one roof in 1991 to realize greater economies of scale and strengthen strategic planning. The Caja Laboral Popular (the bank established in 1959) now focuses on traditional banking services, while its venture capital functions have been taken over by a Central Intercooperative Fund financed with 10 percent of member company profits plus 18 percent of the bank profits.

Originally established in an area relatively poor agricultural in land but rich in iron ore and coal, the Mondragon cooperatives began by making simple heaters and stoves. As of mid-1997, the umbrella Mondragon Cooperative Corporation (MCC) was Spain's leading producer of domestic appliances and machine tools, and Europe's third largest supplier of automotive components. Throughout Mondragon's forty-year history, its governance structure has been highly participatory. A General Assembly of worker-owners elects the board and a Social Council is established in each firm to promote two-way communication between managers and workers. Though its new coordinating organization is voluntary (each firm remains fully autonomous and able to withdraw at any time), strains are beginning to show with the introduction of temporary workers and ongoing talk about the need to sell nonvoting stock, thereby mixing traditional investor-capitalists with Mondragon's nontraditional worker-capitalists.

Italy's Co-op Solution

Northern Italy's ownership solution is equally unusual, if not unique. Support for cooperatives is enshrined in the Italian Constitution as a way to foster "common ownership" and encourage "mutuality without the aims of private speculation." Chief among the co-op's many incentives is an exemption from income tax for amounts allocated to a co-op's capital reserve. In other words, a "supply-side" investment subsidy can be claimed provided the company's assets are not used for "speculative" purposes (i.e., selling the shares) but instead are applied to serve the job creation needs of current and future generations.

The political commitment to this "mutuality" is then leveraged through a 3 percent tax on co-op profits, with the proceeds earmarked to fund mutual funds that provide capital to other co-ops. In their first three years (since 1992), these mutual funds collected reserves totaling more than 100 billion lire ($65 million). The assets of dissolved co-ops are also turned over to these mutual funds. A 1985 law provides financial support to co-ops in crisis or subject to bankruptcy hearing while a 1993 law expanded this support to include all co-ops.

The most interesting aspect of Italian co-ops, however, is not their financial engineering but the social impact that accompanies that engineering. In a groundbreaking study of Italy's modern civic society, Harvard professor Robert D. Putnam found a strong correlation between the more egalitarian, cooperative civic communities of Northern Italy and those features most associated with civic virtue. Citizens tend to deal more fairly with one another and expect fair dealing in return. They anticipate high standards from their government and willingly obey the rules they impose on themselves. In the less egalitarian regions in the South, people are far more likely to expect everyone to violate the rules. Those cynical expectations are confirmed as people are forced to rely more on the police because they lack the horizontal bonds of reciprocity, solidarity and self-discipline.

By contrast, because citizens in the more civic regions are more communal and collective in the way they shape their community, they are able to be more liberal. The irony, Putnam points out, is that "it is the amoral individualists of the less civic regions who find themselves clamoring for sterner law enforcement."[30] He cites the conundrum facing those who naively expect a minimalist government without a government that promotes egalitarian values:

> Yet the vicious circle winds tighter still: In the less civic regions even a heavy-handed government—the agent for law enforcement—is itself enfeebled by the uncivic social context. The very character of the community that leads citizens to demand stronger government makes it less likely that any government can be strong, at least if it remains democratic. (This is a reasonable interpretation, for example, of the Italian state's futile anti-Mafia efforts in Sicily over the last half century.) In civic regions, by contrast, light-touch government is effortlessly stronger because it can count on more willing cooperation and self-enforcement among the citizenry.

By contrast, the less civic, less egalitarian communities are organized hierarchically; public affairs are the business of somebody else—the politicians and the bosses but not me. Political participation is triggered not by collective purpose but by dependency or greed. Participation is stunted in social and cultural associations. Corruption is the norm. Compromise has negative connotations. Representative government becomes less effective. "Trapped in these interlocking vicious circles," Putnam notes, "nearly everyone feels powerless, exploited, and unhappy."

If happiness is a measure of civil success, Putnam's research suggests that citizens who hail from more civic regions are much more satisfied with life. The character of one's community, he finds, is as important to happiness as traditional personal circumstances (family income, religious observance). Share-and-share-alike communities breed more happiness. Overlapping horizontal networks of social solidarity facilitate norms and networks of civic engagement. People are more predisposed to trust, to compromise and to participate. Civic engagement, cooperation and honesty are more common. "Small wonder," Putnam concludes, "that people in these regions are content!"

CHAPTER **18**

Capitalism with Chinese Characteristics

> What is socialism? It means seeking social equality, not that
> the state has to keep a majority stake in every industry.
>
> —*Dong Fureng, senior Chinese economist, September 1997*

The ownership solutions now under way in Eastern and Central Europe are historic, with far-reaching global implications. Yet what goes on there pales in comparison to what ownership solutions may yet emerge as China's fifth of humanity fashions its path to prosperity. One of the greatest difficulties for the United States lies in defining its policy toward a country that is in the throes of redefining itself.

Since the Chinese Revolution of 1949, private ownership of the means of production has been banned based on the classic Marxist view that personal ownership exploits workers. However, reformers and conservatives alike have become increasingly enamored of ESOPs, provided they are designed with "Chinese characteristics." When I first lectured in Beijing in 1987, I couldn't yet grasp how confirmed socialists could embrace employee ownership while rejecting private ownership. On my arrival, I soon discovered that where workers are *themselves* owners, ownership is viewed as nonexploitative, and shareholding is transformed from ideologically suspect *private* ownership into politically correct *public* ownership.[1]

Though cynics see this as semantic gymnastics, I see it as Chinese pragmatism. The Fifteenth Communist Party Congress, convened in Beijing in the fall of 1997, saw this stance evolve even further, as the Party leadership emerging from the first Congress since the death of Deng Xiaoping embraced the notion of a shift to a more general shareholding system.[2] Though the ideologists continued to stress the importance of "public ownership" and the rejection of privatization, president and Communist Party chief Jiang Zemin repeatedly used the phrase "primary stage of socialism" to distinguish the past from what may yet emerge. He also coined a new term—*diversified ownership*— that seemed well crafted to keep the West guessing as to China's intentions.

During the Party Congress, an oft-heard joke made the rounds in Beijing that suggests how some view China's most recent stand on communism versus capitalism. Presidents Bill Clinton, Boris Yeltsin and Jiang Zemin are each driving down a road and their three cars approach an intersection. Mr. Clinton turns right without signaling. So does Mr. Yeltsin. But Mr. Jiang hesitates and asks his passenger, Deng Xiaoping, which way to go. Deng replies, "Signal left and turn right."[3] While that story glosses over many important subtleties influencing reform, it accurately portrays the appeal of market mechanisms as a way to advance living standards alongside socialism's more egalitarian goals.

On the employee ownership front, the Communist Party initially feared that employee buyouts might erode worker and social solidarity by promoting competition among groups of workers. However, the Fourteenth Party Congress (in 1992) embraced employee shares as a pragmatic way to boost worker motivation and enterprise performance without sacrificing socialist collectivity. Chinese-style ESOPs continue to grow at a rapid pace, with estimates ranging from three thousand to thirteen thousand.[4] In 1995, employee ownership received Beijing's blessing as a notion fully consistent with socialist ideology when "employees become masters of the enterprises."

Anecdotal evidence abounds of its success. In an experiment in Zhu Chen Electrical Equipment, a three-hundred-employee generator-manufacturing firm, the state's interest was acquired by the workers in 1993 (except for the land).[5] Within a year, sales had risen by 80 percent. Buoyed by this success, the Zhu Chen city government provided a trained cadre to engineer employee buyouts in 250 other local firms.[6]

With more than three hundred thousand state-owned enterprises, the potential applications of employee ownership are extraordinary. From the workers' perspective, it may be advisable for reformers to move quickly so that workers get in early on what is poised to be one of history's most rapid increases in national wealth creation. Since "market-based socialism" was officially embraced in 1992, China's already-dynamic economy has grown even faster than its heady expansion of the 1980s, with an annual rate of growth averaging 12 percent for 1992–1996 and double-digit growth projected for the balance of the decade.[7] Less than a generation ago, 80 percent of Chinese struggled as farmers working for less than $1 per day. One in three was illiterate. Since then, two hundred million Chinese have escaped absolute poverty, and illiteracy has declined to under 10 percent.

Propertied Prosperity with Chinese Characteristics

A country as immense as China requires a harmonizing theme that can hold it together. Communist ideology has steadily lost its unifying power. Nationalism is the next logical choice, though that, too, will likely prove to be too weak a glue, at least in the absence of persuasive evidence that national policies are fostering broadly shared, country-wide prosperity. At present, that's clearly not the case.

Every country has regional differences in development but China's are dramatic. In 1978, Deng Xiaoping broke up Mao's communes and freed China's peasant farmers to sell their own produce under a "household responsibility system," replacing communes with long-term land leases. That ownership solution enabled 170 million Chinese to escape absolute poverty as farm output grew by 2.6 percent a year between 1970 and 1978, and 6 percent a year from 1978 to 1984. Meanwhile, the agricultural workforce shrank from 71 percent to 53 percent between 1978 and 1994 (a similar transformation in Japan took sixty years). However, as the World Bank noted in 1995, "quick reductions of poverty through agricultural growth were largely exhausted by the end of 1984."[8]

In a second round of ownership reforms, community-controlled industrial enterprises were encouraged to blossom. These "town and village enterprises" (TVEs) absorbed much of the labor liberated by the productivity gains that accompanied farming sector reform. During the 1980s, "special economic zones" were established in southern coastal cities where Beijing relaxed its rules on taxes, labor and foreign investment, allowing firms to operate almost as though they were privately owned. That induced some other cities to demand similar treatment. In combination, these reforms—ownership solutions all—were a primary catalyst for the economic boom that converted the world's most populous nation into an economic powerhouse.

Between 1978 and 1994, China twice doubled its per capita income (in the nineteenth century, it took the United States nearly five decades to double its per capita income). As these reforms phased in, the portion of GDP generated by the state plummeted from 78 percent in 1978 to 34 percent in 1994 even while the output of state enterprises grew and their employment remained roughly the same, with one in five Chinese adults working for the state.

At a time when the cohesive power of communist ideology is at its lowest ebb since the revolution, Beijing's leaders know that the government's legitimacy must be backed by its proven ability to foster an acceptable—and rising—standard of living. At present, more than one in four Chinese (350 million) live in a state of substantial deprivation, subsisting on less than $1 a day according to a 1996 World Bank study. In some areas, the level of privation approaches that of China's great famine of the 1950s when more than 30 million died during Mao's Great Leap Forward, a Marxist-inspired ownership solution consisting of a nationwide system of collectivization. In the mid-1990s, the World Bank found more than 60 million Chinese on the edge of starvation, living on less than sixty cents a day. That's the bad news. The good news is that this marks a dramatic decline from 270 million in 1978, when Deng Xiaoping abandoned Mao's communal ownership solution.[9]

Though submission to authority is a strong tradition in Confucian-influenced China, so is a Taoist tradition of civil protest and rebellion. In a nation founded on the cardinal principle of shared prosperity, that tradition may yet be revived. The ever widening prosperity gap between the eastern and the central-western regions poses dangers of not only rising crime and nascent rebellion but also possible warlordism. The rich-poor gap between coastal and interior regions is also a growing cause for concern.

Unless these trends are brought into synch with China's long-term goals, the progress accompanying its market-based reforms could quickly be reversed. As propaganda department theoretician Li Junru recently claimed, "The fruit of reform could be destroyed in one moment."[10] As it moves toward what leader Deng characterized as "socialism with Chinese characteristics,"[11] China has available to it several adaptable "capitalist" financing techniques (described below) that could ease its way without putting the nation on the path toward an unintended capitalist future.

Capitalist Finance with Chinese Characteristics

To help restrain inflation and finance its deficits, Beijing continues to sell government bonds, including urging (and occasionally forcing) their purchase by workers. The appeal of these bonds could be enhanced by allowing workers to exchange them for shares in their employer. This strategy would simultaneously relieve the government of the need to pay interest while also transforming a portion of China's remarkable savings (40 percent of GDP) into a form where workers' personal efforts could influence the value of their investment.[12] During the early 1990s, France utilized a comparable mechanism, allowing "Balladur bonds" (named after the then French prime minister) to be converted into shares in state-owned enterprises.

Given Bejing's commitment to "public" ownership, policymakers may not be ready for so free-wheeling a debt-for-equity swap. However, allowing workers to gain a stake in companies where they work should cause no ideological nosebleed, even among the most conservative members of the State Council. On an experimental basis, nonemployees could be allowed to swap their government bonds, say, for units in an investment fund holding shares in a portfolio initially limited to companies located in the vicinity of those investors. That would provide a step-by-step means to advance community-oriented shareholding in community-relevant assets (á la TVEs).

Similarly, where companies hold government bonds (a common situation), those could be exchanged for employee-held shares not only in that enterprise but also in closely related companies, such as suppliers or distributors.[13] Such related-enterprise debt-for-shares-swaps could improve business relationships by "ownerizing" their common interests using people-ized cross-shareholding to enhance firm performance.

Western advisers are naive if they expect China's reformers to embrace at this point a laissez faire form of capital markets. The Chinese are aware that during the Allies' post–World War II occupation of Japan, its family-controlled *zaibatsu* were forced by the American-led occupation to convert into publicly traded companies. Within a short period, the companies acquired each other's shares to form corporate cross-ownership groups (*keiretsu*) in which manufacturers and financial companies hold one another's shares as a way of cementing commercial ties. That initiative removed most of the shares from public trading and made the companies largely immune to foreign takeover.[14] Beijing has already authorized the creation of Chinese equivalents to these Asian paradigms, moving to develop a class of *keiretsu*-like industrial powerhouses in beverages, textiles, electronics and autos.

A key ownership issue for China is whether it adopts a property system that all but ensures foreign ownership. Movement in the direction of interlocking industrial (and bank-affiliated) groups seems far more likely—notwithstanding the clear drawbacks that accompany such groups when not subjected to sufficient market discipline—a key factor fueling the financial crisis that swept Asian economies in late 1997 and early 1998.

With its announced commitment to a shareholding system, reformers should now consider whether to include an element of "up-close cross-shareholding." For example, intracompany share purchases might be funded from profit sharing, much like American-style 401(k) plans—but with Chinese characteristics. That would provide a way for workers to diversify (say, initially within a corporate group) while still ensuring that their ownership stake is closely related to their employer. Investment bargaining (wage-for-stock-swaps) could also be encouraged, providing a dampening influence on inflationary pay pressures while offering an opportunity for share bartering among related firms.[15]

Peoplism in the People's Republic

China's reformers have long been intrigued by Japan's people-focused version of market economics. Vice Premier Zhu Rongji, a key reformer and potential successor to Prime Minister Li Peng, has attended seminars in Beijing sponsored by Japan's Finance Ministry and organized by Eisuke Sakakibara, an outspoken advocate of Japan's "noncapitalist market economy" and author of the provocative book *Beyond Capitalism*.[16] Cautioning Mr. Zhu against rapid privatization and a rush to a capital market–dominated financial system, Mr. Sakakibara urged instead reliance on financial mechanisms (principally state-run banks) through which Beijing could retain some influence on the allocation of capital. In 1993, China formed a state development bank, an agricultural bank and an export-import bank.

Western advisors are naive in extremis if they think China's reformers find it appealing to transform China into a financial market–based economy that creates a small group of wealthy capitalists in a nation that has devoted a half-century to egalitarianism, however flawed their means. The Japanese offer persuasive evidence that economic elites are not essential. That sentiment can only be strengthened by the spectacle of plutocratic ownership patterns emerging throughout the Warsaw Pact, often with the advice and assistance of the best economists that the free-enterprise West could muster. At present, Japanese-style "*keiretsu* capitalism" seems much more appealing.

One key challenge that China will face is currently the cause of considerable consternation in Japan's *keiretsu,* in South Korea's corporate groups (*chaebol*) and elsewhere where a more closed capitalism is found, including many of the region's financially troubled economies that emulated features of Japan's *keiretsu* system. Simply put, the difficulty lies in determining when coordination becomes cronyism, when long-term orientation becomes an excuse for poor performance, and when protests against the short-term focus of financial markets become a way to protect coddled companies (and their managers) from market discipline. Where a culture of state-led lending operates alongside open capital markets, the forces of global finance can be unforgiving in their appraisal despite the best of long-term intentions. That became repeatedly clear when, during the 1990s, the IMF expanded its role as guardian of the world's currencies to become a proponent (in South Korea, Thailand, Indonesia, etc.) of banking and financial-sector restructuring in order to shrink the role of the state and give full play to global capital markets.

Swapping an Old Financial Sector for a New

A Chinese version of restructuring went on throughout the mid-1990s. More than one thousand company mergers took place during 1997, most involving firms run by local governments. Beijing is setting up 120 government-approved holding companies and has identified 100 large state-owned firms for conversion into corporations. In September 1997, official reports indicated that more than 10,000 of the nation's 13,000 large and medium-sized firms would be "encouraged to switch to various forms of public ownership."

While it's always risky to predict what China's rulers will permit, the announced intent to move toward a shareholding economy may signal a new ownership solution. Yet despite the proposed shift, a government-run holding company may well continue to be the primary shareholder, at least initially. Nevertheless, given the official embrace of ESOPs, an opportunity to add a worker ownership component now seems at hand.

This shift to a shareholding system is likely to be driven, at least in part, by financial necessity. Many of the recent mergers were made attractive by the government agreeing to pay off much of the debt of troubled companies and exempting the payment of interest on the balance for up to five years. During the early 1990s, the government announced plans that the nonperforming debts of 100 large state enterprises (owed to state banks) would be exchanged for shares in these newly corporatized enterprises. It was envisioned that those shares would be state-owned, at least initially.

The need for some form of debt restructuring is clear. Forty percent of loans are believed to be nonperforming.[17] As a twist on debt-for-shares swaps, those shares instead could be held by state-owned banks—with the idea of shifting China to a banking structure closer to Germany's "stakeholder capitalism" where lenders often hold an equity stake in their clients. With proper training, and aid from bankers with experience in such equity-holding, China's bureaucratic bankers could be trained in the financial skills required for them to become a positive force for economic restructuring.[18] If, with the prodding of those shareholding banks, performance can be improved so that a firm can qualify for a genuine commercial loan (rather than the *policy* loans so common in the past), that loan could be structured as an ESOP loan, with the loan proceeds used to buy those shares for the firm's workers.[19]

Much of China's financial difficulty traces its roots to the financial sector, the soft underbelly of reform. For example, income growth in China's rapidly expanding private sector (particularly its coastal regions) often enters its banking system as savings that earn state-determined rates of interest (four state banks account for 90 percent of banking assets). Three-quarters of bank lending, in turn, is to the state sector as low-interest loans. Because only half those loans are repaid, this credit subsidy (10 percent of GDP since the late 1980s) is equivalent to having the central bank pay for state expenditures. That lack of a hard budget constraint is a defining financial feature of socialist systems. These policy loans fuel an invisible deficit as large as the officially acknowledged budget deficit. That, in turn, causes stubborn inflationary pressures alongside a banking system that is effectively insolvent (its bad debts exceed its capital). To postpone enterprise restructuring only postpones reform of a vicious cycle and ensures the problem will grow in severity.[20]

What China requires is a series of step-by-step policy prescriptions designed to reform the financial sector in ways that (*a*) are ideologically acceptable, (*b*) enhance enterprise performance, and (*c*) can be implemented in a Chinese-like fashion (i.e., gradually). Though many Western advisers have persuaded themselves that the only solution is all-encompassing, all-or-nothing "shock therapy" reform (widely advocated and often administered in Eastern Europe and the former Soviet Union), China's reformers recognize that such counsel, if applied in China, would run the risk of toppling the current reform-prone government. Gradualism remains China's credo.

Hybridized Ownership

China's pragmatic socialism lends itself well to shareholding strategies that address the concerns of both neosocialist legislators and capitalist risk appraisers. Shareholding hybrids could also address a potentially inflationary "currency overhang" due to China's extraordinary personal savings. Reformers worry at the impact should these funds suddenly be converted to consumer demand, bidding up prices. Long frustrated by a lack of investment opportunities, China's workers have routinely snapped up those few shares offered for sale by their employers. In truth, these "shares" are often more akin to bonds, paying a fixed return rather than sharelike dividends that fluctuate based on enterprise earnings.

As of mid-1997, seven hundred Chinese companies, typically the more efficient and profitable ones, were listed on China's two stock exchanges in Shanghai and Shenzhen. Experts agree that the Chinese population has a growing thirst for alternative investment opportunities. Below I describe shareholding hybrids consistent with the goals espoused by reformers.

Community-ization

Beijing presently encourages workers to invest in companies where they work. Where workers are allowed to own a stake in their employer, so too can their extended families by combining family resources for that purpose. As an extension of that policy, reformers could permit *residents* within prescribed areas to buy shares in any company considered appropriate for *local,* community-based ownership. Rather than capital-market "privatization," this might more aptly be characterized as "community-ization."

In addition to fighting inflation by soaking up savings, this mechanism could offer enterprises a much-needed source of cash that they may otherwise seek as loans from an overburdened banking system. Such investment vehicles could also provide a system of decentralized, community-based "feedback," signaling Beijing which companies are viewed locally as most promising. This would mimic the function of capital markets, but without their broader, potentially labor-exploiting aspect loathed by socialist authorities. This would also ensure local investors that their savings are being used to develop enterprises (and jobs) in their local communities rather than flowing into speculative real estate ventures or other projects far removed from local concerns. Likewise, rural savings would become locally "anchored," ensuring that investment funds flow into capital-starved rural development, helping stem the troublesome exodus of rural residents to overcrowded urban areas. A similar approach might well be adapted to Tibet, drawing on that unique culture to craft a locally appropriate ownership solution within larger principles of diversified ownership set up by Beijing.

This regional focus could also help address the concerns of provincial leaders who continue to resist national reforms with attempts to control local resources through "socialist feudalism." A regionally sensitive ownership strategy could provide an attractive means for improving relationships between Beijing and its twenty-two provincial governments, five autonomous regions and three metropolitan areas (plus Hong Kong). A nationally coordinated,

regionally attuned "plan" could help move the provinces back toward integration, an ongoing political challenge for this vast nation.

Serendipitously, this community-ization strategy bears considerable resem-
blance to the familar TVEs. These light industrial groups with shared and often informal ownership (based more on local solidarity than on property
rights), now employ 100 million, accounting for one-third of the rural
workforce, 30 percent of total exports and 40 percent of industrial output.[21]

Hybridized Socialism

China's 305,000 state-owned enterprises (including 118,000 industrial firms)
employ almost 100 million workers. Subsidies provided to the largest 11,000
of these firms cost the government more than it budgets for education and
public health—the two primary human resource investments essential to development.[22] In addition, China is experiencing a classic symptom of economic
progress as higher farm productivity forces people to look elsewhere for employment. The uneven impact of inflation also influences the attractiveness
of urban versus rural areas as residents of rural and inland areas struggle on
largely fixed incomes while those residing in urban and coastal regions typically benefit from frequent wage increases.

The Ministry of Labor projects that the number of displaced peasants could
grow to as much as 400 million by the year 2000. This massive flow of people
is known colloquially as the *mang liu* or "blind flow," similar to a swollen
river. With slightly more conservative figures, the State Planning Commission
forecasts that 44 million young people will enter the job market between 1995
and 2000. It is anticipated that 20 million workers will be shed from state
enterprises and 120 million peasants will head for the cities to seek work,
suggesting the need to create more than 180 million new jobs, mostly in urban areas.[23] The challenge lies in making this transition as smooth as possible
by ensuring that this immense flow does not erupt into instability.

Much as the Communist Party encouraged township and village enterprises as a buffer between rural and urban populations (an earlier ownership
solution), so too it might encourage population-anchoring shareholding initiatives designed to gain for rural folk a stake in enterprises located in or near
rural areas. Simply imposing fines on migrants (as Beijing did in 1995) does
not address the underlying problem. Even more fundamentally, the nation's
socialist ideology will remain under severe strain in the absence of a policy
response to rapidly growing inequality. A comprehensive shareholding strategy could help address that inconsistency.[24]

Ownership hybrids are available that could combine socialist collectivism
with more capitalist-style individual ownership. For instance, as China develops
its energy resources, such as its oil-rich Tarim Basin, some portion of this development (say a royalty interest) could be held by a regionally based general

stock ownership corporation (GSOC).[25] With a state-chartered GSOC, those living in a prescribed region could be assigned a limited number of shares, say with the government granting matching shares for additional purchases. After an initial holding period, the shares could become transferable, with trades limited to region stock exchanges (or to GSOC participants).

Other projects also offer potential candidates for GSOCs. A coal slurry pipeline of hundreds of miles in length is proposed for transporting coal to the Beijing area. That hugely capital-intensive project could, over time, become partially owned by those living in the region. Bilateral GSOCs might be negotiated with China's neighbors. For instance, a China/Vietnam GSOC could be established to hold a royalty interest in those offshore oil fields now claimed jointly by both nations. That ownership solution could help defuse tensions surrounding the development of this natural resource while also advancing notions of shared prosperity.

Economic reform continues to gather momentum, though inflationary pressures and regional financial instability may slow that progress. A comprehensive shareholding strategy could provide an outlet for that inflationary pressure while also providing a platform for assuring the Party faithful that this centrally directed shareholding strategy offers a way for moving China to the next logical stage of socialism. Such a state-engineered, worker-oriented ownership strategy could be designed to resemble precisely what Mr. Deng advocated: "socialism with Chinese characteristics."

Hong Kong and Taiwan: Robust Capitalism Meets Sophisticated Socialism

The future shape of China's market-based socialism became even more interesting on July 1, 1997, when Britain ceded control of thoroughly capitalist Hong Kong. Oddly enough, it may have been an ownership solution (a ninety-nine-year lease) that enabled Hong Kong to outlast Britain's other territorial outposts. Because both parties knew the lease would eventually end, Hong Kong was not seen as simply another colony which likely would have ended in 1949 when Mao Zedong established the People's Republic of China.

Commercial ties between Hong Kong and the rest of China ensure considerable pressure to transcend whatever ideological barriers may separate them. Mainland China has long been Hong Kong's biggest market for both exports and imports. Cross-border investment is also substantial, totaling more than $15 billion as of mid-1996. Also, as Hong Kong's economy has evolved from manufacturing to services, 80 percent of its producers have moved their facilities across the border to Shenzhen and Guangdong, home to over one hundred thousand Hong Kong–invested enterprises.

If ever there was a situation ripe for creative ownership hybridization, it is Hong Kong and its neighbors, China and Taiwan. Bound by business and separated by a fast-evolving ideology, the odds favor the emergence of ownership strategies custom-designed to this unique political environment and these uncommon times. From the perspective of Hong Kong companies, they may be well advised to adopt at least an insurance element of employee ownership to provide political risk insurance against those mainland conservatives who, in the absence of such a worker-owned stake, may be tempted to advocate more traditional ownership solutions, such as nationalization.

Though China's population is fifty times that of Taiwan, Taiwan boasts the world's second-largest foreign-exchange reserves. It is also the world's twelfth largest trader and comes close to doing as much trade with the United States as the mainland. In a period of heightened tensions and occasional saber-rattling by their much larger neighbor, the best stability-enhancing course for Taiwan would be to foster closer economic ties. The Taiwanese already have huge sums invested on the mainland. Particularly useful would be joint ventures in which employees both in Taiwan and on the mainland gain a shared ownership stake. The conscious creation of common economic interests, linked by a common culture, could help smooth today's choppy waters.

The New Chinese Evolution

It is difficult to imagine that China will be able to put the marketization genie back in its bottle. Even extreme optimists would not have dared predict that China could progress so far so fast since Mr. Deng's 1978 demand for "great growth in the productive forces" and his prediction that this change would prove to be a "profound and extensive revolution." He was correct. China's economic reform of the 1980s was described by its leaders as the "bird in the cage"—the steady nurturing of market forces within the overall embrace of a central plan. Now that economic growth has averaged an astonishing 9 percent per year since 1978, it appears that the bird is poised to take wing unless a larger, more flexible cage can be constructed to contain it.

As personal capital accumulation finds its way into entrepreneurship and small-scale businesses, more local jobs will be created, helping absorb migrant laborers. As the successful experiment with town and village enterprises has shown, the provision of a better opportunity can help contain the cost of the "iron rice bowl" (employer-provided housing, health care, etc.). Any increase in local economic opportunity will show up as a decrease in migration. In the broadest sense, it is not just monetary and fiscal reform that China needs but a more equitable sharing in the fruits of that reform. That result is not to be found in traditional prescriptions, whether socialist or capitalist. China requires a reform uniquely its own.

The challenge for Beijing lies in how to combine the dynamism, productivity and efficiency of markets with the social justice concerns of socialism.

A community-focused, up-close shareholding strategy could enable China's market-based socialism to draw from the best of each, creating an economically vibrant system consistent with what the official New China News Agency calls this "crucial period in China's socialist modernization." To non-Chinese this combination may sound like a contradiction. In the Chinese language, however, the symbol for the word *contradiction* is composed of the characters for *sword* and *shield*, implying complementary opposites like the yin and yang of Taoism. China seeks a system that embodies the best of both. Reformers know they need the "sword" of self-interest and market competition to raise living standards. But they also want the "shield" of state-assured social justice to protect those who unfettered free enterprise is notorious for leaving behind. To Western minds, that may appear as conflict, even inconsistency. In the East it looks like a natural search for synthesis.

One reason that the United States has so much difficulty defining its policy toward China is because China is a hugely complex nation in the midst of reconstructing an ill-fitting socialist paradigm to move itself toward a more sensible system. When the dogma of central planning was put aside by Deng Xiaoping in 1978, he conceded that China would "cross the river by feeling for stepping stones." Pragmatism began to displace ideology. From an ownership perspective, that may well prove to be the most prudent path. Unlike many neoclassical economists in the West, economists in the East often have the good sense to realize that they don't have all the answers. Certainly the West has yet to offer a property paradigm that would pass muster by Chinese standards (except for ESOPs and their derivatives). It should come as no surprise if China's still-evolving ownership solution is uniquely Chinese.

Rather than graft a foreign model onto a Chinese root (as China tried to do with its embrace of Soviet-style socialism), today's reformers seem determined to devise a homegrown solution that gives economic substance to what it means to be Chinese. While the West may find the pace slow and the process impenetrable, the answer at which the Chinese arrive may yet provide the economic foundation on which to base more individual, local and regional autonomy, key stepping stones for a more open and democratic society.

Latin America, the Caribbean and the Catholic Church

If you want peace, work for justice.

—*Pope John Paul VI*

Latin America and the Caribbean have long been known for the volatility of their politics. Though political stability and market-based economies are now common in the region, pockets of distinction remain the focus of worldwide attention. Also a dominantly Catholic population could yet be swayed by the church's advocacy of a more just economic order. This chapter reviews recent developments in the region, including a discussion of the key role that may yet be played by a more vigorus and outspoken Vatican.

Cuba is doubtless the world's most determined Marxist-Leninist holdout. Its national motto—Socialism or Death—makes it a particularly fascinating challenge for those who view ownership engineering as a tool that can be used to address a broad range of concerns, regardless of ideology. With its loss of economic support from the Soviet Union, Cuba has stepped up its search for ways to attract foreign investment, particularly in areas that generate foreign exchange, such as tourism, mining, light manufacturing and agriculture. The U.S. trade embargo continues to take its toll. Sugar production plunged from 8.1 million tons in the late 1980s to 3.3 million tons in 1994, the lowest in more than half a century (rising to 4.5 million tons in 1996).

It will come as a shock to anti-Castro Americans to find that Castro has an interest in the U.S.-born ESOP concept. One can only ponder a potential linkage between the lifting of Washington's embargo and Havana's choice of economic reform strategies. For instance, if Castro were to decide that worker ownership is an appropriate solution for Cuba's economic ills, how would the United States respond? What if he announced his intention to model his reform after the ESOP movement in the United States? What if he were also to announce, in the interest of international worker solidarity, that Cuba intends to go the United States one better by limiting U.S./Cuba commercial relationships to ESOP companies? For example, in the allocation of limited landing rights and airport gates at Havana's airport, how would U.S. policymakers respond if Castro announced that landing rights will be limited to those airlines maintaining at least 30 percent employee ownership? That would open Cuba's attractive tourist markets to United Airlines (55 percent ESOP owned), Northwest (37 percent) and TWA (30 percent). What advice are members of Congress likely to receive from the 150,000-plus employee-owners in these airlines?[1]

Worker-Oriented Development

In the interest of opening and reforming Cuba after four decades of economic isolation and political stalemate, how far would U.S. policymakers be prepared to permit the Cuban government to push such a "worker solidarity" concept? Might this provide a useful focus for U.S./Cuban negotiations to discuss conditions for lifting the embargo? At first blush, this may seem fanciful, even far-fetched. But then again, perhaps not. Few doubt Castro's sincerity or his personal devotion to the socialist goal of international worker solidarity. Castro's detractors often forget that the Cuban revolution was one of a very few genuine "people's revolutions." Even now, Castro enjoys a remarkable residual of goodwill in Cuba, even among those now suffering under an antiquated economic system made worse by the U.S. embargo.[2]

Contrary to many socialist populations where state-directed production drew workers to urban centers, Cubans remain relatively well dispersed across the country. That's partly because Castro provided support for a primary education system and built what even Castro's harshest critics acknowledge is the best health care delivery system in the Caribbean through broadly dispersed clinics and hospitals, with an infant mortality rate on a par with the United States (and only half that of Washington, D.C.). This dispersal of both people and enterprises suggests that the Cuban economic environment is ripe both for up-close worker ownership and for decentralized community-oriented (CSOP) and RESOP-type ownership.

Like Marx, Castro does not appear to be unalterably opposed to private ownership. Rather, his rhetorical ire focuses on the injustice of the concentrated ownership that typically accompanies private enterprise. For example, as part of his marathon six-hour-and-forty-three-minute opening address to the October 1997 Communist Party Congress, he argued that he continues to oppose the privatization of state enterprises because "We have no reason to create millionaires, to create enormous inequalities." As Marxist-Leninists, he argued, "we fight not to create individual millionaires, but to make the citizenry as a whole into millionaires."[3]

Though traditional collectivist ownership solutions have never proven capable of realizing the dream that Castro shares with Karl Marx, there is little reason to think the Cuban leader might not be persuaded to experiment with a nontraditional, ownership-sharing version of free enterprise. Indeed, he used the Party Congress as a platform to announce his endorsement of economic experimentation while also opposing it, claiming "the blockade and the effort to drown us don't permit that right now." Yet if ownership patterns are the issue and economic experimentation is acceptable, then the time may be ripe for the international community to take Castro up on his offer.

After four decades of political stalemate, even the most aggrieved Cuban-Americans are beginning to suggest the need for a less confrontational position. A June 1997 poll found a dramatic increase in the number of Cuban-Americans who favor negotiations with the Cuban government: 48 percent compared with 36 percent in a similar 1991 pool. The younger generation, in particular, seems prepared to reassess strategy. For those aged eighteen to twenty-nine, 77 percent favor establishing a dialogue, compared with only 36 percent among those sixty-five and older.[4] Many of those inclined to support a change in policy conclude that, denied the credibility of blaming poor economic performance on the embargo, Castro would have to adapt.

One key question remains: should the international aid community propose such a strategy? For example, should an offer be made of worker ownership technical assistance? The international financial institutions (such as the Inter-American Development Bank) have never known quite how to respond. Development bankers long ago knuckled under to U.S. pressure to isolate Cuba, maintaining a four-decade awkward silence regarding the largest land mass in the Caribbean. An ownership strategy could provide a means for ending this stalemate, providing a focus around which to build consensus for a renewed relationship.

The shift to the right in the political makeup of the U.S. Congress could have a key influence. For example, Senator Jesse Helms, the Republican chairman of the Senate Committee on Foreign Relations, is one of only a few members of the U.S. Congress (other than Russell Long) to propose legislation encouraging employee ownership, including one bill specifically designed to encourage worker ownership in the pursuit of American foreign policy.[5]

Cross-Border Worker Solidarity

Another development that could affect reform in Cuba involves the surprising extent to which worker solidarity cuts across borders. This phenomenon has surfaced with some frequency in recent years, most notably when labor unions in Europe and America supported Poland's Solidarity movement. The AFL-CIO has long been intimately involved in anti-Communist efforts in the region, including support for a Ronald Reagan–led effort to promote employee ownership in the region. That effort merits a brief description as it may serve as a useful precedent.

In 1986, the Congress commissioned a presidential task force report to identify how U.S. efforts could encourage widespread private ownership in

Latin America and the Caribbean. The overall political assessment was straightforward: countries in the region tend to lurch between unstable extremes of concentrated ownership—ownership in the hands of a few private families or ownership under the control of a few public ministries (or a military regime). What emerged from this Reagan-era task force was a guide to how ESOPs and similar financing techniques could be used to build a property-owning middle class supportive of both market economies and democratic governments.[6] Embroiled in contentious disputes about his policies in the region, Reagan took great delight in the report, consistent with his support a decade earlier when he rhetorically inquired in a 1975 radio commentary: "Could there be a better answer to the stupidity of Karl Marx than millions of workers individually sharing in the ownership of the means of production?"

Reagan was particularly enthused about an ESOP established for campesinos at La Perla, a nine-thousand-hectare coffee plantation located in Guatemala's Quiche Province, then one of the principal areas of leftist guerrilla activity. In the early 1980s, communist insurgents announced their arrival in this remote highland area by murdering La Perla's owner. In the ensuing search for a peaceful "middle road" solution, the owner's two sons sought U.S. help in establishing an ESOP while also diversifying into cardamom and macadamia nuts, key cash crops. Using development assistance to endow their cobbled-together ESOP (and finance their new crops), the brothers diluted their ownership stake by issuing to the ESOP new shares, enabling the workers to gain a 40 percent stake, their shares paid for largely out of future farm profits.

Shortly thereafter, on 1 March 1985, 120 armed communist insurgents attacked the estate and for five hours took control of its center until 200 armed worker-owners staged a counterattack, driving the rebels back off what the campesinos now considered "their" land. Several were killed on both sides. Contrary to the expected response, where farmers eagerly join the guerrillas in overthrowing the oppressive landlords, these campesinos instead took up arms against their leftist "liberators."[7] Soon thereafter, a contingent of contrite guerrillas returned to inquire if they could become a part of this new ownership experiment. That dramatic turn of events captured the imagination of those looking for an alternative to failed land reform models and anxious for a new paradigm that could rid the region of instability. Reagan's task force report was dedicated to La Perla's employee-owners.

Cross-Party Political Support for an Ownership Solution

Strong support for the report also came from Reagan's congressional nemesis, Democratic Speaker of the House Jim Wright, who otherwise opposed most everything Reagan stood for in Central America, including his secret support of the Nicaraguan contras. Well before the era of ESOPs, the Texas congressman urged that American investors build plants in the Dominican Republic to can and freeze fruits and tomato paste for local consumption, substituting domestic production for more expensive imports. The key political ingredient, in Wright's mind, was his proposal that investors set aside shares both for plant workers and for the farmers providing the fruit and tomatoes (an early ESOP/RESOP hybrid).[8] Two decades later, Wright returned to that theme, characterizing Reagan's task force report as an "imaginative approach," particularly its key recommendation: the use of ESOPs in conjunction with debt-for-equity swaps, suggesting:

> It appeals to the very basic truth in human nature which Lee Iacocca discovered when, at Chrysler's lowest ebb, he distributed a large body of stock among the employees. It inspired their wholehearted cooperation and helped revive that great corporation.
>
> The idea would be to encourage foreign lenders to exchange non-performing government loans in state-owned companies for equity in those companies, with the agreement to sell or transfer a substantial portion of that equity to an employee ownership trust. What better way to promote the advantages of capitalism than by spreading its base, letting the workers have a piece of the action and discovering that they can be capitalists too? What better way to refute the Marxist claim that private enterprise is evil and that its goal is merely to exploit the workers?
>
> And what better way to reassure a host country in Latin America, resentful of foreign ownership and domination of companies, that a majority of the ownership will stay right there in their own lands, enriching the fabric of their local society?[9]

Costa Rican president Oscar Arias was also among the task force report's vocal supporters. Recent recipient of the 1987 Nobel Peace Prize for his efforts in mediating the Central American peace process, Arias threw his considerable prestige behind the recommendations, advocating employee ownership in several high-profile speeches. In a surprising move, the AFL-CIO supported the report's recommendation advocating the duty-free import of trade-sensitive goods (shoes, textiles, handbags) provided those goods are manufactured in companies that are partly employee-owned, reasoning that the union's long-term commitment to worker solidarity should override short-term concerns about threats to the jobs of American labor union members.

The Papal View of Property

The Vatican could be the "wild card" in influencing change in the region's ownership patterns, particularly if Pope John Paul II should decide to bring the Church's moral muscle to bear in the region. Since 1891 and Pope Leo XIII's release of *Rerum Novarum* ("The Condition of Labor") at the height of the industrial revolution, a series of concerned pontiffs have issued social teachings on the proper role of property.[10] Those include a 1931 proclamation by Pope

Pius XI on the fortieth anniversary of *Rerum Novarum* (at the height of the Depression) insisting that "no man can be at the same time a good Catholic and a true socialist."[11] In 1961, on the seventieth anniversary of *Rerum Novarum*, the same year as (Catholic) President Kennedy's disastrous Bay of Pigs invasion of Cuba, Pope John XXIII directed his attention to "one very important social principle":

> *Economic progress must be accompanied by a corresponding social progress, so that all classes of citizens can participate in the increased productivity. . . . From this it follows that the economic prosperity of a nation is not so much its total assets in terms of wealth and property, as the equitable division and distribution of this wealth. . . . Experience suggests many ways in which the demands of justice can be satisfied. Not to mention other ways, it is especially desirable today that workers gradually come to share in the ownership of their company, by ways and in the manner that seem most suitable.*[12]

In 1967, Pope Paul VI issued a direct challenge to concentrated ownership, suggesting (in *Populorum Progressio*) that "Private property does not constitute for anyone an absolute or unconditional right. No one is justified in keeping for his exclusive use what he does not need, when others lack necessities." With Pope John Paul II's publication in 1981 of the encyclical *Laborem Exercens* ("On Human Work"), the Vatican insisted that both Marxism and conventional capitalism were badly flawed: "The Church's teaching on ownership diverges radically from collectivism as proclaimed by Marxism and 'rigid capitalism.'" He then went on to urge "associating labour with the ownership of capital, as far as possible," concluding on a revealing note of advocacy: "Every effort must be made to ensure that in this kind of system also the human person can preserve his awareness of working 'for himself.' If this is not done, incalculable damage is inevitably done throughout the economic process, not only economic damage but first and foremost damage to man."

This ownership-oriented trend in Catholic social teachings continued on the one hundredth anniversary of *Rerum Novarum* when Pope John Paul II again challenged both socialist and capitalist ideologues to devise a new, more equitable form of economics, noting:

> *. . . what is being proposed as an alternative is not the socialist system, which in fact turns out to be state capitalism, but rather a society of free work, of enterprise and of participation. Such a society is not directed against the market, but demands that the market be appropriately controlled by the forces of society and by the State, so as to guarantee that the basic needs of the whole of society are satisfied.*[13]

In support of his point that "the Marxist solution has failed," he notes "the historical experience of socialist countries has sadly demonstrated that collectivism does not do away with alienation but rather increases it, adding to it a lack of basic necessities and economic inefficiency." At the same time, he offered no solace to doctrinaire capitalists, noting: "There is a risk that a radical capitalistic ideology could spread which refuses even to consider these problems in the a priori belief that any attempt to solve them is doomed to failure, and which blindly entrusts their solution to the free development of market forces." Lest anyone misconstrue his message that a new economics is required, he concludes: "It is unacceptable to say that the defeat of so-called 'real socialism' leaves capitalism as the only model of economic organization."*

Reform and the Church

With an estimated one billion Catholics worldwide, including dominantly Catholic populations throughout Latin America, the Caribbean and parts of Europe and Africa, the church's social doctrine on ownership could have widespread implications as policymakers search for a "third road." The church is clearly calling for a more inclusive form of economics, one capable of improving the conditions of the "vast multitudes [who] are still living in conditions of great material and moral poverty."[14] As for Cuba, the implications could be immediate. The church could nudge Cuban policymakers to embrace policies and programs designed to "associate labour with the ownership of capital" (though there is no indication Pope John Paul II did so during his January 1998 visit to Cuba). Or, should Castro decide to lead Cuba in this direction, he could point to his worker ownership reforms in seeking Vatican support for lifting the U.S. embargo. This new current in an old stream could prove to be a tempting legacy for the Cuban leader, perhaps even a retirement goal.

Latin America and the Caribbean offer an especially fruitful focus for ownership solutions, particularly for those who seek relief from the region's plutocratic past. Extreme economic disparities and political volatility have long characterized the region. Escape from that debilitating pattern requires financial engineering that, serendipitously, can take its bearings from the region's long-dominant purveyor of social values: the Catholic Church.

---

* In April 1997, the Pontiff stressed again the "persistent scandal of serious inequalities" and, worried at the dangers attending the "exorbitant power of the global market," he cautioned about the effects of "an unbridled market which, under the pretext of competitiveness, prospers by exploiting man and the environment to excess."

CHAPTER 20

South Africa: Overcoming Economic Apartheid

> Perhaps the dominant feature of the South African economy is its great disparity in income and wealth distribution.
>
> —*U.S. Department of State, Agency for International Development*

Apartheid, translated literally, means "apartness" or "separateness." The recent end of South Africa's *political* apartheid left in place a dramatic *economic* apartness. Average white income is eight times that of nonwhites. In a nation where 90 percent of the population is nonwhite, a white minority owns 90 percent of South Africa's assets; 70 percent of which is held in fewer than 10 large corporations. The five biggest corporate groups control 82 percent of the Johannesburg stock exchange.[1] Eighty percent of the land is held by 30 percent of the population. A long history of educational apartheid ("Bantu") means that this white minority also possesses most of the human capital required to sustain the nation's modern economy as well as the professional skills needed to design and implement the changes required to bring an end to the economic component of apartheid.

Also it should be understood that a vast morass of multiple bureaucracies employed (in 1994) a staggering two million of the nation's five million whites. As part of negotiations leading to a peaceful transition, these people will retain their jobs until 1999, though without any incentive to do their jobs well. In addition, two-thirds of South Africans are under age thirty in a population of forty-two million that is projected to reach fifty-nine million by 2010 (not counting illegal immigrants from the north who are now streaming into the country). To keep up with population increases, South Africa must grow an unrealistic 6 percent a year, which dooms any strategy that relies on growth alone to lift the poor.

In this environment, it's difficult to imagine a more certain formula for breeding political disillusionment than to see pre-apartheid property rights maintained alongside post-apartheid political rights. Yet this destabilizing gap cannot be bridged by either of the two conventional remedies: Marxist-style expropriation or Keynesian-style income redistribution. After gauging the economic and financial environment of the 1990s, the politically dominant African National Congress (ANC) came to the same conclusion. To fulfill its agenda, the ANC/ Mandela government recognized that their social justice goals would require a market-oriented approach. Otherwise they would provoke further capital flight, worsen a troublesome "brain drain" and increase the trepidation voiced by already-timid foreign investors.

The first initiatives focused on the broadening of land ownership and on housing, including an impossibly optimistic goal of 1 million new homes by 2000. Their ownership goal is reflected in a macroeconomic strategy known as GEAR, for growth, employment and redistribution. Yet the goal of broader ownership is certain to confront the standard dilemma: (1) how to make investors of those with few funds to invest (the bulk of the ANC's constituency), and (2) how to encourage broader wealth distribution without forcibly redistributing already-owned wealth (thereby stimulating capital flight, etc.).

In a February 1996 National Framework Agreement with the three major trade union groups, the Mandela-led "Government of National Unity" committed itself to a restructuring of state-owned assets in a way that will "redistribute wealth" while facilitating "genuine black economic empowerment." However, that leaves intact the far more prevalent nonstate sector. At present, a white-dominated economic structure controls South Africa's business and financial sectors while a nonwhite-dominant government structure controls the policy environment affecting those sectors. This guarantees a certain tension for the constructive engagement required to change a system that, decades in the making, may take considerable time to change.

Shaping an Empowerment Policy

If ownership remains separate and apart from the experience of nonwhites, ANC members will eventually ask whether apartheid has genuinely been eradicated or merely eroded. The U.S. State Department's Agency for International Development summarized the challenge thus: "It can easily be argued that economic empowerment is the single most important long-term concern facing South Africa, and that it will be impossible to deal effectively with the enduring legacies of apartheid until economic empowerment is first addressed."

It's impossible to imagine an economic empowerment strategy worthy of the term absent a healthy component of nonwhite ownership participation. Properly implemented, communicated, managed and administered, ESOP-like ownership schemes could make a positive contribution not only to peaceful change (unions were the core of the ANC's support) but also to improved economic performance. Most new jobs will continue to be generated within the informal economy for some time to come. However, sustained economic growth in all sectors is the only alternative to the difficult dilemma facing ANC leaders who may otherwise be pressured to look for ways to redistribute income and possibly wealth.

If the ANC goes the conventional economic empowerment route I've encountered elsewhere, the rhetorical commitment to broad-based ownership will soon face financial reality. The usual result is a thin veneer of newly minted owners, particularly among the most politically well-connected. Cynics suggest this is precisely what is unfolding, as politically well-connected non-white businessmen purchase valuable assets at discount prices. In some cases, they are lent the purchase money. An analogous strategy (labeled "people's capitalism") emerged in the United States during the Nixon administration when his urban economic development strategy helped create a few wealthy non-white owners of inner-city businesses, leaving those who worked for them participating not as shareholders but solely as jobholders. Franchise operations have traditionally been prime candidates for this "facade capitalism"—fast-food eateries, soft drink bottling plants, photo-processing outlets, and so on.

Solidarity brought the ANC to power. Maintaining that solidarity will require a combination of both political and financial skills as strategists look for a way to tread that fine line between encouraging the creation of new capitalists and not unduly upsetting the property rights of the old capitalists. On that score, South Africa's dominantly white capitalists have moved quickly to foster a stability-enhancing corps of new black owners. In one high-profile $900 million deal, Anglo American Corporation, the nation's largest company, offered a 48 percent stake in a holding company ("Johnnic") to the National Empowerment Consortium made up of miner, rail, textile and food-service unions. The purchase money was lent by South African banks, insurers and union pension funds. Although the shares were sold at 11 percent below the market price, critics suggest that this discount was more than compensated for by the fact that this sale co-opted people close to the government, ensuring that no antibusiness legislation would be passed. They cite as an example the fact that the ANC has ceased its talk of nationalization while leaving in place price-fixing cartels that reportedly will enable Anglo to gain considerably more than it gives up through this discount sale.

How Long the Honeymoon?

South Africa has long had the most well developed economy in Africa, with paved roads, telecommunications, a well-established legal and banking system, a cadre of skilled professionals, and so on. Plus South Africa is the obvious place from which to focus on the rest of southern Africa. In short, South Africa is rightly viewed as the commercial jewel of sub-Saharan Africa. The Johannesburg stock exchange ranks thirteenth worldwide in total capitalization. This economically modern nation now has a modern (i.e., representative) political system. Yet the day will arrive when political participation without economic participation rings hollow. If post-apartheid South African capitalism does not prove itself genuinely inclusive, no one should be surprised if the ANC membership insists that its leaders return the movement to its socialist roots.

In my experience, the peaceful transformation of a nation's ownership pattern is a long-term endeavor, one not susceptible to a quick fix without destabilizing the property rights of both old and new owners. Several high-visibility pilot projects could be crucial in buying the new government some time to make what will inevitably be a lengthy transition in an environment where ANC supporters have high hopes for dramatic and rapid change. Mining offers an obvious opening, accounting for some 10 percent of GDP. Though nonwhite employment in this sector has shrunk 27 percent from a decade ago, gold mining still accounts for 8 percent of formal jobs. Perhaps most importantly, the chief miners' union (NUMSA) has long been the ANC's strongest supporter. In addition, mining has always been an enormously powerful and highly visible force in the economy, represented by such historically dominant family fiefdoms as the Oppenheimer family's Anglo American and the De Beers groups.

In one highly contentious proposal, the ANC proposed a new property law standard whereby mineral rights would belong not to the landowner (as under current law) but to the state, as in key mining countries such as Australia, Canada and Chile. That would have gained for the Mandela government more control over the nation's resource base. As one possible ownership strategy, the government's rights could be deeded to a General Stock Ownership Corporation in which all South Africans own a personal stake, with mining companies required to pay to the GSOC a tonnage-based royalty.[2] While on a per capita basis, that may not amount to a large sum, it may well provide enough, say, to pay for school uniforms and books. Stakeholder enrollment could be coordinated with voter registration while ongoing shareholder communication could provide a way to raise financial literacy rates. Similarly, a policy environment could be provided that encourages extraction companies (such as Anglo American and De Beers) to include a significant ESOP in their companies.

In an attempt to keep the core of their corporate fortunes intact, current owners of these and other major South African firms are prepared to share ownership in certain corporate appendages. This so-called "unbundling" also offers an opportunity to use ownership-broadening financial techniques. With 30 percent of listed shares held in institutional hands, South Africa also provides an environment in which institutional investors may be persuaded to favor investments in firms that adopt performance-enhancing employee participation programs. A portion of institutional funds might also be invested in microcredit facilities as a way to stimulate jobs in the informal sector.

Rethinking Land Reform

Agriculture offers another opportunity to de-racialize ownership. Land has long held a special meaning for Black South Africans, as reflected in slogans adopted both by the ANC (*"Mayibuye iAfrika!"*—"Come back, Africa!") and by the rival Pan African Congress *("Izwe Lethu!"*—"The land is ours!"). Under apartheid, some 3.5 million people were forcibly removed from their land by the white government between 1960 and 1980 and ordered into black "homelands." Those displaced by government policy want a new policy that will return their land, most of which is now farmed by whites. However, South Africa's new bill of rights promises compensation to any owner whose land is taken by government action. That ensures an unaffordable land empowerment process for the fiscally constrained government.

Historically, land reform worldwide has been characterized by sharp drops in productivity as farmers are given small, economically nonviable plots and left without support for credit, marketing, transportation or even assistance in gaining rudimentary agricultural skills. Large-scale commercial farming currently accounts for 90 percent of the value-added component in South African agriculture. Unless ANC supporters want to settle for subsistence farming (albeit an improvement for many), they may be well advised to consider packaging land reform in a nontraditional way.

For instance, they could urge multifamily groups to jointly own a farm as a corporation or a cooperative, thereby capturing economies of scale (in purchasing, marketing, transportation, access to credit, etc.). Useful alliances could also be created with suppliers and distributors. For example, employee-owned corporate farms could be ownership-linked to other firms with which they have long-term relationships (fertilizer companies, trucking firms, retail outlets, etc.). A more fully integrated, cross-ownership strategy could help advance broad-based black economic empowerment while also reducing economic risk and advancing social and racial harmony.

Development experts are also urging South Africa to make better use of its natural resources, including the exploitation of its beautiful terrain and wildlife by attracting eco-tourists. Though this is destined to play only a minor role in the long-term development strategy, it's useful to consider how even this niche might be organized to include a harmonizing ownership component. For example, to attract tourists with an environmental orientation, the founders of Conservation Corporation are collaborating with South African landowners—who are also shareholders in the venture—to create large wildlife habitats, allowing wild animals to replace the crops and cattle that previously utilized the land.[3]

In short, a widely acceptable, stability-enhancing ownership pattern is likely to emerge only over the long term, and only as policymakers implement a range of ownership-broadening initiatives. Perhaps more so than any other country, the South African government should establish a Ministry of Capital Ownership as an ownership-focused counterpart to the Ministry of Labor. Its goal would be to acknowledge today's property rights while also pressing an agenda to steadily broaden tomorrow's. Without such a sustained and institutionalized policy focus, economic empowerment may wither while economic apartheid endures.

On the day in 1993 when Nelson Mandela and former president Frederik de Klerk jointly received the Nobel Peace Prize, Bishop Desmond Tutu (the 1984 recipient) declared, "Once we have got it right, South Africa will be the paradigm for the rest of the world." Certainly South Africa has that potential. Perhaps the greatest danger lies in the possibility that it falls short of that potential because it pays insufficient attention to the institutional changes required to evoke a genuinely inclusive ownership solution.

CHAPTER 21

Islamic Ownership: The Vice-Regents

God the glorified has ordained
the support of the poor
in the wealth of the rich,
so no indigent goes hungry
but for what a rich man enjoys.
And God Most High
will question them about that.

—Hadrat 'Alī (598–661 B.C.), translated by T. Cleary

slamic countries number thirty-seven worldwide, accounting for 20 percent of the world's population (1.2 billion people). Islam's proponents are valiantly (sometimes violently) struggling to reconcile Western notions of commerce with fundamental Muslim tenets. In this chapter, we consider how "Islamic economics" could play a role not only in advancing an ownership solution but also in harmonizing Islamic values with those of the Judeo-Christian West.

Islam includes at its core a commitment to social justice. Its teachings aspire to create societies that eradicate poverty, fulfill human needs and ensure an equitable distribution of income and wealth. The goal is not equality but an avoidance of gross inequality along with an injunction that wealth should not become "a commodity between the rich among you." That presents a problem, because the ownership-concentrating closed system of finance operates with total disregard for religious preferences. Capitalism is just as happy to create plutocracies in Qatar as in Quebec.

Unraveling the Islamic Riddle

The historical heart of the Muslim faith is found in the Middle East, a region that remains a riddle to most in the West. Among the nineteen countries in the area studied by New York–based Freedom House, all but five are rated as "not free" where leaders have served, on average, more than two decades. Given the democratic West's rejection of political monarchies (with some notable exceptions, such as Jordan), it remains difficult for Americans to fathom the notion of royalty—kings, princes, sheiks, emirs and such—dominating a nation's natural resources (largely oil) while its citizens live dependent on their largesse. More difficult yet is for those steeped in democratic values to imagine that a citizenry would choose such an arrangement, unless they can comprehend no better alternative.

The Middle East is burdened by some of the world's fastest-growing populations and slowest-growing economies. From 1981 to 1990, personal income in Arab countries fell by more than 2 percent a year. With jobless rates among the world's highest, incomes have grown only slightly since. In addition, Arab political culture, as perceived in the West, continues to be defined by pervasive corruption, stringent censorship and a rampant disregard for civil liberties.

Cynicism, even despair, is now widespread, particularly among Muslim youth, who know that change could bring improvement to lives long defined by status quo politics. As elsewhere, exclusion breeds extremism. Comparisons with living standards in more open societies are revealing. In Oman, the literacy rate is 30 percent; that compares with 93 percent in Costa Rica, where life expectancy is ten years longer. Saudi Arabia has fifteen times the per capita income of Sri Lanka but a lower literacy rate. The development and the human rights contradictions grow steadily more difficult to reconcile with both Muslim and Christian values, including America's eloquent silence regarding the treatment of dissidents in a region it has long considered too strategically important to embarrass. As the Dalai Lama notes, things in Tibet would be quite different if it were well endowed with oil.

The evidence suggests that many of the Persian Gulf's royal families are reasonably generous, overseeing their petrol-dollar-dominated economies to afford an acceptable lifestyle for those under their care, much as in feudal Europe the vassals were reasonably well looked after by the nobility of that era. However, symptoms of discontent and unrest abound as declining medical services, crowded classrooms, endemic unemployment and a weak infrastructure stir calls for reform, particularly among those who view royal rule as lacking in social justice and thwarting modern democracy.

Historically, such social environments (i.e., royalty alongside the restless) have bred Marxist-inspired, socialist-style ownership solutions. The response among modern-day Muslims instead has been a call for a return to their religious roots. When an Islamic-based political party scored a victory in Turkey in December 1995, the West recoiled in disbelief. Yet often a pro-Islamic vote can be interpreted not so much as anti-Western sentiment as a vote opposing economic, social and political inequities.

Islamicized Recycling of Petrodollars

A closely related issue accompanies the immensity of the funds generated by the sale of oil from the Islamic Middle East. Commencing in the mid-1970s, the accumulation of these enormous sums brought with it an ongoing need to reinvest these "petrodollars," an original stimulus to the globalization of capital markets in the Persian Gulf's worldwide search for financial returns. Under fundamental Islamic teachings, those funds (representing the blessings of Allah) should be invested with a strong sense of social responsibility and in a way that helps lift mankind from the degradations of poverty and hunger to a life of comfort and happiness.

From that perspective, one can easily understand the consternation of those in Islam who see instead a world undergoing a capital market-led globalization grounded in materialism and largely devoid of human values. Add to that an ownership patterning that suggests a selfishness of epic proportions and one can see the clear conflict with the Islamic ideal of an economic system that reflects values suited to the welfare of humanity as a whole—and as a way to foster cooperation and mutual goodwill.

It is because all of humanity is seen by Islam as a single family that devout Muslims consider the charging of fixed interest (*riba*) exploitative. Money should not be made from money because interest forces the user of financial capital to bear all the risk, unjustly rewarding those who own the capital. To demand payment regardless of the circumstances is considered exploitative, akin to demanding "a pound of flesh." *True* Muslims, according to the Qur'an, should only make money from sharing in the risks born by their brethren.

In many Islamic countries, traditional interest-based lending can be found alongside financiers who operate more like merchant bankers, taking risks alongside their clients. Many banks offer both Islamic and non-Islamic funds. Neither socialism nor capitalism, Islamic economics is difficult to categorize, and, indeed, observance of the injunction against *riba* is sporadic.[1] In some locales, Muslim clerics accept a distinction between reasonable interest (which is OK) and unacceptable usury, though interest of any sort is banned, at least in name, in Sudan and Iran. According to Harvard University's Islamic Finance Information Program, in mid-1997, the Muslim world had 133 Islamic financial institutions in 24 countries. Although most are located in Pakistan, Sudan and Indonesia, they also include an offshore Islamic banking subsidiary wholly owned by Bahrain which was set up by Citibank.[2] Practical experience has spawned many variations on this theme.[3] However, the core notion of risk-sharing remains strong, with its strength increasing as Islam continues its expansion along with a return to its traditional roots.[4]

Throughout its population (the same size as China's), the Islamic world is struggling with a fast-widening gap between its haves and its have-nots, but with one key difference: Islamic teachings prohibit the use of wealth in ways that divide those who comprise the Muslim family. The Quranic law on inheritance is explicit in its insistence that wealth "circulate" through society.

One fruitful strategy would ensure that the region's petrodollars are systematically recycled and "Islam-icized." This Muslim-derived financial capital could be deployed worldwide in a way that economically empowers the people of those countries where the funds are invested. Thus, for example, the Muslim leaders of Saudi Arabia or Bahrain could invest equity in enterprises abroad, with an understanding that they would later exit those investments through ownership-broadening financing techniques such as ESOPs, RESOPs, GSOCs, etc.[5]

The potential impact of Islamic economics is not lost on the West. Deposits at Islamic banks, mostly in the Middle East and Southeast Asia, are growing at 15 to 20 percent a year with approximately $100 billion in current assets in mid-1997 and capital of almost $5 billion (up from zero two decades ago).

The Islamic banking sector enjoys double-digit growth.[6] Commercial banks in the region (including numerous Western banks) are opening Islamic "windows" to attract Muslim funds.[7] To date, however, the growth of Islamic banking suffers from two key limitations: a lack of innovation and a lack of standardization. Financial product standardization (essential for securitization) could flow from a thematic focus on financial products that foster ownership-sharing capital structures, encompassing Muslim notions of risk-sharing by all parties involved.

For instance, a Qatar-wide GSOC could retain a warrant in each of the non-Qatar companies in which Qatar invests its petrodollars, permitting the GSOC later to buy shares in that company at a price agreed to today. A little-known precedent exists in the West. In return for the U.S. government granting the Chrysler Corporation a $1.2 billion loan guarantee in 1979, Chrysler was required to provide the federal government with warrants to buy Chrysler stock—recognizing that U.S. taxpayers were taking a risk by guaranteeing Chrysler's loan. Initially valued at $6 per share, those warrants were later exercised at $72 each, with the proceeds dedicated to general revenues.

A GSOC for all citizens of Qatar could hold warrants in companies in which their petrodollars are invested in Islamic countries worldwide, thereby enabling Qatar's citizens, over time, to accumulate a diversified portfolio of equities throughout the Islamic world. This would advance the notion of cross-border brotherhood within the Muslim faith while also potentially recruiting non-believers to the Islamic message of shared prosperity. Some portion of the proceeds from the sale of those warrants could be earmarked to fund specific social services such as the education and training required to provide Qatar's citizens (or Muslims elsewhere) with the skills they will need as Gulf nations exhaust their base of nonrenewable natural resources or as alternative fuel sources become more cost-effective.

A Brotherhood of Co-Owners

This ownership pattern–sensitive investment strategy has the potential to enhance both development and camaraderie across Islam's many nations. For instance, Muslims comprise 62 percent of the inhabitants of China's Xinjiang Province (a sparsely populated area three times the size of France). Once known as East Turkestan and regarded as part of Turkic Central Asia, the Chinese took it over in 1949 and encouraged the Han, China's primary ethnic group, to settle in this "new dominion" (the literal translation of *Xinjiang*). The Han population has since grown from 5 percent to 38 percent in a population of 16 million.

Although the region has abundant natural resources (coal, copper, gold, iron and oil), the median 1996 per capita annual income for the minority rural Muslim population was $90.50, less than one-fourth that of the region's urban residents, mostly Han. Kashgar, the province's cultural and religious center located near the northeastern border of Pakistan, has more than 9,500 mosques. Less than 25 percent of Kashgar's residents have running water. What few jobs are created by local resource-extracting firms are reserved largely for the Chinese settlers. The economic plight of the native Uighurs cries out for help from fellow Muslims.

Though Xinjiang produced 10.4 million metric tons of crude oil in 1993, all profits flowed to Beijing. Reflecting conventional capitalist thinking, Chinese leaders say only that the central government, not Xinjiang's residents, invested the funds required to locate and extract the oil. Like populations elsewhere who find themselves rich in natural resources but poor in investment capital, Xinjiang's residents could not develop on their own. Islamic petrodollars could fill that financial void while ESOPs, GSOCs, and similar stakeholder structures could fill the "social capital" void by ensuring that local Muslims gain a stake in local development—and in a way consistent with China's goals of market-based socialism and diversified ownership.[8]

Absent such a helping hand, these Muslims will continue to eke out a spartan agricultural living among the politically favored Chinese while their local resource base supports the living standards of those in Beijing. China's policymakers may welcome this Islamicized rural development strategy as an experiment in stemming the exodus of struggling rural residents into China's overcrowded urban areas. In addition, Xinjiang has been under subtle siege since a Uighur separatist killed 16 Chinese policemen in November 1996. Subsequent bombing attacks included bridges, buses and an oil refinery. Beijing suspects that Uighurs have links with Pakistan's Kashmiri militants. Though Uighurs are Muslims, they view their cause not as Islamic so much as anticolonial, a stance not without some irony for the communist Chinese.

Xinjiang is important to Beijing not so much because of its resources (its oil reserves were once hoped to rival those of Saudi Arabia) but because it borders former Soviet Central Asia and the gas reserves of Uzbekistan. Plus it could become the site of a pipeline to carry Turkmen gas to fuel China's economic growth. China's first preference would be to find its own energy sources. Otherwise, it could be importing as much as 1.7 million barrels of oil a day by the year 2000. Absent that windfall, it needs a compliant Xinjiang as an avenue both for importing oil and gas and for exporting manufactured goods to Central Asia. Muslims in the region may yet come to the aid of both the Uighurs and the Chinese, applying Islamic finance to ensure that their fellow Muslims share in the wealth that seems destined otherwise to pass them by.

A Stakeholder Peace in the Middle East

The West Bank and the Gaza Strip offer another opportunity for a demonstration of the potential of Islamic economics.[9] Development may yet proceed in this volatile area provided a fragile peace can endure and political stability can attract the private capital required to fund that development. The one factor that has thus far escaped scrutiny is the most obvious one: development *for whom*? If, for example, absentee investors—whether Jewish or Muslim—provide needed financial capital and then stay on indefinitely as absentee owners, they will have missed a unique opportunity to apply ownership-broadening financing techniques in an area that needs all the harmony-fostering creativity it can muster. Similarly, an opportunity will be missed if those known locally as the *athria falastin* (the monied elite of Palestine) are allowed to dominate the local economy, ownership-wise. That appears to be a real risk as many Palestinians resent the lavish living standards that seem to be affordable by many among the ten thousand Palestinians who accompanied Yasir Arafat's return from exile in Tunis.

Harvard University Professor Leonard Hausman argues that "The relevance of business as a builder of peace has been missed in the Arab-Israeli peace process. If in September 1993, Yasir Arafat and Yitzhak Rabin had agreed to get one hundred Israeli businesspeople and one hundred Palestinian businesspeople each to put up $2 million in joint ventures and one hundred such ventures developed, we'd be further along. There would be mutual interest in the development of the economy, there would be jobs . . . there would be solid relationships between Israelis and Palestinians."[10]

By ensuring that those *living in the area* share a tangible economic stake, an ownership pattern–sensitive approach could help defuse the "them versus us" stance that has long plagued Palestine. Rest assured, the inclusion of an ownership element will add an additional layer of complexity and cost. It may even slow the process. However, this long-simmering animosity is ancient. It needs a well-considered solution designed for the long term. Time taken now to create a system of shared risk, responsibility and reward could do much to ensure that this delicate, oft-broken truce becomes an enduring and prosperity-inducing peace.

Similar cross-cultural, prosperity-sharing models could advance peace efforts in other areas where Muslims are under stress, such as in the divided territory of Kashmir, the predominantly Muslim area fought over and divided by Indian and Pakistani troops in 1947. Or in the former Yugoslavia where Serbs, Bosnian Muslims and Croats are struggling to identify common ground on which to build a peaceful future. An ownership-participation strategy could provide not only a base for confidence-building, it could also serve as an ideological counteroffensive against those who might rule as Communists, Mafioso, warlords or some combination.

Fostering Communitarian Capitalism

Other projects also provide opportunities for the application of Islamic economics. For instance, Muslim-dominated Azerbaijan aims to construct a pipeline from its inland oil fields to the open seas. A combination of Islamic capital and an ownership system consistent with Islamic principles could go a long way toward assisting this struggling nation in completing an infrastructure asset that is desperately needed if this newly independent Muslim state is to generate the foreign exchange required for development. Fellow Muslims residing in capital-providing countries might well retain a stake (perhaps through a GSOC), thereby fostering long-term, cross-border economic bonds.

For a world hooked on hydrocarbons, it's difficult to overstate the potential importance of the oil reserves lying beneath Azerbaijan, Turkmenistan and the Caspian Sea. Proven reserves beneath Azerbaijan's portion of the Caspian total 17 billion barrels, equivalent to the North Sea field off Britain. Geologists confidently predict that another twenty to thirty billion more barrels remain to be found. The oil-rich northeastern portion of the Caspian belongs to newly independent Kazakhstan, with ten billion barrels of proven reserves and perhaps three times that not yet confirmed. Estimates of total reserves in the Caspian and surrounding area run as high as two hundred billion barrels.[11]

What's at stake is not only trillions of dollars but also the shape of geopolitics surrounding this key resource and, potentially, the environmental consequences of its use. For example, because Azerbaijan has no outlet to sea lanes, it is evaluating its options of oil pipeline routes to access world markets. Each presents its own set of problems, due not only to the high costs accompanying the difficulties of distance and terrain but also because of environmental concerns and rampant regional instability. In addition, any route is likely to upset the political sensibilities of at least one of the regional powers. The most direct route to the Persian Gulf would be to link into Iran's existing network of pipelines—the route announced by Turkmenistan in December 1997.[12]

The global view of mankind that underlies Islamic economics may hold a clue to reconciling Islamic teachings with oil-derived development. If this 200 billion barrel natural asset is viewed as a gift of Allah granted for the benefit of all humankind, then all the nations of Islam have an obligation to ensure that this is the end to which it is put. With political will, its development could be organized in such a way that it advances economic development not only in Azerbaijan and its neighbors but also throughout this long-troubled region where instability, injustice and a lack of development have long been inseparable partners.

Imagine, for example, if the region were to coalesce around the goal of putting this natural bounty to the purpose of building harmony and prosperity in the four neighboring countries of Iran, Iraq, Syria and Turkey—including a component that benefits the immense Kurdish population found in each. Imagine further if the leaders of neighboring Russia, Jordan, Kuwait and Saudi Arabia were to press this initiative as a means for combining peaceful development, access to energy and regional cooperation in this center of Islamic culture.

In addition, Muslim leaders in the region cannot be unmindful of the environmental implications of burning 200 billion barrels of carbon-based fuel. The Qur'an mandates that this resource be made available on a basis that does not endanger the earth. What that implies for an environmentally sound development strategy is more difficult to discern. At a minimum, a sensitivity to emission-absorption rates is called for, and perhaps a set aside of oil revenues for the research and development of fuel conservation methods, cleaner-burning engines and alternative energy sources.

In the Muslim view of the world, sovereignty can belong only to Allah. Although political sovereigns are a useful social fiction, they too must comply with Islam (*Islam* literally means the submission of all creatures to their creator). In the current global mix of strengths and weaknesses, assets and liabilities, the Muslim world has been gifted with abundant hydrocarbons while the Christian West is rich in science and technologies: manufacturing technologies, financial technologies, organizational technologies and so on. If it is to the benefit of all mankind that these riches should be put to use with the goal of attaining harmony, tranquility and peace (a Muslim tenet), then multi-cultural, collaborative (and green) development is a must.

It would be a source of great richness indeed if this development effort were to advance not only global peace and cross-cultural tolerance but, in the process, help wean mankind off this inherently limited and environmentally disabling resource. Perhaps most important, however, would be the demonstration effect that such an effort might have for all humanity. Dr. Martin Luther King Jr. described well the challenge we face: "Through our scientific genius we have made of the world a neighborhood; now through our moral and spiritual genius we must make of it a brotherhood." It is in this domain that Islamic economics could make a real and lasting difference.

A Reformed and Resurgent Islam

An historic analogy may help describe what could yet emerge from this focus on Islam-influenced ownership patterns. Five centuries ago, the Reformation, in its disillusionment with the previous order, released a pent-up surge of individualism and creativity. That, in turn, laid the foundation for what we now know as democracy and free-enterprise capitalism. At that time too it seemed that people were casting off orthodoxy and returning to their religious roots in a way that threatened the status quo. Yet in retrospect, it's clear that this return to the old spawned something radically and wonderfully new.

Today's resurgence of Islam includes a litany of very Western ideas, including individual responsibility, reliance on market mechanisms, a commitment to economic and social justice—plus quite specific injunctions mandating care for the environment. A Muslim mainstream is anxious to join the modern developing world while keeping their values intact. What we may be seeing is the beginning of a fundamental overhaul of the economic and social systems underlying Islam. If so, the result could produce something quite novel: clearly not socialism yet certainly not the oligarchic capitalism so common in the Islamic world of today. This still-emerging hybrid thus far lacks a label, though "communitarian capitalism" seems an obvious candidate, and a description consistent with Muslim tenets.

Islamic teachings give full scope for the crafting of quite modern solutions to problems on which direct guidance is not provided in the Qur'an. In essence, the Muslim faithful view economics as based on man's obligation to organize his affairs in accordance with the will of God as his representative (his vice-regent) on Earth. Islam's primary inspirational texts (the Qur'an and the Sunnah) suggest that happiness and peace can only be attained if man's mundane pursuits are suffused with moral purpose. What Islamic economists seek is a moral version of modern capitalism.

Culture- and ideology-spanning economic initiatives could provide common ground to focus on a range of collaborative efforts between Islam and the Judeo-Christian West. Absent a conscious effort to develop such collaborations, current tensions seem destined to fester and perhaps escalate. In the conscious attempt to meld Western finance with Islamic values, the two cultures are certain to discover a new richness in the transcendent values they share.

Epilogue

Every creature shares in the dignity of causality that God has shared with all creatures.

—St. Thomas Aquinas

The Ownership Solution is an attempt to assist readers in viewing two very old ideas—free enterprise and private ownership—in a very new way. My goal has been to stay within the traditions that accompany these ideas, using the term *tradition* in the same way that Martin Buber suggests: "a change of form within the same stream." Nowhere do I suggest a destination. Instead I propose only what I see as a more hopeful direction—a trajectory, not a preconceived end point.

More broadly, I see that those of us from the more prosperous "mentor" economies are not providing models of sustainable development worthy of emulation abroad. For reasons I do not comprehend, policymakers worldwide (both corporate leaders and those in public office) choose to ignore financial techniques that could improve the relationships that people have with their economy, with their workplace, with their government and, perhaps most importantly, with their environment and with each other. It is in these relationships that we will find the key to societal and environmental health, as well as the route to sustainable prosperity and enduring harmony.

World Bank President Jim Wolfensohn points out that today five billion people live in market economies—up from one billion just ten years ago. Characterizing inclusion as "the key development challenge of our time," he notes that "in too many countries, the poorest 10 percent of the population has less than 1 percent of the income, while the richest 20 percent enjoys over half. . . . *If we do not act, in thirty years the inequities will be greater.* With population growing at eighty million a year, instead of the three billion living on under $2 a day, it could be as high as five billion. In thirty years, the quality of our environment will be worse. Instead of 4 percent of tropical rain forests lost since Rio, it could be 24 percent. In thirty years, the number of conflicts may be higher. Already we live in a world which last year [1996] alone saw twenty-six interstate wars and twenty-three million refugees. One

does not have to spend long in Bosnia or Gaza or the Lakes District of Africa to know that without economic hope we will not have peace. Without equity we will not have stability. Without a better sense of social justice our cities will not be safe, and our societies will not be stable. Without inclusion, too many of us will be condemned to live separate, armed, and frightened lives."[1]

Although a blueprint might be drawn for what I think is a more inclusive, more just, and more sustainable ownership system, the truth is that people who live thirty years or one hundred years from now will do whatever they please. The concept of prosperity may be very different by then. All I can offer during this time of complex transition is a few observations that I hope might better enable us to deal with these challenges within an economic model in which the human heart is no longer so clearly in conflict with itself. Joseph Campbell, noted mythologist and psychologist, once urged that we "create a future image of what humankind can be." That enables us to then live into that image. The anthropocentric, self-centered caricature of "economic man" advanced by radical market theorists is but one half of the "two selves that swell within our breast" (to paraphrase the words of Goethe's *Faust*).

Granting dominance to only one of mankind's dimensions has drawbacks that have become steadily more apparent as world trade and global capital markets expand and as the notion of self-interest is exposed to other cultures, such as Islam, where it is viewed as not only potentially corrosive of core social values but even depraved, perhaps even blasphemous. In a similar way, indigenous peoples have long cautioned that neither the secular nor the sacred exist in isolation but in relation to each other. The policy challenge, as well as the challenge for business leaders, lies in evoking an appropriate balance as each of us does our own small part to define the new reality into which we are moving. I remain quite hopeful. At long last, we are becoming conscious of our condition and of our role as cocreators of our condition.

In the United States, we are blessed with a culture of openness, optimism and options. That will serve us well in our search for an ownership solution. On the one hand, that solution needs to reflect the everyday reality that market exchange will continue to be made on the basis of self-interest. That fundamental mechanism is a key ingredient by which economic progress is advanced worldwide. The naiveté of the Left has long been reflected in their attempts to construct a system to change human nature to achieve social justice instead of nurturing an economic environment that evokes social justice while accommodating human nature.[2]

On the other hand, it may require a Copernican shift to jolt America out of today's market-myopic fixation in which, in the appraisal of former New York Governor Mario Cuomo, Americans have been "seduced by a new mythology that insists that the strongest among us are sufficient unto themselves and the rest are not worth the bother."[3] The corporate entity, in particular, is often single-mindedly mission-oriented, operating with sometimes shockingly little concern for the risks its financial-return agenda imposes on the world around it, including many stakeholders who are put at risk without any voice in the matter or the risk imposed on the voice-less environment.

From the perspective of systems design, the goal of *The Ownership Solution* is to evoke a system that ensures, as Adam Smith envisioned, a genuinely "self designed" economic life for as many people as possible. That requires a commercial environment that is better capable of incorporating the wishes of those whose lives are affected by the economic forces that surround them. We are only at the beginning stages of understanding how to foster such a system. At the very least, however, we must think more broadly and more deeply about how property—as an inherent feature or "property" of free enterprise—can be engineered to generate a better result.

Needed: An Enlivening Social Contract

Much like the Buddhist notion of work as "right livelihood" is intended to deepen humankind's appreciation, gratitude and humility, so too could the notion of "right ownership" be applied in a similar way, redirecting mankind's acquisitive instinct into economic and social patterns more in keeping with fundamental notions of economic and social justice, and better able to foster a shift in consciousness from a person-centered to a more bio-centered world view.[4] Wall Street may be correct that "money is smarter than people"—but only in the same sense that water is smarter because it follows the path of least resistance. We know that water can be diverted, dammed and redirected so that its potential for damage is contained as we harness its capacity for good. The challenge for capitalism lies in fashioning a social contract that can channel financial capital's return-seeking properties in a way that better balances financial with other goals—social, fiscal, political, cultural, environmental.

Ownership engineering provides a means for ensuring that decisions affecting peoples' lives are no longer left solely in the abstract domain of pricing or in the hands of an oftentimes detached financial and managerial elite. Today's ecological challenge goes far deeper than the issue of discharges and emissions. It's also about how the economic domain can better provide what we want without endangering what our descendants need. Genuine stewardship requires a signaling system composed of something more than monetary units of reckoning. It also calls for personalized, localized and humanized relationships that afford those affected an opportunity to give voice to their deepest concerns. St. Thomas Aquinas recognized this in advancing his notion of "the dignity of causality." Everyone wants to feel that they are, at least in some small part, a cocreator.

Psychologists dating back to Freud have known that human beings need to feel that they can have an impact on their personal environment. While the demands of return-seeking capital have their place, they also must be kept in their place. And while a "level playing field" has about it an intellectual elegance, as does the abstract notion of a laissez-faire economy, it's time to recognize that we can no longer take cultural cohesion for granted—there is no invisible hand that creates equal opportunity. While it's bad news that capitalism tends to concentrate capital ownership, it's good news that it need not, and that the tools are at hand to ensure that it will not.

A people-based, feedback-intensive, self-organized, self-designed system is what Adam Smith envisioned—and the lack of which Karl Marx found so unsettling in his critique of finance capitalism. The challenge lies in designing an economic signaling system that incorporates that feedback at every conceivable stage so that humane, sustainable economic behavior emerges. Thus far, we have not fielded an economic science capable of displacing the myth of the isolated, individual self. That myth is sustained, even nurtured, by a social contract that views the needs of self as somehow separate and removed from the larger community and nature. It is in the resolution of that false dichotomy that an ownership solution can play a part.

Toward a New Common Sense

Two hundred years ago, it seemed impossible that population would not outrun food supply, yet an end to starvation is now well within our grasp—if only we organize to end it. One hundred years ago, it seemed unlikely that humankind could attain universal literacy, yet that objective too is now a feasible goal—if only we choose to achieve it. Fifty years ago, it seemed implausible that we would see Jung's notion of the collective unconsciousness made widely comprehensible, even visible—yet global media has the reach, the capacity and the potential for humans to be witness to their behavior as a species—both the noble and the nefarious—shining the light of global awareness on every aspect of the human psyche—provided we choose to turn this new technology to that use.

Thirty-five years ago, it seemed doubtful that a global consciousness could emerge, yet now the compelling imagery of a fragile earth adrift in space has laid the imaginative groundwork for just that—if only we muster the will to build on that foundation. A short decade ago, it seemed impossible that the tense standoff between capitalism and communism would end—yet we now live in the midst of that change—though it remains to be seen whether humankind is sufficiently mature to insist that ideology never again divide it.

The pieces are now in place to evoke a greater sense of global community and cross-cultural tolerance. What's required is support for those inquiries and conversations by which mankind crafts a new common sense about how humans can live together peaceably, prosperously and sustainably. Serendipitously, this challenge corresponds with the view of the world now advanced by modern physics where terms such as group consciousness, collective knowing, learning fields, fields of knowing, empathic fields, morphic resonance and so on are much in use.[5]

In layman's terms, quantum physics confirms that organizational learning (such as what takes place through democratic institutions) is how thought participates in creation. Those subtle "fields" of consciousness—including those that emerge in the dialogue that takes place in congregations, civic clubs, boardrooms and parliaments—are the intangible "stuff" of the universe that generates statutes, corporate by-laws, codes of conduct and such. When fully engaged, this self-reflective state can work dramatic change as it accesses the knowledge and wisdom that lies dispersed throughout the community.

One key weakness of present-day capitalism is that it suffers from a peculiar brand of reductionism that overlooks the textures, the tones and the qualities of relationships that often matter far more to the long-term health of human communities than more easily quantifiable benchmarks, such as those found in the domain of finance. It is in the steady *co*-evolution of both consciousness and culture that the future of capitalism will be forged.

We saw this co-evolving, self-organizing phenomenon at work in the field of consciousness that emerged (with the help of the media) to end the Vietnam War, to advance civil rights and, for that matter, to enact supply-side economics. Modern physics confirms Jung's notion that the collective unconscious is not only a psychic repository of past experiences; it is also a potential source of intelligence, insight and guidance. Yet it can also serve as the source of collective madness (witness Hitler and the Holocaust), the carrier of collective habit and tradition (for both good and ill), and the breeding ground for the embrace of ideas that can go terribly wrong. The field itself is neutral; it responds to the human intentions that animate it. Therein lies the role of free will and vision, and the role in advancing awareness and social progress that is played by leadership, both individual and collective.

Quantum Capitalism

Approaching this notion from a spiritual perspective, Buddhist monk Thich Nhat Hanh insists that "Communities of mindful living are crucial for our survival and the survival of our planet."[6] The goal as I see it—consistent with the new physics—is to cultivate this field of collective knowing in our various human communities in order to set the stage for the emergence of new organizational forms that better serve our goals. That's why I resist the temptation to become attached to any one ownership form or solution. Doubtless there are multiple solutions based on a multitude of possibilities, as we've seen in the worldwide review undertaken in this book.

To return to our beginning and to the "seventh-generation" standard for sustainability that I suggested guide our deliberations, ponder for a moment the 1854 reply of Chief Sealth ("Seattle") to the proposal by President Franklin Pierce that the chief agree to sell two million acres of Indian land in the Northwest. In questioning how something they consider sacred could be sold ("If we do not own the freshness of the air and the sparkle of the water, how can you buy them?"), the chief offers an early version of quantum mechanics: "This we know: All things are connected. Whatever befalls the earth befalls the sons of the earth. Man did not weave the web of life; he is merely a strand in it. Whatever he does to the web, he does to himself."

Ownership might itself be envisioned as a "field" of sorts—a collective agreement about the importance of private property as a handy fiction for ensuring human connectedness. Where it works well, that personal stake advances mindfulness; it evokes accountability; it aligns self-interest with the collective interest; it energizes individual and organizational learning; and it enhances the functional intelligence of the species. That's a very ambitious agenda I admit, but one that we fail to pursue at our peril. Indeed, I suggest that much of today's violence—physical, psychological, environmental—stems from a collective crises of disconnectedness—a sense of being apart from rather than a part of.

Yet that lack of connectivity is not some immutable law inscribed in the organizational DNA of capitalism and fixed for all time. Quite the contrary. Capitalism's current exclusiveness and disconnectedness is nothing more than a habit that has steadily solidified from within to become a force that, like any habit, can be broken. Over time, connectivity and community can be reengineered back into a system that we have allowed to become not only disconnected but dispassionate, unconcerned, even uncaring. Father Thomas Berry suggests that our modern sense of angst stems from the polarity between the conscious (to which we are connected) and the unconscious—which is profoundly disturbed by today's lack of unity, community, belonging and connectedness—in the very broadest sense.

"Our secular, rational, industrial society," argues Berry, "with its amazing scientific insight and technological skills, has established the first radically anthropocentric society and has thereby broken the primary law of the universe, the law of the integrity of the universe, the law that every component member of the universe should be integral with every other member of the universe and that the primary norm of reality and of value is the universe community itself in its various forms of expression. . . ."[7] One key goal of *The Ownership Solution* is to evoke a breakthrough to a capitalism that fosters a more mindful living.[8]

Though the quantum revolution in physics occurred in 1927, it wasn't until the mid-1970s that it became a subject of general discussion.[9] Unlike the latest trend in fashion or politics where change infiltrates the popular consciousness practically overnight, the implications of this fundamental change in science are only just beginning to seep into the social sciences. Even now, the mechanistic paradigm continues to dominate perception, diagnosis and prescription, and nowhere more so than in economics where the ideology of technological progress and a steady rise in GNP underlies all. Rather than a sense of sacred unfolding, or being drawn by some unseen force toward an inner, intuitive goal—like an acorn attracted to its maturity as an oak—an economy instead is viewed as an essentially purposeless, mechanistic, inanimate and soulless process, pushed along from behind by the purposeless and soulless forces of indefinite growth and expansion for their own sake.

My hope is that this book might accelerate a much-needed maturing of both economic science and capitalism so that their internal mechanisms might be re-envisioned in light of the insights now available through the new sciences. I suspect that the route to an integral and soulful economics lies through the participatory knowing available only through a genuinely shared capitalism. As theologian Matthew Fox phrases the challenge: it's "time we grow our soul larger." Through that field of a shared, participatory knowing, I believe a more compassionate and more sustainable capitalism will emerge. The era of attempting to find truth from the neck up is fast drawing to a close. That approach, while helpful, lacks the wholeness that can come only through integrating the valid concerns of both the head and the heart.

In addition to that broader, deeper, more integrated knowing, it's also essential that capitalism—as a system—develop a more respectful listening attuned to the impact of human activity on living systems. Our sometimes mindless striving for steadily rising living standards has put an unsustainable burden on nature. St. Thomas Aquinas reminds us that insight comes from not one but two volumes, both the written word and the world of nature. Stuck in a verbal and mental construct (capitalism even traces its roots to the Latin word *capitalis*, or head), we've become strangers to ourselves, wedded to a system that unwittingly divides the indivisible in a futile attempt to pretend that mankind can exist apart from nature.

This path may well lead us, at least temporarily, through a period of anger, grief and mourning. The anger will emerge from the shared consciousness of what we've allowed our "unconscious capitalism" to do—to ourselves, to our fellow man, to our children and to nature. The genetic defects, the needless cancers, the stunted growth of chemically abused children, the denuded landscapes, the endangered aquifers, the depleted oceans, the lost species, . . . The list is an endless recitation of senseless tragedy bred of blind human self-absorption whose cause lies deep within the very paradigm on which we base our standard of living. Its origins put this element of the human psyche beyond even the reach of the soothing balm of human forgiveness.

Underlying that is, I expect, an intuitive remorse, a shared sense of guilt, regret and sadness that may well benefit from a period of communal mourning.

Though that's a very different way of thinking about leadership and politics, those who can guide us through such a healing will serve a useful, unifying purpose. That's because the mindfulness now required of capitalism requires a shared sense of human connectedness that resonates at the most profound levels of personal experience. A period of shared mourning might help introduce the human community to itself.

A Template for Future Generations

This book suggests the broad outlines of an uncommon social contract, one like we've not seen to date—one that focuses not only on quantities but also on qualities. My hope is that the notion of ownership as a tool for fostering economic, social and ecological "connectivity" might provide a useful focal point to inject a harmonizing and humanizing element into the fractious, disconnected and often disempowering notions that characterize so much of today's decision-making, both in politics and in business.

As an American, I sense that we badly need fresh means for injecting vitality and meaning into the seemingly mundane activity of everyday market exchange. Fundamentally, we need a design that is itself enlivened with *spiritus* ("life-breath"). That requires new ways to evoke a sense of belonging and aliveness, along with a renewed sense of place and social commitment so that people become more alert to their opportunities to serve—and so that they take those opportunities seriously. That, in turn, requires an economic environment that empowers them sufficiently that they can *afford* to offer their service. My hope and expectation is that this opportunity, in turn, might evoke a sense of gratitude for a system that allows them that opportunity. That, I think, is what is meant by the transition to a service economy.

This suggested redesign of the social contract, necessarily a step-by-step process, is meant primarily for the benefit of the next generation. What parents are to their children, a nation's institutional design is to future generations. The financing mechanisms and the ownership-broadening techniques I offer are essentially hollow. At best, they are only vehicles to carry the intentions of the generation that now has its hands on the policy levers in both the public and private sector. If this generation (my generation) wants its children to embrace a worldview that sees humankind as inescapably interdependent and as "part of" rather than "over" the Earth, we need to demonstrate by our actions that we do indeed have an obligation to future generations.

If the "price of freedom is eternal vigilance," certainly that must be true for sustainability as well. As we better understand humankind's connectedness to all of creation, our entrancement with industrially driven consumption may begin to release its hypnotic hold, particularly if we have the good sense to use the medium of television to awaken us to the full extent of the costs of our consumption and bring to an end our species' isolation in the larger ecosystem. This change in scale—enabling the human consciousness to fully realize its place in life's larger pattern—awaits us as one of our key challenges.

At present, humankind is in a groping phase, trying to find its way from an adolescent, self-centered worldview to a more mature and integral perspective that reflects the realities of current science. We're early on in this shift, paradigm-wise. This is a time of unparalleled challenge because today's shift presents us with a challenge not only to our economic system but also to the worldview that underlies it. What the new physics confirms is what Chief Seattle warned almost 150 years ago: the wealth of any nation is inseparable from the wealth of all nations, as well as to the ecosystem that ultimately underlies that wealth. "Continue to contaminate your bed," he cautioned, "and you will one night suffocate in your own waste."

Despite the "fictions of Wall Street bookkeeping," as Father Berry puts it, "the earth is a faithful scribe, a faultless calculator, a superb bookkeeper; we will be held responsible for every bit of our economic folly."[10] Once the damage is done, there can be no reprogramming of our endocrine, immune or brain systems. Once our chemicals have forced the soil to produce beyond its natural rhythms, we are certain to live in a world where nature's life-giving qualities have been dissipated. This is no longer some abstract conversation about costs and benefits or the relative merits of production methods. The degradation of our habitat is now beginning to generate degraded humans. We've already irreversibly put our children at risk—and our children's children. Yet our worldview remains locked into so small a frame of reference that we seem incapable of seeing the whole, forgetting that, as indigenous peoples, ancient mystics and modern physicists all remind us, the whole is as necessary to the understanding of the parts as the parts are necessary to the understanding of the whole.

There's ultimately little choice but to yield to the wisdom of the universe. By my reckoning, that means we need nothing less than a feat of worldwide awareness and education to break out of today's exploitative anthropocentrism to something akin to biocentrism, or at least something well beyond today's milquetoast versions of man-apart environmentalism.

Even the notion of humankind could usefully be revisited so that we reconceive ourselves not as simply another being on the earth (one step removed from the ape) but as God's vice-regent (in the Islamic view) or as a dimension of the universe in whom the universe reflects on itself. It is in that context that our personal deliberations (including even your reading of this book) are an integral part of what will emerge as our children's world of tomorrow. That's why today's leaders need to set the stage for mutual understanding and mutual agreement on how to proceed, including a recognition that today's leadership is now necessarily collective. The crafting of a successful response to our social and ecological challenges requires an awakening to our inherent capacities for collective knowing, collective foresight and collective action.

Well before modern psychology, naturalist Ralph Waldo Emerson reflected on what he called the "oversoul" that could arise in earnest conversation: "In all conversations between two persons, tacit reference is made, as to a third party, to a common nature. That third party or common nature is not social; it is impersonal; it is God. And so in groups where debate is earnest, and especially on high questions, the company becomes aware that the thought rises to an equal level in all bosoms, that all have a spiritual property in what was said, as well as the sayer. They all become wiser than they were. It arches over them like a temple, this unity of thought. . . . All are conscious of attaining to a higher self-possession. It shines for all.[11]

It is in that spirit that I leave for your reflection a consideration of what role an ownership stake might play in facilitating participation in the conversations that count in your community. In looking back over more than two decades of rumination on this distinctly social notion, I now see the wisdom in a theory once espoused by British philosopher Fritz Schumacher. "Knowledge," he cautioned, "obliges you. If you don't use it, it poisons you." I only hope that any knowledge you may have gleaned from this book will now be put to good use.

I invite readers to contact me with their thoughts, suggestions and comments c/o The Gates Group, 1266 West Paces Ferry Road; Suite 505; Atlanta, Georgia 30327; USA. Those inclined to support this work are urged to send their tax-deductible contributions to the nonprofit Center for Ownership Solutions at the same address. An acknowledgment of receipt will be provided. (Visit our web site at www.ownershipsolution.com.)

Making Assets Accountable

This appendix expands on Chapter 4 ("Putting the 'Own' Back in Ownership").

There was a time when, if an institutional investor was dissatisfied with an investment, he would take what became known as the "Wall Street walk," selling the shares to signal his displeasure. Now the mammoth size of these investors (pension trustees, mutual fund managers) makes this remedy infeasible, even unwise. Institutions are often a company's single largest shareholder. To a remarkable extent, they *are* the market. Thus, any attempt to unload shares could cause share prices to plummet before institutions could fully unload their holdings, the financial equivalent of shooting themselves in the foot.

The three largest pension plans in the United States are now TIAA/CREF (a nationwide plan for teachers and researchers), the California Public Employees Retirement System (Calpers) and New York State's state and local systems. Their combined June-1997 holdings totaled $381 billion. In addition to the difficulties they confront in selling, many of them are, in effect, permanent shareholders. Because their pension obligations mature decades into the future, they hold securities for very long periods.

Faced with these realities, the question then becomes, how can they best influence corporate performance? Many of them lack the staff, the expertise and even the interest to exercise traditional ownership rights in a direct, sustained and responsible fashion. For instance, New York State fund is run by the state comptroller, an elected official with a relatively small staff of civil servants. Calpers invests in hundreds of companies. Its trustees cannot possibly sit on that many boards of directors, attend hundreds of shareholder meetings or evaluate thousands of quarterly financial statements. TIAA/CREF indexes two-thirds of its stock portfolio, actively managing only about one hundred stocks. But even one hundred companies is a lot to monitor, much less influence.

Even if an institutional investor *were* qualified to act, it would face a "collective choice" dilemma. If New York's comptroller devotes resources to improving a company's performance, the benefit will be spread among all shareholders, even though only New York incurred the costs. Much like small investors, these big investors are inclined to be "rationally ignorant." Because they realize so little benefit from exercising their atomized voting rights, they have often elected not to become informed enough to vote. Stymied by this dilemma yet prodded by government policymakers to "do something," institutional investors began to consider how best they could exercise their dormant ownership rights. As we shall see, that hugely important, little-understood and largely invisible struggle continues to consume the institutional-investor community in its search for an ownership solution.

If You Can't Walk, You Better Talk

One of the early policy prods came in the mid-1980s, when the pension branch of the Department of Labor announced that it viewed voting rights on pension-held shares as having real economic value. Thus, pension trustees would be expected to vote their shares rather than remain rationally ignorant, and they would have to vote in the best interests of the pension beneficiaries. Because the only lawful purpose of pension plans is to accumulate funds for retirement, that became an obligation to vote to maximize financial returns.

Pension reform legislation enacted in 1974 laid the groundwork for the quandary facing institutional investors, who now have no choice but to devise ways to exercise their ownership "voice." The very concept of the corporation as personal property has long assumed that those who own the property (the stockholders) will oversee the board of directors who, in turn, will oversee day-to-day managers. With the growth of distant and rationally ignorant shareholders, this system of checks and balances began to unravel. As a result, companies were not being managed to maximize shareholder value (as reflected in the price of their shares).

Economists suggest that this was a predictable "agency cost" accompanying the abdication of ownership by remote, uninvolved pension trustees. Out of this "ownerless" environment emerged the leveraged buyout (LBO) and the hostile takeover, often combined in the same transaction as LBO artisans spotted underperforming companies and took them over. With a government mandate that trustees should maximize the value of pension assets, pension trustees were left with little choice when faced with an offer to buy a company. If a premium was offered over the shares' current market value, trustees felt obliged to sell.[1] This dilemma converted institutional investors into virtually certain sellers for anyone offering to buy shares at a premium. That obligation to sell, in turn, practically guaranteed that any share bid above the current price would put a company "in play" by making it susceptible to a takeover, either by the original bidder or by someone else making a higher offer. Pension-plan trustees soon became pawns in a pricing game in which their discretion was limited largely to one issue: who would pay the most for their shares.

At this point a great divide developed within the ranks of the giants in the institutional arena: the public-sector versus the private-sector pension plans.

Public-sector pension trustees were largely unconcerned with the potentially disruptive impact of takeovers on corporate managers and directors. Their focus was solely on financial returns. Plus, any increased return for state-sponsored plans meant less taxpayer dollars required to fund their plans, a political plus. Those managing corporate-sponsored plans saw it differently. After all, it was their fellow managers and directors who bear the brunt of this new scrutiny and accountability—and who live with the stress and personal trauma of coping with an environment characterized by the specter of hostile takeovers.*

With the Wall Street Walk no longer a possibility; with disruptive, debt-laden hostile buyouts falling into some disfavor (though they've recently come back); and with many states responding favorably to executives' pleas for takeover protection, institutional investors turned their attention to how they might exercise their ownership voice to improve the performance of companies in their portfolios.

In an ongoing attempt to upgrade the quality of corporate governance, a movement has emerged that centers on a series of board-related changes. Each focuses on transforming directors' relations with the corporation. The four primary changes: (1) using more "outside" directors and bringing to the board more diversity; (2) removing management directors from key board committees; (3) splitting the posts of chief executive officer and chairman of the board; and (4) ensuring that directors own shares in the companies they oversee so that their interests are aligned with those of the shareholders. Let's briefly review each of these.

Outside Directors

The trend toward the use of outside, nonexecutive directors reflects an attempt to separate the overseers (company directors) from the overseen (company executives), a key principle of trusteeship. Thus, institutional investors are pushing for more independent directors, for more diversity among board members, for periodic board-led reviews of senior managers, and for the board appointment of an experienced "lead director" who could run the board during a management crisis. This movement toward director independence is well advanced, with some companies going so far as to disqualify company executives as candidates for board membership. The diversity movement is driven by the realization that some 63 percent of outside directors of the largest one thousand U.S. companies are chief executive officers of other companies. Overall, CEOs sit on an average of two boards each. The concern is that their admittedly worthwhile experience may be offset by a mindset that thinks more in terms of the interests of managers than of shareholders. The

---

* A 1997 executive survey by staffing company Robert Half International Inc. found that the number one fear of most executives is job loss because of a merger or acquisition. Reported in *The Wall Street Journal,* 11 November 1997, p. 1.

overall goal of these two changes is to bring to corporate oversight a broader range of views. However, as *The Economist* notes: "The idea that there is a kind of ideal non-executive, simultaneously disinterested and expert, is as beguiling—and improbable—as the notion of the wise old king dispensing justice from beneath a shady tree."[2]

Reformed Board Committees

Board reform also focuses on the makeup of certain key committees of the board, particularly the nominating committee, the compensation committee and the audit committee. The panel that nominates board members is commonly chaired (or dominated) by the chief executive officer or other insiders. Although the shareholders elect directors from among those nominated, this nominating power effectively enables managers to select those charged with their oversight, an arrangement not well designed to provide either a check or a balance.

The compensation committee, charged with setting pay and benefits of executives, is often similarly staffed. Within the relatively small fraternity of top corporate executives, those serving on compensation committees (typically CEOs of other companies) know that the pay established for executives in one company will be used as a benchmark to set pay in other companies, including their own. Given such a cozy arrangement (with its "racheting up" effect on management pay), it should come as no surprise to find that during the 1980s, chief executives' pay grew far faster than either corporate profits or production workers' wages.

In an indirect attempt to address this issue, the Securities and Exchange Commission issued rules requiring that companies include in their annual report three items meant to shine light on this murky area. The rules require a chart in the annual report listing the pay and benefits of the top five executives, including stock grants and stock options along with an estimation of their value. The second is a statement from the board's compensation committee summarizing the rationale for this level of compensation, in the hope that boards will find it more difficult to award pay raises (or stock options) unless linked to performance. The third requirement is a disclosure of cross-directorships among board members, so that shareholders and potential investors can better evaluate for themselves the extent of this mutual back-scratching and lack of diversity.

The last area of board-committee concern is the audit committee, charged with providing the board an independent assessment of the company on a wide range of issues—financial, managerial, strategic, and so on. Because of the intended oversight function of the board, independence may be the most critical for this committee. It is not unusual for key shareholders to serve on both the board and the audit committee. At Coca-Cola, for example, billionaire Warren Buffett, an 11 percent shareholder, serves on both.

The main culprit behind poor corporate performance, according to Harvard Business School professor Michael Jensen, is the failure of these key internal control systems. The board's lack of accountability shows up as managerial empire-building, missed opportunities, the cross-subsidization of marginal operations within a corporate group and an unwillingness to confront the pain (restructuring, paring product lines, etc.) required to compete in the global marketplace.

Overseer and Overseen

Another area of concern focuses on the common practice whereby one person serves as both CEO and chairman of the board (charged with oversight of the CEO). John Nash, president of the National Association of Corporate Directors, estimates that 40 percent of America's Fortune 500 largest industrial companies will soon have split the jobs of chairman and CEO. Institutional investors are also concerned with how directors are financially linked to the company. As Adam Smith pointed out over two centuries ago:

> The directors . . . being the managers of other people's money than of their own, it cannot be well expected that they should watch over it with the same anxious vigilance with which the partners in a private co-partnery frequently watch over their own. . . . Negligence and profusion, therefore, must always prevail, more or less, in the management of the affairs of such a company.

With increasing frequency, institutional investors address this issue with an ownership solution: they want to know that their funds (and the company's managers) are being monitored by boards made up of directors who have some of their own wealth at risk in the company. In the past, directors were typically compensated with per-meeting fees (and expenses) in addition to a range of benefits, typically including health care and a pension. The latest trend is to provide company shares as part or all of directors' benefits packages, either as share grants or in the form of share options. A prestigious Blue Ribbon Commission on Director Compensation formed by the National Association of Corporate Directors devised a 1995 plan to link board pay more closely to shareholders' interests. The primary recommendations: (a) pay directors primarily in company stock, "with equity representing a substantial portion, up to 100 percent," (b) set a substantial stock ownership target and deadline for each director, (c) abolish all board member benefits programs because they tend to reward longevity rather than performance, (d) ban outside directors or their firms from providing professional or financial services, and (e) fully disclose each director's pay and perquisites in the proxy statement.

A 1996 Towers Perrin survey of proxies in 250 of the largest U.S. industrial companies reveals that 80 percent included stock in the compensation of their board directors (in 1985, only 3 percent used stock to pay directors).[3] At its most extreme, this director-targeted ownership solution pays directors *solely* in shares, a strategy now used at Travelers Insurance and Scott Paper Company.[4] A similar ownership solution has long been used to attract and retain high-performing managers and other top performers, typically through a combination of stock grants and stock options.

Aligned Managers/Director-Owners

The drawbacks inherent in separating ownership from control were first chronicled six decades ago, at a time when the development of capital markets coincided with a drift away from "proprietor capitalism" and toward "managerial capitalism." This phenomenon predates the 1930s, when Adolph A. Berle and Gardiner Means wrote their classic text, *The Modern Corporation and Private Property*, describing the "atomization" of ownership and the rise of professional managers over whom absentee owners exercised less and less influence. Business historian Alfred Chandler later characterized this system as "managerial capitalism" in his Pulitzer Prize–winning chronicle of American industry, *The Visible Hand*.

This dramatic change was a two-sided coin, accompanied by both costs and benefits. The benefits included the ability to amass ever larger sums of financial capital through the capital markets, a helpful ingredient in raising the funds required for costly, multiyear investment projects. In addition, access to capital markets gave potential investors access to diversification and liquidity, which lowered risk, thereby reducing the cost of capital as investors became willing to accept lower rates of return. Separating the owner from the role of owner-manager also greatly expanded the pool of potential managers and led to the development of a steadily expanding group of professional managers, a still-growing and increasingly crucial service sector.

Though these managers may not have been personally well-to-do (at least at the outset), they quickly discovered that separation of ownership from control offered them an opportunity to behave as though they were. Corporate "empire building" became an early symptom of managerial excess. Lavish living soon followed. After the 1989 takeover of RJR Nabisco, the new owners sold what was known as "Ross's Air Force" of twenty-six planes, including eleven personal jets (Ross Johnson was RJR's longtime chairman and CEO). At American Express, a 1994 shuffle in the upper echelons resulted in exposing (and disposing of) ousted chief executive James Robinson's plush Manhattan penthouse suite, in which shareholders had invested some $12 million. Top executives also became notorious for moving corporate headquarters from long-established locales to communities closer to their homes or even to their vacation homes, such as Scott Paper Company's relocation from Philadelphia to Boca Raton, Florida.[5]

Due in part to such managerial excesses, several public-sector institutional investors (led by Calpers) banded together to oppose one of the more obvious abuses of management prerogatives: efforts to entrench themselves with techniques designed to impede hostile takeovers. These investors reckoned that capital markets should be given full play, particularly in light of their return-oriented mandate as pension trustees. Typically, takeover defenses involved changes in corporate voting rights or in the company's capital structure when an uninvited offer was made for the company's shares (such as diluting the acquirer by issuing more shares).

The managerial abuses associated with the divorce of owners from operators seemed to become more extreme as the institutionalization of ownership became more extreme. Although the current response to this trend takes many forms, the most common response is to address these divided loyalties by ensuring that managers and directors are linked to the company not only as employees but also as employee-owners, ideally as significant owners. Needless to say, this switch in emphasis from fear to greed attracted the enthusiastic support from those it was meant to incentivize.[6] Proponents suggest that success in addressing this agency cost dilemma (i.e., by creating more "inside" owners) is proven by the upward shift in share values seen in those companies that encourage such "active" ownership strategies (i.e., by key insiders), regardless of whether that ownership comes through leveraged buyouts or through executive share schemes.[7]

It is not at all clear either (*a*) that today's executive-focused ownership schemes need to be as generous as they are, or (*b*) that they are working as intended. For instance, when shares decline in value below the option purchase price (known as an "underwater" option), companies frequently grant new options to replace the old. Such "risk-free" ownership is not the sort enjoyed by traditional proprietors whose stake these schemes are meant to mimic. More generally, it is clear that this tightly targeted ownership solution (limited to top managers and directors) is not, in itself, sufficient to stimulate the performance required in today's globally competitive environment. Something more is needed.[8]

Rent-an-Owner

Another ownership strategy focuses on what Wall Street calls "relationship investing" or, for the more skeptical, "rent-an-owner." The basic premise is simple. An institutional investor places a sum of money, say $500 million, with an investment banking firm. That firm then buys meaningful stakes in several companies, ideally acquiring enough to merit a seat on the board of directors. The firm then acts as a surrogate voice for the institution, thereby providing the active, inside, hands-on component of ownership currently lacking among institutional investors. The firm also provides technical market-analysis in initially selecting the investment and ongoing advice regarding corporate strategy, finance, governance and so on, with the goal of assisting the institutional investor in focusing on improving rather than changing (or "churning") their investments. Ideally, the investment bankers invest their own funds as well, insuring that they also are at-risk proprietors. Typically, the firm charges an annual fee and shares in any increase in share value above a prescribed floor.

Numerous investment-banking firms propose to provide this "surrogate ownership" service to the institutional investor community. Lazard Freres's "Corporate Partners" was one of the first when it took a negotiated ownership position in Polaroid in the 1980s at a time when the company was under the pressure of a hostile takeover bid. However, this strategy, too, has severe limitations. For instance, the advantage of additional inside information may be offset by a loss of liquidity because of legal limitations on the ability of insiders to trade shares based on information not generally available to outsiders. This strategy also suffers from a classic "free rider" problem. Instead of other investors developing their own monitoring strategy, they may elect to ride on the coattails of this effort, buying or selling in lockstep with those they know are privy to better information.

In addition, this "insider" service is already being provided in a limited way, both by the opportunity to invest in various leveraged-buyout funds and by the opportunity to buy a stake in quoted companies that, in turn, specialize in such investing. For example, both Warren Buffett–directed Berkshire Hathaway and U.K.-headquartered Hanson Industries offer an opportunity to invest in a business whose sole purpose is to identify undervalued companies in which to invest and, with more hands-on, motivated management, increase the value of investors' shares.

This particular ownership solution frequently sounds better in the general explanation than in the fine print. For instance, such "relationship" investors often insist on acquiring a specially tailored class of high-dividend-paying preferred shares granting them priority both in liquidation and in their claim on corporate earnings (Lazard's strategy at Polaroid). This preferred stake creates a potential conflict between their ownership stake, with its focus on short-term results, and that of other shareholders who hold more risky common stock.

Finance Model, Market Myopia or Total Wealth Creation

In closing this appendix, it may prove useful to return to the issue with which we began Chapter 4: how to put the *own* back in ownership. In an attempt to broadly characterize the various reasons why corporate governance systems frequently produce less than terrific results, Brookings Institution economist Margaret Blair offers three revealing clusters of arguments categorizing the key viewpoints influencing this crucial area.[9]

The first cluster she calls the "finance model," which argues that absentee shareholders lack sufficient influence over management, leading to poor performance and lavish executive living. This group views with favor the activism of institutional investors, hopeful that their actions will wield a positive influence. Thus, finance-model adherents support a broad range of reform proposals to enhance shareholder voice and restrain managers and directors in, for example, their ability to compensate themselves (say with stock options), unless that compensation is based on criteria linked to proven performance in enchancing shareholder value.

The second cluster, broadly characterized as "market myopia," is comprised of those who object to the fact that the shareholder focus on short-term profits and share value is at the expense of building the company for the long term. In their view, shareholders have too much power, and management needs to be shielded from an overemphasis on short-term stock prices. This group, too, generally views with favor the activism of institutional shareholders, but in the hope that this largely permanent shareholder group will tend to take a longer-term view.[10]

Market myopia supporters look for ways to shield management and boards from the excessive influence of short-term-oriented financial markets. Those include proposed changes to the firm's environment, such as abolishing quarterly reports and imposing transaction taxes to discourage frequent trading. They also propose corporate-focused changes, such as electing directors for longer terms, developing alternative measures of performance, using broader definitions of corporate assets, overhauling investment budgeting methods (for instance, to include employee training) and generally ensuring that long-term value creation takes precedence over short-term stock prices.

The third set of arguments (previewed in Chapter 4) suggests that share-value maximization for those providing *financial* capital may not produce the best possible results for society as a whole. This view directly challenges the historical notion that those who put up risk capital should be considered the only owners. Instead, Blair proposes that the boundaries of firms be redesigned to create a greater sense of proprietorship for all those who have put assets at risk, not just those who have put *financial* assets at risk.

Accountability and the Global Corporation

This accountability issue has substantially broader implications than those generally taken into consideration by a financial analyst trying to justify the merits of investing in one corporation rather than another. The emergence of global challenges (such as the environment), along with the globalization of trade, capital markets and the corporate entity itself, has not been matched by a globalization of laws affecting corporate policymaking. There is no such thing as global corporate law. For the most part, the corporate entity roams the world freely, constrained by local, not international, law.

To date, this has meant that each country tailors its scope of corporate responsibility to its peculiar priorities. Public-policy oversight is practically nonexistent in certain countries. In the United States, for example, the bulk of major corporations are chartered in Delaware, a state known for its laissez-faire attitude toward corporate behavior. In a frenzied attempt to bolster sagging tax revenues and create jobs, other states actively court corporate headquarters by aggressively competing in a regulatory "race to the bottom."[11] That suggests a major challenge for those who would impose accountability from *outside* the corporate entity.

The trend toward more "inside" ownership continues to gather momentum. As Professor Jensen points out, having insiders *without* ownership is now widely regarded as a wasted opportunity to improve enterprise efficiency. In a similar vein, World Bank economist David Ellerman points to the desirability of ensuring that "effort relevant" investors (managers, employees, suppliers, distributors) hold much of a corporation's equity, leaving its debt securities to those whose efforts have little or no operational impact. Overall, the trend toward more consciously engineered, ownership-based accountability seems certain to continue.

From a political perspective, the fear of concentrated financial power is likely to prove a barrier to the pursuit of other possible avenues of accountability. Although it is technically and legally feasible for institutional investors to jointly bring pressure to bear on the management of poor-performing companies, the specter of coordinated action by these modern-day "multibillionaires" is certain to raise eyebrows, particularly in a financial environment in which their influence is becoming steadily more apparent. Sensing this might well be the reaction, several of the larger institutional players now make a point of staying well clear of even the perception of collaboration or cooperation, fearful that they may invite scrutiny, criticism and regulation should any move be made in that direction. That, too, suggests more interest in promoting indirect, insider-focused means for making institutionalized assets more accountable.

Dissecting Modern Ownership

This appendix "dissects" modern corporate ownership into its components. The goal is to clarify what the term *ownership* means by illustrating how bits and pieces of ownership can be created and conveyed.

Any ownership solution must include an effort to define it. For instance, during the early 1990s, contingents of Russian and Ukraine managers traveled to Duke University's Fuqua School of Business for a management-development program. In the session on privatization of state-owned enterprises, I routinely began by asking the participants, "What is ownership?" Without exception, the answer was "control." Those familiar with the Russian psyche will hardly find that surprising. Though control is certainly one element of ownership, that fails to paint the complete picture. Due to the enormous diversity and flexibility in ownership structures, particularly within its most common commercial form, the corporation, the term *ownership* can be misleading, in the same way that use of the generic term *dog* transcends the obvious discrepancies called up by the names poodle and Great Dane.

Peruvian economist Hernando De Soto suggests that ownership confers "the right to use, enjoy and dispose of property." Even that is only a partial dissection. To fully understand the formulation of an ownership solution, we need to examine each of its parts. In complexity theory, it's well known that innovations usually involve assembling known building blocks in new ways.[1] This appendix describes the key building blocks from which corporate ownership solutions are constructed.

At the outset, it should be noted that corporate shares represent a proportional part of the corporation, with each share embodying a mix of seven categories of rights: liquidation rights, appreciation rights, transfer rights, income rights, voting rights, information rights and certain public rights. Below I describe each of these rights.

Liquidation Rights. Ask an economist to describe the rights accompanying corporate shares and the response will likely be "residual rights"—meaning shareholders have a right to share in whatever is left over (the residual) after all other creditors are paid. Where "preferred" shares are part of a corporation's capital structure, those shares have a priority claim over the "common" shares in carving up the corporate carcass should the company's affairs be wound up and the assets sold.

Russia's lack of enforceable liquidation rights was one of the first stumbling blocks on the road to economic reform. In economist Douglass North's terminology, they lacked "fully functioning" property rights. A key missing ingredient: a fully functioning bankruptcy law. If a loan went sour, Russian banks had no reliable way to force a company into liquidation, with the hope of recovering its funds by selling the collateral. Because the liquidation right lacked the force of law, the property rights weren't fully functional.

Appreciation Rights. The ability to capture any increase (appreciation) in the value of a company's shares is a key attraction of shareholding, particularly in a buoyant stock market. Nowhere has that been more obvious than in the United States, where the market has soared to record heights for seven consecutive years. The ability to run the risk of any decrease in the value of corporate shares (and to harvest any gain) is at the heart of capitalism's risk/reward system. Any increase in value is typically realized by eventually selling the shares and pocketing the capital gain. This component of ownership is easily and often split off into a separate ownership right. Corporate executives are routinely granted stock options allowing them to buy shares in the future at a price set today. A 1997 study by the National Center for Employee Ownership found that over 5 million U.S. employees now work for companies that provide stock options to most of their employees.[2]

The exercise of an option may be linked to the passage of time, to a certain event or to some aspect of enterprise performance, such as repayment of debt (a common feature of leveraged buyouts) or a measurable benchmark of performance, such as achieving a target rate of profitability, cash flow or return on investment. Quite often, a minimum time period must lapse before an option can be exercised. These "golden handcuffs," ensure that valued employees will forfeit options if they quit early. Where options are granted on a periodic or "rolling" basis, these handcuffs may be perpetual. In the 1980s, it became common for top executives in the United States and Britain to be granted additional options (or an accelerated right to exercise outstanding options) when their company was taken over (commonly known as "golden parachutes"). Thus, poor management performance could itself lead to takeover speculation, accompanied by a sharp rise in the share price, handsomely rewarding key executives for their poor performance.

Transfer Rights. As De Soto points out, ownership generally implies the right to "use, enjoy and dispose" of the property. However, if, for example, a company wishes to use stock ownership to link the fortunes of the company and its employees, experience suggests that where those shares are immediately transferable, cash-strapped employees often will sell their shares and pocket the cash, severing the hoped-for linkage. Thus, if long-term employee shareholding is the goal, some type of "lock-in" is advisable to restrict transfer. That restriction, in turn, implies a lower share value, partially offsetting the appeal of appreciation.

In the case of an ESOP, the employees' shares are inaccessible while they are being paid for with the proceeds of an employer loan. Without that restriction, any required repurchase of shares *from* employees might impair the company's financial ability to purchase shares *for* employees. Transfer rights can be restricted in other ways, as well. For example, the United Steelworkers negotiated a "right of first refusal" in several labor contracts, whereby, should someone offer to buy a company, the company is obliged to grant employees several months to submit a competitive bid.

Income Rights. Every corporation has a variety of claims on its income. These claims are generally "layered" according to their priority. Payments due on a bank loan are senior to those due holders of less senior "subordinated" debt, which in turn, will take priority over dividend payments to the last-in-line "residual" claimants: the shareholders. Shareholders, in turn, will be paid dividends on a similarly layered basis, depending on whether they are holders of ordinary ("common") shares or more senior "preferred" shares.

The corporation became the world's preeminent commercial organization largely because of this "layer cake" design determining the rights and responsibilities, risks and rewards of various stakeholders. Privatization is commonly defined as a transfer of control over a company's cash flows from the state to private hands. Of course, income rights do not entitle an owner to income. Even quite sizable wealth holdings may not be accompanied by a sizable income. In Hawaii, the Robinson family owns land on the islands of Niihau and Kauai valued at more than a half billion dollars. Yet the vast bulk of the land is undeveloped and much of the income (generated largely from farming and cattle) is committed to pay property taxes. Despite being asset-rich, the Robinsons are income-poor.

Voting Rights. Voting rights, a key element in determining corporate control, are viewed by many as the most important component of ownership—as the comments by Russian managers suggest. Issues affecting voting and control are referred to generally as "corporate governance," which, broadly defined, sets the ground rules for determining who exercises control under what circumstances, who is subjected to what risks and who harvests what rewards. During the turn-of-the-century heyday of the so-called robber baron capitalists, governance of the corporation was largely a one-person show. Those owner-operators were actively involved in day-to-day management, using their appointed "surrogates" largely to administer rather than guide the corporation. With many of those early fortunes now in foundations or split among heirs with often widely divergent degrees of involvement, much of the modern debate on governance focuses on this separation of ownership and control and how to maintain accountability (described in Appendix A).

Information Rights. Access to corporate information has value, including potential value in the hands of competitors who may wish to profit from that information. Thus, even publicly listed corporations often divulge only limited amounts of information on a narrow range of subjects. Nevertheless, access to a certain amount of information is an implied right of ownership. Securities laws, for example, require minimum levels of disclosure before shares may be offered for sale except to sophisticated investors. On the other hand, trading on "inside" information is severely constrained.

Steelworkers bargained successfully for the right to name a board member to each of the six largest integrated steel companies, thereby assuring themselves of access to board-level information. In a similar development, many of the better-performing companies are now turning to "open book management," reasoning that honesty is the best information policy and that an informed workforce will be better motivated to enhance company performance.[3]

Public Rights. Despite often heated debates about the merits of public versus private ownership, the bittersweet truth is that government is a preferred shareholder with a "golden share" in every corporation worldwide. Let me explain. Once a corporation has paid its allowable expenses, including setting funds aside for depreciation, the next claimant on its revenues is not the preferred shareholders but the government. If that claim is not paid (i.e., akin to a preferred "dividend"—in the form of taxes), the government can exercise its implied golden share (i.e., implied under federal tax law), seize the company's assets and liquidate them to satisfy that claim.

Explicit golden shares are commonly found where government retains an interest following the privatization of a state-owned enterprise. For example, the government of Ghana retained a golden share enabling it to block any takeover of its partially privatized Ashanti Goldfields Company. Likewise, in the privatization of British Telecom, the Thatcher government initially retained a golden share permitting it to force the sale of shares by anyone accumulating more than 15 percent of the company.

This appendix has intentionally focused on the rights that accompany corporate ownership. Readers may rightly ask about the corporate responsibilities that accompany those rights. Suffice it to say that the responsibilities are few. With the exception of those activities either banned by government (child labor) or mandated by government (minimum wage, job safety, etc.), the corporate entity operates largely in a do-as-you-please environment.

Invoking control or jurisdiction is fraught with difficulties, both philosophical and practical. DeAnne Julius of Royal Dutch Shell acknowledged the dilemma when she pointed out: "In any fundamental sense, only people have nationalities."[4] How is a transnational firm's nationality to be defined? By the nationality of those who benefit from its success? By that of its shareholders? Its employees? Where the firm is chartered? Where it produces most of its goods? Where it generates most of its sales or profits? "An Anglo-Saxon economist would choose the nationality of its shareholders as the best criterion," Julius suggests. "A German or Japanese economist—and most politicians—would prefer the nationality of its workforce." In a very fundamental sense, the transnational corporation need answer only to its owners.

Core Ingredients in Any Ownership Solution

This appendix reviews the basic design issues that arise in structuring an employee stock ownership plan and expands on matters discussed in Chapter 5 ("Up-Close Capitalism— The Employee Ownership Solution").

Plan Establishment, Coverage and Participation

Key design issues in structuring an employee stock ownership plan include who initiates action: the company, the employees, current shareholders or the government. For instance, Hungarian ESOP law requires a lengthy, employee-initiated twelve-step process. Poland and Russia require that a minimum number of employees endorse an ESOP, whereas in the United States, Britain and Jamaica, an ESOP may be initiated by any party, though it is most commonly the sponsor company that plans, designs and implements it.

Employees' shares may be held directly or by a trust-like vehicle such as an escrow account, a foundation or an employees' association. In Egypt, for example, 320 ESOPs were in place in mid-1997 with shares held by shareholder associations. Or employees can hold the shares directly, perhaps with a transfer restriction prohibiting sale before a designated time or event.

In determining who gets what in an ESOP, employees often receive allocations relative to their pay or based on a formula that awards points for a combination of pay and service, enabling companies to recognize the contribution of longer-service, lower-income employees. In some countries, employees' shares "vest" (become nonforfeitable) over a period of years. Similarly, ESOP laws typically allow the exclusion of certain employees, such as those under a certain age, the newly hired or those working part-time. Also, unionized employees may well be excludable unless they agree to participate, recognizing that any other route would interfere with their right to bargain over terms and conditions of employment. Significant shareholders may also be ineligible (for example, Jamaica excludes those who already own 5 percent of the shares).

Voting and Control

The voting of shares is often a bone of contention, particularly where shares are not yet fully paid up. This is far from a mere theoretical issue. For instance, a company may fund a "leveraged" ESOP with the proceeds of a loan, with shares allocated to employees' accounts as the loan is paid. During this period, who votes the not-yet-paid-for shares if another company makes an offer to buy the company? Typically, those shares are voted either in proportion to the votes on allocated shares or in accordance with however the majority vote their shares.

Research by the National Center for Employee Ownership found that employees place surprisingly little value on the voting component of ownership. Their concern leans more to the ESOP's financial features, with a preference for large annual contributions and a steadily increasing account balance. They also prefer that their employer consult with them on workplace- (versus boardroom-) related issues—where they feel their competence is underutilized.

Corporate governance in employee-ownership companies has long been a nagging issue. If, for example, employee-shareholders as a group comprise a significant stake in a company, the question arises as to whether that entitles the employees (or the ESOP trustee) to a board seat. One view insists that it does, while another suggests that this inappropriately assumes that employees are a homogeneous group rather than reflecting a range of views and opinions, like other shareholders. Critics also worry that the organizational requirements for selecting an employee board member would mimic those for establishing a labor union, a procedure that nonunion companies may resist, thereby discouraging them from establishing an ESOP.

More generally, some commentators reject the notion of "constituent" board members, arguing that boards are intended to represent the interests of *all* shareholders. Supporters counter that employees' views are excluded only at great cost to company performance, while others insist that alternative means are available for soliciting that feedback. The concept of supervisory boards, much utilized in Germany, offers a potential compromise, with employees participating in a supplemental board that oversees a more traditional managerial board. Another view proposes the mandatory use of "cumulative voting," whereby each employee's share has as many votes as there are board seats open for election, enhancing the likelihood that employees can pool their shares and elect a board representative.

Rights, Liquidity and Value

Diversification is also an ongoing issue. Employee-ownership advocates note that ESOP-style ownership provides workers with an asset that they know, and one in which their personal effort may well have some impact on value (versus assets held in a broadly diversified pension plan). Whereas one camp worries about exposing employees to risk, others suggest that this element of risk is just what is intended so that employees' attitudes and motivations are aligned with those of other shareholders. Some point out that risk is never eliminated from an economic system; it is only shifted around. Thus, some risk should appropriately be placed with those whose personal performance is crucial to performance. Compromises are typical. For example, U.S. law requires that an ESOP sponsor company provide employees an option to diversify 25 percent of their ESOP balance as they reach age fifty-five and another 25 percent at age sixty.

The liquidity of ESOP shares presents one of the most challenging tasks for both employee and employer. For those companies without readily tradable shares, a careful balance must be sought. On the one hand, employees eventually want cash for their shares. On the other hand, if the sponsor company is required to repurchase those shares, care must be taken not to overwhelm the company with either the magnitude or the timing of this liability, thereby adversely affecting the value of shares held by others, including other employee-owners. In the United States, ESOPs are permitted an extended period to pay out amounts due employees. Jamaica eases this burden by allowing companies a tax deduction both for the original share purchase *for* employees and the subsequent share repurchase *from* employees. Jamaica also defers any repurchase obligation on the part of the employer until the shares are first offered for sale to other employees.

That brings the issue of valuation fully into view. Where a company's shares are actively traded on an established exchange, their value is readily known, though employees may fare well or poorly depending on whether they sell their shares in good times or bad. The valuation of nontraded shares raises a host of thorny issues, particularly in environments lacking the appraisal skills commonly found in developed countries. The issue is largely one of competence and objectivity; ESOP-related rules generally require that valuations be done by experienced personnel who are independent of the company. The likelihood of mischief in this area is legendary, both at the outset, when the appraisal may determine the amount of tax relief allowed the employer, and later, when shares are repurchased from employees or exchanged for a more diversified portfolio, which may affect the amount of tax imposed on the employee or his estate.

Education, Expectations and Purpose

Of all the many challenges facing the implementation of ESOPs, perhaps the greatest lies in the area of education and training. Though we live in the age of global capitalism, no country (including the United States) educates its people to become capitalists. None. At best they are educated to be workers, and often not well even for that. The concept of owning a paper asset (shares) is foreign to many. In addition, employees often have unrealistic expectations about what it means to be a shareholder: some equate it with a "get rich quick" scheme, while others imagine it entitles them to take over management of the company. Unrealistic expectations can be the undoing of even the most carefully engineered ESOP. In the best of circumstances, all parties involved acknowledge that managers have the right to manage and employees have the right to be managed right.

Disputes regarding the purpose of employee ownership can also prove challenging. Entrepreneurs may view employee ownership as an attractive alternative to the outright sale of the company. Or as an alternative to an exchange of their shares for shares of another company. An ESOP may allow them simultaneously to generate liquidity for a new venture while also retaining a controlling interest in their current venture. Bankers may view ESOPs as a new lending opportunity and as a way to offer a broader range of services to their clients, including lending and trustee services.

Workers may see shareholding as another component in their compensation package, supplementing other employer-provided benefits such as health care or a pension. Or they may see it as a way to secure their jobs and anchor the company's physical capital. Or they may view it as a way to supplement their income with dividends or profit sharing. Labor union leaders may see it as a way to deliver a victory to their members in difficult times, or as a way to access financial information to better inform union strategists what is needed to preserve jobs or protect their members' pensions.

Managers may view the concept quite differently, depending on their position in the company. Operations managers may see employee ownership as a component of a total quality management program and as a way to foster an environment in which everyone has both something at risk and some way to share in the rewards. Mid-level supervisors, on the other hand, may view employee ownership as a threat, particularly if accompanied by workplace participation schemes that alter current management practices.

Policymakers may view employee ownership as a way to improve economic performance and competitiveness, thereby enhancing tax revenues to offset the cost of ESOP tax incentives. Or they may see employee ownership as a component of a broader strategy to promote broad-based asset holdings as an antidote to the fiscal strains accompanying entitlements. Or it may be seen as a politically helpful element in building a constituency for privatization or for free enterprise more generally. Or it may be viewed as a populist-inspired response to the concentration of wealth, or as a way for constituents and communities to empower themselves economically.

The challenge lies in recognizing that not all of these goals may be attainable, at least not at the outset. Over time, as an employee ownership program is designed, implemented and matures, these various agendas may be fulfilled to greater or lesser degrees. In the interim, however, these diverse viewpoints can be an ongoing source of debate among the various parties involved. This is best anticipated and resolved with an early statement of goals and objectives, both short- and long-term. Quite commonly, ESOP companies publish a corporate "vision statement" for this purpose, often with substantial input by all affected parties.

Institutional Challenges

Adapting ESOPs or other employee ownership schemes to developed countries may pose an array of political, social and financial challenges, but in those countries at least the institutional framework (legal, financial, regulatory) is usually in place and fully functioning. That often is not the case for developing countries or for those countries making the shift from command to market economies. The financial community may well lack resources to support ownership-transfer transactions, particularly where (as is often the case) the creditworthiness of companies is questionable or, due to poor accounting or bookkeeping practices, is simply unknown. Add to that the potential need for restructuring, plus the new and uncertain impact of employee ownership, and the institutional barriers can be quite daunting.

Similarly, the government may lack the fiscal capacity to provide financial encouragement for ESOPs, particularly where structural-adjustment agreements with international financial institutions limit the government's policy discretion. In addition, the ongoing need to finance a social safety net, often badly frayed, can place constraints on policymakers' ability to offer concessions to encourage employee ownership, particularly in the form of stock accumulation incentives for those who are already relatively well-off (i.e., those holding secure jobs and working for profitable companies). More fundamentally, it may take time to develop supportive institutions, particularly in those countries with little experience with corporations and weak capital markets. That can be further complicated by a lack of those key institutions that make a market possible, including a system of secure and transferable property, enforceable contracts and a reliable currency.

A development policy designed to alter something as fundamental (and emotional) as property rights also has the potential to create social tensions and insecurities, particularly among those few to whom ownership has typically been limited. In addition, traditional systems of property rights, including communal property rights (particularly common in the agricultural sector) may prove difficult to replace even where, from an efficiency viewpoint, corporatized groupings of farmland could yield economies of scale (in purchasing, marketing, access to financing, etc.) not presently available either through communal systems or through small-parcel family farming.

The lack of accurate or reliable company information can also pose a barrier, both to implementation and to the protection of potential owners. A tradition of closed and secretive family companies can impede both implementation and the willingness to share information. Notions of fiduciary obligation may also be new or not yet fully developed, posing a challenge to the indirect or trust-type holding of employees' shares. In addition, employee ownership may bring little if any new financial capital to the company, while possibly constraining other potential investors in making needed changes in the organization, such as layoffs and other forms of restructuring. Employee ownership may enhance or detract from a firm's attractiveness to potential investors depending on the circumstances, including the recent history of labor relations both within the company and within the overall political environment.

Where the political goal is substantial employee ownership, considerable training and management assistance may be required. Significant employee ownership in highly capital-intensive companies such as telecommunications or power generation may be financially impractical or socially inequitable. Price volatility can also be a concern, particularly where employees own a stake in companies heavily impacted by world commodity prices. Employees may also be skeptical of any proposal to make them co-owners, particularly in those countries with a colonial heritage or where exclusion from ownership has long been a fact of life. A lack of professional competence can also plague both policy design and implementation, particularly in such key service areas as law, accounting, appraisal and investment banking. Needed regulatory oversight may put an additional strain on public administration services already lacking sufficient staffing, funding, motivation and competence.

APPENDIX

GDP: What Gets Measured Gets Managed

Economics is the science of the measurable.[1] As a result, financial quantities often take precedence over more human-valued qualities, while gains in dollar-denominated measures, such as gross domestic product (GDP), are frequently put ahead of values that are more difficult to measure—community, civility, social trust, civic engagement, corruption, environmental sustainability and so forth. For this reason, the fashioning of ownership strategies requires a word about GDP—the gauge to which policymakers most often look in calibrating economic policy. Gross national product (GNP) was first used to estimate wartime productive capacity. It originated as a crude way to measure transactions in which money visibly changed hands through consumer spending, business investment, government purchases or foreign trade.

Nobel economist Simon Kuznets, an early proponent of the GNP concept, cautioned from the outset against overreliance on this imperfect measure, warning in 1934 that a nation's welfare can "scarcely be inferred from a measurement of national income." Yet more than six decades later, this yardstick continues to blur the distinctions between quantity and quality, between costs and benefits, between short and long term and between genuine accretions to wealth and unsustainable environmental practices. "Goals for 'more' growth," Kuznets warned, "should specify more growth of what and for what." Had he been more conscious of environmental and ownership issues, he might have added "from what" and "for whom."

Nowadays, the implicit assumption is that people are better off when spending is on the rise. That makes for certain perverse measures of progress. The cleanup expense of the Exxon *Valdez* oil spill, the costs of the O. J. Simpson murder trial, outlays for prison construction and rising fees paid divorce lawyers—each implies real progress. Working longer hours may require that parents shift childcare from the home to a paid daycare center, suggesting a rise in GDP but possibly a lower quality of life for both parent and child. Costs and benefits are given equal weight. Income and expense, even assets and liabilities—all are washed out by a measure that translates any dollar-denominated exchange into an economic "good," even if those exchanges reflect a weakening of the social glue that binds the nation together. It can even signal rising prosperity (because more money is changing hands) while much of the population is losing ground.[2] From 1973 to 1993, GDP rose 55 percent while real wages plunged almost 14 percent.[3]

Though GDP serves a useful function, it's a deceptive measure by which to set an economy's course. In evaluating the success of economic policy, University of Maryland economist Herman Daly suggests that present market measurements (such as household income and GDP) overlook what is often most important to people. "The quality of all his relationships," Daly argues, "defines the individual far more than what he consumes during a certain period."[4] Gary Becker, 1992 Nobel laureate economist, calculates that people devote about sixty hours a week to some productive use without engaging in market transactions—whether household chores or involvement in community activities. "We don't measure the value of all that," he says, "though it is precisely the accumulation of those values that we teach our children." Northwestern University professor emeritus Robet Eisner, former president of the American Economic Association, suggests that the inclusion of nonmarket transactions would add some 50 percent to our conventional measure of GDP.[5]

GDP falls short on other measures as well. From an ecological perspective, Daly points out that GDP views the Earth as though it were a business in liquidation, because policy accounting is fundamentally at odds with business accounting. For instance, as an oil company drains its reserves, the company can claim a depletion allowance, enabling the company to reduce its taxable income because it has less of the asset (oil reserves) with which to produce income. However, as that oil is sold, the depletion of that finite resource shows up as a *gain* in GDP. Moreover, its use may well be degrading the air, water, etc. Similar accounting skews global asset accounting. As international fishing exhausted the fisheries of the Georges Bank near Newfoundland, each nation counted that loss as a gain in national prosperity.[6]

Perpetual-Motion Economics

Perhaps most pernicious from an environmental perspective, reliance on GDP generates signals suggesting that conservation and habitat protection come only at the expense of progress and prosperity. That is analogous to saying that the oil company's depletion allowance (or the depreciation allowed for its oil-drilling equipment) must come at the expense of the business, when in truth it is the only way to ensure the future of the business. Perhaps oddest of all, GDP analyzes only a circular closed system of financial exchanges that take place from households to firms and back again, with no inlets or outlets, almost like a perpetual-motion machine. Daly points out that "it is exactly as if a biology textbook proposed to study an animal only in terms of its circulatory system, without ever mentioning its digestive tract. . . . Real animals have digestive tracts that connect them to their environment at both ends. . . . But in economics there is only the circulatory system."[7]

This oversight has spawned a new concept in economics, broadly known as "entropic flow" (from resources to waste) or "throughput." That puts a name to something we already know, namely that there is a one-way flow from environmental resources through firms and households and back to environmental sinks. The entropic throughput of matter and energy is a much more fundamental exchange than the circular exchanges measured by GNP— yet it escapes policy accounting. Throughput is a potential Trojan horse for conventional economics because, as Daly notes, once admitted into the paradigm, its hidden army of implications attacks nearly every assumption undergirding policymaking and economic science.[8] GDP, in particular, begins to look decidedly deficient as a measure of sustainable progress.

Measuring Both Progress and Regress

Even legitimate, environmentally sound growth can mask national policies that pamper a well-to-do elite while everyone else goes hungry or suffers under a repressive regime. A nation's seed corn could be stripped out, shipped abroad, converted to hard currency and deposited in the Swiss bank account of a corrupt ruler—and GNP/GDP would count that a win for the economy as a whole. Alternatives to GNP/GDP have been discussed for years. The gross progress indicator (GPI) attempts to assign monetary values where values are intrinsically difficult to assess (the prevalence of crime, the use of volunteers, the loss of leisure, etc.). The idea is that at least some estimate of value is more reasonable than zero.[9]

Redefining Progress, a San Francisco policy institute, publishes the GPI documenting twenty-five years of almost uninterrupted economic decline, contrasted with the official estimate of a 4.2 percent growth rate in GDP over the same period. Though the GPI confirms an upward curve in the economy from the early 1950s until about 1970, it finds a gradual decline of 45 percent since then. According to the institute, "the GPI reveals that much of what we now call growth of GDP is really just one of three things in disguise: fixing blunders and social decay from the past, borrowing resources from the future, or shifting functions from the traditional realm of household and community to the realm of the monetized economy. . . . The GDP operates like a business income statement that adds expenses to income instead of subtracting them. It is oblivious to the difference between progress and regress, loss and gain. . . . The GDP spirals ever upward by adding everything, making no distinction between costs and benefits, well-being or decline."[10]

In the absence of a proper measure of economic progress, we are unlikely to live within the limits of the natural world. Add to that today's remote-control, by-the-numbers, financial-return-driven decision-making and we have a certain formula for unsustainability, by any measure. As the economic system's feedback loops are currently wired, misinformed policymakers are incapable of making sensible policy choices. The ongoing globalization of both trade and finance makes it all the more urgent that we implement more sensible systems for signaling us both when things are going well and when they are going wrong. GPI staff pinpoint the problem:

> It is no accident that the social and environmental realms that have suffered such erosion in recent decades are precisely those that our systems of national accounting fail to address. Accounting drives policy, for business and the nation alike. It defines the issues that policy-makers seek to address. If economic indicators provide no feedback regarding matters crucial to human health and well-being, these will continue to be undermined by misguided policies. . . . It is important to recognize that the GDP deals with such questions already—in a misleading and backdoor way. It assigns to social and ecological capital an implicit and arbitrary value of zero. To use the GDP as a measure of progress is to assume that families and communities and the natural habitat add nothing to economic well-being, so that the nation can safely ignore their contributions, and, in fact, their destruction can be regarded as economic gain.[11]

In *The Ecology of Commerce*, Paul Hawken makes the case for a complementary signaling system if we are to manage our way toward a sustainable free enterprise:

> The massive inefficiencies of industrialism are not more apparent because they are masked by a financial system that gives improper information. . . . Instead of markets giving proper information, everything else is giving us proper information: our airsheds and our watersheds, our soil and riparian systems, our bodies and health, our society, inner cities and rural counties, the breakdown of stability worldwide and the outbreak of conflicts based on environmental shortages. All these are providing the information that our prices should be giving us but don't.

Notes

Introduction and Overview

1. For wealth distribution, see Edward N. Wolff, *Top Heavy: A Study of Increasing Inequality of Wealth in America* (New York: Twentieth Century Fund, 1995). For income distribution in sixteen industrial countries, see *Income Distribution in OECD Countries* (Washington, D.C.: Organization for Economic Cooperation and Development, November 1995).

2. In 1759, Glasgow University professor Adam Smith published *The Theory of Moral Sentiments*, a treatise on ethics that dealt with the role of "human sympathy" as the core of moral judgment. In 1776, he published *The Wealth of Nations*, his treatise on laissez-faire economics (what he called the "System of Natural Liberty") in which he focused on the role of "self-love" in the complex motivations underlying human action. Man's "self-interest" (the modern term) is encompassed in Smith's broader theory of ethics because, he believed, a proper regard for one's own happiness is a necessary element in virtue.

3. Mortimer Adler suggests that Jefferson's omission of any reference to property may reflect an attempt to ensure that the Declaration would be open to whatever means subsequent governments might discover in their effort to promote the general welfare. Mortimer J. Adler, *Haves Without Have-Nots* (New York: Macmillan, 1991).

4. In truth, most of the fertile land was by then already in private hands and no longer a part of the public domain. Many tracts were in remote areas and no provision was made for even elementary agricultural training. By 1890 only one of every three homesteaders had occupied his land long enough to obtain the deed to it. Much of the homesteaded land fell into the hands of large estate owners.

5. Alexis de Tocqueville, *Democracy in America* (1840).

6. Douglass C. North and Robert Paul Thomas, *The Rise of the Western World* (London: Cambridge University Press, 1973). The boundaries of this notion are now hotly debated, as the patenting of life forms (through patents granted on human genes since 1980) is being attacked by a broad base of religious groups as reducing life to its marketability and commoditization.

7. Although Whitney's invention was successful, patent infringements ruined his business. He then turned to the manufacture of firearms, later demonstrating to the U.S. government that, through the mass production of interchangeable parts, large numbers of muskets could be manufactured in a short time and repaired without delay, providing an early indication that government procurement can be a stimulus both to innovation and to wealth accumulation.

8. The concept of property rights continues to evolve and expand. In March 1995, the U.S. Supreme Court ruled that companies may claim property rights (in the form of trademarks) for certain colors associated with their products, holding that the Lanham Act of 1946 should be construed broadly in interpreting its language that trademarks include "any word, name, symbol, or device, or any combination

thereof." Administrative judges and trademark officials have authorized trademarks for particular shapes (a Coca-Cola bottle), sounds (the NBC network's distinctive chimes), and even smells (a peculiar scent of plumeria blossom on a sewing thread).

9. The notion of the commons retained its resonance within the thirteen original colonies, where the term *commonwealth* was used to describe three of the original thirteen states—Virginia, Massachusetts and Pennsylvania.

10. Some cities (New Haven, Jersey City) have securitized their unpaid property tax bills, cleaning out their inventory of unpaid bills by selling them at a discount, much as merchants sell their accounts receivable to financiers known as "factors." Other cities (New York) are borrowing against taxes due. For instance, investors (such as pension funds) will lend the city sixty cents for every dollar of unpaid tax bills.

11. WorldWatch Institute reports that, when measured by GNP, the number of the one hundred largest economic units in the world that are nations numbers forty-nine, while those units that are corporations (measured by revenues) number fifty-one. *WorldWatch* (May/June 1997), p. 39.

12. Adler, *Haves Without Have-Nots,* p. 41. See also Louis O. Kelso, "Karl Marx: The Almost Capitalist," *American Bar Association Journal* (March 1957).

13. John Maynard Keynes, *The General Theory of Employment, Interest and Money* (New York: Harcourt, Brace and World, Inc. First Harbinger Edition, 1964), p. 110.

CHAPTER 1
Disconnected Capitalism

1. All U.S. institutions held $11.1 trillion at the end of the second quarter of 1996, accounting for 21.4 percent of all outstanding U.S. assets, up from $6.3 trillion in 1990 and $673 billion in 1970. This represents a sixteenfold increase since 1970. By comparison, total U.S. financial assets grew less than twelvefold over the same period (from $4.6 trillion to $58.8 trillion). *Institutional Investor Report* (New York: The Conference Board, January 1997).

2. *Pensions and Investment Age* (22 January 1996). A 1995 Goldman, Sachs report predicted that the institutional fund management business will soon be dominated by no more than twenty-five companies, each with managed assets of at least $150 billion. As of July 1996, Goldman Sachs had $85 billion under management, including $23 billion for two British Coal pension funds. Merrill/Mercury Asset Management had $382 billion in managed assets. The February 1997 merger between Morgan Stanley and Dean Witter created a firm with $271 billion in managed assets. Globalization is bringing further consolidation. In June 1997, Zurich Group, the Swiss insurer, bought Scudder Stevens & Clark. The new entity has combined assets of more than $200 billion.

3. The other five are Kampo (the Japanese postal insurance system), Fidelity, Axa, Barclays and Merrill/Mercury Asset Management. Reported in "Swiss Merger Stirs Up Financial Industry," *Wall Street Journal,* 9 December 1997, p. A3.

4. The total number of mutual funds swelled from 1,430 in 1990 (when their total assets were about $1 trillion) to more than 8,100 by July 1997.

5. James M. Poterba and Andrew A. Samwick, *Stock Ownership Patterns, Stock Market Fluctuations, and Consumption.* Brookings Papers on Economic Activity, vol. 2 (Washington, D.C.: Brookings Institution, 1995), pp. 295–357, 368–372. Reprint (New York: National Bureau of Economic Research, 1995), no. 2027.

6. According to a 1992 Survey of Consumer Finances for the Federal Reserve and the Internal Revenue Service (utilizing different techniques), the portion of the

nation's wealth in the hands of the richest 1 percent of Americans declined to 30.4 percent from 37.1 percent from 1989 to 1992 and the next richest 9 percent saw their share of the wealth grow to 36.8 percent from 31.2 percent, while the bottom 90 percent of Americans saw their wealth rise to 32.8 percent in 1992 from 31.8 percent in 1989, a statistically insignificant increase. Reported in *The New York Times*, 13 March 1996, p. D1.

7. "Politics into economics won't go," *The Economist* (11 May 1996), p. 26.
8. A 1996 commission chaired by Michael Boskin (chairman of President Bush's Council of Economic Advisers) concluded that the consumer price index had been overstating inflation by one percentage point a year. If true, the commission claims, then average hourly earnings have risen by 13 percent from 1973 to 1995 instead of having fallen by 13 percent as official statistics indicate. For a contrary view characterizing the conclusions as "highly debatable," see Jeff Madrick, "The Cost of Living: A New Myth," *The New York Review*, 6 March 1997, pp. 19–24.
9. See Alan B. Kruger, "The Truth About Wages," *The New York Times*, 31 July 1997.
10. Reported in *The Wall Street Journal,* 31 December 1997, p. 1.
11. Quoted in "Who Killed the Middle Class," *New Yorker,* 11 October 1995, p. 113.
12. Lester C. Thurow, "One nation, divisible," *The Boston Globe*, 9 July 1997.
13. Jim Carrier, "Sailing the High-End Seas," *The New York Times,* 24 January 1998, p. B1.
14. See Appendix D ("GDP: What Gets Measured Gets Managed") suggesting twenty-five years of almost uninterrupted economic decline.
15. Anticipating the revisionists, the UN took care to point out that "even with lower fertility and slower population growth, per capita incomes would have fallen in many countries."
16. *Human Development Report 1996.* (New York: United Nations Development Program), p. 3.
17. In its July 1996 ranking, *Forbes* magazine identified 446 billionaires worldwide. Its July 1997 list is limited to the top 200 billionaires, though it identified nearly 500, up from 96 ten years earlier when the rankings were started. *Forbes*, 28 July 1997.
18. According to the World Bank's assessment: "There is a substantial risk that inequality between rich and poor will grow over the coming decades, while poverty deepens." *World Development Report* (Washington, D.C.: The World Bank, 1995).
19. "Report from Chiapas, Mexico," Seva Foundation 1995/1996 Annual Report (Berkeley, California), p. 9.
20. "Toward a Politics of Hope," Fifth Annual E. F. Schumacher Lectures (October 1985). Lappe also points to a startling parallel in the United States during the 1970s. With record agricultural exports topping $40 billion in one year and a wholesale shift to large-scale capital and chemical-intensive farming, the top 1 percent of farmers (as measured by sales) increased their share of net farm income from 16 percent to 60 percent. Subsequently, the number of rural Americans living in mobile homes increased by 52 percent between 1980 and 1990.
21. See also Melvin L. Oliver and Thomas M. Shapiro, *Black Wealth/White Nation* (New York: Routledge, 1997).
22. See Adler, *Haves Without Have-Nots.* Adler argues that justice "may suggest the setting of a reasonable maximum to protect the common good against the eroding effects of self-serving interests." See also William Greider, *Who Will Tell the People?* (New York: Simon & Schuster, 1995); Philip M. Stern, *Still the Best Congress Money Can Buy,* rev. ed. (Washington, D.C.: Regnery Gateway, 1992). In 1976, the U.S. Supreme Court upheld limits on the contributions that candidates for federal

office can accept, indicating that such limits were justified because they helped safeguard the integrity of the election process. However, the court rejected any restriction on how much candidates can spend, indicating that spending is itself a form of political speech and is thus protected by the First Amendment to the U.S. Constitution.

23. University of Chicago professor Kevin M. Murphy, winner of the 1997 John Bates Clark Medal from the American Economics Association, is credited with identifying the growth in demand for skilled labor—as opposed to the rise in supply or decline in demand for unskilled labor—as the principal cause of the widening gap in wages between blue- and white-collar workers.

24. *Economic Report of the President* (Washington, D.C.: Council of Economic Advisers, 1997), p. 391. Medicare is projected to run out of funds in 2002. Starting in 2010, when baby boomers begin to retire, Medicare rolls will rapidly double to about 70 million people in 2030.

25. "The visible hand," *Economist*, 20 September, p. 17.

26. This is not meant to suggest that "economic man" cannot rationally promote non-self-interested goals that he may value. Indeed, this "self-love" passage indicates " . . . that what Smith is doing here is to specify why and how normal transactions in the market are carried out, and why and how division of labour works, which is the subject of the chapter in which the quoted passage occurs." Amartya Sen, *On Ethics and Economics* (Cambridge, Mass.: Blackwell, 1987), p. 23.

27. Theo Colborn, Dianne Dumanoski and John Peterson Myers, *Our Stolen Future* (New York: Plume, 1997).

28. Michael Lerner, "Crossed Signals: Synthetic Chemicals and the Coming Health Revolution," *Whole Earth*, Summer 1997, p. 77.

29. See *Tomorrow's Company: The Role of Business in a Changing World* (London: Royal Society for the Arts, 1995).

30. Myron S. Scholes, "Stock and Compensation," *Journal of Finance*, July 1991.

31. Sam Brittan, *Capitalism with a Human Face* (London: Edward Algar, 1995), p. 59.

32. Arguing against Alexander Hamilton's view, Thomas Jefferson cautioned that "money, not morality, is the principle of commercial nations."

33. See Charles Hampden-Turner and Alfons Trompenaars, *The Seven Cultures of Capitalism* (New York: Currency Doubleday, 1994).

CHAPTER 2
Reconstructing Capitalism

1. "The libertarian good society lies . . . in the maximum dispersion of property compatible with effective production." Henry C. Simons, *Economic Policy for a Free Society* (Chicago: University of Chicago Press, 1948).

2. From 1976 to 1986, the share of national income flowing to the poorest 10 percent of U.S. households, already a meager 1.1 percent, dropped by 20 percent. More than 25 million Americans (nearly one in ten) could qualify for food stamps while 38 million lived below the official poverty line, including one of every five children. Those at the bottom who thought it could not possibly get any worse were repeatedly proven wrong.

3. See note 7, chapter 1.

4. Juliet B. Schor. *The Overworked American* (New York: Basic Books, 1992). This may understate the decline in living standards, as many families maintained purchasing

power with two employed spouses working more total hours, eroding family and leisure time.

5. Alan B. Krueger, "The Truth About Wages," *The New York Times*, 21 July 1997.

6. It surfaced again in a welfare reform bill enacted in the fall of 1996 which deprived legal immigrants of a range of benefits. According to the Emma Lazarus Fund, although legal immigrants represent only 6 percent of those on public assistance, they were targeted for more than 40 percent of the cuts.

7. This comes at a time when the number of primary and secondary students is projected to grow to 56 million by 2004, up from the 1971 "baby boom" peak of 51 million (and 47 million in 1991). A combination of immigration and aging baby boom children assures continuing pressure on school districts around the country, particularly in the southern portions of immigration-flooded Florida, Texas and California.

8. Historian William Manchester, in *The Glory and the Dream*, chronicles that period, noting that it was not until 1938 that Roosevelt quit trying to balance the budget, asking Congress in mid-April for $3 billion to increase public works, relief, flood control and housing. Manchester suggests that FDR "was perhaps the only politician in the country who thought of economics as a moral problem." Roosevelt's coinage of the phrase *New Deal* in his 1932 speech accepting the Democratic nomination was a combination of Theodore Roosevelt's Square Deal and Woodrow Wilson's New Freedom, plus adviser Stuart Chase had just published a book titled *A New Deal.*

9. See Milovan Djilas, *The New Class* (New York: Praeger, 1957); Friedrich A. Hayek, *The Road to Serfdom* (Chicago: Phoenix, 1944).

10. Serendipitously, a major reform of employee-benefit law soon reached the Finance Committee, to which Long appended Kelso's ESOP proposal. The first ESOP incentives were contained in the Employee Retirement Income Security Act of 1974 (ERISA). Based on a tax ruling, Kelso had already twice adapted employee-benefit plans for use as techniques of finance for clients in California. The first ESOP (in 1956) facilitated a partial ESOP buyout of a Palo Alto–based newspaper chain (described in Chapter 5). The second enabled a fertilizer manufacturing facility to become owned largely by its farmer-customers. See Stuart M. Speiser, *A Piece of the Action* (New York: Van Nostrand Reinhold, 1977) for an overview of the early development and evolution of ESOPs, including an account of Louis Kelso's pioneering work.

CHAPTER 3
Why Does Capitalism Create So Few Capitalists?

1. *Employee Stock Ownership Plans—Interim Report on a Survey and Related Economic Trends* (Washington, D.C.: U.S. General Accounting Office, February 1986), table 16.

2. Allowing people to buy shares on a before-tax and tax-deferred basis has become a major stimulus to the accumulation of personal capital in institutional hands, including the significant growth of 401(k) plans.

3. *Statistical Abstract of the United States* (Washington, D.C.: U.S. Government Printing Office, 1992), p. 434.

4. Gabriel Kolko, *The Triumph of Conservatism: A Reinterpretation of American History, 1900–1916* (New York: Macmillan, 1963).

5. The notion that lower taxes and investment subsidies would pay for themselves was first made popular by economist Arthur Laffer and commentator Jude Wanniski. Laffer is best remembered for his bell-shaped "Laffer curve" depicting his claim that, as tax rates fell, productive activity would rise, along with tax revenues. With the help of *Wall Street Journal* editorial page writer Robert Bartley, who hired Wanniski in 1972, and Irving Kristol, publisher of *The Public Interest*, a neoconservative journal, supply-side economics steadily gained key converts in policy circles, including Ronald Reagan.

6. Between 1983 and 1993, foreign sales of U.S. Treasury bonds rose from $30 billion to $500 billion. In the fiscal year ending June 30, 1995, foreigners bought 65.6 percent of newly issued Treasury securities.

7. This is not meant to suggest that government debt cannot be used for good purposes. Even the Continental Congress borrowed $11 million from the Dutch to fund the American Revolution. Alexander Hamilton later issued new federal bonds to redeem those debts (by then held by speculators) over the objection of Thomas Jefferson who, when he became president, borrowed $15 million to finance the Louisiana Purchase. The point is not whether taxpayer-secured debt is good or bad; the point is to identify when the benefit of public debt accrues to private parties and to consider whether the number of beneficiaries is sufficiently broad.

8. *Economic Report of the President* (Washington, D.C.: Council of Economic Advisers, 1997), p. 390. It has become popular to focus not on the total debt burden but on the deficit (the amount of debt added each year to the total debt). Thus, the 1996 deficit was "only" 1.4 percent of GDP versus 2.7 percent in 1980 and 6.1 percent in 1983—at the height of supply-side economics. "We could afford Ronald Reagan once," notes Herbert Stein, chairman of President Richard Nixon's Council of Economic Advisers. "We cannot afford him again." Herbert Stein, "It's Reaganomics," *The New York Times*, 11 February 1996, Sec. 4, p. 1.

9. "I have estimated that 71 percent of the wealth of households in 1989 was traceable to gifts and inheritances (with 29 percent traceable to household savings). This was up from 47 percent of the wealth of households in 1962 traceable to intergenerational transfers and 65 percent in 1983." Edward N. Wolff, "The Recent Rise in the Concentration of American Wealth: A Cause for Alarm?" Ibid. at p. 78.

10. *Statistics of Income* (Washington, D.C.: Internal Revenue Service, 1989). Of course, individuals, sole proprietorships, partnerships and other entities also claim depreciation deductions. This analysis focuses on the corporate entity because most commercial assets in the United States are held in corporate form.

11. Edward N. Wolff, Ibid.

12. Harvard economist Lawrence Summers (now undersecretary of the U.S. Treasury) and Boston University's Laurence Kotlikoff found that at least 46 percent of contemporary wealth accumulations are attributable to inheritance.

13. Bruce Bartlett, "Income Gap Between Poorest and Richest Rises," *The New York Times*, 20 June 1996, p. A1.

14. Contrary to the predicted impact, new investment actually stagnated and then declined over the following two years, rebounding only in 1984 with the help of a worldwide economic recovery. Business expenditures on new plant and equipment rose 0.4 percent in 1982 and declined 1.5 percent in 1983 before growing 16.4 percent during 1984 in conjunction with a worldwide economic expansion. *Economic Report of the President* (Washington, D.C.: Council of Economic Advisers, 1991).

15. Michael Jensen, "A Revolution Only Markets Could Love," *The Wall Street Journal*, 3 January 1994.

16. Supporters of LBOs suggest that their beneficial results showed up in the fact that during the 1980s the equity value of public firms grew from $1.4 trillion to $3.0 trillion. Ibid. LBO detractors were portrayed as ill-informed naysayers, pessimists and roadblocks on the path to progress. In a series of congressional hearings, experts predicted that this diversion of corporate cash to debt repayment would erode research and development, siphon off resources from internal projects, soak up management time, and force firms to reward managers based on financial criteria rather than on strategic criteria grounded in what managers perceived as best for the long-term health of the company. With the benefit of hindsight, a 1996 study confirmed those fears. See Michael Hitt, "The Market for Corporate Control and Firm Innovation," *Academy of Management Journal*, 39, no. 6 (1996).

17. "A Fragile Redwood Deal," *The New York Times*, 3 October 1996. In order to resolve a decade-long controversy that slowed Hurwitz's tree harvest and caused him considerable public embarrassment, in October 1996 the state and federal government agreed to pay him $380 million in cash and government property (i.e., swapping his land for other government-owned land) to convert the most sensitive acreage into a public preserve.

18. See John B. Shoven and Joel Waldfogel, eds., *Debt, Taxes and Corporate Restructuring* (Washington, D.C.: Brookings Institution, 1990).

19. Only 0.78 of 1 percent of such transactions included an ESOP, and the majority of those were attributable to a few large transactions. Source: The ESOP Association, Washington, D.C.

20. A record number of Americans declared bankruptcy in 1996 (more than 1 million); many due to credit card debts. Total household debt reached the $5.4 trillion mark in mid-1997, with the share of disposable income committed to debt service passing 18 percent. Among lower- and moderate-income families, debt is higher still.

21. Data based on research by Securities Data Company.

22. The deals of the 1990s are driven less by investment bankers and more by corporate strategists looking for partnerships, such as Westinghouse acquiring CBS to metamorphose into a media company. Leveraged buyout transactions in the 1990s use relatively less debt (60 to 70 percent) rather than the more highly leveraged debt-to-equity ratios of the 1980s, while appreciated stock became a common form of payment. "Financial buyers" acquired approximately $22 billion in companies in 1996. Hostile corporate bidders acquired their targets only 38 percent of the time between 1994 and May 1997, down from 48 percent in 1988–1993.

23. The dramatic run-up in the stock market provided many firms a powerful currency to spend: their own pricey shares. Witness WorldCom's $37 billion buyout of MCI Communications in November 1997. At the end of 1997, the Dow Jones Industrial Average ended higher for a record sixth successive year, including back-to-back gains of 33.5 percent in 1995 and 26 percent in 1996. A rising stock market lifts the value of company shares, making deals easier to do, which in turn stimulates speculation about other takeover candidates, which again lifts stock prices, facilitating even more deals. As a result, acquisitions are now often structured not as cash purchases but as stock swaps, with shareholders of the acquired firm receiving payment in the form of newly issued shares in the acquiring firm, which, unlike cash, have the attractive habit of becoming more valuable in the seller's hands.

24. Findings of 1996 survey by *The Washington Post*, Kaiser Family Foundation and Harvard University. Reported in *The Washington Post National Weekly Edition*, 24–30 October 1994.

25. Results of a survey commissioned by Merrill Lynch, reported in "Tuned Out, Turned Off," *The Washington Post National Edition*, 5–11 February 1996, p. 6.

26. See Robert D. Putnam, *Making Democracy Work—Civic Traditions in Modern Italy* (Princeton, N.J.: Princeton University Press, 1993), pp. 109–129. Putnam's research confirms that the presence of civic virtue is more prevalent in more egalitarian communities where the horizontal bonds of collective reciprocity and solidarity evoke a light-touch government able to count on more willing cooperation among a citizenry who value civic engagement and are much happier.

27. See Richard G. Wilkinson, *Unhealthy Societies—The Afflictions of Inequality* (London: Routledge, 1996), pp. 13–28.

28. Peter T. Kilburn, "Health Gap Grows, with Black Americans Trailing Whites, Studies Show," *The New York Times,* 26 January 1998, p. A16.

29. See Robert Ashford, "The Binary Economics of Louis Kelso: A Democratic Private Property System for Growth and Justice," in John H. Miller, ed., *Curing World Poverty—The New Role of Property* (St. Louis: Social Justice Review, 1994).

CHAPTER 4
Putting the "Own" Back in Ownership

1. Others may also swell these institutional holdings, such as U.S.-educated foreigners who bequeath monies to U.S. institutions. See "A Hong Kong Builder Gives $100 Million to Princeton," *The New York Times*, 10 November 1995, p. 1.

2. This trend was given another boost by the Congress in 1996 with the revival of favorable tax rules governing private charitable foundations (nonprofit organizations with typically only one source of funding). Unlike a public charity where the donor typically loses control over how the proceeds are spent, the donor or his family retains control and can apply those funds to uses that may or may not be broadly representative of the community. See "A Tax Break Prompts Millionaires' Mad Dash to Create Foundation," *The Wall Street Journal*, 27 January 1997, p. 1.

3. Personal communications (1980–1996). Two books from that era did predict a steady increase in the role played by U.S. pension plans. See Peter Drucker, *Pension Fund Socialism* (1976); Jeremy Rifkin and Randy Barber, *The North Will Rise Again* (Boston: Beacon Press, 1978).

4. Overall, institutional assets grew 10.9 percent from 1970 to 1980 and 12.9 percent from 1980 to 1990. *Institutional Investor Report*, Ibid.

5. *The Brancato Report* (Fairfax, Va.: The Victoria Group, September 1996). Mutual funds held 21.8 percent of that. As a percentage of total mutual fund assets, foreign equities accounted for 4.0 percent in 1995 ($72 billion), up from 1.7 percent in 1990 ($26.7 billion). Pensions and endowments invest approximately 5.3 percent of their total assets in foreign equities ($259 billion in 1995). With the U.S. economy now accounting for 36 percent of worldwide equity, risk-diversification experts suggest a global weighting of portfolios, arguably investing only 36 percent of their funds in the United States. In January 1995, the Coca-Cola Company announced that it was abandoning the labels *international* and *domestic* as a way to describe their business. Coca-Cola now considers itself a global company, suggesting to investors that they need not buy an international portfolio because by investing in Coca-Cola they are investing globally.

6. Ibid., p. 73.
7. This is a subtle but crucial distinction. Although pension funds held $4.95 trillion in mid- 1996 assets, the investment of 56.1 percent of those assets is delegated to external fiduciaries to manage, including investment advisers, investment companies, insurance companies and banks. *Institutional Investor Report*, Ibid.
8. "Riding Wall Street on Autopilot: Investors Rush to Index Funds," *The New York Times*, 28 January 1997, p. 1.
9. William M. Mercer, Inc., "1995/96 Long-term Incentive Compensation Survey Results," (William M. Mercer, Deerfield, Illinois), p. 6. The median shares reserved for the stock option program is 8 percent, though this number is slightly skewed by the high use of options in small emerging companies.
10. Judith H. Dobrzynski, "New Road to Riches Is Paved with Options," *The New York Times*, 30 March 1997, p. F 10.
11. See Bruce Orwal, "Eisner Exercises 7.3 Million Disney Stock Options," *The Wall Street Journal*, 4 December 1977, p. A3; Bruce Orwall and Joann S. Lublin, "How Eisner Cashed In," *The Wall Street Journal*, 5 December 1997, p. A4. Mr. Eisner's 1996 options reportedly could net him $300 million if the share price grows only 5 percent a year during his ten-year contract.
12. "Putting Aside a Billion While Making a Company Thrive," *The New York Times*, 13 October 1996, p. 14. From the perspective of their own self-interest, investors may have few qualms about this version of employee ownership: a thousand dollars invested in Coca-Cola stock when Mr. Goizueta took over in 1979, with dividends reinvested, was worth $52,000 in 1996. On the other hand, giving a CEO full credit for the rise in a company's stock is only marginally less ludicrous than giving a political leader full credit for a rising stock market.
13. Robert H. Frank and Philip J. Cook, *The Winner-Take-All Society* (New York: Martin Kessler Books/The Free Press, 1995).
14. Mark Landler, "Who America Pays to Play Top Executives," *The New York Times*, 25 August 1996, p. E4.
15. "High Performance Workplaces: Implications for Investment Research and Active Investing Strategies," Report to the California Public Employees' Retirement System, May 30, 1994, Gordon Group, Inc. ("Gordon Report"): "There is a strong correlation between corporate policy in the arena of workplace practices and the general quality and effectiveness of management."
16. As part of its investment criteria, the California Public Employee Retirement System now prefers such feedback-focused firms. See Richard Pascale, Mark Milemann, and Linda Gioja, "Changing the Way We Change," *Harvard Business Review* (November-December 1997).
17. Edward Regan and Joe Gibson, "The Decline and Revitalization of Corporate America," *The Aspen Institute Quarterly* (Summer 1991): 90.
18. The Gordon Report cautions that institutions distinguish between those policies that enhance employee voice and those that amount to a transfer of wealth from stockholders to employees.
19. Economists David Levine and Laura Tyson confirm that "participatory arrangements that offer workers no stake in returns have not been successful." "Participation, Productivity and the Firm's Environment," in Alan S. Blinder, et al., *Paying for Productivity* (Brookings, 1990). See also Peter Kardas, "Comparing Growth Rates in Employee Ownership Companies to Their Participatory Competitors," a report for Washington State Department of Community Development (February 1994) lending "support to the theory that the combination of employee ownership and

significant participation makes it possible for employee ownership companies, on
average, to have an advantage unavailable to their competitors."
20. This indirect activism also recognizes that *direct* activism has some very practical
limits, including the reluctance of those managing corporate pension funds to do
anything that might disrupt the lives of their corporate colleagues. This passivity
is important because the $3.6 trillion in assets of corporate-sponsored pension
plan assets is more than twice that of more activist-prone public sector plans ($1.4
trillion). Institutional Investment Report, Ibid., p.15. Harvard Business School
professor Michael Jensen, a specialist on corporate governance, concludes that a
more thoughtful approach to accountability is called for, arguing that "institutional activism is never going to amount to much" because it works mainly
through "public embarrassment in the press," and "the press isn't interested in
middle-market companies."
21. Sam Brittan, *Capitalism with a Human Face* (London: Elward Elgar, 1995).
22. Mahbub ul Haq, remarks to the State of the World Forum (San Francisco), 4–9
November 1997.
23. See Steven Greenhouse, "Nike Shoe Plant in Vietnam Is Called Unsafe for Workers," *The New York Times,* 8 October 1997, p. 1.
24. See Neil Ulman, "A Main Forest Firm Prospers by Earning Eco-Friendly Label,"
The Wall Street Journal, 26 November 1997, p. 1.
25. Robert A. G. Monks and Neil Minow, *Power and Accountability* (New York:
Harper Collins, 1991).
26. See John J. Sweeney, *America Needs a Raise* (New York: Houghton Mifflin, 1996).
27. *Estimates of Federal Tax Expenditures for Fiscal Years 1997–2001.* Joint Committee on Taxation, 26 November 1996, Table 1.
28. "Program-related investments" are growing in popularity among foundations in
their search for better ways to leverage the impact of their funds.
29. In the 104th Congress, legislation was introduced (H.R. 1594 "The Pension Protection Act") meant to nullify an interpretive bulletin by then Labor Secretary
Robert Reich that encourages economically targeted investments.
30. Roberta Romano, "Public Pension Fund Activism in Corporate Governance Re-
considered," *Columbia Law Review* (May 1993).
31. In a survey of the 139 largest nonfederal public pension plans, 50 of the 119 respondents reported that they had invested $19.8 billion (2.4 percent of their as-
sets) in ETIs to promote housing, real estate or small business development. These
investments included bond purchases, loan purchases, private placements, certificates
of deposit and venture capital. Projected yields on venture capital sometimes
lagged benchmark investments. The report was unable to reach definitive conclusions about the economic effects of ETI because of a lack of data. See *Public Pension
Plans—Evaluation of Economically Targeted Investment Programs* (Washington,
D.C.: U.S. General Accounting Office, March 1995).
32. Actuarial assumptions include such variables as life expectancy, expected turnover,
retirement dates, anticipated investment returns, projected rates of inflation and
other factors based on experience and on general statistical data.
33. Wal-Mart structured its compensation schemes so that many of its senior executives and store managers accumulated significant assets.
34. Margaret Blair, *Ownership and Control: Rethinking Corporate Governance for
the Twenty-First Century* (Washington, D.C.: Brookings Institution, 1995). See
also Appendix A.

35. *The Seven Cultures of Capitalism* with Alfons Trompenaars (New York: Currency Doubleday, 1994).
36. "Charles Handy Sees the Future," *Fortune,* 31 October 1994. Ranging even more broadly, George Goyder argues that "it is iniquitous to give control over an organization dependent upon the daily cooperation of free men and women to absentee landlords from now until doomsday." George Goyder, *The Just Enterprise* (London: Adamanitine Press, 1987). Corey Rosen, executive director of the National Center for Employee Ownership, notes that in today's radically restructured workplace, "you need people to think and act like owners." You also need a reward system consistent with that role. "It's also a matter of ethics," Rosen insists. "If workers are supposed to act like businesspeople, then they should reap the rewards that businesspeople normally receive."
37. The Teacher's Insurance and Annuity Association—College Retirement Equities Fund has 1.8 million participants at some sixty-one hundred colleges, universities and other nonprofit educational institutions. Reflecting the trend toward both global diversification and the global sensitivity to these issues, senior staff warn that their activism will increasingly focus on Europe and Japan, where the fund has significant holdings. In mid-1997, half of its $93 billion variable-annuity stock account was invested in stocks tied to the Russell 3000 index, which is composed of the nation's three thousand largest public companies, with the balance split between foreign and domestic stocks it hopes will outperform the market.
38. Kay contrasts this with more traditional business relationships where the pursuit of short-term gain is valued over continuity and stability. A key weakness of such behavior: the immediate appropriation of wealth often takes priority over its creation. *Foundations of Corporate Success: How Business Strategies Add Value* (London: Oxford University Press, 1993). He argues that the other key sources of advantage are (1) innovation (largely replicable by other companies), (2) reputation (typically brand names), and (3) strategic assets such as government-sanctioned monopoly rights that inhibit market entry (such as airport gates). See also Janelle Barlow and Claus Moller, *A Complaint Is a Gift—Using Customer Feedback As a Strategic Tool* (San Francisco: Berrett-Koehler, 1996).
39. Extolling the advantages accompanying long-term producer-supplier relationships found in Japan's *keiretsu* (corporate groups)—lower transaction costs, reciprocal learning, a willingness to make relationship-specific investments, etc., Princeton professor Alan Blinder suggests that this "looks more like matrimony rather than a series of one-night stands." Alan S. Blinder, "Should the Former Socialist Economies Look East or West for a Model?" (mimeo) International Economics Association, Moscow (1995).
40. The importance of such relationships was anticipated by Robert Axelrod and others conversant in game theory and the development of cooperative strategies. "The foundation of trust," Axelrod argues, "is not really trust but the durability of the relationship." *The Evolution of Co-operation* (New York: Penguin Books, 1990). Similarly, James C. Collins and Jerry I. Porras, *Built to Last—Successful Habits of Visionary Companies* (New York: Harper Business, 1994), documents that the success of long-lasting companies is attributable not to corporate leadership but to the fact that they have strong company *cultures* capable of surviving in spite of rather than because of their leaders.
41. *Capital Choices—Changing the Way America Invests in Industry*, A Research Report Presented to the Council on Competitiveness and Cosponsored by the Harvard Business School (1992).

42. Kevin Kelly, *Out of Control* (Reading, Mass.: Addison-Wesley, 1994).
43. Michael Rothschild. *Bionomics—Economy as Ecosystem* (New York: Henry Holt and Co., 1990).
44. *Tomorrow's Company: The Role of Business in a Changing World* (London: Royal Society for the Encouragement of Arts, Manufactures and Commerce, June 1995). Absent that inclusive approach, the report suggests that the corporation also puts at risk its license to operate, thereby jeopardizing both short- and long-term financial performance.

CHAPTER 5
Up-Close Capitalism—The Employee Ownership Solution

1. See Jeffrey R. Gates and Jamal Saghir, "Employee Stock Ownership Plans (ESOPs)—Objectives, Design Options and International Experience," CFS Discussion Paper Series, No. 112 (September 1995). Washington, D.C.: The World Bank.
2. This account is drawn from a combination of historical records and personal communications with Russell B. Long, from 1980 to the present.
3. T. Harry Williams, *Huey Long* (New York: Vintage/Random House, 1969).
4. On 30 April 1935, straw ballots printed on 3-by-5 cards were mailed out, with 100,000 addressed to an upscale sample of telephone owners and 49,742 sent to recipients of unemployment benefits. Respondents had no idea they were replying to a poll by a national political party because the postcard's return address was a Washington, D.C., post office box registered to "The National Inquirer." Only responses from the 100,000 mailing were tallied. Edwin Amenta, Kathleen Dunleavy and Mary Bernstein, "Stolen Thunder? Huey Long's 'Share Our Wealth,' Political Mediation, and the Second New Deal," *American Sociological Review*, October 1994.
5. Ibid. In *The Return of Thrift* (Free Press, 1996), Phillip Longman argues that Social Security was enacted largely as a counter to costlier demands for universal old-age assistance touted by physician Francis Townsend (1867–1960) and his ten million followers. FDR proposed to limit the government's financial exposure by restricting benefits to those who had first paid payroll taxes to the program.
6. See A. J. Liebling, *The Earl of Louisiana* (Louisiana State University Press, 1960). His life was later chronicled on film in a 1992 feature-length film starring Paul Newman as Earl and focusing on his notorious affair with stripper Blaze Starr.
7. Russell B. Long, personal communication, October 1995. Assistant secretary of labor and chairman of the technical board of the President's Commission on Economic Security (1934–1935), Altmeyer then became a member of the Social Security Board, serving as chairman (1935–1946) and commissioner (1946–1953).
8. Louis O. Kelso, personal communication, April 1976.
9. Private gross fixed nonresidential investment totaled $807 billion in 1996, made up of $213 billion in nonresidential structures and $594 billion in producers' durable equipment. *Economic Report of the President* (Washington, D.C.: U.S. Government Printing Office, February 1997), Table B-16.
10. See Marshall N. Carter and William G. Shipman, *Promises to Keep: Saving Social Security's Dream* (Washington, D.C.: Regnery Publishing, 1996).
11. Quoted in Lee Altenberg, "Beyond Capitalism: Leland Stanford's Forgotten Vision," *Sandstone and Tile* 14 (1) (Winter 1990): 8–20 (Stanford Historical Society, Stanford, Calif.) citing Robert S. Brookings, *Economic Democracy: America's Answer to Socialism and Communism* (New York: MacMillan, 1929) and *The Way Forward* (New York: MacMillan, 1932).

12. The ESOP concept originated with a twelve-hundred-page manuscript written by Louis Kelso while stationed with the U.S. Navy in the Panama Canal Zone near the end of World War II. His working title was "The Fallacy of Full Employment." Kelso later shelved his manuscript while the Congress was debating passage of the Full Employment Act of 1945, resurrecting it after meeting with philosopher Mortimer J. Adler who persuaded him that it should be published. With Adler's assistance, the manuscript was rewritten, condensed (to 265 pages) and published in 1958 as *The Capitalist Manifesto* with Adler as coauthor. Louis O. Kelso and Mortimer J. Adler, personal communications, circa January to October 1976.
13. *Viewpoint* (a syndicated radio broadcast), February 1975.
14. Joseph Blasi and Douglas Kruse, *The New Owners* (New York: Harper Collins, 1991).
15. Professor James E. Meade (1907–1995), a Nobel Laureate economist, advocated a "labor-capital partnership" in which employees would be paid partly in company shares.
16. These accounts taken from "How About Some Horror Stories," *Employee Ownership Report* (Oakland: National Center for Employee Ownership, November/December 1997), p. 15.
17. Eric Bates, "Private Prisons," *The Nation*, 5 January 1998, p. 11.
18. This provision was restricted in 1989 and then repealed in 1996 in conjunction with legislation raising the minimum wage. Effective 1 January 1998, "Subchapter S" corporations are permitted to establish ESOPs under the Small Business Protection Act of 1996.
19. See Louis O. Kelso and Patricia Hetter, *Two-Factor Theory: The Economics of Reality* (New York: Vintage, 1967). Originally published as *How to Turn 80 Million Workers into Capitalists with Borrowed Money*.
20. Within management ranks, ownership is even further concentrated. In 78 percent of the 7,000-plus publicly traded companies, the five most senior executives control three-quarters of all management stock. In only 256 of these companies do the top five managers control less than 40 percent.
21. ESOPs and stock bonus plans account for about $300 billion of that total, with the balance held via profit-sharing and 401(k) plans ($250+ billion and 2–3 million employees) plus broad-based stock options (5 million employees with $200 billion). "Statistical Profile of Employee Ownership." Oakland: National Center for Employee Ownership, May 1997. The tax expenditure cost of encouraging ESOPs is about $1 billion per year. "Estimates of Federal Tax Expenditures for Fiscal Years 1997–2001," by the staff of the Joint Committee on Taxation, November 28 1996.
22. Approximately 4 percent of existing plans are terminated each year.
23. The early work of 1996 Nobel Laureate economist James Mirrlees showed that an optimal tax system must be "incentive compatible" so that tax rates encourage productive people to work harder. The National Center for Employee Ownership reports that approximately 3 percent of ESOP participants give up pension plans for their ESOP while 5 percent involve wage concessions.
24. As of 1991, approximately 1,000 publicly traded firms (about 15 percent of all listed companies) had at least 4 percent employee ownership, with an average employee ownership of 12.2 percent. That represents the largest single block of shareholders in 41 percent of these companies. Those companies with at least 4 percent employee ownership represent 30 percent of the public market and about 20 percent of the jobs. Approximately half of the 8.6 million employees working for

these corporations are also employee owners. Of the "Fortune 100" largest U.S. companies, 33 have 12 percent average employee ownership while at least 4 percent employee ownership is found in 27 percent of the "Fortune 500" industrial companies and 20 percent of the "Fortune 500" service firms. Joseph B. Blasi and Douglas Kruse, Ibid.

25. "ESOPs: How the Average Worker Fares." Oakland: National Center for Employee Ownership, 1990. A 1991 study found that ESOP leveraged buyouts fared considerably better than non-ESOP buyouts. "The Record of ESOP LBOs in the 1980s." Oakland: National Center for Employee Ownership, 1991. A quarterly "Employee Ownership Index" tracks public companies with more than 10 percent employee ownership. Though the index shows a high correlation of employee ownership with performance, that does not prove *causation*. The link between ownership patterns and performance continues to generate volumes of research, no one of which is conclusive. However, the sheer weight of the published work suggests this linkage is both real and significant. (The U.S. index has outperformed other indexes for the last six years.) Britain also has an index, though it tracks only 30 companies (the U.S. index has 351). The U.K. index has also outperformed the market over the period 1992 to 1997, growing from a base of 100 to 311 while an all share index grew from 100 to 179. "Employee Ownership Report." Oakland: National Center for Employee Ownership, November/December 1997, p. 13.

26. Reported in Carolyn T. Geer, "Sharing the Wealth, Capitalist-style," *Forbes*, 1 December 1997, p. 158.

27. Ibid., pp. 165–167.

28. Ibid., pp. 171–176.

29. John Maynard Keynes viewed diversification with some reticence, believing it a mistake to try to spread risk by spreading too much among enterprises "about which one knows little and has no special reason for confidence."

30. John Case, "A Company of Businesspeople," *Inc.*, April 1993, p. 79.

31. Carolyn T. Gerr, "Turning Employees into Stockholders," *Forbes*, 1 December, p. 154.

32. Sue Burzawa, "'How Much Participation?' Is a Question Each ESOP Company Must Answer for Itself," *Employee Benefit Plan Review*, July 1997, p. 48.

33. "Employee Ownership and Corporate Performance," Oakland: National Center for Employee Ownership, 1995.

34. Half the company's profits are credited annually to employees' accounts (to accumulate until retirement) while another portion (7.5 percent) is used to buy shares from departing employees, ensuring that the shares are liquid while also providing a way to bring new employees aboard as repurchased shares are redistributed to all employees. This "recycling" helps keep the market liquid, motivates employees to keep a sharp eye on profits and favors those with longer service.

35. Frederick F. Reichheld, *The Loyalty Effect* (Cambridge, Mass.: Harvard Business School Press, 1996).

36. In a similar vein, World Bank economist David Ellerman urges that we reject the mechanistic view that a company (or a country) is somehow like an electric motor that runs at the same speed and capacity regardless of who owns it. David Ellerman, *Property and Contract in Economics: The Case for Economic Democracy* (Cambridge, Mass.: Blackwell, 1992).

37. In July 1996, the Teamwork for Employees and Management Act ("Team Act") was passed by the Congress and vetoed by President Clinton who said it "would undermine the system of collective bargaining." The Team Act reflected one version of the December 1994 recommendations of the Commission on the Future of

Worker-Management Relations that suggested amendments to the National Labor Relations Act to ensure that nonunion employee participation programs are not found to violate the act's ban on company-dominated unions "simply because they involve discussion of terms and conditions of work or compensation."

CHAPTER 6
New Property Paradigms

1. See John Holland, "Complexity Made Simple," First Annual Stanislaw Ulam Memorial Lecture reported in *The Bulletin of the Santa Fe Institute*, Winter 1994. See also Holland, *Hidden Order: How Adaptation Builds Complexity* (New York: Addison-Wesley, 1995).

2. League ownership rules presently have as a goal a single profit-motivated individual as the owner of at least 30 percent of each NFL franchise. Green Bay's "commons" ownership solution is protected under a "grandfather" clause.

3. See Jeffrey R. Gates and David E. Reid, "Translating Your ESOP Abroad," *Financial Executive* (July/August 1994).

4. Regardless of the organizational structure, an ownership strategy could enhance performance by promoting ownership within the corporate parts (such as employees owning shares in their employer) or by fostering ownership of parent company shares. Where organized as alliances (often the case for the largest multinationals), employees could be allowed to gain an ownership stake in each of the allied companies.

5. See discussion of Professor John Kay's notion of "corporate architecture" in Chapter 4 ("Putting the "Own" Back in Ownership").

6. Note that this structure could prove abusive in a monopolistic environment where, for example, a processing plant dominates the economy and forces its suppliers and distributors to make firm-specific investments.

7. I encountered an almost identical situation while on assignment in Casablanca, where Morocco's largest dairy used an ESOP/RESOP combination to buy out a 40 percent foreign investor. As the loan was paid (largely from company earnings), a component of stock ownership accrued to both employees and the farmers who supplied the company with milk.

8. See Ian Hargreaves, *Sharper Vision* (London: DEMOS, 1993). The BBC generated additional revenue by selling its programs, or by proceeds from coproduction with other companies, including American public television stations. In 1996, the BBC announced plans to expand its reach worldwide and to add substantial new commercial revenue to its public broadcasting coffers. For example, 1998 will see the launch in the United States of a commercially supported cable channel ("BBC America") that will generate income from its joint venture with Discovery Communications for which Discovery is putting up all the investment, at least $550 million over five years. The BBC will also co-own several new commercial cable channels being sold around the world by Discovery. See Lawrie Mifflin, "A BBC Cable Channel Headed for the U.S.," *The New York Times*, 9 December 1997, p. B1.

9. Jeanne Pohl Smith, "Fifteen years of dividends add up." *Juneau Empire, 20th Aninversary, Permanent Fund Edition* (25 February 1997), p.2.

10. Quite commonly, resource-rich economies also experience a shrinkage in their traded-goods sector—due largely to an appreciation in its exchange rate (undermining competitiveness) along with a diversion of both capital and labor into extraction (often low-skilled) and away from manufacturing and other value-added production.

11. See "The Natural Resources Myth," *Economist*, 23 December 1995, p. 87.
12. A similar self-financing concept (the community investment corporation) could enable residents to gain access to equity and real estate profits in local for-profit real estate development companies.
13. Another downside of a natural resource endowment is the temptation for a nation's people to forgo an education.
14. Terry L. Anderson, "How the Government Keeps Indians in Poverty," *The Wall Street Journal*, 22 November 1995.
15. Federal legislation enacted in 1987 required states to enter into good faith negotiations with Indian tribes to allow them to operate games of chance that are not prohibited by state law. Nationwide, gaming revenue in more than 270 casinos, bingo halls and other gambling facilities on Native American land totaled more than $5 billion in 1995 and was growing $1 billion a year.
16. See Thomas Kuhn, *The Structure of Scientific Revolutions* (Chicago: University of Chicago Press, 1962).

CHAPTER 7
Toward a Workable Work Ethic

1. Nobel laureate economist Robert Solow documents that the labor market is as much a social as an economic institution, in *The Labor Market as a Social Institution* (Cambridge, Mass.: Blackwell, 1990).
2. "Most indigenous ceremonies, if you look to their essence, are about the restoration of balance. That is our intent: to restore, and then to retain, balance. Nature itself continually tries to balance, to equalize." Winona LaDuke, *Learning from Native Peoples*, Thirteenth Annual E. F. Schumacher Lectures, 23 October 1995 (Great Barrington, Mass.: E. F. Schumacher Society).
3. In July 1995, Intuit Corporation announced that American Express, Smith Barney and seventeen of the largest U.S. banks are joining it to enable customers to conduct online financial transactions: banking, credit card services, brokerage services, financial planning and more. The implications for employment levels in financial services are enormous, particularly now that 40 percent of homes have a personal computer and most have an online service.
4. *U.S. Code*, vol. 15, sec. 1021.
5. The notion of government serving as employer of last resort resurfaced again in the 1970s as the Humphrey-Hawkins Full Employment Act (never enacted).
6. "O Governor, Won't You Buy Me a Mercedes Plant," *The New York Times*, 1 September 1996, sec. 3, p. 1.
7. Ibid. The subsidies became a political issue in Alabama's 1994 gubernatorial race. After Governor James E. Folsom Jr. was defeated by Fob James Jr., James renegotiated portions of the pact, including canceling the state's $75 million order for twenty-five hundred cars. Folsom hoped to shift some of the cost to the federal government by calling out the Alabama National Guard for a "training exercise" (i.e., clearing and leveling the land), an effort that was halted after complaints from the congressman representing that area.
8. Charles V. Bagli, "Tax Breaks Proliferating to Keep Corporations in New York City," *The New York Times*, 17 October 1997, p. A20.
9. Timothy Egan, "Old-Fashioned Town Sours on Candymaker's New Pitch," *The New York Times*, 6 October 1997, p. 1.

10. Ibid. Arthur J. Rolnick, research director for the Minneapolis Federal Reserve, proposes that Washington tax as income 100 percent of any such subsidies.

11. Alabama originally planned to relieve Mercedes and its employees from income tax during the company's debt-repayment period. That plan would have redirected funds that, under a state court order, were earmarked to improve Alabama's schools. Governor James retreated from this strategy after a legal challenge was threatened by the Alabama Education Association. After a court ruling, he also withdrew a proposal to divert state oil and gas revenues to Mercedes.

12. Overall, 30 percent of the world's labor force was either unemployed or under-employed. Unemployment in the fifteen European Union nations increased in 1995 to 11.3 percent of the workforce, compared with 2 percent in the 1960s.

13. Wage inequality has widened significantly over the past decade and a half in those countries that have deregulated their labor markets—most notably the United States, Britain, Australia and New Zealand. For instance, the United States allowed its minimum wage to fall to 34 percent of the median wage, whereas France's minimum wage hovers closer to 60 percent. Higher unemployment in France led to the conclusion that there must be a tradeoff between jobs and equality: countries with the widest wage differential should enjoy the lowest rates of unemployment. Alas, the trade-off is not that simple, as it fails to take into account other factors, such as education and training, which vary across countries. See "Earnings Inequality, Low-Paid Employment and Earnings Mobility," *OECD Employment Outlook* (Washington, D.C.: OECD, 1996).

14. In introducing his public-works programs in 1935, President Roosevelt expressed his belief that public-works employment was far superior to the "dole," because pay for no work was a "narcotic, a subtle destroyer of the human spirit." In accepting the nomination of the Democratic Party in 1936, Roosevelt explained why, to address human need during the Depression, he had broken his promise to balance the budget: "Governments can err, Presidents do make mistakes. Better the occasional faults of a Government that lives in a spirit of charity than the constant omissions of a Government frozen in the ice of its own indifference."

15. Austrian economist Friedrich von Hayek cautioned that a chief cause of inflation is that, without *continued* government spending, policymakers cannot maintain people in the jobs to which they have been drawn by the (inflation-fueling) spending of the past. One key reason that Keynesian economics fell into disfavor was the rise of the "rational expectations" school of economics led by 1995 Nobel laureate Robert Lucas of the University of Chicago, who argued it was unlikely that governments could stimulate lower unemployment with demand-side remedies (except over the short term) because employers would anticipate (and discount) the potential inflationary effect.

16. Relying on game theory, Nobel laureate economist Robert Solow argues that the unemployed do not readily lower their wage rates for the simple reason that, once employed, they still want to enjoy a decent income rather than contribute to the creation of a low-wage world for everyone. See Robert Solow, *The Labor Market as a Social Institution* (Cambridge, Mass.: Blackwell, 1990).

17. Truman Bewlay. Presentation to the Happiness Conference, London School of Economics, 1993.

18. For example, a firm may be unwilling to invest in new hires because relatively high interest rates reduce the value of the income those new workers could generate for the company. A company could earn more by investing in risk-free government

securities. Edmund Phelps, *Structural Slumps: The Modern Equilibrium Theory of Unemployment, Interest and Assets* (Cambridge, Mass.: Harvard University Press, 1994).

19. Two of this era's most successful investors, Warren Buffett and Charles Munger, have a substantial portion of their investment portfolios invested in Gillette (15.3 percent and 13.2 percent, respectively). "$45,000 a Share, $1,500 a Share or $264 a Share," *The New York Times*, 8 June 1997, p. F4.

20. Another factor stems from recent trends in corporate downsizing and reengineering. Many of its most vocal proponents are having second thoughts, including Stephen Roach, chief economist of Morgan Stanley, once an advocate for the "rightsizing" of workforces as a means to revive American productivity. One of the key downsizing challenges, he now concedes, is to find a way to restrain costs without tearing out the innovative heart of a company, as much reengineering has risked doing. Despite Roach's change of heart, managers in downsized firms are reluctant to go along, fearful that the next downturn may leave them overstaffed. "Jobs and Wages Revisited," *Economist*, 17 August 1996, p. 62.

21. Full-employment policymakers will search in vain for a for-profit company whose managers seek a production method that requires more man-hours. Note, however, that the nonprofit sector is in great need of man-hour-intensive work, such as childcare, tutoring, elderly care, teaching aides, surrogate parenting, library assistants and so forth. Jeremy Rifkin predicts that rapid growth in this third sector marks "the dawn of the post-market era." Jeremy Rifkin, *The End of Work* (New York: Jeremy Tarcher, 1995).

22. Samuel Brittan, "Pay and Jobs in a Global Economy," *Financial Times,* 22 September 1994.

23. "Knowledge workers" was coined by Peter Drucker in his 1959 book, *Landmarks of Tomorrow.*

24. See William Greider, *One World, Ready or Not* (New York: Simon & Schuster, 1997); Jerry Mander and Edward Goldsmith, eds., *The Case Against the Global Economy* (San Francisco: Sierra Club Books, 1996).

25. *Workers in an Integrating World,* World Development Report (Washington, D.C.: World Bank, June 1995).

26. Arthur contends that economics is at a pivotal point in its development. Because "all the sciences are intertwined," economic science must look more holistically at "how elements together produce patterns or structure" in a process-dependent world that is always evolving. Interview in *The Bulletin of the Santa Fe Institute* (Winter 1994), p. 5. See W. Brian Arthur, *Increasing Returns and Path-Dependence in the Economy* (Ann Arbor, Mich.: University of Michigan Press, 1994). See also M. Mitchell Waldrop, *Complexity: The Emerging Science at the Edge of Order and Chaos* (New York: Simon and Schuster, 1992).

27. Mickey Kaus, *The End of Equality* (New York: Random House, 1992).

28. Peter F. Drucker, "The Age of Social Transformation," *Atlantic Monthly*, September 1994.

29. Within an occupational elite, there may be a cognitive elite that is even more prosperous. At least that is one theory suggesting a new social stratification by cognitive ability that, left unchecked, "will lead the United States toward something resembling a caste society." In the most controversial element of this theory, the authors propose that (due largely to genes) "the cognitive elite has a better chance of preserving its intellectual capital from generation to generation than the old elite had of preserving its money" (because the cognitive elite will tend to intermarry,

breeding a subsequent generation of the cognitively superior). See Richard J. Hernstein and Charles Murray, *The Bell Curve: Intelligence and Class Struggle in American Life* (New York: Free Press, 1994). Quotes excerpted from "The Aristocracy of Intelligence," *The Wall Street Journal,* 10 October 1994.

30. Po Bronson, "Silicon Valley, the Workers' Paradise," *The Wall Street Journal,* 25 January 1997 p. A19.

31. See Victor Hanson, "Labor Is What Others Do for Us," *New York Times,* 2 September 1996.

32. Many of the costs of this steady rise in economic distress are indirect, long-term and personal. For instance, medical research confirms that mental stress, such as that associated with economic insecurity, releases hormones that damage the body's immune system.

33. During the mid-1980s, the military and intelligence communities of China and Pakistan worked together in a global smuggling network, coordinated by the Central Intelligence Agency, to ship billions of dollars in U.S.-manufactured arms to Afghan guerrillas fighting Soviet troops, who invaded and occupied Afghanistan from 1979 to 1989.

34. Variations on this theme create dangers worldwide. For example, Bahrain recently became the first Gulf state to own a navy frigate. Although the $200 million warship (the USS *Jack Williams*) was a gift from the United States, Bahrain paid $50 million to job-creating U.S. shipyards and armaments firms to upgrade the ship's combat capabilities.

35. Dramatic savings may be available through "green design." See Ernst Ulrich von Weizsacker, Amory Lovins, and L. Hunter Lovins, *Factor Four* (London: Earthscan, 1997).

36. *Economic Report of the President* (Washington, D.C.: Council of Economic Advisers, 1994).

37. The Washington, D.C.–based Economic Policy Institute reports that one-third of American workers are now in so-called nonstandard jobs (part-time, temping, day work and self-employed).

38. Traditionally, temporary-services employment has been very sensitive to the business cycle, which is consistent with the industry's role as a buffer for firms that find it costly to adjust their permanent employment levels in the face of what may be temporary changes in demand. See Lewis M. Segal and Daniel G. Sullivan, "The Growth of Temporary Services Work," *Journal of Economic Perspectives,* Spring 1997, pp. 117–136. With growth in the contingent workforce (temps, part-timers and the self-employed) identified as the primary cause of the decline in health and retirement coverage, the Teamsters (and other unionists) viewed the UPS strike as an attack on employers' scaling back of their responsibilities to employees.

39. William Bridges, *JobShift* (Reading, Mass.: Addison-Wesley, 1994). See also William Bridges, "The End of the Job," *Fortune,* 19 September 1994, p. 62.

40. See Kevin Kelly, "New Rules for the New Economy," *Wired,* September 1997, p. 140.

41. Jessica Lipnack and Jeffrey Stamps, *Virtual Teams: Reaching Across Space, Time, and Organizations with Technology* (New York: Wiley, 1997).

42. One of the key transaction costs here is the need to create and maintain appropriate financial information that passes muster from the perspective of securities regulation. Although the Securities and Exchange Commission has done much to streamline this process for equity offered through employee benefit plans, additional efficiencies are required to make this more cost-effective. The advent of networked computers and e-mail means that compliance with disclosure requirements could

be accomplished on a virtually paperless basis (for example, using company-specific Web sites on which required information would be posted).

43. Buckminster Fuller, *I Seem to Be a Verb* (New York: Bantam Books, 1970).

CHAPTER 8
Reinventing Labor Unions

1. The United Steelworkers was not established until 1942 at a Constitutional Convention called by the Steelworkers Organizing Committee (SWOC) of the Congress of Industrial Organizations. The SWOC began its efforts in 1936. A predecessor organization, the Amalgamated Association of Iron, Tin and Steel Workers, founded in the 1880s, was absorbed by the SWOC.
2. It is anticipated that the merger will be completed in the year 2000.
3. An analogous situation has emerged in Israeli kibbutzim, where Sephardic Jews from Arab countries became workers in (rather than members of) kibbutzim established earlier by Ashkenazi Jews from Western Europe.
4. See Christopher Mackin, "Ownership and Industrial Relations," *Perspectives on Work*, April 1997, p. 66.
5. Testimony before the Joint Economic Committee of the U.S. Congress (20 February 1967).
6. Lynn Williams, president of the United Steelworkers (retired), personal communication, March 1996.
7. Recent research suggests a need to revisit the relative risks of shareholding versus jobholding. Brookings economist Margaret Blair found that losses experienced by displaced workers are far higher for long-term employees. Workers who lost their jobs due to plant closings or layoffs in the mid-1980s earned 14 percent less on their next job. "But the longer the worker had held his previous job, the greater the earnings loss. Thus, workers who had 11–20 years of seniority earned 28 percent less on their next job while those with 21 or more years of seniority earned 44 percent less." In short, layoff puts at risk what may well be a worker's primary investment: his or her firm-specific skills, experience and seniority. Margaret Blair, Ibid.
8. See Christopher Mackin, "Beyond the Contract: Taking on Ownership." *Workplace Topics*, July 1991 (AFL-CIO Department of Economic Research); Thomas A. Kochan and Paul Osterman, *The Mutual Gains Enterprise* (Cambridge, Mass.: Harvard Business School Press, 1994).
9. See C. F. Sabel, "Studied Trust: Building New Forms of Cooperation in a Volatile Economy," *Human Relations* 46, no. 3 (1993). Studied trust describes a midway point between distrust and unquestioning faith.
10. The Steelworkers typically insist that investment bargaining be kept separate from that of pensions, using the ESOP as the focus of negotiations only on current pay and benefits to ensure that retirement funding remains largely unaffected. They also insist on shares with full voting rights and, where the company is unlisted, require that shares be valued by an independent appraiser. See AFL-CIO Industrial Union Department Guidelines on ESOPs, 1987. Their bargaining typically includes a preference for convertible preferred shares.
11. See Robert Kanigel, *The One Best Way: Frederick Winslow Taylor and the Enigma of Efficiency* (New York: Viking, 1997).
12. Source: Bureau of Labor Statistics.
13. See David Cannon, *Generation X and the New Work Ethic* (London: DEMOS, 1995).
14. See "UAL Corporation," Harvard Business School Case Study 9-295-130 (19 April 1995). Boston: Harvard Business School Publishing.

15. See "Matters of Scale," *World Watch*, May/June 1997.

16. See Wynne Goodley, "The U.S. Balance of Payments, International Indebtedness and Economic Policy: A Policy Brief," Jerome Levy Economics Institute of Bard College, August 1995.

17. Stuart Kauffman, *At Home in the Universe* (New York: Oxford University Press, 1995), p. 282.

18. See Greider, *One World, Ready or Not*, pp. 442–443.

19. Labor Force Statistics from the Current Population Survey, Bureau of Labor Statistics, Table B-1.

20. Segal and Sullivan, "Temporary Services Work."

21. A precedent can be found in the Steelworkers' successful bargaining to create the Institute for Career Development in its 1989 bargaining round. Financed by a ten-cents-an-hour levy and jointly administered by a board comprised of people from both the union and the major companies (with locally based joint committees), the institute focuses on basic skills training: literacy, numeracy, computers, etc.

22. "Politics into Economics Won't Go," *Economist*, 11 May 1996, p. 26.

23. Geoff Mulgan and Helen Wilkenson, "Well-being and Time" in *The Time Squeeze* (London: DEMOS), Issue 5/1995.

24. The patent on this financial product is held by consultant Francis Vitagliano and Franco Modigliani, M.I.T. professor emeritus and Nobel laureate in economics.

25. This seeming paradox fuels a worldwide impetus for free trade and open markets. In part, that movement is driven by the interests of financial capital whose owners (accurately) see that closed labor markets tend to fuel inflationary pressures.

26. Given the increasingly crucial role played by knowledge, World Bank economist David Ellerman suggests that perhaps we need a knowledge-based ESOP, to give knowledge workers greater ties to the company so that the company has an incentive to invest more in their human capital development. Perhaps workers put up some of the money for training (that is matched or augmented by company funds) but it goes to buy them stock which is only released when they have stayed with the company for a requisite period. This could, he suggests, set off a virtuous circle whereby motivated trainees (it's partly their money) gain more human capital matched by legal capital (shares), which become worth more as their personal productivity is enhanced. Dr. David P. Ellerman, personal correspondence, 21 October 1997.

27. Joel Garreau, "Ten Commandments for Planners," *Whole Earth Review*, Winter 1995, pp. 64–66. See also Daniel H. Pink, "Free Agent Nation," *Fast Company*, (December–January 1998), p. 131.

28. Kevin Kelly, "New Rules for the New Economy," *Wired*, September 1997, p. 140.

29. Linton Weeks, "Wonder Woman of the Cyberworld," *The Washington Post National Weekly Edition*, 10 November 1997, p. 10.

SECTION 2
A Capitalism That Works for Everyone

1. The term *biosphere* was coined by Russian biologist V. I. Vernadsky in the 1920s; *The Biosphere,* inspired philosopher and paleontologist Teilhard de Chardin (1881–1955) to coin the term *noosphere* (from *nous,* or consciousness) to capture his notion of a steadily spreading consciousness through which humanity would become more aware of its interdependence, leading to a more highly evolved stage of humanization ("ultra-hominisation"). In an unpublished text (*The Future of Money: Beyond Greed and Scarcity*), Bernard A. Lietaer coins

the term *cybersphere* to suggest that the emergence of a global network of information and telecommunications may yet provide the means to realize Teilhard's
vision.

CHAPTER 9
Making Money

1. Alan Watts, "Wealth vs. Money," *Playboy*, December 1968, p. 209.
2. The U.S. Federal Reserve began as a regional network of lenders of last resort,
   limited to accepting bank notes ("bankers' acceptances") based on the production, warehousing, transportation, etc., of real, productive goods and services.
3. Although the Federal Reserve Act forbade the reserve banking system from purchasing private "financial" paper (i.e., non-real bills), no such limitation was
   placed on the purchase of the government's debt obligations.
4. As Chapter 3 indicates, this conventional analysis misconstrues the saving issue,
   overlooking the fact that business saving in the United States now outpaces personal saving three to one. Note also that all permutations of "expenditure taxes"
   (sales taxes, value-added taxes, consumed-income taxes) preserve intact the key
   component of business saving: depreciation and its dominant role in fueling
   closed-system financing and concentrated ownership.
5. In 1961, Kelso published *The New Capitalists* (coauthored with Mortimer J.
   Adler) with the revealing subtitle *A Proposal to Free Economic Growth from the
   Slavery of Savings* (New York: Random House, 1961; reprint, Westport, Conn.:
   Greenwood Press Publishers, 1975).
6. Some lenders are more concerned with traditional collateral such as real estate
   and other property that can be readily liquidated in case of loan default. Others
   are "cash-flow lenders," more concerned with the borrower's revenue-generating
   capacity (typically its "EBIT"—earnings before interest and taxes), secured with
   loan covenants ensuring that those revenues are applied to loan repayment.
7. John Maynard Keynes, *The General Theory of Employment, Interest and Money*.
   Repr. (New York: Harcourt Harbinger, 1964), pp. 376–377. Keynes saw the need
   for financial engineers but had concerns about their fees. Thus, Keynes advocated
   six decades ago "a scheme of direct taxation which allows the intelligence and
   determination and executive skill of the financier, the entrepreneur *et hoc genus
   omne* (who are certainly so fond of their craft that their labour could be obtained
   much cheaper than at present), to be harnessed to the service of the community
   on reasonable terms of reward." Ibid. Wall Street bonuses totaled $12 billion for
   1997, up 30 percent over 1996. See Patrick McGeehan and Anita Raghvan, "Wall
   Street Investment Bankers, Traders May See Year-End Bonuses Leap by 30%,"
   The Wall Street Journal, 3 December 1997, p. C1.
8. The needs for both speculative loans and government debt paper could be met
   from the existing pool of accumulated savings ("past savings"), paying market-
   determined rates of interest. To ensure that the nation's access to credit is not limited in extraordinary circumstances (such as during a war), the Federal Reserve
   Act could, for example, allow the financing of government IOUs based on a
   supermajority vote (say two-thirds) of the Congress. A similar limitation is now
   favored by those who wish to limit the government's power to tax or spend. "The
   inflationary bias of direct or indirect monetization of the public debt would be
   eliminated since increased money supply would be matched and exceeded by the
   value of the increased production of goods and services." Dr. Norman A. Bailey,
   "Fed Should Share the Wealth," *Journal of Commerce*, 27 October 1989.

9. In the midst of the Depression, former Brookings Institution President Harold Moulton offered a similar insight, albeit from the demand side. He argued that the demand for capital goods (machinery, equipment, etc.) is derived from the demand for consumer goods produced by that machinery and equipment. But where, he wondered, could the funds be found for capital expansion if consumption was expanding while savings (the source of investment capital) was declining? Moulton's answer: "From commercial bank credit expansion." "Such expansion relieves the possibility of shortage in the 'money market' and enables business enterprises to assemble the labor and materials necessary for the construction of additional plant and equipment." Harold G. Moulton, *The Formation of Capital* (Washington, D.C.: The Brookings Institution, 1935), p. 107. "[T]he expansion of capital occurs only when the output of consumption goods is also expanding; and ... this is made possible by the [simultaneous] expansion of credit for production purposes." Ibid., p. 118.

10. As William Greider explains: "If the central bank held a substantial portion of its portfolio in private commercial debt paper, the financing for real enterprises in the productive economy, the central bankers would presumably have greater concern for whether their policies were threatening those enterprises with failure. The Fed's portfolio of U.S. debt paper, in other words, permits greater detachment from the real economic consequences." Greider, *One World, Ready or Not*, p. 438. Funds raised by the U.S. Treasury from the Federal Reserve are virtually cost-free, as the bulk of the interest that the Treasury pays on the bonds it sells to the Fed are returned to it each year as Fed-generated "profits."

11. Kelso's plan should not be confused with populist William Jennings Bryan's "easy money" policy of 1896 (following the "Panic of 1893") advocating the unlimited coinage of silver at a ratio to gold of 16:1. Nor should Kelso's plan be confused with the flexible-currency system advanced by Charles W. Macune, economic theorist and organizer of the populist Farmers Alliance of the 1880s. Macune's "sub-treasury plan" proposed that the government underwrite farmers' cooperatives through government-owned warehouses ("sub-treasuries"), which would buy farmers' crops through the issuance of low-interest federal "sub-treasury certificates" that the farmers could then sell for cash based on their personal needs. This would have allowed farmers to regain some control over their lives by providing a means both to avoid the rock-bottom prices prevailing at harvest time and to escape the high-interest crop lien system. See Lawrence Goodman, *Democratic Promise: The Populist Moment in America* (Oxford: Oxford University Press, 1976).

12. The general "fungibility" (interchangeability) of money and credit makes any credit- or money-expansion mechanism a potentially inflation-fueling challenge.

13. Kelso's unorthodox view of money and credit is also intended to lower the cost of capital where used to address both supply-side and demand-side (income stimulation) concerns. Access to reserve banking he views as a "public good" for which only a modest charge should be levied, in addition to whatever fees are required to fund the commercial banking sector's charge for evaluating and monitoring loans. In addition, a fee would be charged for insuring that portion of the loan risk not covered by private-sector credit insurance underwriters. For this last function, he recommends the establishment of a "capital diffusion reinsurance corporation." See Louis O. Kelso and Patricia Hetter Kelso, *Democracy and Economic Power* (Cambridge, Mass.: Ballinger, 1986). On this point, the Kelsos argue that the function of personal saving in the banking system is to serve an insurance function, as a cash cushion to guard against the risk of loan default. For example, U.S. banks are required to maintain a certain level of "capital sufficiency," typically

cash deposits ("reserves") equal to at least 6 percent of outstanding loans. If the function of reserves is insurance, Kelso argues that an insurance mechanism be constructed to address that need through a private-sector reinsurance company. Its costs could be covered by premiums paid by commercial lenders to protect up to 75 to 90 percent of the losses on such loans, similar to loan-default insurance offered by the Mortgage Guarantee Insurance Corporation, with the premium included in the annual interest charged by lenders.

14. As a percentage of total domestic financial assets, the commercial banks' share has dropped from more than half to only a quarter over the past seventy years. Source: Federal Reserve Board. The same trend is unfolding worldwide. Whereas banks once had 70 percent of the world's financial assets, they now account for only 30 percent. A World Bank study disclosed that total bank assets in the United States equal only 50 percent of GDP, compared with, for instance, 100 percent in Malaysia, 150 percent in Japan and 170 percent in Germany. The U.S. bond markets totaled 110 percent of GDP, compared with 90 percent in Germany, 75 percent in Japan, 50 percent in Korea and less than 10 percent in Thailand and Indonesia. Reported in Alan Murray, "Asia's Financial Foibles Make American Way Look Like a Winner," *The Wall Street Journal*, 8 December 1997, p. 1.

15. Keynes recognized a mismatch and tension between the long-term time horizon of producers (who are motivated by the prospect of future sales) and financiers, who have much shorter time horizons as they trade in the most liquid of assets in a world in which commitments can be quickly unraveled based on constantly changing assessments of risk. Mexico offers a classic case, as its early 1990s growth was financed with inflows of cash from abroad. In 1994, when financial confidence collapsed, so did the economy as that cash raced back home, leaving Mexico to cope with plummeting living standards as it slashed public expenditures and turned to the IMF and the U.S. government for financial support.

16. The United States already allowed unfettered access to its financial markets. Edmund L. Andrews, "Accord Is Reached to Lower Barriers to Global Finance," *The New York Times*, 13 December 1997, p. 1. Some systems theorists caution that the emerging world trade system is a self-reinforcing feedback loop destined to unleash "success to the successful"—in the sense that the more money you have in the bank, the more interest you earn, the more money you have in the bank. See Donnella H. Meadows, *Whole Earth Review*, Winter 1997, p. 78.

CHAPTER 10
Capitalism as if Our Children Mattered

1. Nicholas D. Kristof, "Across Asia, a Pollution Disaster Hover," *The New York Times*, 28 November 1997, p. 1.
2. World Commission on Environment and Development, *Our Common Future*, also known as the Brundtland Commission Report (New York: Oxford University Press, 1987). This same standard was embraced by the President's Council on Sustainable Development.
3. David Brower, *Let the Mountains Talk, Let the Rivers Run* (San Francisco: Harper Collins West 1995), p. 16.
4. Murray Gell-Mann, *The Quark and the Jaguar* (New York: W. H. Freeman, 1994).
5. See Fritjof Capra, "A Systems Approach to the Emerging Paradigm," in Michael Ray and Alan Rinzler, eds., *The New Paradigm in Business* (New York: Jeremy Tarcher, 1993).

6. "World Scientists' Warning to Humanity," Union of Concerned Scientists, Cambridge, Mass., 1992.
7. The United Nations Intergovernmental Panel on Climate Change, composed of twenty-five hundred scientists from around the world, reports that the scientific community is confident that global climate change is in progress and that at least some of the change is due to human action, particularly the burning of coal, oil and wood. See William E. Stevens, "Scientists Say Earth's Warming Could Set Off Wide Disruptions," *The New York Times*, 18 September 1995, p. A1.
8. See "Clinton on the Global Environment: Some Progress but Much More Still to Be Done," *The New York Times*, 28 June 1997, p. A7 (transcript of address to UN environmental conference in which President Clinton commits to the development of limits "that will significantly reduce our emission of greenhouse gases"). For a review of the politics of climate change, see Robert Repetto and Jonathan Lash, "Climate Change," *Foreign Policy*, Fall 1997, p. 84.
9. In August 1997, British Petroleum, the world's third largest oil company, broke ranks with other fossil fuel producers, announcing that there is now sufficient scientific evidence to warrant concern about whether human activity (primarily the burning of fossil fuels) is changing Earth's climate. See William E. Stevens, "Industries Revisit Global Warming," *The New York Times*, 5 August 1997, p. 1.
10. The "Kyoto protocol" anticipates the use of flexible mechanisms for meeting these limits, including an international system of emissions trading (agreement on the principles, rules, guidelines and operations of the trading system was deferred until a meeting set for November 1998 in Buenos Aires). See Peter Passell, "Trading on the Pollution Exchange," *The New York Times*, 24 October 1997, p. B1; "Excerpts from Clinton Comments on Plan to Reduce Gas Emissions," *The New York Times*, 23 October 1997, p. A14. William K. Stevens, "Tenitive Accord Is Reached to Cut Greenhouse Gases," *The New York Times*, 11 December 1997, p. 1.
11. John M. Broder, "Clinton Adamant on 3rd World Role in Climate Accord," *The New York Times*, 12 December 1997, p. 1.
12. See Jeremy K. Leggett, ed., *Climate Change and the Financial Sector: The Emerging Threat, the Solar Solution* (Munich: Gerline, Akademie Verlag, 1996).
13. In 1994, the National Marine Fisheries Service estimated that 40 percent of the nation's commercial fish species are overfished. In New England, the agency estimates that the overfishing of cod, haddock and flounder have already cost fourteen thousand jobs and $350 million a year in lost revenue. The industry seems now to have accepted what its critics have said for years: to save the industry, it is necessary first to save the fish. John H. Cushman Jr., "Panel Recommends Virtual End to Fishing Fleet in Georges Bank," *The New York Times*, 27 October 1994, p.1.
14. Jonathan Friedland, "Fish Stories These Days Are Tales of Depletion and Growing Rivalry," *The Wall Street Journal*, 25 November, 1997, p.1.
15. Legislation can play a key role. For instance, since enactment of national air-quality standards, the number of Americans living in areas that failed federal standards has been cut by half. Since 1970, the number of American rivers and lakes that are safe for fishing and swimming has increased from one-third to two-thirds. The dumping of sludge in the oceans is now illegal, landfills are safer, and certain endangered species have staged substantial comebacks.
16. This figure was agreed to at the International Conference on Population and Development ("The Population Summit") convened in Cairo in 1994.
17. Note, however, that recent UN reports have revised fertility rates downward. See *World Population Prospects: The 1996 Revision* (New York: United Nations,

1996). Fertility has dropped below the replacement rate in nineteen less-developed countries. Current projections suggest that global population will top out at about 8.5 billion in 2050 and start declining. See Ben J. Wattenberg, "The Population Explosion Is Over," *The New York Times Magazine*, 23 November 1997, p. 61.

18. James Q. Wilson, "Capitalism and Morality," *Public Interest,* Fall 1995.

19. From a financial perspective, the precautionary principle mandates that corporate managers identify, quantify and manage risks in order to enhance the value of the corporation for its shareholders. From an environmental perspective, where there are threats of serious or irreversible damage, the lack of full scientific certainty should not be used as a reason for postponing cost-effective measures to prevent environmental degradation.

20. Stephan Schmidheiny with the Business Council for Sustainable Development, *Changing Course: A Global Business Perspective on Development and the Environment* (Cambridge: M.I.T. Press, 1992). In 1995, the council merged with its counterpart in the International Chamber of Commerce to become the World Business Council for Sustainable Development.

21. Matthew Connelly and Paul Kennedy, "Must It Be the Rest Against the West?" *Atlantic Monthly*, December 1994.

22. James C. Collins and Jerry I. Porras, *Built to Last* (New York: Harper Business, 1994).

23. Sara Van Gelder interview, *In Context*, no. 41.

24. See G. Bennett Stewart III, *The Quest for Value.* (New York: Harper Business, 1991). Economic value added (EVA) is what remains of profits after taxes once a charge for the capital employed in the firm is deducted. EVA turns a company's value into the valuation of a series of individual projects rather than (as, say, with free cash flow methodology) treating corporate valuation as one large and protracted capital budgeting exercise. Market value added (MVA) is the dollar spread between a company's market value and its capital. "Maximizing MVA should be the primary objective for any company that is concerned about its shareholders' welfare. A company's EVA is the fuel that fires up its MVA." Stewart, p. 153. Total shareholder return measures the change in a firm's market capitalization over a one-year period plus dividends paid expressed as a percentage of its initial value.

25. See Steve Lerner, *Eco-Pioneers—Practical Visionaries Solving Today's Environmental Problems* (Cambridge, Mass.: M.I.T. Press, 1997).

26. Barry A. Stein, "Decentralizing the American Economy," in Harold S. Williams, ed., *The Uses of Smallness* (New York: Rodale Press, 1978).

27. Kevin Kelly, *Out of Control: The Rise of Neobiological Civilization* (Reading, Mass.: Addison-Wesley, 1994).

28. *Economic Report of the President* (Washington, D.C.: Council of Economic Advisers, 1997), p. 318.

29. Seth Schiesel, "The No. 1 Customer: Sorry, It Isn't You," *The New York Times*, 23 November 1997, p. BU 1.

30. Reported in *The Economist,* 11 November 1995, p. 74.

31. In 1996, acquisitions of private companies totaled nearly $80 billion, an 84 percent increase from 1995 and the most ever, accounting for 12 percent of the dollar volume of domestic mergers and acquisitions, up from 8 percent of the 1995 total. "Time to Go," *The Wall Street Journal*, 28 February 1997, p. 1 (citing research by J. P. Morgan & Co.).

32. In the typical spin-off, a company gives its shareholders stock in a subsidiary, which becomes an independent company. The transaction is not taxed because, technically, the shareholders owned stock in both companies before the transaction.

With the size of today's spin-offs, often totaling a third of a company, these transactions might more accurately be called breakups.

33. Source: Securities Data Corporation.

34. "Spinning Away," *Time*, 26 August 1996, p. 30.

35. See in Chapter 5 ("Up-Close Capitalism—The Employee Ownership Solution") a description of the "Employee Ownership Index," suggesting superior portfolio performance where employee-ownership firms are included.

36. A Fannie Mae-like financial facility could ease this process, acquiring these notes as investments in conjunction with the partial "privatization" of Social Security. The institutional investor community may be well advised to provide the debt capital used to finance this employee equity participation strategy, perhaps with warrants attached.

37. See discussion in Chapter 6 ("New Property Paradigms").

38. "The Natural Step" (chaired by Paul Hawken) promotes a framework for understanding and solving environmental problems, suggesting that in order for society to bring its metabolic flows into alignment with sustainable limits, the amount and type of waste must change considerably.

39. Ray Anderson, personal conversation, July 1997. Anderson argues that "financial institutions must get outside their comfort zones also by becoming third-party participants in the strange concept of a lease without a term." Ray C. Anderson, *The Journey from There to Here: The Eco-Odyssey of a CEO* (Atlanta: The Peregrinzilla Press, 1995).

40. "Declaration of Interdependence," *Wired*, January 1997, p. 162.

41. Gunter Pauli, *Breakthrough* (London: Epsilon Press Limited, 1996), p. 99.

CHAPTER 11
Community Without the Communism

1. See Francis Fukuyama, *The End of History and the Last Man* (New York: Free Press, 1992).

2. Francis Fukuyama, "The Economics of Trust," *New Republic*, 14 August 1995.

3. See James O'Toole, *The Executive's Compass: Business and the Good Society* (New York: Oxford University Press, 1993).

4. Quoted in *Business Ethics*, January/February 1995.

5. See David Cannon, *Generation X and the New Work Ethic* (London: DEMOS, 1994).

6. Of course, non-self-interest goals may also incorporate values worth seeking, an issue addressed at the intersection of economics and ethics. Of late, ethics has been largely ignored by the more radical of Adam Smith's fans in their search for simple answers to issues that Smith, an accomplished moral philosopher, suggested lie in the complexity of the human psyche. See Sen, *On Ethics and Economics*.

7. See Max DePree, *Leadership Is an Art* (New York: Bantam Doubleday Dell, 1989); *Leadership Jazz* (New York: Bantam Doubleday Dell, 1992).

8. DePree's theme finds support in John Block's best-seller, *Stewardship: Choosing Service over Self-Interest* (1993) in which Block explains: "Stewardship is the willingness to be accountable for the well-being of the larger organization by operating in service, rather than in control, of those around us."

9. The spreading popularity of "best places to work" is evidenced by the fact that *Fortune* and *Business Week* also now publish lists.

10. John Paul II, *Laborem Exercens* (1981).

11. "No More Mr. Nice Guy," *The Washington Post National Weekly Edition,* 18–24 December 1995, p. 10.
12. See Amitai Etzioni, *The Spirit of Community* (New York: Touchstone, 1993); *The New Golden Rule* (New York: Basic Books, 1996).
13. America's steady increase in rates of incarceration is consistent with Robert Putnam's finding of a high correlation between inequality and a rise in various symptoms of a lack of good citizenship, including higher rates of criminality and corruption. See Robert D. Putnam, *Making Democracy Work.* The state of Florida now spends as much on corrections as on colleges. In California, the number of prisoners has grown from 19,000 in the mid-1970s to 150,000 in 1997. A 1997 study of Washington, D.C., found that half of the black men there between the ages of eighteen and thirty-five are under the control of the criminal justice system on any given day. California spent 2 percent of its budget on prisons in 1980 and 9 percent in 1994. By 2002, that figure is projected to top 16 percent, according to a Rand Corporation estimate. "Main Street Finds Gold in Urban Wave," *Los Angeles Times,* 9 October 1996, p. 1.; Fox Butterfield, "Crime Keeps on Falling, but Prisons Keep on Filling," *The New York Times,* 28 September 1997, p. 1.
14. See J. Russell Smith, *Tree Crops: A Permanent Agriculture* (Washington, D.C.: Island Press, 1950).
15. Gary Paul Nabhan, *Cultures of Habitat* (Washington, D.C.: Counterpoint, 1997), pp. 1–2.
16. Sociologist Paul Ray identifies the emergence of an "Integral Culture" that "manifests a distinctive toleration for ambiguity—beyond either/or." He notes that "compared to the rest of society, the bearers of Integral Culture have values that are more idealistic and spiritual, have more concern for relationships and psychological development, are more environmentally concerned, and are more open to creating a positive future." His most surprising finding: these "Cultural Creatives" make up 24 percent of the adults in the United States, or about 44 million people—"bigger than any comparable group seen at the birth of any previous social renaissance." The overall male-female ratio is 40:60. Paul H. Ray, "The Rise of Integral Culture," *Noetic Sciences Review* (Spring 1996).
17. A 1993 survey by the New York–based Families and Work Institute found that seven in one hundred American workers care for disabled spouses, relatives or friends over the age of fifty. Research shows volunteering and charity as particularly satisfying activities, more even than sports and music. Cited in Geoff Mulgan and Helen Wilkenson, "Well-being and Time," *The Time Squeeze* (London: DEMOS, 1995).
18. In the United States, 80 million citizens volunteer some 1 billion hours each year. However, an October 1994 report by Independent Sector found that Americans, concerned about their financial well-being, are donating less time and less money to charities. In May 1997, a nationwide program (America's Promise) began to enlist volunteers, led by retired General Colin Powell.
19. See Jeremy Rifkin, *The End of Work* (New York: Jeremy P. Tarcher/Putnam, 1995). Rifkin predicts a "post-market era" fifty years hence, when most Americans will receive their economic livelihood in the form of voucher payments in return for community service, with the vouchers financed by value-added taxes on high-tech goods and services.
20. Kelso and Adler, *The Capitalist Manifesto.*
21. See Jane Jacobs, *Cities and the Wealth of Nations* (New York: Random House, 1984).
22. The depressions of the 1870s and 1880s were harbingers of a monetary crisis that manifested again in the Depression of the 1930s, when the Farmer's Home

Administration (FHA) was established to replace some of the rural capital that had flowed to the cities to finance the industrial revolution.

23. See Robert Swann and Susan Witt, *Local Currencies: Catalysts for Sustainable Regional Economies* (Great Barrington, Mass.: E. F. Schumacher Society, 1995).

24. Ibid., p. 3.

25. These small-scale attempts to create and retain money (and credit) in local communities is a manifestation of a larger social movement known as "bioregionalism" based, in part, on the writings of Fritz Schumacher, who argued that "production from local resources for local needs is the most rational way of economic life." See E. F. Schumacher, *Small Is Beautiful* (New York: Harper Colophon, 1973) and *A Guide for the Perplexed* (New York: Harper & Row, 1977); see also Barbara Brandt, *Whole Life Economics* (Philadelphia: New Society Publishers, 1995).

26. "Mixed Signals," *The Wall Street Journal,* 18 June 1997, p. 1.

27. For an overview of this subject and a resource guide, see a collection of articles and interviews in *YES! A Journal of Positive Futures,* Spring 1997, pp. 28–40.

28. Bernard A. Lietaer, *The Future of Money: Beyond Greed and Scarcity.* See also, Bernard Lietaer, "Community Currencies: A New Tool for the XXIst Century," *World Business Academy Perspectives* (Winter 1994), pp. 80–97.

29. Ibid., p. 112.

30. Cited in Christopher Plant and Judith Plant, eds., *Green Business: Hope or Hoax?* (Philadelphia: New Society Publishers, 1995), p. 103.

31. Robert Swann and Susan Witt, Ibid., p. 4.

32. "Thinking Locally in a Global Economy," *Berkshire Trade and Commerce Monthly* (November 1997).

CHAPTER 12
The Politics of Ownership

1. *New York Times*–CBS News poll reported in *The New York Times,* 2 March 1995. In an August 1995 poll, U.S. voters indicated they would prefer by three to one to continue with imbalanced budgets rather than change Social Security. *The New York Times,* August 12, 1995.

2. In 1990, 13.8 percent of the voters came from families with incomes under $15,000. In 1992, they declined to 11.0 percent." Adam Clymer, "Class Warfare? The Rich Win by Default," *The New York Times,* 11 August 1996, Sec. 4, p. 1.

3. Arthur Schlesinger, "Fascism's Lengthening Shadow" *The Wall Street Journal,* 27 December 1993.

4. Today's crisis in politics may also be grounded in its tendency to blame individuals rather than the system in which they live. In the current environment of glorified individualism, people are expected to pledge themselves to market values where everything is reduced to an exchange relationship, even in their personal lives. If you're unsuccessful, then it must be your fault. If you're not driven by material ambition, something is amiss. If you don't have a job, you must be irresponsible. If you don't serve my needs, I'll find someone who will. That limited framework for human meaning breeds cynicism and a sense of isolation, even hopelessness, while also undermining personal relationships and social solidarity. See Michael Lerner, *The Politics of Meaning: Restoring Hope and Possibility in an Age of Cynicism* (Reading, Mass.: Addison-Wesley, 1996).

5. "Two Pillsburys Get Together on a Political Theory," *Minneapolis Tribune,* 2 July 1972. Charlie later authored the first law journal note on ESOPs: "Employee

Stock Ownership Plans: A Step Toward Democratic Capitalism," *Boston University Law Review* (March 1975).

6. *Barron's*, 21 July 1975.

7. *Forbes*, 1 May 1975.

8. Quoted in "Riches for All," *National Observer*, 25 May 1974.

9. Radio commentary, 20 July 1974.

10. *Toronto Star*, 26 June 1975.

11. *San Francisco Business*, January 1976.

12. *Village Voice*, 28 April 1975.

13. *The Whole Earth Catalog*, Spring 1970.

14. *Berkeley Daily Gazette*, 16 July 1971.

15. *Esquire*, December 1973.

16. Kelso's advocacy was not helped by the fact that a U.S. thoroughbred named Kelso (descended from the legendary Man o' War) was voted horse of the year for five consecutive seasons (1960–1964). Owned by Mrs. Richard C. Du Pont, Kelso had won a record $1,977,896 when he retired with an ankle injury in 1967, the same year that Louis O. Kelso and Patricia Hetter published their first book together making the case for ESOPs (*Two-Factor Theory: The Economics of Reality*).

17. Remarks to a joint meeting of the American Economic Association and the American Financial Association in San Francisco, 28 December 1983.

18. *Business Week*, 19 June 1989.

19. Remarks to Executive's Club, Chicago, Illinois, 13 September 1988.

20. George F. Will, "Joining the Side You're On," *The Washington Post*, 5 December 1996.

21. "OPM Wants to Sell Background Check Operation to Agency Employees," *The Washington Post*, 11 June 1995, p. A4. In August 1996, the office was incorporated as U.S. Investigative Services, Inc. Its seven hundred current employees own 91 percent of the company, with the balance owned by eleven managers. A noncompetitive three-year contract eased the transition (and the financing of the ESOP) while maintaining employment (10 percent of the personnel either stayed on with the oversight staff, transferred to another agency or retired). See "Live Long and Prosper," *The F.E.D. Newsletter* (La Jolla, Calif.: the Foundation for Enterprise Development), Fall 1997, p. 1. This strategy also surfaced in 1988 when George Bush's Commerce Department told private companies interested in running its National Technical Information Service that, if chosen, they would have to guarantee existing workers' jobs for six months and provide them stock in the operation. See "Federal ESOP?," *The Wall Street Journal*, 23 February 1988. See also "Methods to Privatize Appropriate State Government Functions Through the Development and Promotion of Employee-Owned Companies (ESOPs), Richmond Va.: Report of the Secretary of Administration and the Commonwealth Competition Council, 1998.

22. *The Washington Post*, 31 December 1969, p. C1.

23. See Richard N. Goodwin, "Has Anybody Seen the Democratic Party?" *The New York Times Magazine*, 25 August 1996, p. 33.

24. See Michael J. Sandel, "America's Search for a New Public Philosophy," *Atlantic Monthly*, March 1996, p. 52.

25. Ibid., p. 68.

26. See Laurence Zuckerman, "Tiny Turbine: The Next Generator?," *The New York Times*, 2 December 1997, p. C1.

27. Ronald A. Heifetz and Donald L. Laurie, "The Work of Leadership," *Harvard Business Review*, January–February 1997, p. 124.

28. Ibid., p. 134.
29. Ibid.
30. Joseph Jaworski, *Synchronicity—The Inner Path of Leadership* (San Francisco: Berrett-Koehler, 1996), p. 182. Jaworski takes as his model for leadership the findings of modern physics where, for example, David Bohm may have phrased best the challenge of leadership in summarizing a key principle of physics (Mach's principle): "The whole is as necessary to the understanding of its parts, as the parts are necessary to the understanding of the whole." Or, as Bell's theorem proved: "the world is fundamentally inseparable." See pp. 77–83.
31. Ibid., p. 116.
32. Duane Elgin, *Collective Consciousness and Cultural Healing,* A Report to the Fetzer Institute (Kalamazoo, Mich.: The Fetzer Institute, October 1997), p. 26.
33. Paul Kennedy, *Preparing for the Twenty-First Century* (New York: Random House, 1993).

SECTION 3
Toward A Twenty-First-Century Capitalism

1. "The extent to which the state embodies trust, participation and inclusion is the extent to which those values are diffused through society at large." Will Hutton, *The State We're In* (London: Vintage, 1995).
2. Arthur M. Okun, *Equality and Efficiency: The Big Tradeoff* (Washington, D.C.: The Brookings Institution, 1975).
3. Beginning in 1974 with enactment of the Employee Retirement Income Security Act, setting nationwide rules governing tax-qualified deferred compensation plans.
4. William A. Galston, *Liberal Purposes: Goods, Virtues, and Diversity in the Liberal State* (Cambridge: Cambridge University Press, 1991).

CHAPTER 13
Reinventing Capitalism

1. During the 1948–1951 period, the sixteen nations of the Organization for European Economic Cooperation (and West Germany) experienced a rise in their GNPs of 15 to 25 percent.
2. "Nearly all the great names of European business—Renault, Pechiney and Dassault in France; Volkswagen and Daimler-Benz in Germany; Fiat in Italy; plus Norse Crown Canning in Norway—were started or restarted with American assistance after the war." "The Marshall Plan's Success," *The Washington Post National Weekly Edition*, 2 June 1997, p. 8.
3. Letter to *The Washington Post*, 20 July 1976.
4. Groundwork for this initiative is already in place. Under line-item veto legislation that became effective 1 January 1997, the president may strike specific spending or tax breaks from congressional bills without rejecting the entire legislation. In effect only until 2004, the law allows the president to cancel any tax break that affects fewer than one hundred taxpayers.
5. Joint Committee on Taxation, *General Explanation of the Economic Recovery Tax Act of 1981* (Washington, D.C.: GPO, 1981), p. 401. In 1981, in consultation with Senator Russell Long, I drafted an amendment to this act directing the Treasury to prepare a biannual "ownership impact statement" (assessing the impact on ownership patterns of the supply-side tax incentives) to be issued two

months prior to congressional elections. At the last moment, Long decided not to introduce the amendment for fear of embarrassing then Finance Committee chairman Bob Dole, who led the congressional push for enactment of the bill. Soon thereafter, Dole won election as Senate majority leader, based in substantial part on the political support he garnered among his Republican colleagues in conjunction with passage of that bill.

6. For instance, such a survey could confirm (or disprove) the allegation that in Brazil some 35 million acres owned by a propertied elite lie fallow while millions of Brazilians either crowd into densely populated urban squalor or engage in environmentally damaging subsistence farming in the Amazon Basin.

7. Where title is unclear (a common circumstance in developing countries), that information would prove useful in identifying where institutional support may be needed to formalize titling and registration procedures.

8. Tim Weiner, "For First Time, U.S. Discloses Budget on Spying: $26.6 Billion," *The New York Times*, 16 October 1997, p. A17. This all-inclusive budget encompasses both the agency itself, which employs seventeen thousand and spends an annual $3 billion, and a cache of funds drawn upon by other federal intelligence agencies, including the National Security Agency, which conducts global eavesdropping, and the National Imagery and Mapping Agency, which makes pictures and maps from space. See David Wise, "The CIA's Midlife Crisis," *Washington Post*, National Weekly Edition, 22 September 1997, p. 21.

9. This monitoring effort is led by Medea (Measurements of Earth Data for Environmental Analysis), made up of sixty scientists in universities and industry who advise U.S. intelligence agencies on the use of secret data to study the environment. "U.S. Will Deploy Its Spy Satellites on Nature Mission," *The New York Times*, 27 November 1995, p. 1. Note also that the Framework Convention on Climate Change (negotiated as part of the 1992 Rio "Earth Summit") requires that signatory countries conduct ongoing inventories of emissions.

10. See William Perry, Bobby Inman, Joseph S. Nye Jr. and Roger K. Smith, "American Strategy in the 1980s," *The Aspen Institute Quarterly* (Summer 1991). In September 1997, an American multi-billionaire with a long-time interest in environmental matters (Atlantan Ted Turner, founder of Cable News Network) agreed to give the United Nations $100 million per year over the next ten years. A portion of those funds might fill this monitoring gap, including an ongoing CNN assessment of the relationship between ownership patterns and the impact of development on the environment.

CHAPTER 14
Reengineering Capitalism for Inclusion

1. See "The Majority Leader's Lure to the Maritime Crowd—Trent Lott's Championing of Shipping Subsidies Coincides with a Boatload of Recent Contributions," *The Washington Post National Weekly Edition,* 7 July 1997, p. 11.

2. Evidence of early military influence remains in computer jargon, such as "booting up." Government-assisted development of information technology provides a window into the murky world of government-assisted wealth accumulation and the tangled issue of how most appropriately to divvy up a nation's wealth into that which benefits everyone and that which benefits a few. Nathan Myhrvold, Microsoft technology chief, acknowledges that computer architecture as we know it was invented at the Princeton-based Institute for Advanced Study, which was

founded with tax-exempt funding provided by the family behind Macy's department stores. As Myhrvold puts it, "We're *collectively* richer for these generous gifts of intellectual property" (emphasis added). Nathan Myhrvold, "What's the Return on Research," *Fortune*, 8 December 1997, p. 88.

3. In a 27 June 1997 address to a United Nations environmental conference, President Clinton pledged that the United States would have solar panels on 1 million more roofs by 2010. Reported in *The New York Times*, 28 June 1997, p. 7

4. *Forbes*, 14 October 1996, p. 120; 13 October 1997, p. 182.

5. No one has yet attempted to quantify the private wealth accumulation attributable to the $1 trillion Reagan-era military buildup, when defense spending grew by 160 percent between 1983 and 1989. Budget Director David Stockman reports that, under pressure from Defense Secretary Caspar Weinberger, Reagan agreed to a 10 percent increase in real growth in Pentagon spending over six years (he had promised 5 percent during his election campaign). The Committee on the Present Danger and other conservative groups had accused Jimmy Carter of "unilateral disarmament" based on his 1980 defense budget (a key reason Carter proposed a 5 percent increase in his 1981 budget). In a budgetary oversight, Stockman mistakenly calculated that agreed-to annual growth rate based not on the lean Carter budget of 1980 but on Reagan's already pumped-up Pentagon budget for 1982, providing a much higher base year on which the agreed-to increase was computed. Once the new growth rates were announced (and Stockman realized his mistake), there was no turning back, particularly after Reagan had campaigned on the issue of a "window of vulnerability."

6. "The Sky, the Limit," *The Wall Street Journal*, November 18, 1996, p. A1. See also "McDonnell Douglas Chief Says Loss of Big U.S. Job Makes Mergers Easier," Ibid., p. A4.

7. Until a mid-1990s public offering diluted its ESOP holdings to 20 percent, Avondale Industries qualified as one of the twenty-five largest companies in the United States, with at least 30 percent of its shares owned by its employees. In 1997, the ESOP trustee decided to sell the plan's remaining company shares. Any ownership-pattern conditions associated with defense contracting should include not only direct contractors but also those to whom work is subcontracted or outsourced.

8. David Rogers, "Congress Approves Defense Bill Laden with Add-ons for Firms in GOP States," *The Wall Street Journal*, 26 April 1997, p. A2.

9. Christina Zampas, "Advancing the Rule of Law through Legal Education," *Open Society News*, Spring 1997, p. 12.

10. "Our Flying Pork Barrel," *Forbes*, 28 July 1997, p. 42.

11. For a first-person account of these conflicts, see "Ex-Manager Describes the Profit-Driven Life Inside Columbia/HCA," *The Wall Street Journal*, 30 May 1997, p. 1.

12. In one of the more blatant displays of just how tightly closed this access can be, the Federal Communications Commission proposed in mid-1992 (an election year) that $1 billion in licenses to open seventeen hundred new television stations be reserved for current station owners, along with a change increasing by 150 percent the number of radio stations these owners could accumulate. Under public scrutiny, the proposal was withdrawn. The 1995 budget reconciliation bill granted existing television station a second channel to carry out the transition to a new generation of advanced high-definition (HDTV) services.

13. Katharine Graham, publisher of *The Washington Post*, reports that, in the midst of the 1970s Watergate scandal (in which *Post* reporting helped end the political career of President Richard Nixon), four separate challenges were filed to the

renewal of the *Post*'s licenses of their two Florida television stations. Katharine Graham, *Personal History* (New York: Knopf, 1997).

14. In a subsequent PCS auction, the FCC allowed firms to pay 10 percent down and payments over ten years. Though the FCC nominally raised $10.2 (of the $23.1) billion, many of these start-up companies, initially backed by Asian investors, have been unable to raise sufficient funds to fulfill their obligations. As this book was going to press, an "ownership solution" was under construction that, under the terms of a World Trade Organization agreement, would allow foreign companies to own 100 percent of American communication companies (instead of the current limit of 25 percent), enabling these fledgling firms to raise more foreign capital to make good on their purchases.

15. "How the West Stopped Bruce Babbitt," *Economist*, 21 May 1994, p. 34.

16. *Hard rock* is a mining industry phrase used to distinguish the extraction of nonfuel minerals ("hard rock") from fuel-bearing minerals such as coal.

17. Employment in metals, iron ore, and copper industries declined from 149,800 in 1980 to 76,700 in 1994. *Facts About Minerals 1995* (Washington, D.C.: National Mining Association), p. 48.

18. Reported in *The Wall Street Journal*, 19 February 1997, p. 1.

19. Stephen Moore and Dean Stansel, Ibid.

20. See Michael D. Young, "The Design of Fishing-Right Systems—the NSW Experience," *Ocean and Coastal Management* 28, nos. 1–3. (1995), pp. 45–61.

21. Terry Baker, director of Enterprise Development for City of Indianapolis (personal conversation), 1 July 1997. See "In Privatizing City Services, It's Now 'Indy-a-First-Place,'" *The New York Times*, 2 March 1995, p. A8.

22. The Postal Services's share of the "correspondence and transaction market" declined 18 percentage points between 1988 and 1996 (from 77 percent to 59 percent) and is expected to drop another 5 percent by 2002. "Putting the Byte on Stamps," *The Washington Post National Weekly Edition*, 7 July 1997, p. 32.

23. *The Citizen's Charter*, Prime Minister Report to the Parliament (London: HMSO, 1995). Available through the London-based Adam Smith Institute.

24. The spread of free trade has been a boon to owners of capital worldwide, partly because global dispersal of the world's industrial base (along with access to lower-cost labor) has stagnated or eroded the incomes of workers in high-wage countries. See Jerry Mander and Edward Goldsmith, eds., *The Case Against the Global Economy* (San Francisco: Sierra Club Books, 1996).

25. The Ex-Im Bank was established in 1934 as a way to promote U.S. exports and stimulate employment. The U.S. government stands behind Ex-Im Bank guarantees, which can be provided either to the exporting company or to a foreign buyer of American exports. Several major multinational companies have launched a campaign to eliminate the "local content" requirements that currently accompany the bank's loans and guarantees. If this initiative succeeds, critics suggest that U.S. taxpayers would, in effect, be subsidizing the dismantling of their industrial base, leading to a further loss of high-wage jobs, ensuring an erosion of domestic market demand, and widening disparities between America's rich and poor as these firms globalize their workforces while using taxpayer-subsidized capital to build their balance sheets. See William Greider, "Who Governs Globalism?" *American Prospect*, January-February 1997, p. 73.

26. This requirement could be a cost-effective way to stimulate U.S. competitiveness by fostering ownership-motivated work environments. See Michael Porter, *Capital Choices* (Washington, D.C.: U.S. Council on Competitiveness, 1992).

27. This effort followed on from a law signed by President George Bush in 1992 which invigorated a little-known Commerce Department entity called the Trade Promotion Co-operation Council and mandated that it liaise among those federal agencies charged with helping exporters.

28. Quoted in *The Economist*, 25 February 1995. The Commerce Department also has a program offering trade development assistance loans, in which success is measured in jobs.

29. See Walter Pincus and George Lardner Jr., "Ambassadorships For Sale: $250,000 Each," *Washington Post National Weekly Edition*, 3 November 1997, p. 9.

30. Section 1042 of the Internal Revenue Code permits the tax-free reinvestment of proceeds from the sale to an ESOP of shares meeting certain requirements provided the proceeds are "rolled over" into approved securities. This could be amended to include, within limits, funds contributed to a federal political campaign, thereby linking campaign financing to some broader social good.

31. Stephen Moore and Dean Stansel, Ibid.

32. The Wine Institute, the trade association of California wineries and a primary advocate of the program, reports that exports of California wine have increased in the last ten years to $300 million a year from $25 million. "Corporate Welfare's New Enemies," *The New York Times*, 2 February 1997, p. E6. In a related development, on 25 June 1997, the U.S. Supreme Court upheld a New Deal–era marketing program (the Agricultural Marketing Agreement Act of 1937) that requires individual agricultural companies to help pay for industrywide advertising (*Glickman v. Wileman Brothers & Elliott*, No. 95-1184).

33. The primary agreements are the General Agreement on Trade and Tariffs (GATT), the World Trade Organization, and the Multilateral Agreement on Investment.

34. See Colin Hines and Tim Lang, *The New Protectionism* (New York: New Press, 1995).

35. Typically, a government grant was made to a revolving loan fund managed by a regional economic development agency, which in turn made ESOP loans.

36. By law Fannie Mae is limited to the secondary market (i.e., it cannot originate mortgage loans) and no loan can exceed $227,000 (for 1998).

37. U.S. antitrust law provides that a successful plaintiff may be able to recover treble damages. A portion of this penalty could take form as an extension of credit to the entity being divested. For instance, the divesting company could be required to accept a non-interest-bearing note from the divested entity, structured to enable employees of the divested firm to acquire a portion of the shares.

38. The Justice Department and the Federal Trade Commission have been operating for years under "merger guidelines" that set out economic criteria for appraising mergers, beginning with an identification of the market the merger will affect. Thus, for example, a federal judge blocked Staples Inc.'s acquisition of Office Depot Inc. in June 1997 because the office-superstore market was a distinct segment in which the combination of two market leaders would lead to higher prices.

39. The growing frustration with the steady spread of monopoly power in this arena has caused some communities to build their own cable companies. See Barnaby J. Feder, "Some Local Cheers for 'Creeping Socialism,'" *The New York Times*, 4 October 1997, p. B1.

40. See also Don Hazen and Julie Winokur, eds., *We the Media* (New York: The Now Press, 1997).

41. James Gleick, "Making Microsoft Safe for Capitalism," *The New York Times Magazine*, 5 November 1995; Steve Pearlstein, "When Does Big Mean Being Too Big?" *The Washington Post National Weekly Edition*, 3 November 1997, p. 22.

42. John Markoff, "Tomorrow, the World Wide Web! Microsoft, the PC King, Wants to Reign Over the Internet," *The New York Times*, 17 July 1996, C1.

43. See "How to Control Microsoft," *The New York Times*, 18 November 1997, p. A22; Bill Gates, "Why the Justice Department Is Wrong, *The Wall Street Journal*, 10 November, 1997, p A24.

44. In its July 1995 consent decree with the Justice Department allowing Microsoft to develop "integrated software products," the company agreed to cease a discounting practice that discouraged personal computer makers from installing rival operating systems and agreed that sales of Windows 95 would not be conditioned on an agreement that makers refrain from using a competing product. See "Netscape Widens Microsoft Antitrust Allegations," *The Wall Street Journal*, 21 August 1996, p. B8.

45. At the end of fiscal year 1996, Social Security trust fund reserves stood at $499.5 billion. That compares with Social Security obligations of $8 trillion to $10 trillion—benefits that workers have earned to date. Reserves are projected to reach $2.87 trillion by 2018 and then gradually be depleted until they run out, in 2029 (thereafter pay-as-you-go tax receipts are projected to cover only 77 percent of benefits). This $65 billion "surplus" meant that, for fiscal year 1996, the U.S. government's budget deficit was $144 billion instead of $209 billion. By investing that $65 billion in government bonds, Social Security is "funded" by purchasing one form of government obligation (to make payments on government bonds) to cover another form of government obligation (to make Social Security payments).

46. Projections for slower growth in the workforce or workers' earnings would put pressure on a pay-as-you-go financing system that has long relied on a steady expansion in both the workforce and earnings. If current trends persist, by the year 2040 there will be fewer than 2 taxpaying workers for every Social Security recipient (compared with 3.3 in 1997 and 7 in 1950). Between 1990 and 2030, the number of Americans over age sixty-five will double, while the working population is projected to grow by only 25 percent. Raising the eligibility age for full benefits could help, but the 1983 amendments already raised it to sixty-six in the year 2020 and to sixty-seven in the year 2030 (though life expectancy has increased by fourteen years since Social Security was enacted in 1935).

47. See "High Performance Workplaces: Implications for Investment Research and Active Investing Strategies," *Report to the California Public Employees' Retirement System*, ("Gordon Report") (Gordon Group, Inc., May 30, 1994).

48. All Chilean workers (except military and the self-employed) are required to contribute 10 percent of their monthly salary plus an additional 1 percent to cover the premium for compulsory life and disability insurance and another 1.5 percent to 2.0 percent to cover the costs of twenty private mutual fund groups known as Administradora de Fondes Pensiones (AFPs). AFP funds increased from 0.9 percent of Chilean GDP ($300 million) in 1981 to 10 percent of GDP in 1985 ($2.8 billion) and 43 percent of GDP by 1994 ($22.3 billion). Dimitri Vittas, "Strengths and Weaknesses of the Chilean Pension System," The World Bank (May 1995). In 1994, the funds held 55 percent of all government bonds, 59 percent of corporate bonds and 62 percent of mortgage bonds. Though the funds held 11 percent of all Chilean equities, shares in privatized utilities accounted for 83 percent of those holdings. In the early years, when the Chilean stock market was powered by inflows of fresh AFP cash, investment returns averaged 12.5 percent. The 1996 return of 3.5 percent is likely more indicative, particularly given tight investment limitations. The Chilean system also includes three government guarantees: a minimum pension benefit for those who have participated for twenty years (creating

a strong incentive to hide income), a minimum profitability for the funds, and the guaranteed payment of annuities promised by failed insurance companies. The transition cost of the Chilean plan was paid for, in part, with what was then a budget surplus of 5 percent of GDP.

49. With the issuance of its report in January 1995, the commission ceased to exist.

50. The draft report was leaked 17 February 1996, on the eve of the New Hampshire presidential primary. See "Can Retirees' Safety Net Be Saved?" *The New York Times,* 18 February 1996, p. A1. The final report was released 6 January 1997. See "Social Security Report Opens Debate," *The Wall Street Journal,* 7 January 1997, p. A2.

51. The report indicates that the current payroll tax rate is only 2.2 percentage points short of the amount required to meet Social Security's seventy-five-year target. Much of the initial bad news centers around how shortfalls are made up. With 84 percent of current Social Security taxes now paid out as current benefits, only one-sixth of tax revenues are available for investment. If both the tax rate (12.4 percent) and the tax base ($68,400 in 1998) remain the same while tax collections are invested in the stock market, this deficit will have to be made up. The "transition cost" of shifting from one system to another is estimated at between $3 trillion and $4 trillion. Other potential remedies include higher tax rates or a higher base of taxable salary, later retirement, reduced benefits, amending (or capping) the cost-of-living adjustment and increasing taxes on benefits received. Additional savings could be generated by reducing future benefits promised to workers not yet nearing retirement and, in return, allowing them to pay in less payroll taxes, provided those funds are locked into investments for retirement. Two key changes (taxing Social Security benefits the same as pensions and revising the way inflation is computed) could trim approximately two-thirds off this projected multi-trillion-dollar deficit. Government financing could also play a part, such as requiring that these funds continue to buy government bonds (an approach used in privatizing Chile's public pension system) and issuing to participants Chilean-like, government "recognition bonds" as they transfer to the new system, with the value of those bonds based on the present value of benefits accrued under the previous system.

52. The World Bank Group's Multilateral Investment Guarantee Agency (MIGA) unwittingly contributes to this process, offering insurance against the political risk that, for instance, a power developer is not allowed to continue to charge agreed-to electricity rates.

53. See Peter Carlson, "The Ultimate Player," *The Washington Post National Weekly Edition,* 29 July–4 August 1996, p. 6.

54. Kevin Sack, "Taking Turns, GOP Takes Care of the South," *The New York Times,* 18 November 1997, p. 1.

55. See "Dole, Gingrich and the Big Ethanol Boondoggle," *The Wall Street Journal,* 2 November 1995.

56. Lorraine Adams and Charles R. Babcock, "The Majority Lender's Lure to the Maritime Crowd," *The Washington Post,* Weekly Edition, 7 July 1997, p. 11.

57. See "Smoke and Mirrors," by Common Cause (Washington, D.C., March 14, 1996), documenting that tobacco industry political giving topped $20 million in political action committee and "soft money" from 1986 through 1995, including a record $4 million in off-election year 1995.

58. David J. Kramer, "The Risk-Free Loans," *The Washington Post,* Weekly Edition, 2 June 1997, p. 23.

59. According to the U.S. General Accounting Office, the control of airport gates by the nation's largest airlines has resulted in ticket prices at ten of the nation's largest

airports that are 31 percent more expensive than at other airports. Since 1969, the Federal Aviation Administration has limited the number of takeoff and landing slots at O'Hare, National, Kennedy and La Guardia, effectively ceding control of these public assets to a few privately owned airlines. Reported in *The New York Times*, 13 November 1996, p. A2.

60. Jackie Calmer, "How Cash, Caucuses Combined to Protect a Fuel on the Hill," *The Wall Street Journal*, 18 August 1997, p. 1.

61. A 1995 report by Stephen Moore and Dean Stanse of the Washington, D.C.–based Cato Institute ("Ending Corporate Welfare As We Know It") provides one of the more recent chronicles of this relationship.

62. "In Political Money Game, The Year of Big Loopholes," *The New York Times*, 26 December 1996, p. 1.

63. Brown's notorious use of Commerce Department discretion for Democratic fundraising sufficiently raised the ire of Republican congressional leaders that they introduced legislation to abolish the department in 1996. Clinton's appointment of Brown followed a trail blazed by many others, including Richard Nixon in 1972 with his Commerce Department appointment of Maurice H. Stans, his campaign finance manager, and George Bush in 1988 with appointment to Commerce of his campaign manager, Robert A. Mosbacher. When accused that he was openly rewarding campaign contributors with participation in trade missions, Mosbacher replied, "That's part of what the system has been like for 160 years." Ibid.

64. James Q. Wilson, "Democracy Needs Pork to Survive," *The Wall Street Journal*, 14 August 1997. Note, however, that the need for political bargaining does not imply that the bargains struck must benefit solely the well-to-do.

65. See Hilary F. French, *Partnership for the Planet: An Environmental Agenda for the United Nations* (Washington, D.C.: Worldwatch Institute, 1995).

66. The Asia Pacific Economic Cooperation forum (APEC) contains in its "non-binding investment principles" an environmental provision similar to that in NAFTA.

67. Another potentially relevant analog is found in the World Intellectual Property Organization, which helps rationalize and reconcile international agreements in this area, where conventions are often overlapping and complex.

68. Environmentalists have long argued for pollution taxes, carbon taxes, discharge fees and so forth, in the hope of taxing noxious behavior out of the marketplace. While taxing "bads" has merit, it is difficult to imagine that such a program could be agreed to and implemented on a worldwide basis in the time frame relevant to the rapid emergence of the environmental problems they identify. I suggest a two-track approach: initiatives that discourage noxious use while also fostering an ownership environment in which more people gain the right to influence the use of those inputs that cause pollution. See Robert Repetto and Duncan Austin, *The Costs of Climate Protection: A Guide for the Perplexed* (Washington, D.C.: World Resources Institute, 1997).

69. "World Trade Group Orders U.S. to Alter Clean Air Act," *The New York Times*, 18 January 1996, p. C5.

70. Arthur Koestler, *Janus: A Summing Up* (London: Pan Books, 1978).

71. See Elizabeth Sahtouris, "The Biology of Globalization," *Perspectives on Business and Global Change* (Burlington, Calif.: World Business Academy, September 1997), p. 27. See also Elizabeth Sahtouris, *Earthdance—Living Systems in Evolution* (Alameda, Calif.: Metalog, 1996).

72. Ibid., p. 32.

73. Ibid., p. 32. This phenomenon may be the "living system" source of the world-wide emergence of networks of special interest nongovernmental organizations (NGOs) and the role they play in the operations of networks of international organizations (the UN, the World Bank, etc.).
74. Ibid., p. 37.
75. George Kennan (under the pseudonym "X"), "The Sources of Soviet Conduct," *Foreign Affairs,* July 1947, p. 582.
76. See William Drozdiak, "Down with Yankee Dominance," *The Washington Post National Weekly Edition*, 24 November 1997, p. 15.
77. President Woodrow Wilson, remarks at Independence Hall, Philadelphia, July 4, 1914.
78. Arthur Schlesinger Jr., "Has Democracy a Future?" *Foreign Affairs*, September/October 1997, p. 2.
79. Ibid., p. 11.
80. Margaret Wheatley, *Leadership and the New Science* (San Francisco: Berrett-Koehler, 1992), p. 146.
81. Margaret Wheatley, *A Simpler Way* (San Francisco: Berrett-Koehler, 1996), p. 36. In support of this theme, Wheatley notes that Werner Heisenberg, one of the fathers of quantum physics, describes the world of modern physics as one divided not "into different groups of objects but into different groups of connections." Margaret Wheatley, *Leadership and the New Science,* Ibid., quoted at p. 71. From Heisenberg's quantum perspective, the world "appears as a complicated tissue of events," in which connections of different kinds alternate or overlap or combine and thereby determine the texture of the whole. Werner Heisenberg, *Physics and Philosophy* (New York: Harper Torchbooks, 1958), p. 107.
82. Josef Joffe, "How America Does It," *Foreign Affairs*, October/November 1997, p. 13.
83. Ibid., p. 27.
84. Quoted in William Drozdiak, "Down with Yankee Dominance," Ibid.
85. Arthur Schlesinger, Jr., "Has Democracy a Future," Ibid., p. 12.
86. Margaret Wheatley, *Leadership and the New Science,* Ibid., pp. 64–65

CHAPTER 15
Creating a Capitalism That Creates More Capitalists

1. Many of these incentives will be most attractive to larger corporations. Tax returns of American corporations with assets of $250 million or more represent less than 1 percent of all corporate tax returns. However, these 6,798 returns account for 76 percent of total corporate income taxes after credits. Statistics are from a 1996 Internal Revenue Service report, based on an examination of 1993 corporate tax returns. Reported in *The Wall Street Journal*, 20 November 1996, p. A1.
2. Economists often complain that corporate income-tax policy favors debt over equity because the interest expense of debt holders is tax deductible, whereas dividends paid to equity holders are not. Efforts to "integrate" the corporate and the personal income tax (for example, by allowing the corporation a deduction for dividends paid) would have a substantial negative fiscal impact. Perhaps more important, however, it has thus far proven impossible to portray such proposals as a grassroots issue, due largely to prevailing ownership patterns. Regardless of whether the financial playing field is level or tilted, the primary players on that field are those few with ready access to the closed system of finance, either through

their cash or through their collateral to secure debt. Corporate integration could be linked to broadened ownership efforts: for example, taxable companies could claim a partial tax deduction on dividends paid if they were moving toward partial employee ownership. A limited version of corporate integration was achieved in 1984 for firms through a provision permitting a corporate tax deduction for dividends paid on ESOP-held shares.

3. The currently "subsidized" component of depreciation (i.e., the amount of depreciation claimable in excess of that generally allowed under a useful life concept plus that allowed due to expensing) has an estimated tax expenditure cost of $157.8 billion over the fiscal years 1997–2001.

4. The Senate report on the Revenue Act of 1962 characterized the ITC as the "central element" in a bill meant to stimulate economic recovery. "This investment credit, coupled with the depreciation guidelines recently liberalized by the administration, by stimulating capital formation will provide growth in the economy consistent with the principles of a free economy." Senate Report No. 1881, August 15, 1962 (to accompany H.R. 10650).

5. In one of the many tax policy changes of the early 1980s, the investment tax credit (originally intended for machinery and equipment but denied to structures) was expanded to include "single-purpose agricultural and horticultural structures"—such as chicken coops used (like machines) to "produce" broilers for processing and sale by Perdue, Tyson, Holly Farms and others. See *General Explanation of the Economic Recovery Tax Act of 1981,* p. 78.

6. For those countries without a capital gain tax, policymakers could impose the tax, allowing relief when transactions are structured to advance broader ownership.

7. U.S. law provides a blend of all three, allowing individual shareholders of unlisted companies to defer tax on the sale of their shares provided (*a*) the proceeds are reinvested in securities of U.S. operating companies, (*b*) an ESOP is the buyer and (*c*) the ESOP acquires "qualifying" employer securities (generally the best class of common shares or preferred shares convertible into such shares). In addition, this tax deferral is limited to the sale of shares in a company that achieves a minimum threshold of 30 percent ESOP ownership.

8. This provision was included in S. 1755, "The Employee Stock Ownership Promotion and Improvements Act" (introduced 19 November 1993). The bill was sponsored by Senator Jeff Bingaman, Democrat from New Mexico.

9. For couples with incomes below $41,200, the rates would be 8 and 10 percent.

10. McCaw reportedly pocketed approximately 10 percent of that amount.

11. The Congress has often debated the use of a capital gain tax cut to lure investment capital into inner-city businesses (through "enterprise zones" or "empowerment zones"). A typical proposal would cut the capital gain tax when some portion of the proceeds is reinvested in distressed urban areas. The ownership element would require that this reinvestment also create employee-owners in those businesses. Or the proceeds could be reinvested in a mutual fund that, in turn, would invest in such companies. Or condition the tax cut on a combination of geography (inner-city investment), demographics (jobs for inner-city residents), and ownership participation (by that targeted group or by those residing in the community). See Jeffrey R. Gates and Robert L. Woodson Sr., "Jobs and Ownership Are the Answers to Urban Ills," *Los Angeles Times,* Washington edition, 7 August 1992.

12. The Federal Reserve reports that mutual funds supplied more than one-fifth of all the capital to U.S. credit markets between 1991 and 1994. Mutual funds have also helped sustain record-high levels of initial public offerings of securities, providing

small- and medium-sized businesses with access to equity capital. U.S. banks are struggling with the shift from being lenders to becoming capital-market firms—a key factor in the ongoing consolidation of banks nationwide.

13. The Bank of England lobbied successfully for the abolition of reserve requirements in 1980, helping set off a credit boom. Since that policy lever was forfeited, Britain's central banking system has run largely based on shifts in interest rates. See Will Hutton, *The State We're In* (London: Vintage, 1995).

14. In 1995, 31,564 Americans were affected by federal estate taxes, raising $15.1 billion, up from $7.5 billion a decade earlier. By 2007, according to Congress's Joint Tax Committee, approximately 73,200 estates will be affected, with revenue from estate and gift taxes rising to an estimated $35.3 billion. This estimate was made prior to 1997 amendments reducing estate tax levies.

15. Liability for the payment of estate taxes could be assumed by an ESOP in exchange for a transfer from the estate to the ESOP of shares of an equal value. The ESOP-sponsoring company could then pay the taxes over an extended period. Until its repeal as part of a revenue-raising exercise, an ESOP incentive reflecting these features was included in the U.S. tax code. As a variation on this theme, ESOPs could be treated as "charitable remainder" trusts. Thus, for example, a decedent could be allowed to leave a life estate for a spouse, with those funds remaining at the surviving spouse's death transferred to an ESOP on the same tax-favored basis as though the monies were left to charity.

16. Similar incentives could be enacted at the state level. In 1974, Minnesota became the first state to provide that an ESOP could qualify as a charitable organization for purposes of state inheritance and gift tax law. Act of 15 March 1974. Chapter 157 Minn. Sess. L. Serv. 228.

17. "Estimates of Federal Tax Expenditures for Fiscal Years 1997–2001" by the staff of the Joint Committee on Taxation (26 November 1996), Table 1.

18. Some critics of concentrated ownership suggest that allowing the passage of immense fortunes from one generation to another runs counter to fundamental democratic notions of a classless society. Others urge the periodic breakup of large family fortunes as a way to recapture for society a portion of that wealth attributable to the infrastructure and culture that contributed to its accumulation (highways, schools, court systems, etc.). Still others rely on an analogy to the natural order, pointing to the fact that the life-giving nutrients for one species are often derived from the death or decay of another. Any change in the stepped-up basis rules of current law will encounter significant record-keeping challenges.

19. Previously, the exemption was $600,000; that has now been increased to $1.3 million for family farms and businesses and to $1 million for other estates.

20. Note also that the tax expenditure attributable to the exclusion from tax of investment income on life insurance and annuity contracts is projected to total $115.8 billion during fiscal years 1997–2001. Joint Committee on Taxation, Ibid.

21. In 1975, three-quarters of employees' retirement plans promised fixed benefits (defined benefit plans). By early 1997, according to the Employee Benefits Research Institute, more than half of company-sponsored retirement plans were defined contribution plans. More than 44 million people participate in tax-qualified defined contribution plans, up from 12 million in 1975.

22. Joint Committee on Taxation, Ibid.

23. "Effort-relevant" owners is a phrase coined by World Bank economist Dr. David Ellerman. Personal correspondence (May 1996).

24. See description of related enterprise share ownership plans (RESOPs) in Chapter 6 ("New Property Paradigms").
25. The National Center for Employee Ownership estimates that employees owned about $250 billion in employer stock through 401(k) plans as of May 1997.
26. Under U.S. law, tax incentives directed at encouraging employee capital accumulation are conditional. Unless an employee benefit plan can be shown to benefit a broad base of employees (versus just those who are highly compensated), the tax incentives are withdrawn.
27. Likewise, a credit is allowed for dividends received from foreign subsidiaries of domestic corporations in cases where their earnings have been subject to foreign tax. This indirect tax credit could be limited to subsidiaries that meet a minimum threshold of broad-based share ownership.
28. "A recent survey of the *Forbes 400* suggests that about half of great fortunes in the United States are inherited. . . ." Edward N. Wolff, "The Recent Rise in the Concentration of American Wealth: A Cause for Alarm?" *The Aspen Institute Quarterly* (Winter 1994), p. 78.
29. Those opposed to progressive income taxes oppose them because they do what they're designed to do. For example, according to the Internal Revenue Service, those ranked in the top 50 percent by income paid 98 percent of individual income taxes in 1994, up from 92 percent in 1985. The top 50 percent also had about 85 percent of the income. The top 1 percent, ranked by income, paid 28 percent in 1994, up from 21 percent for 1985. For 1996, individual income taxes accounted for 48 percent of total IRS collections while corporate taxes represented 12.5 percent (compared to 24 percent in 1960) and estate and gift taxes 1.2 percent. Without including the impact of estate tax cuts, the Treasury Department estimates that the 1997 tax cut directs 50.3 percent of its benefits to the top 20 percent of income earners (i.e., those with annual incomes exceeding $93,222).
30. John Maynard Keynes, "Economic Possibilities for Our Grandchildren" in *Essays in Persuasion* (New York: W.W. Norton Company, 1963), p. 369.
31. France had an annual wealth tax in place for six years during the mid-1980s and Ireland for three years during the 1970s. In none of the OECD countries does the wealth tax presently account for more than 2.3 percent of total tax revenue (Switzerland), and typically it accounts for less than 1 percent. In combination, a direct wealth tax and estate tax together provide an average 0.7 percent of total tax revenue among OECD countries. Edward N. Wolff, "The Structure of Wealth Inequality and Prospects of a Wealth Tax in the United States," A Report to the Twentieth Century Fund, January 1994.
32. The possibility of transferring financial wealth holdings across borders suggests a need for caution and/or international coordination lest a taxpayer living in one country purchase asset holdings in another country. Recognizing that capital mobility, most countries have kept their tax largely in line with others.
33. For instance, in 1994, for a married couple with two children, Germany imposed a flat rate tax of 0.5 percent on all accumulations above $129,000, with exclusions for household effects, automobiles, savings (up to $4,600), pensions, life insurance (up to $4,600) and unincorporated businesses (up to $58,000, with the excess taxed at 75 percent). Switzerland has a threshold of $56,000 for couples, with a sliding tax rate commencing at 0.5 percent (up to $83,000) and 0.30 percent for any accumulations over $1,113,000; exclusions are allowed for household effects and pensions. Wolff, "Structure of Wealth Inequality," p. 80.

34. Ibid.
35. Andrew Carnegie was the first prominent wealthy American to state publicly that the rich have a moral obligation to give away their fortunes: "Men who continue hoarding great sums all their lives, the proper use of which for public ends would work good to the community, should be made to feel that the community . . . cannot . . . be deprived of its proper share." See Andrew Carnegie, *The Gospel of Wealth* (1889). During his lifetime, Carnegie gave away over $350 million.
36. Where a corporation claims a tax deduction for the interest expense incurred in conjunction with an equity-reducing transaction (such as a leveraged buyout or a recapitalization), a portion of that deduction could be disallowed unless the transaction is structured so that a minimum percentage of the equity becomes owned by a broad base of employees.
37. Jack Stack, *The Great Game of Business* (New York: Doubleday Currency, 1992).
38. For example, the New York Center for Employee Ownership and Participation actively promotes employee ownership, sponsoring seminars and convening conferences. It also offers modest financial assistance and serves as a clearinghouse for employee ownership information.

SECTION 4
Coping with Global Capitalism

1. See Donald Sassoon, *One Hundred Years of Socialism* (New York: The New Press, 1997).
2. John C. Edmunds, "Securities: The New World Wealth Machine," *Foreign Policy*, no. 104 (Fall 1996), p. 118.
3. Hernando De Soto, *The Other Path* (New York: Harper & Row, 1989). In developing countries, titled land accounts for 70 to 80 percent of family assets, yet more than 90 percent of rural land and 50 percent of urban property are not protected by formal titles.
4. De Soto also documents the frustration of Peruvian officials who want to encourage the rural poor to substitute legal crops for coca, the feedstock for cocaine. So long as their plots remain informal (untitled and unregistered), government officials cannot implement an enforceable crop-substitution program with them. In the interim, sulfuric acid, kerosene and toluene used to produce coca paste are being dumped into the Amazon Basin.
5. See *Structural Adjustment and Inequality in Latin America: How IMF and World Bank Policies Have Failed the Poor* (London: Oxfam UK, September 29, 1994).
6. James D. Wolfensohn, *The Challenge of Inclusion,* Ibid., p. 19.

CHAPTER 16
The Development Dilemma

1. Remarks of Gustave Speth, administrator of the United Nations Development Program, at the Microcredit Summit (Washington, D.C., February 4–6, 1997).
2. Dr. Norman Bailey, Institute for the Study of the Americas (April 1994). The Washington, D.C.-based Inter-American Dialogue estimates that the ranks of the poor increased during the 1980s by 50 million people, adding to the 130 million poor counted in 1980.
3. "Monitoring Economic Progress," World Bank Report (September 17, 1995).

4. *World Development Report 1996*. New York: United Nations Development Program.
5. *Adjustment in Africa: Reforms, Results and the Road Ahead* (Washington, D.C.: World Bank, March 1994).
6. *The World Bank, The East Asian Miracle, Economic Growth and Public Policy* (New York: Oxford University Press, 1993), p. 3.
7. Remarks at State of the World Forum, 4 October 1996 in San Francisco.
8. See Appendix D ("GDP—What Gets Measured Gets Managed"), challenging GDP as a proper measure of progress.
9. See Herman Daly and John B. Cobb Jr., *For the Common Good: Redirecting the Economy Toward Community, the Environment and a Sustainable Future* (Boston: Beacon Press, 1994).
10. See *Expanding the Measure of Wealth* (Washington, D.C.: The World Bank, April 1997).
11. Valuation concepts present an instructive challenge. For example, the monetized world of transactions and exchanges in the rich countries (as reflected in capital markets) captures one aspect of reality, while the purely physical accounting of natural assets captures another. Thus, for example, the ratio of monetary to nonmonetary assets in high income economies is 3:1, while that of Latin America and the Caribbean is 1:3. Serageldin, *Sustainability and the Wealth of Nation*, pp. 12–13.
12. "World Bank Develops New System to Measure Wealth of Nations," World Bank Press Release (17 September 1995).
13. *Human Development Report 1992* (New York: United Nations Development Program), 1992.
14. For example, Professor Mary Corcoran found that boys who grow up poor earn 41 percent to 63 percent less per year than boys from middle-income households. Reported in *The Wall Street Journal*, 6 August 1997, p. 1.
15. Key donor countries (such as the United States) enacted policies consistent with this philosophy. For example, the U.S. Department of Commerce created the "Big Emerging Market" concept in 1993 whereby the United States and American businesses (with Commerce Department prodding) focused their attention on ten or so of the most attractive emerging markets (such as those in Central and Eastern Europe). At the same time, the United States reduced its support for those countries not on the "most wanted" list. Critics suggest that this strategy amounted to the United States "cherry picking" the ripe emerging markets to the advantage of U.S. trade while absolving itself of any responsibility for the less dynamic "nonemerging" nations. See Stephen-Gotz Richter, "How America Stiffs the World," *The New York Times*, 27 August 1996.
16. Quoted in "The Outlook," *The Wall Street Journal*, 15 September 1997, p. 1.
17. In an attempt to measure the political factors that really matter to business, researchers identified two: whether business leaders had to cope with unexpected changes in laws or policies and whether they expected government to stick with their announced policies. See Stephen Knack and Philip Keefer, "Institutions and Economic Performance: Cross-Country Tests Using Alternative Institutional Measures," *Economics and Politics,* November 1995. See also Silvio Borner, Aymo Brunetti and Beatrice Weder, *Political Credibility and Economic Performance* (New York: Macmillan Press, 1995).
18. Hugh Peyman, "For Emerging Economies, Thrift Doesn't Always Pay." *The World Paper* (Boston), September 1997, p. 3.
19. Alison Sander, "Global Communications: Where Is the Technology Taking Us?," (Boston: Cambridge Transnational Associates), unpublished paper prepared for State of the World Forum (San Francisco, 4–9 November 1997), p. 6.

20. Margaret Wheatley, *Leadership and the New Science,* Ibid.
21. Remarks at State of the World Forum (San Francisco, 4–9 November 1997).
22. Ibid.
23. See Shann Turnbull, "Democratic Capitalism: Self-Financing Local Ownership and Control," *Human Systems Management* 12, no. 4, 1993.
24. *Portfolio Investment in Developing Countries,* Stijn Claessens and Sudarshan Gooptu, eds. World Bank Discussion Paper 228 (December 1993). Emphasis added. A report by the "Group of Thirty" found that foreign portfolio investment in Latin America has substituted for domestic savings. *Latin American Capital Flows: Living with Volatility* (Washington, D.C.: Group of Thirty, 1994).
25. The United Nations Development Program documents that "the traditional view that economic growth in the early stages is inevitably associated with deteriorating income distribution has been proved false." The UN's *Human Development Report 1996* offers the "new insight" that an equitable distribution of public and private resources can enhance the prospects for further growth. "The assertion that the benefits of growth in the early stages would inevitably be skewed towards the rich rested on two principal arguments. The first came from Nobel laureate Simon Kuznets, who said that inequality would first rise, as workers left agriculture for industry, and then fall as industrial production became more widespread. The second was advanced by Nicholas Kaldor, who emphasized the importance of savings. He argued that the only way to finance growth would be by channeling the initial benefits into the pockets of rich capitalists. Since they have the higher propensity to save, only they could provide the funds for investment. These hypotheses have been disproved by recent evidence of a positive correlation between economic growth and income equality (as represented by the share of the poorest 60 percent of the population). Japan and East Asia pioneered this form of equitable development, and China, Malaysia and Mauritius have been following a similar route more recently."
26. *Human Development Report 1996.* (New York: United Nations Development Fund), p. 9.
27. Hazel Henderson and Alan F. Kay, "Introducing Competition to the Global Currency Markets," *Futures* (London), May 1996.
28. A June 1992 report by former World Bank vice president Willi Wapenhans concluded that the gap between policy and practice (in the environmental area) at the World Bank is due largely to what he called the bank's "pervasive preoccupation with new lending." Portfolio Management Task Force, "Effective Implementation: Key to Development Impact," World Bank, Washington, D.C., November 3, 1992.
29. "As a matter of policy, the (World Bank) does not reschedule payments, and it has suffered no losses on the loans it has made. It has earned a net income every year since 1948." *The World Bank Annual Report 1995,* Ibid., p. 4.
30. This could be a particularly useful exercise for the World Bank Group's International Finance Corporation and for the Inter-American Development Bank's Inter-American Investment Corporation. Ownership patterns are impacted in both donor and developing country by the contracts granted (for planning, construction, engineering, maintenance, etc.).
31. This insensitivity is surprisingly deep-seated. See *Bretton Woods: Looking to the Future* (Washington, D.C.: Bretton Woods Commission, July 1994). This 50th Anniversary Report recommends an increased emphasis on loan guarantees, cofinancing and innovative financing techniques plus better institution building, a renewed focus on sustainability and better aid coordination. Though each of those goals would be advanced with a more ownership pattern–sensitive development strategy, that aspect goes unmentioned.

32. Higher "hurdle rates" also have the effect of directing investments into resource-extraction industries where investment risk is often less—in part because access to hard currency is easier (i.e., in global commodity markets). The lack of capital markets also impacts the nature of investments. For example, a large dam can take ten years or more to plan and build whereas a coal-fired plant can be operational in eighteen months. In energy-starved Asia where demand for electricity is growing at 8 percent a year, the demand for fuel-powered plants is growing twice as fast as that for hydroelectric plants—largely because independent power producers are much more cautious about putting money into longer term hydroelectric projects. Where capital market development includes pension funds, access to that long-term capital could become a funding source for cleaner energy, including hydro and solar.

33. To assist in directing savings into small-scale, job-creating businesses, locally organized mutual funds could provide an opportunity for community (or region-wide) residents to invest in a pool of nearby companies. Such "micro-cap funds" (i.e., designed to invest in companies with very small market capitalizations) are growing in popularity in the United States, where there are now about ten thousand micro-cap or small-cap public companies. Because Wall Street generally overlooks this sector, market inefficiencies are common, suggesting a supporting role for public policy (and/or development-bank assistance).

34. In each of the more than twenty countries in which I have worked, I made a point of visiting the local stock exchange. In the typical case, it's a smallish room open for trading a few hours two or three days a week. The "floor" of the exchange usually consists of a few chairs and a chalkboard on which are listed a dozen or so companies plus a few government bond issues. At the outset, participants in these exchanges are typically drawn from local elites who are already participants in that country's version of the closed system of finance, with the exchange serving initially as a means for generating liquidity and diversification.

35. Ninety-four percent of borrowers are female, mostly "solidarity groups" (typically five per group), with each woman signing as a coguarantor for the other four. No one of the five can qualify for another loan until the loans of all five are repaid. A five-year study shows that loan recipients soon double their income and, after five years, manage to climb above the poverty line. All figures as of October 1996.

36. Muhammad Yunus, "The Empowerment of the Poor," remarks at State of the World Forum, 4 October 1996 in San Francisco.

37. In 1995, a consortium of development banks pledged approximately $300 million to fund microcredit programs, projecting that in ten years the programs would reach 7.5 million women and their 38 million family members. Dr. Mohammad Yunus advocates a novel microcredit funding mechanism. He notes that donor countries are cutting their foreign-assistance budgets while dozens of developing countries are saddled with foreign debt, much of which was contracted by undemocratic governments and used for questionable purposes. Interest payments on that debt continue to shift much-needed hard currency to global financial institutions, exacerbating the creation of a large and growing underclass. Dr. Yunus proposes that debtor countries pay local currency into a local microcredit fund managed by women's groups in local communities, with those funds lent to micro-enterprises of those attempting to escape poverty through self-employment. For each sum of local currency deposited into this microcredit fund, foreign lenders would agree to reduce foreign debt by an equivalent amount of hard currency.

38. Ismail Serageldin, "Helping Out with Tiny Loans," *The Journal of Commerce*, 4 February 1997.

39. "Tuned Out, Turned Off," *The Washington Post National Edition*, 5–11 February 1996, p. 6.
40. "Democracy, Capitalism and Morality," *The Wall Street Journal*, 27 December 1994.
41. Harvard University commencement address, 1 June 1997, reported in *The New York Times*, 2 June 1997, p. 1. See also *Averting the Old Age Crisis: Policies to Protect the Old and Promote Growth* (Washington, D.C.: The World Bank, 1994).

CHAPTER 17
Reinventing Capitalism in Europe

1. In truth, it is unfair to attribute to Marx the failures of Soviet-style socialism as he had little to say about the actual operations of a socialist economy. He is most aptly remembered as a critic of nineteenth-century economics (what he labeled "capitalism"). See John Cassidy, "The Return of Karl Marx," *New Yorker*, 20 and 27 October 1997, p. 248.
2. Many of these avowedly "employee-owned companies" are rapidly evolving into management buyouts where, shortly following privatization, managers begin to acquire employees' shares. On the basis of a 1993 survey of 142 such companies created during the 1990–1991 period, insiders own a majority of the shares in 85 percent of the firms. As a general rule, more than 50 percent of the employees participated in the buyout. Managers own approximately 40 percent of the shares, whereas blue-collar workers own some 30 percent. In 40 percent of the companies, at least 51 percent of the shares are held by ten or fewer employees (i.e., managers). Pawel Ruszkowski and Julian Pankow, "Experiences with Management-Employee Buyouts in Poland," a paper developed for the fifth International Employee Ownership Conference, Merton College, Oxford, 5–8 January 1995.
3. Czech privatization required that 3 percent of the shares be set aside in a national property fund to finance restitution claims from those who could prove ownership of assets nationalized by the Soviets.
4. As of mid-1997, at least ten senior banking officials had been charged with embezzlement or other financial crimes. Dozens of investment managers have looted assets without reprimand. In March 1997, a single fund manager embezzled 1.3 billion crowns (U.S.$40 million). As of early 1997, 750,000 Czechs, fully 7 percent of the population, had been stripped of their investments. "Czechs Offer Peek at New Corporate East," *The Wall Street Journal*, 8 May 1996, p. A10.
5. *Current Aspects of the Czech Capital Market* (Prague: Ministry of Finance, 1997).
6. Reported in Jane Perlez, "Market Place: A U.S. Fund Manager in Prague Has Found Privatization Corrupt," *The New York Times*, 3 December 1997, p. C1, quoting Howard I. Golden, president of Central European Privatization Fund.
7. Jane Perlez, "For the Czechs, the Fairy Tale Is All Over Now, " *The New York Times*, 1 December 1997, p. 1.
8. The Gdansk shipyard, home to Solidarity, closed in March 1997, one of the first state-run enterprises that the Polish government decided to close. At the time, the shipyard was owned 60 percent by the government and 40 percent by the workers.
9. Drawing on the ESOP's self-financing concept, Hungary enacted legislation in 1992 allowing employees to purchase a company's shares with (tax-deductible) company profit-sharing payments spread over a fifteen-year period, with an optional three-year interest-payments-only grace period. A required down payment of 2 percent, 15 percent or 25 percent was pegged to the average per-employee price

of those shares proposed for ESOP financing. The interest rate was set at 3 percent (plus the intermediary bank's 4 percent margin). Banks could lend up to 85 percent of the share value. At the end of 1994, approximately two hundred Hungarian companies had implemented ESOPs covering more than sixty thousand employees.

10. With a 15 percent down payment and installment payments over a three-year period. Installments could be made in cash, with privatization vouchers or from future company earnings (reflecting the ESOP's self-financing concept). In addition, managers were allowed to buy 5 percent of the shares on a preferred basis. For unincorporated companies (such as shops), employee groups could participate in auctions by buying at a 30 percent discount from the offering price, with 25 percent down and the balance paid over three years.

11. Between 1993 and 1996, employees sold some of their holdings but remained majority owners in 65 percent of the large privatized firms. See Joseph R. Blasi, Maya Kroumova and Douglas Kruse, *Kremlin Capitalism* (Ithaca, N.Y.: ILR Press, 1997).

12. Reported in *Economic Justice Monitor* (April 1995) published by the Center for Economic and Social Justice, Arlington, Virginia.

13. *Washington Times*, 24 September 1994.

14. *Financial Times*, 11 December 1995, p. 2.

15. "How Western Investors Won a Coveted Stake in Russian Gas Concern," *The Wall Street Journal*, 16 January 1997, p. 1.

16. Although the law set a maximum $2.5 million limit on campaign spending, members of the Yeltsin campaign concede that its leaders spent $100 million (opponents put the figure at about $500 million).

17. Quoted in "Russia's New Tycoons," *The Washington Post National Weekly Edition*, 20 January 1997, p. 12.

18. "Charting the Communist Collapse," *The Washington Post National Weekly Edition*, 20 January 1997, p. 28.

19. Grigory Yavlinsky, "Shortsighted," *New York Times Magazine*, 8 June 1997, p. 66.

20. George Soros, "The Capitalist Threat," *Atlantic Monthly*, February 1997, p. 45.

21. In determining whether a member country has achieved the "sustainable convergence" required for entry into the European single currency (the euro), five "Maastricht criteria" are laid down: price stability, low long-term interest rates, exchange-rate stability, and a sustainable government financial position defined as (*a*) a budget deficit not exceeding 3 percent of GDP and (*b*) a ratio of public debt to GDP of no more than a "reference value" of 60 percent. See Edmund L. Andrews, "Hostile Bids and Mergers Rise in Europe," *The Wall Street Journal*, 14 October 1997, p. C1; John Rossant, "Why Merger Mania Is Rocking the Continent," *Business Week*, 27 October 1997, p. 64.

22. Only about 5 percent of Germans hold shares. Instead, savings are routinely channeled through banks into industrial loans rather than through mutual funds into shares where shareholder pressure might generate higher financial returns. This risk-averseness has historical roots: twice this century Germans have lost their savings in currency reforms. Also, the high-profile flotation of Volkswagen shares in 1960 (which later dipped below their original offering price) contributed to turning a generation of Germans against equities.

23. Commencing 18 November 1996, the $11.5 billion raised by the sale of 20 percent of the company was used to reduce the firm's $70-plus billion debt, a substantial portion of which was incurred in modernizing former East Germany's phone system and shifting to digital technology. As of December 1996, the company had

sold 713.7 million shares or 26 percent of the company, including 23.7 million shares sold to Telekom employees (0.86 percent).

24. A Fannie Mae-like financial intermediary (or a bank) could purchase those notes and bundle them for resale.

25. These ESOP notes could be bundled and sold as securities ("securitized"), providing Germans with another debt instrument in which to invest, through a debt instrument that fosters broad-based equity ownership.

26. Many German firms have funded their pensions not with cash or other assets but with book reserves (an unfunded promise to pay). Germany's baby boom generation will soon begin to exert a strain on German companies as those pension obligations fall due. Any strategy that puts more appreciating, income-producing assets into German hands can help relieve that fast-emerging pressure. These pension plans could also invest in ESOP notes.

27. "G.M. Success in an Unlikely Place," *The New York Times,* 31 October 1994.

28. The banks counter that, if they were to sell their stakes, capital gain taxes would be punitive because those shares were acquired at well below what they would now fetch in the market. Consequently, the capital gains tax bite would erode their reserves because the shares were carried on the books at fair market value. Thus, after paying taxes, they would be required to replenish their capital by selling equity in a distressed and already equity-shy stock market.

29. Russia's largest banks favor the "German model" in which banks have considerable regulatory control over the securities industry. That's partly because they know that, contrary to the German system, Russian banks would not face the limitations on bank power exerted by the German government.

30. See Putnam, *Making Democracy Work,* pp. 109–116.

CHAPTER 18
Capitalism with Chinese Characteristics

1. Others suggest that, in the Marxist system, capital is capital only if in the hands of a distinct capitalist class. See Joseph A. Schumpeter, *Capitalism, Socialism and Democracy* (1950).

2. See "Major Shift for Communist China: Big State Industries Will Be Sold," *The New York Times,* 12 September 1997, p. 1.

3. Reported in "A Great Tiptoe Forward," *The New York Times,* 17 September 1997, p. 1.

4. See George Tseo, "Chinese Economic Reform and Employee Ownership," *Journal of Employee Ownership Law and Finance,* Fall 1995, pp. 159–191.

5. Ibid. Early reforms in the state-owned enterprise sector took the form of a "contract responsibility system" whereby, once state firms had produced for the central plan, managers could sell their product on the open market. Then came the "modern enterprise system," which aimed to separate the state as owner from day-to-day management while also imposing financial discipline, encouraging firms to restructure and merge, and exposing them to competition.

6. Ibid.

7. See *The Chinese Economy: Fighting Inflation, Deepening Reforms* (Washington, D.C.: The World Bank, 1996); and Harry G. Broadman, ed., *Policy Options for Reform of Chinese State-Owned Enterprises* (The World Bank, 1996).

8. Progress also proved difficult to sustain because household responsibility grants farmers the right to what they produce on the land while title to the land remains

vested in the collective. That undermines the incentive to make long-term investments, hampers crop diversification and reduces opportunities to realize economies of scale—a key factor in agricultural productivity.

9. Though his words later came back to haunt him during the ideological purity
purge of the early-1970s Cultural Revolution, Deng revealed his pragmatic streak
even then, declaring, "It doesn't matter whether the cat is black or white, as long
as it catches mice."

10. Reported in *Business Week*, 1 September 1997, p. 53.

11. Two-thirds of all investment in China continues to flow into state-owned factories
run by Communist Party appointees, up from 61 percent in 1990. Beijing policymakers are reportedly determined to preserve no more than 1,000 large state-owned
companies on the socialist model; the balance (99,000) reportedly will be sold,
merged or put into bankruptcy.

12. Workers' savings are a key factor keeping China's banks afloat; any loss of confidence could be disastrous because the reserves held by Chinese banks are
miniscule. See Seth Faison, "Beijing on the Brink?" *The New York Times*, 27
November 1997, p. A10.

13. See discussion of "RESOPs" in Chapter 6 ("New Property Paradigms").

14. Globalization is bringing changes both to Japan's *keiretsu* system and to
Germany's "corporatist" system. For example, ongoing financial deregulation in
Japan has resulted in cross-holdings declining to 46 percent of all shares in 1997,
down from 52 percent in 1992, according to Goldman, Sachs & Co. See "Japan's
Slow-Motion Economic Revolution Takes Shape," *The Wall Street Journal*, 18
September 1997, p. A11.

15. For example, employees might be allowed to elect to receive their compensation
partly in employer shares (a form of savings) later swapping those shares for securities (stocks *or* bonds) of related enterprises. This ownership-facilitated relief from
inflationary pressures need not be limited to payroll costs. For example, if the
shares were tradable (even with geographic restrictions), employees could apply
sale proceeds toward their purchase of housing, a costly employee benefit now
often provided by state-owned enterprises.

16. Eisuke Sakakibara, *Beyond Capitalism* (Washington, D.C.: Economic Strategy Institute, 1993).

17. The People's Bank of China conservatively estimates that at least 22 percent of
the nation's loans are nonperforming.

18. The Industrial and Commercial Bank of China (ICBC) employs more than
500,000. A 1997 World Bank report (*China 2020*) found of the four large state
banks that "their accounting risk management, and credit analysis systems are
woefully inadequate, and the quality of their portfolio is unknown."

19. See Jeffrey R. Gates, "Capitalist Tools for Chinese Workers," *Financial Times*, 17
February 1994, p. 13. In the current reform environment, retailers and others with
strong export markets have fared best while those faring worst are state-owned
enterprises hard hit by the credit squeeze. In lieu of payment, many companies
are holding uncollectible receivables, bank guarantees, promissory notes or even
bartered goods. Such nonbank debts could also be targeted for this swap strategy. Enterprises receiving loans from state-owned banks often on-lend those funds
to other state-owned firms at interest rates upward of 20 percent. These so-called
"triangular debts" totaled a staggering $120 billion at the end of 1996, a four-
fold increase over two years earlier. Those loans, too, could be converted to shares,
raising the politically sensitive issue of just who should own those shares.

20. Brookings Institution China scholar Nicholas Lardy suggests that the banking system's recapitalization be borne by the taxpayer. The ratio of domestic government debt to GDP is 6 percent, which is low by international standards. Lardy estimates that the cost of recapitalization would be roughly 35 percent of GDP. If the government issued bonds to cover the cleanup costs, China's debt-to-GDP ratio would be 40 percent or so, a figure Lardy suggests is manageable. He suggests that those bonds be acquired by newly recapitalized banks. See "The Long March to Capitalism," *The Economist*, 13 September 1997, pp. 23–26.

21. The non-state sector's contribution to industrial output increased from 22 percent in 1978 to two-thirds in 1995, with TVEs and other cooperatives accounting for more than 70 percent of this output.

22. One of China's primary educational deficiencies is its inadequate number of students at the university level. For a discussion of essential "market-complementary initiatives," see Jean Dreze and Amartya Sen, *India: Economic Development and Opportunity* (Oxford: Oxford University Press, 1996).

23. Reported in *The Economist*, 14 October 1996, p. 39.

24. According to the Ministry of Agriculture, the income ratio for rural peasants and urban residents widened from 1:1.7 in 1985 to 1:2.4 by 1991. In the industrial sector, the seaboard's share of gross output value increased from 60 percent in 1982 to 83 percent in 1990. Also, urban workers are better positioned to increase their nonwage income. The proportion of national income claimed by urban workers grew 9.3 percent between 1979 and 1984.

25. See description of GSOC in Chapter 6 ("New Property Paradigms").

CHAPTER 19
Latin America, the Caribbean and the Catholic Church

1. Note that this preference would provide companies with a bankable "asset" (i.e., this newly opened market) against which they could borrow funds to develop this route, using those funds to implement an ESOP.

2. See Debra Evenson, *Revolution in the Balance* (Boulder, Colo.: Westview Press, 1994).

3. As quoted in Larry Rohter, "Cuba's Party Peers Ahead, Chooses to March in Place," *The New York Times*, 12 October 1997, p. Y6.

4. Results of biannual poll by Florida International University reported in Mireya Navarro, "As Old Cubans Die, Young Pragmatists Emerge," *The New York Times*, 6 December 1997, p. 1.

5. On 13 November 1989, Senator Helms introduced an amendment to the pending Foreign Assistance Act permitting the Polish-American Enterprise Fund and the Hungarian-American Enterprise Fund to be used for the establishment of ESOPs.

6. Conceived by the Arlington, Virginia–based Center for Economic and Social Justice, this effort was chaired by Ambassador J. William Middendorf II. I was retained by Ambassador Middendorf to draft the report.

7. "Guatemalan Peasants Fight Off Rebels on Model Land-Reform Estate," *The Washington Times*, 10 April 1985.

8. Jim Wright, *Worth It All* (New York: Brassey's, 1993); personal communication, May 1995.

9. Jim Wright, remarks to Caribbean Basin Initiative Conference in Miami, 30 November 1987.

10. See Jeffrey R. Gates, "Capitalism and Human Dignity: The Ownership Imperative," *America*, 19 October 1996.

11. *Quadregesimo Anno* ("On Reconstructing the Social Order"), 1931.
12. *Mater et Magistra* ("On Christianity and Social Progress"), 1961.
13. *Centesimus Annus* ("The Hundredth Year"), 1991.
14. Ibid.

CHAPTER 20
South Africa: Overcoming Economic Apartheid

1. *The Economist*, 7 October 1995, p. 20.
2. For a description of GSOCs, see Chapter 6 ("New Property Paradigms").
3. See Terry L. Anderson and Donald R. Leal, "The Rise of Enviro-Capitalists," *The Wall Street Journal*, 26 August 1997.

CHAPTER 21
Islamic Ownership: The Vice-Regents

1. Devoutly Islamic financial institutions deploy their capital more like merchant bankers than lenders, making various forms of profit and loss-sharing arrangements in place of more traditional notions of predetermined interest. Examples include equity raising, leasing (*ijara*) and working capital (*istisna*). In the assessment of Robin Leigh-Pemberton, former governor of the Bank of England, Islamic banking is "a perfectly acceptable mode of investment, but it does not fall within the long-established and well understood definition of what constitutes banking in this country." Quoted in "Islamic Banking," *Financial Times* survey, 28 November 1995
2. In Saudi Arabia, the ruling family's moral authority is grounded in its Islamic credentials though the financial system is conducted along Western lines. With the rise of fundamentalism, that is changing. At the end of 1995, the Saudi's National Commercial Bank, the country's largest financial institution with almost $20 billion in assets, had converted 15 percent of its outlets into Islamic branches, with more conversions in process. Ibid.
3. Because many bank depositors have little taste for risk-taking and long-term investments, Islamic banks provide products with predetermined rates of short-term return, such as commodity trades and trade financing (for example, a middleman might be paid to buy goods for an Islamic bank and resell them at a predetermined price). Islamic leasing (*ijara*) allows project financiers to purchase assets (say of a power plant) and lease them back to the project sponsor at a markup and on a deferred-payment basis over the lease term. With an *istisna* structure, a project's suppliers might be funded, with the Islamic bank holding title to the equipment until satisfaction of an agreed-to deferred payment structure when title would be conveyed.
4. Islamic finance specialist Aziz Ali Mohammed cautions that equity suggests Islamic banking should also ensure protection for the saver. At a minimum, the saver's purchasing power should be preserved, either by indexing or some other means . Absent that basic requirement, non-interest-based lending can quickly become unsustainable, particularly in an inflationary environment. Aziz Ali Mohammed, "Holier Than Thou Banking," paper prepared for Money Matters: Financing Social Development in the Islamic World, Cairo, 1–2 October 1997.
5. See Chapter 6 ("New Property Paradigms"). Such techniques could also be included at the outset. Note, however, that even equity investments can mean indirect interest-based lending if the company is leveraged in the traditional sense. Traditional interest-based leveraged financing could instead be structured along

Islamic lines by, for example, providing that the employees' stake be paid for with future earnings and profits of the enterprise.

6. See Sara Khalili, "Unlocking Islamic Finance," *Infrastructure Finance*, April 1997, p. 19.

7. Innovation is needed to broaden the scope of financial products that can pass the Islamic litmus test imposed by advisory panels of religious scholars and clerics ("Shari'a boards" comprised of Muslim clerics who interpret Islamic teachings). Without standardization, it becomes difficult to package financial instruments and sell them into Islam's broader financial markets, boosting bank liquidity. To date, Malaysia has made the most progress. More than thirty financial institutions now offer dual banking services, with non-Islamic and Islamic financial services available side by side, along with an interbank market in Islamic financial products (critics claim that Malaysia's interbank financial products are not Islamicized because they are based on short-term government paper).

8. See discussion in Chapter 18 ("Capitalism with Chinese Characteristics").

9. Jewish economics also has a prescription against the lending of money for interest. The Bible's book of Exodus cautions: "If you lend money to my people, to the poor among you, do not act toward him as a creditor; exact no interest from them." Jewish "free loan societies" have long been a little-known part of the social fabric of the United States. See "Jewish Loan Societies Rethink the Tradition of Helping All Comers," *The Wall Street Journal,* 11 September 1997, p. 1.

10. Peter Alan Harper, "Bringing peace through profit," *Japan Times*, 2 November 1997, p.10.

11. Stephen Kinzer, "A Perilous New Contest for the Next Oil Prize," *The New York Times*, 21 September 1997, Sec. 1, p. 1.

12. The simmering political conflicts in this resource-rich region often have an economic dimension. For example, in November 1997, the Clinton administration persuaded Russian President Boris Yeltsin to pressure Gazprom, a major Russian company, to postpone a proposed $3 billion bond offering to explore for natural gas in Iran. Steven Erlanger, "Russian Partner in Iran Deal Postpones Its Bond Offering," *The New York Times*, 12 November 1997, p. A10. In secessionist Chechnya, Russian and Chechen leaders reached an accord in November 1997 splitting transit fees on the initial oil that will flow from Azerbaijan through Chechnya to the Russian port of Novorossisk on the Black Sea. Stephan Kinzer, "A Perilous New Contest for the Next Oil Prize," Ibid.

Epilogue

1. James D. Wolfensohn, *The Challenge of Inclusion*, Ibid., p. 6 (emphasis added).

2. "The task of transmuting human nature must not be confused with the task of managing it." John Maynard Keynes, *The General Theory*, p. 374.

3. Mario Cuomo, *Reason to Believe* (New York: Simon & Schuster, 1995).

4. See Steve Lerner, *Eco-Pioneers* (Cambridge, Mass.: MIT Press, 1997).

5. For a review of the literature, see Duane Elgin, "Collective Consciousness and Cultural Healing," Ibid.

6. Thich Nhat Hanh, Arnold Kotler (ed.), *A Joyful Path: Community, Transformation and Peace* (San Francisco: Parallax Press, 1994).

7. Thomas Berry, *The Dream of the Earth* (San Francisco: Sierra Club Books, 1990), p. 202.

8. See Stuart Kauffman, *At Home in the Universe* (New York: Oxford University Press, 1995).

9. See Fritjof Capra, *The Tao of Physics* (Berkeley: Shambhala, 1975; 3d ed., 1991)

10. Thomas Berry, *The Dream of the Earth*, Ibid., p. 74.

11. Ralph Waldo Emerson, *Essays* (New York: Thomas Nelson and Sons, [no date, taken from the essay on the "Oversoul"]) p. 202. Cited in Duane Elgin, "Collective Consciousness and Cultural Healing," Ibid., p. 5.

APPENDIX A
Making Assets Accountable

1. Court cases soon made it clear that trustees could not decline without breaching their fiduciary duty unless confident that the company's performance would improve enough to recover that premium in the foreseeable future.

2. "Punters or Proprietors?" *The Economist*, 5 May 1990.

3. See also survey conducted by Pearl Meyer & Partners, reported in *The Wall Street Journal*, 19 January 1995.

4. Note that Scott Paper was acquired in mid-1995, creating substantial capital gains both for its directors (who had to approve the acquisition) and for CEO Al Dunlap who was brought in less than a year earlier and who reportedly netted more than $100 million from his stock-heavy compensation package.

5. "Follow the Leader," *The New York Times*, 13 October 1995, p. C1.

6. This ownership solution faces a variant of the "collective choice" dilemma: any single manager can act to improve corporate performance but, if successful, will recover only a pro rata share of any benefit (i.e., as reflected in share value). Thus, direct perquisites (pay, club memberships, chauffeurs, private dining rooms, etc.) will continue to be attractive to managers, particularly given both the uncertainty that improved corporate performance will be reflected in share prices and the diffused impact in any case. There is little evidence that managerial ownership has replaced the immediate payoff of "perks" and an array of management privileges. Indeed, stock options may simply be just another perquisite. See Lynn Brenner, "The Myth of Incentive Pay," *CFO*, July 1995, p. 26.

7. But see Judith H. Dobrzynski, "New Road to Riches Is Paved with Options—Investor Activism Lifts Executive Pay," *The New York Times*, 30 March 1997, p. F1.

8. On November 12, 1996, a Blue Ribbon Commission on Director Professionalism, a panel created by the National Association of Corporate Directors, issued a "best practices" report urging a broad range of board-related reforms, including imposing term limits on directors and limits on the number of boards on which directors can serve. Other suggestions reiterated several rudimentary standards, such as having a majority of outside directors, paying them at least partly in stock and requiring them to own shares. Other recommendations include the selection of only directors who possess financial literacy, a definition of director independence and an ongoing evaluation of both directors and the board as a whole. Joann S. Lublin, *The Wall Street Journal*, 12 November 1996, p. B1.

9. Margaret Blair, *Ownership and Control: Rethinking Corporate Governance for the Twenty-First Century* (Washington, D.C.: Brookings Institution, 1995).

10. Note, however, that whereas institutional investors may take a long-term view, they frequently utilize investment managers who are hired and fired based on short-term results.

11. See Monks and Minow, *Power and Accountability*.

APPENDIX B
Dissecting Modern Ownership

1. See Holland, *Hidden Order*.
2. See *The Stock Options Book* (Oakland, Calif.: National Center for Employee Ownership, 1997).
3. See Jack Stack, *The Great Game of Business*.
4. DeAnne Julius, *Global Companies and Public Policy: The Growing Challenge of Foreign Direct Investment* (London: Royal Institute of International Affairs, 1990).

APPENDIX D
GDP: What Gets Measured Gets Managed

1. Paul Samuelson concedes in *Economics*, his best-selling college textbook: "Economics focuses on concepts that can actually be measured." See also "What Is Prosperity," *Whole Earth Review*, Summer 1995.
2. On the other hand, Federal Reserve chairman Alan Greenspan is among those who believe that GDP understates economic progress by understating the impact of technology on quality and productivity (for instance, today's computers offer more computing capacity at a lower price). GDP can serve some valid purposes, such as investment planning if you are a business executive or setting money supply targets if you are chairman of a central bank.
3. As noted in the first chapter, a dispute rages over whether the 1996 Boskin Commission is correct in suggesting that shortcomings in the computation of the CPI (consumer price index) understate wage growth.
4. See Herman E. Daly, *Steady-State Economics,* 2d ed. (Washington, D.C.: Island Press, 1991).
5. Further complicating this computation is the fact that GDP is presumed to measure final product produced for the market. Thus, for example, if a city hires a policeman to patrol its streets, that is considered final, but if that same person is hired by a local business to patrol its production plant, that is considered intermediate and is not counted. However, all government purchases of goods and services are considered final products. Professor Eisner asks: "In both cases, are the police services not intermediate? But if they are, what about our more than $300 billion in annual military expenditures? Are they not intermediate?" Robert Eisner, "What Counts and How to Count It," *The Wall Street Journal*, 12 November 1996.
6. From 1990 to 1995, the sturgeon population of the Caspian Sea, source of 95 percent of the world's black caviar, plunged from 200 million to fewer than 60 million, improving short-term GDP (but degrading long-term GDP) of all five Caspian states: Azerbaijan, Iran, Kazakhstan, Russia and Turkmenistan. "The Caspian Caviar Crisis: Killing Too Many Fish," *The New York Times*, 23 December 1995, p. C1.
7. Herman Daly, "Nicholas Georgescu-Roegen: The Revolutionary Economist," *Adbusters*, Spring 1996, p. 61. See Nicholas Georgescu-Roegen, *The Entropy Law and the Economic Process* (Cambridge, Mass.: Harvard University Press, 1971).
8. See Herman Daly, *Steady-State Economics*. Ibid.
9. Clifford Cobb, Ted Halstead and Jonathan Rowe, "If the GDP Is UP, Why Is America Down," *Atlantic Monthly*, October 1995.
10. Clifford Cobb, Ted Halstead and Jonathan Rowe, *Redefining Progress* (San Francisco: Redefining Progress, September 1995). The genuine progress indicator includes estimates of over twenty-five aspects of economic life that GDP ignores.
11. Ibid., p. 8.

Index

Page numbers followed by n or nn refer to footnotes and endnotes.